Power and Impotence

Studies in Critical Social Sciences Book Series

Haymarket Books is proud to be working with Brill Academic Publishers (www.brill.nl) to republish the *Studies in Critical Social Sciences* book series in paperback editions. This peer-reviewed book series offers insights into our current reality by exploring the content and consequences of power relationships under capitalism, and by considering the spaces of opposition and resistance to these changes that have been defining our new age. Our full catalog of *SCSS* volumes can be viewed at https://www.haymarketbooks.org/series_collections/4-studies-in-critical-social-sciences.

Series Editor
David Fasenfest (Wayne State University)

Editorial Board
Eduardo Bonilla-Silva (Duke University)
Chris Chase-Dunn (University of California–Riverside)
William Carroll (University of Victoria)
Raewyn Connell (University of Sydney)
Kimberlé W. Crenshaw (University of California–LA and Columbia University)
Heidi Gottfried (Wayne State University)
Karin Gottschall (University of Bremen)
Alfredo Saad Filho (King's College London)
Chizuko Ueno (University of Tokyo)
Sylvia Walby (Lancaster University)
Raju Das (York University)

Power and Impotence

A History of South America Under Progressivism (1998–2016)

Fabio Luis Barbosa dos Santos

Haymarket Books
Chicago, IL

First published in 2019 by Brill Academic Publishers, The Netherlands
© 2019 Koninklijke Brill NV, Leiden, The Netherlands

Published in paperback in 2020 by
Haymarket Books
P.O. Box 180165
Chicago, IL 60618
773-583-7884
www.haymarketbooks.org

ISBN: 978-1-64259-371-6

Distributed to the trade in the US through Consortium Book Sales and Distribution (www.cbsd.com) and internationally through Ingram Publisher Services International (www.ingramcontent.com).

This book was published with the generous support of Lannan Foundation and Wallace Action Fund.

Special discounts are available for bulk purchases by organizations and institutions. Please call 773-583-7884 or email info@haymarketbooks.org for more information.

Cover design by Jamie Kerry and Ragina Johnson.

Printed in the United States.

10 9 8 7 6 5 4 3 2 1

Library of Congress Cataloging-in-Publication data is available.

*This book is dedicated to Méri,
who was with me on journeys she didn't make*

Contents

About *Power and Impotence*   XI
Acknowledgements   XII

Introduction   1
  1 The 'Progressive Wave'   1
  2 A National Approach   4
  3 A Methodological Note   8

1 **Venezuelan Revolution: Underdevelopment despite an Abundance of Foreign Exchange**   10
  1 Introduction   10
  2 Underdevelopment with Abundance of Foreign Exchange Reserves   11
  3 Bolivarian Revolution   18
  4 Dilemmas of the Venezuelan Revolution   23
  5 Crisis   28
  6 Final Thoughts   34

2 **Conciliation and Order under 'Lulaism' in Brazil**   37
  1 Introduction   37
  2 Preamble   37
  3 Strategies of Accumulation: Neodevelopmentism or Neoliberalism?   39
    3.1 *Conciliation and Order*   39
    3.2 *Neodevelopment*   41
  4 The Lulista Way of Regulating Social Conflict   46
    4.1 *Articulation of Two Consensuses*   46
    4.2 *Conservative Modernization*   49
  5 Lulism in Crisis   55
    5.1 *From the June Days to Mobilizations for Impeachment*   55
    5.2 *Impeachment*   59
  6 Final Thoughts   60
    Post-scriptum: the 2018 Brazilian Presidential Elections   64

3 **Kirchnerism and Impasses of the Bourgeois Way in Argentina**   70
  1 Introduction   70
  2 Perón and Peronism   71

  3 From the 'National Reorganization Process' to Neoliberal Democracy 73
  4 Kirchner Governments 79
  5 Cristina Kirchner 85
  6 Final Thoughts 88

4 **The Process of Change in Bolivia: Creative or Destructive Tensions?** 92
  1 Introduction 92
  2 The Variegated Society between Revolution and Dictatorships 93
  3 Democracy and Neoliberalism 97
  4 Revolutionary Conjuncture 100
  5 The Process of Change 103
  6 Final Thoughts 118

5 **Ecology versus Capitalism: Dilemmas of the Citizen Revolution in Ecuador** 121
  1 Introduction 121
  2 Ecuadorian Formation 122
  3 From Re-democratization to Alianza País 124
  4 Political Economy of the Citizen Revolution 128
  5 Final Thoughts 135

6 **The Deposition of Lugo in Paraguay and the *Brasiguayo* Question** 138
  1 Introduction 138
  2 The Agrarian Question and Brazilian Presence in Paraguay 139
  3 Soy and *Brasiguayos* 142
  4 The Lugo Presidency (2008–2012) 147
  5 The Agrarian Question in the Lugo Government 150
  6 The Political Judgment 152
  7 Final Thoughts 154

7 **Brazil and the Political Economy of South American Integration** 156
  1 Introduction 156
  2 Open Regionalism versus Developmental Regionalism 157
  3 Political Economy of Developmental Regionalism 159
  4 Developmentalism in Crisis 165
  5 The Petista Order in South America 168
  6 Final Thoughts 169

8	Chile and the Political Economy of the Real Neoliberalism 171
	1 Introduction 171
	2 Between the Popular Front and the Chilean Way to Socialism 171
	3 From Dictatorship to Protected Democracy 175
	4 Political Economy of the Concertación 180
	4.1 *Concertación in Power* 180
	4.2 *Macroeconomics* 185
	4.3 *Education* 186
	4.4 *Labor Relations, Poverty and Debt* 189
	4.5 *Pension Fund Administrators* 191
	5 Crisis 193
	6 Final Thoughts 194

9	Perversion and Trauma: Impasses of Contemporary Peruvian Politics 198
	1 Introduction 198
	2 New Left and United Left 199
	3 Alanism and United Left 203
	4 Sendero Luminoso 205
	5 Fujimori 210
	6 Fujimorista Legacy 214
	7 Final Thoughts 218

10	War and Peace in Colombia in Historical Perspective 221
	1 Introduction 221
	2 Background 222
	3 Roots of Violence 224
	4 Insurgency and Counter-insurgency in the 1980s 229
	5 Neoliberalism and Parapolitics 232
	6 The War Party in Power 235
	7 Dilemmas of the Peace Process 239

11	Where is the Cuban Revolution Going? Dilemmas of Primitive Socialism 244
	1 Introduction 244
	2 Revolution against Underdevelopment 245
	3 Reform or Update? 252
	4 Current Dilemmas 257
	5 Final Thoughts 262

Conclusion 270
1 The Movement of History 270
2 Regional Integration 276
3 Nine Propositions 279
   3.1 *Integration Is a Dimension of the Latin American Revolution* 279
   3.2 *History Requires its Own Solutions to its Own Problems* 280
   3.3 *Latin American Integration Will Be against the Economy* 281
   3.4 *Development Must Be Equal and Combined – with the People and the Planet* 282
   3.5 *Progress Is Walking with your Own Legs, with your Head Where your Feet Step* 284
   3.6 *Values not only Opposed to, but Different from, those of Capitalism* 286
   3.7 *Equality in the Workplace against Capital* 288
   3.8 *A Strong State that does not Eat Me* 289
   3.9 *There Is no Alternative to Popular Power* 290

Bibliography 293
Index 331

About *Power and Impotence*

It is to the enormous credit of this author that he has gone where few other writers would have dared to tread. From a courageous and remarkable survey of ten different countries of South America – the continent that witnessed the rise and decline of the 'Pink Tide' – Fabio Luis has distilled crucial lessons relevant not just to that part of the world but relevant for the Global South as a whole. He has powerfully highlighted the perils of merely moderating the thrust of neoliberal developmentalism rather than breaking with it altogether no matter how high the risk of 'disorder' this might seem to entail. This book is a great learning experience and a must read!
  – *Achin Vanaik, Professor (Retired) of International Relations and Global Politics, University of Delhi*

Fabio Luis presents a sober and incisive account of the flow and the ebb of the 'pink tide' across South America through an impressive analysis of recent political history in all but one of the countries on the continent, concluding that the pattern of 'permanent counterrevolution' in Latin America prevents a viable reformist path to development. It is a book that should be studied by all who are interested in the trajectory of an alternative to neoliberal politics in the Global South.
  – *Karl von Holdt, University of the Witwatersrand*

This book examines critically, in great detail, the 'pink tide' in nine Latin American countries, as well as the changing political and economic circumstances in Cuba. This is a key resource for understanding the recent political dynamics in one of the most important and influential regions in the world. Indispensible!
  – *Alfredo Saad-Filho, Professor of Political Economy, King's College London*

The shadows of Latin American progressivism emulate the darkness when the sun declines and the lights that marked an era fade. That's what this book is about, which offers a powerful and enlightening analysis of this historical period.
  – *Alberto Acosta, Former President of Constituent Assembly of Montecristi, Ecuador*

Acknowledgements

My fieldwork refers to different research and extension projects. As a Fellow of the Institute of Applied Economic Research (IPEA), I was investigating the issue of *brasiguaios*[1] in Paraguay when President Lugo was deposed in 2012. Beginning in 2014, I was in Venezuela, Colombia, Bolivia, Peru, Cuba, Argentina and Chile within the framework of the Universidade Federal de São Paulo (UNIFESP) Latin American Reality extension program. This is a project that brings together groups of students and teachers around an agenda of academic and political education culminating in collective field research involving visits and interviews with popular leaders as well as political and intellectual personalities. The program is supported by the Pro-Rectory of Extension of UNIFESP, which deserves special thanks.

The Memorial of Latin America offered its facilities for the project activities, before and after the trips, besides organizing the electronic publication of its results. Fundação de Apoio à Pesquisa do Estado de São Paulo (FAPESP) supported the research project 'Neodevelopmentalism or neoliberalism: Brazil and the sense of South American regional integration', process no. 2014 / 05549-3. This support enabled me to undertake additional research in the following countries: Venezuela, Ecuador, Bolivia, Peru and Uruguay. The chapter on regional integration is based on the results of this research. And lastly, the interviews in Ecuador were done in 2011 within the framework of a project similar to the Latin American Reality, but carried out outside the university, for which I updated the data and bibliography later.

I am grateful to the following institutions, colleagues and students who participated in the different projects: Pedro Barros, Verena Hitner, Felippe Ramos, Daniel Feldman, Pietro Alarcón, Hector Mondragón, Carol Ramos, Nilson Araújo, Luis Pinto, Rodrigo Chagas, Regiane Bressan, Daniel Carvalho, Gilberto Maringoni, Agustín Espinosa, Fabiana Dessoti, Vivian Urquidi, Bruna Muriel, Salvador Schavelzon, Luciana Sousa, Marcelo Carvalho, Carlos Alberto Cordovano, Joana Salem, Patrícia Mecchi, Vanderlei Vazelesk, Fabio Maldonado, Silvia Adoue, Luis Fernando Ayerbe, Plínio de Arruda Sampaio Junior, Frei Betto, Carlos Eduardo Carvalho and Vitor Schincariol, in addition to the students who participated in the different projects. Outside of Brazil, my thanks go to all quoted in the respective chapters, as well as to Miguel Tinker Salas, Rodrigo Chagas, Salvador Schavelzon, Javier Gomez, Bernardo Sorj, Michael Löwy,

---

1 Brazilians living in Paraguay, some of whom have assumed a leading role in the soybean business.

ACKNOWLEDGEMENTS

Marcelo Santos, Clécio Mendes, and Julio Gambina, all of whom were among the critical readers of different chapters. Further thanks to my colleagues at various academic journals, in which versions of some of these texts were published. Isabel Loureiro and Daniel Feldman read and commented on the whole manuscript. A special metion goes to SWOP at Wits University for their financial support of copy editing this manuscript. I want to thank David Kane for translating my work into English, as well as Dale McKinley and Monica Seeber who did the copy editing. Finally, I should thank Alfredo-Saad Filho for his support and David Fasenfest who was an invaluable partner as an editor. Thank you.

Who wants to keep order?
Who wants to create disorder?
Brazilian rock band Titãs, *'Disorder'* (1988)

Introduction

The purpose of this book is to contribute to a critical assessment of the so-called 'progressive wave' of South America. This expression refers to the succession of leaders identified with the left and elected in reaction to neoliberalism in past years: Hugo Chávez in Venezuela (1998); Luís Inácio Lula da Silva in Brazil (2002); Néstor Kirchner in Argentina (2003); Tabaré Vázquez in Uruguay (2005); Evo Morales in Bolivia (2005); Rafael Correa in Ecuador (2006); and, Fernando Lugo in Paraguay (2008).[1] Except for the latter, all were reelected and/or chosen their successors. In Chile, socialists took over the *Concertación*[2] with the election of Ricardo Lagos (2000). Only in Peru and Colombia, for reasons explored in the book, can one say that the political alternation turned to the right during this 'progressive wave'.

In December of 2015, when Bolivarianism in Venezuela suffered a crushing defeat in parliamentary elections, during the same month in which Argentina elected president Mauricio Macri, it seemed that the progressive wave was giving way to a reactionary hangover. This perception was consummated with Dilma Roussef's impeachment in Brazil the following year. Although the Frente Amplio still ruled Uruguay, Morales presided over Bolivia and Correa's chosen successor was elected in Ecuador in 2017, it was clear that the political initiative had changed hands. How are we to understand these developments? Are they a reaction to the change advanced by previous governments, or has progressivism simply run out of steam amid frustrated expectations, haunted by falling commodity prices and allegations of corruption? What can this experience tell us about wider trends in contemporary history?

1   The 'Progressive Wave'

The 'progressive wave' emerged as a reaction to the socially deleterious effects of globalization and neoliberalism in South America. From a global perspective, it was an attempt, from the periphery, to stop the movement towards barbarism that characterizes contemporary capitalism.

---

1   This book originally appeared in Portuguese as *Uma história da onda progressista sul-americana (1998–2016)*. São Paulo: Elefante, 2018.
2   Coalition led by Christian Democrats and Socialists, which governed Chile since the end of Pinochet's dictatorship.

However, this reaction was limited by the very conditions of the degradation of the social fabric and of the international conjuncture in which it tried to assert itself. The result was projects for change that accepted the parameters of the inherited system, aiming at better renegotiating the global insertion of their countries, as well as the situation of the socially disqualified – the 'excluded' that they often represented. For this moderate political reason, pragmatism and interest converged at different levels between an unfavorable assessment of the correlation of forces for change and mere accommodation to power. In short, with the possible exception of Venezuela, it was decided to face barbarism along the path of least conflict.

This path accepted and supported the prevailing link between neoliberalism and progress. The progressive wave was neoliberal not only because it was subordinated to the dictatorship of structural adjustment, but because it introjected the neoliberal 'way of the world' that characterizes it, reducing politics to management techniques with a mercantilist logic. At the same time, it was progressive not because it was necessarily left-wing, but because it shared a worldview that identified the confrontation of underdevelopment with economic growth, a peripheral version of the ideology of progress.

As a result, progressive governments have linked structural adjustment to the myth of economic growth; financialization to primary exports; and, capitalization of the poor to imported consumption. In an attempt to placate capitalist voracity, it sought the lowest common denominator between globalization and sovereignty in the international sphere, and between neoliberalism and integration of the population on the domestic level.

Interpreted on its own terms, the wave seemed successful at first. Economic growth fueled by rising commodity prices facilitated targeted policies that mitigated poverty, while business prospered as ever, resulting in relative social peace. Brazilian 'neodevelopmentism', 'serious' capitalism in Argentina, the 'process of change' in Bolivia, the 'Citizen's Revolution' in Ecuador and the Lugo government in Paraguay, all pursued the philosophical stone of an inclusive neoliberalism, in the hope of forging amalgams from which nations would arise – as was the case in the past with the utopia of a dependent development.

However, early in 2018, progressivism looked like dust on the travelled path, gradually descending on the trail where the train of history was advancing. Wherever one looked, inclusive neoliberalism gave way to social dispossession, while conciliation gave way to class warfare. Beyond the criticisms, mistakes and correct actions that could be pointed out in each case, the direction of the movement was clear: the progressive bid was insufficient to stop, let alone reverse, the vortex towards barbarism.

In this sense, what was happening in Cuba was revealing. Isolated by its politics and geographical location, the destiny of the island was always connected to that of its regional surroundings. Twenty years of progressivism later, Cuba wrote a constitution in which the word 'communism' was eliminated. The progressive wave, which began by the rewriting of constitutions to re-found nations (in Venezuela, Bolivia, Ecuador), ended up rewriting a unique experience of a leftist sovereign nation in the region.

The paradox went further though: while the countries that rode the progressive wave advanced in different rhythms and tempos toward entrenched states of criminalization of politics and economic insulation, in Colombian fashion, countries that were not governed by progressivism evolved timidly in the opposite direction. For example, progressive fronts did well in the presidential elections in Chile, Peru and Colombia between 2016 and 2017, while López Obrador reached the presidency in Mexico in 2018.

In spite of the encouragement it may bring to the left in these countries, this more recent progressive ascent should be interpreted not as an indication of change, but as its opposite. Twenty years later, at a time when both the harmlessness of progressivism to threaten the system and its relative effectiveness to manage social contestation became evident, a breach opened in countries where the forces of change have been most stifled in recent decades that will surely nurture the illusions of many and certainly not lead to any systemic change. López Obrador will be the first thrown to the lions, facing as he is, the monumental Mexican crisis.

Placed face-to-face, the past and the future, progressivism and reaction emerge in this light as different representations of, but not contrary to, the barbarism toward which the planet is heading. The failure of national developmentalism in the periphery, followed by the disintegrating effects of neoliberalism in all spheres of existence from economics to political culture, moves the whole of the Third World toward this destiny.

To give two examples: the degradation of Nehruvian nationalism associated with the Congress Party in India, which embraced neoliberalism in the 1990s, was succeeded by the rise of Hindu nationalism, a ideology with totalizing ambitions, reactionary and at the same time modernizing. In South Africa, the African National Congress, which has run the country since the end of apartheid has degenerated, as witnessed during the administration of Jacob Zuma, into an organization that has 'captured' the state for private purposes, while societal violence and inequality has intensified. Wherever you look in the Global South, the picture is bleak: economies impervious to change, social disintegration, the downgrading of politics and cultural alienation. Concentration of wealth, social abandonment, repression and obscurantism are the hallmarks of contemporary history.

Analyzed in light of this worldwide trend, progressive governments in South America emerge as attempts to civilize the train of history using common sense and concerted action. It was believed that it was possible to tame capitalist development on the periphery, or at least moderate its speed and direction. Without questioning the directional path, they adopted economic growth as north, based on the paradigm of the development of productive forces. As a result, instead of applying the brake on the train of progress, as Walter Benjamin put it, these governments accelerated it; instead of driving it as they expected, they were dragged along and, in some cases, defenestrated.

The moral of the story is that progressivism does not lead to change and it will take more than good will to realise it. Contrary to impressions, derailing this train will not lead to barbarism, but actually may be the only way to avoid it. It is necessary to dismantle the order that progressivism intended to civilize, or there will be no more civilization. If order is progress, as stated on the Brazilian flag, then disorder is urgent.

2   A National Approach

The Latin American left demands an informed analysis of the progressive wave, in order to answer questions of political relevance for the present and for the future. This contribution is organized around chapters addressing each South American country, including those that have not identified with progressivism, with the exception of Uruguay. This national approach is complemented by a discussion of the process of regional integration led by Brazil, which also permeates the chapter on Paraguay. The book also incorporates a discussion about Cuba, an inescapable reference of any process of change in the region and ends with some final reflections.

The questions that guide the analysis of progressive governments are political: Have these governments been effectively progressive in helping to overcome inequality and dependence? What is the scope and limits of the change pursued? What relations did they establish with both popular forces and the ruling classes? In historical perspective, is it possible to identify a political functionality from the point of view of the reproduction of the system? And finally, what are the links between the progressive processes and the reaction that one now sees?

In relation to Chile, Peru, and Colombia, different and more specific questions arise: Why in these countries has neoliberalism not been challenged, even rhetorically? What happened to the popular camp and to the left? Is the continuation of armed struggle in Peru and Colombia in the 1990s relevant to explaining the constraints to progressivism? Is Chile a case of the success of neoliberalism? And, more recently: in light of the progressive wave, do the left-wing fronts that grew during the elections in Peru in 2016, in Chile in 2017 and in Colombia in 2018, have a promising future? Overall, the question that arises is: What lessons can be drawn from the progressive wave for left politics on the subcontinent?

A chapter on Cuba is included because since the triumph of the revolution in 1959, the island has somehow affected every process of change in the subcontinent and vice versa: the revolution's margin of maneuver is conditioned by its regional environment. Further, an analysis that aims to contribute to counter-hegemonic politics needs to incorporate the Cuban experience. In this chapter, the central question is: What is the meaning of the ongoing changes on the island? Put another way, we must ask whether there is a capitalist restoration underway in Cuba. Underlying this analysis is an attempt to reflect on the actuality of revolution in Latin America.

Beyond each national process, the progressive wave recovered the ideals of subcontinental unity, associated with sovereignty and development. The constitution of the Union of South American Nations (UNASUR) in 2008 is the main expression of this movement, which nevertheless focused on South America and not on Latin America as intended in the Bolivarian Alternative for the Americas (ALBA), launched a few years earlier. An analysis of regional integration allows us to discuss the synergies and constraints between different national processes. Indeed, part of the hope that the progressive wave aroused was the possibility of convergence between governments, fostering changes difficult to posit in isolation; for example, challenging the hegemony of the United States.

From this point of view, the character of the Brazilian Workers Party (PT) governments was decisive in determining the general meaning of the process, since in addition to the political and economic importance of Brazil, the country demanded the leadership of a regional integration that it sought to model in the image of its domestic policy. We must then ask several questions: What were the underlying interests in a South American integration led by Brazil? How did this leadership interact with governments who had different orientations at the time, like Chávez in Venezuela and Uribe in Colombia? How should we interpret the consensus around the creation of UNASUR and the Initiative for the Integration of Regional Infrastructure of South America (IIRSA)? What does this process of regional integration, to which all the countries of South America have adhered, reveal about the reach and limits of the progressive wave? And correspondingly, what are the scope and limits of integration embraced by such governments?

The central hypothesis of the book is that the progressive wave makes explicit the narrow limits to change within the overall political and socioeconomic system in Latin America. The possibility of modifying these societies without facing the roots of problems, which are linked to dependence and inequality inherited from the colonial past, limits change to the surface of politics. It must be noted however, that electoral change is functional to bourgeois democracy and to the ruling classes, especially at a time when the pattern of domination, described by Florestan Fernandes as the 'Autocratic Bourgeois State', is shaken.[3]

It was in contexts with these characteristics that progressive governments were elected. In some cases, neoliberalism was openly contested, as in Argentina, Bolivia, or Ecuador, where popular uprisings toppled presidents. In others the protest was latent, as in Brazil or Uruguay, where those who inaugurated structural adjustment were punished with successive electoral defeats. From this point of view, the progressive wave can be seen as another chapter in the historical book of the permanent counterrevolution that characterizes class domination in Latin America. Despite the originally good intentions of the progressive wave, the counterrevolution has imposed itself as a law of gravity on the narrow purposes of change. Often, the low ceiling for reform has become the very ground of progressivism.

The impossibility of reform as a path associated with the antipopular, antidemocratic, and anti-national character of the ruling classes, is not a new or original hypothesis in Latin American thought. Almost one hundred years ago, the Peruvian José Carlos Mariátegui enunciated the antinomy between bourgeoisie and nation in his country, while Florestan Fernandes explained with academic rigor, decades later, why it was so. However, it is one thing to know something in theory and another to realize it in practice. In this respect, the analysis of the progressive wave gives historical concreteness to the

---

3 Fernandes refers to a State impermeable to popular interest, an institutional correlation to the 'closed circuit' of bourgeois politics in dependent capitalism, which condemns the people to a world of 'political minimums'. This pattern of domination refers to the economic impotence of the dependent bourgeoisie, which is compensated for by political omnipotence necessary to ensure the exploitation of labor and devastation of natural resources. In this circumstance, bourgeois politics is articulated around a negative objective: the monopoly of politics. The Autocratic Bourgeois State is the main instrument of this pattern of class domination, which translates into a permanent counterrevolution, consolidated in the Brazilian case with the coup of 1964. Since then, the bourgeois project has been reduced to renegotiating the conditions of underdevelopment around an anti-national, antipopular and antidemocratic modernization. The counterrevolution becomes a building block of bourgeois domination, forbidding space for change within the order. (Fernandes 1975a, 1975b, 1976, 1981).

proposition that the pattern of class struggle that characterizes dependent capitalism in Latin America makes reform not a viable path to overcome underdevelopment.

From a political point of view, it is as important to note this movement in the progressive wave as it is to understand it. To this end, two main strategies are adopted in this book: historical contextualization and the dynamics of class struggle, which involves analyzing the relationship of governments with the dominant classes and with popular sectors. This approach emphasizes the internal determinations of each process, referring the political démarche to the movement of history and the pattern of class struggle. From this perspective, although imperialism and the role of the United States are inescapable realities, I observe that this presence was not decisive in the unfolding of the processes covered, with exceptions such as Plan Colombia and the ineffable blockade of Cuba. The United States did not play a key role in overthrowing Lugo in Paraguay or Rousseff in Brazil, as was the case with Jacobo Arbenz in Guatemala or Salvador Allende in Chile during the Cold War. Even the instability that characterizes the Bolivarian process since the election of Maduro in 2013 is mainly related to internal dynamics.

The requirement of contextualization imposes a historical framing to the chapters in which the different countries are addressed, referring the period of the progressive wave to the specific dilemmas of each situation: underdevelopment with an abundance of foreign exchange reserves in Venezuela; 'sociedad abigarrada', or a variegated society in Bolivia; violence in Colombia; primitive socialism in Cuba, and so on. This look back is important to assess the scale of the challenges faced, because if progressives were elected in reaction to neoliberalism, the problems they faced have deeper roots. But it is also fundamental to understand the countries that have not leaned to the left: for example, the Shining Path and Fujishock, or Unidad Popular and the Pinochet dictatorship – quite different processes among themselves – to explain why the Peruvian left shrank and the Chilean left froze.

At the same time, it is necessary to inquire as to why these processes ended up succumbing to the system, even where there was a remarkable potential for radicalization, as in Bolivia. Beyond the seduction of power, there is a correlation between the political timidity of these governments and the defeat of the historical movement that precedes them. As a chapter of the world counter-revolution, the Latin American counterrevolution in the context of the Cold War liquidated revolutionary but also reformist projects, generating the conditions for the imposition of neoliberalism which, in turn, consolidated such a process. As a result, the bourgeois order in Latin America is reaffirmed as a permanent counterrevolution.

In this reality, there is no middle ground: managing the system requires joining with the rich and dominating the poor. There are different ways of exercising this domination, but exploitation, alienation, and dependence are always there. In this perspective, while progressive governments illustrate the constraints of breaking with the permanent counterrevolution, the countries in which politics did not lean towards progressivism are the counter-argument: i.e., it is the permanent counterrevolution without a pink interlude.

To reconstitute the dynamics of the recent class struggle in different countries, I turned to field research, in addition to the established bibliography. All chapters, including those dealing with regional integration, refer to conversations, interviews and visits, most of which are cited. Those that are not, as in the case of Ecuador, are because I have no record.

3 A Methodological Note

This methodological note sets out the limits of the book's scope. There is no chapter on Uruguay because this was the only South American country where I did no field research. On the other hand, there is a chapter on Cuba, because it is a necessary reference for any reflection on change in contemporary Latin America. Initially there was not a chapter about Brazil, given that I recently wrote a book about my home country. However, faced with the opportunity to make this book accessible to an audience that does not read Portuguese, I added a chapter on Brazil, elaborating on an article co-authored with Ruy Braga. It is the only chapter that does not rely on systematic fieldwork.

Beyond the national chapters, I include the project of regional integration of successive PT governments for two reasons: to make explicit the character of Brazilian foreign policy and the integration it promoted; and, because this is a fertile angle to analyze the interactions between South American countries, both to the left and right of the progressive spectrum. In this light, the moderating role of PT governments becomes evident, in the dual meaning of the term: as mediator between radicals and reactionaries (like Chávez in Venezuela and Uribe in Colombia respectively); but also, as actors who pressed for moderation rather than the radicalization of change. At the same time, the '*Brasiguayo*' question illuminates the contradictions of the Brazilian project, which in the Paraguayan case contributed to an unfortunate outcome.[4] This

---

4 This refers to the sensitive issue of Brazilian agribusiness empowerment in Paraguay, which opposed the agenda of land reform that was proclaimed, albeit half-heartedly, by the Lugo government deposed in 2012. See Chapter 6.

approach assumes that the PT governments have played a decisive role in defining the reach and boundaries of the progressive wave.

Finally, there is a chronological limitation. Field research and the writing up of original drafts were carried out at different times. Although I propose 2016 as the year in which the progressive wave process ran out, not all chapters end there; some advance to 2017. The chapter on Ecuador uses an update based on secondary sources because extensive fieldwork had been done in 2011. In the case of Colombia, the chapter was drafted at the end of 2014, for which I only added a note related to the defeat of the public consultation on the peace process. Here, the analysis presented offers elements to explain the result, such as the resonance of Uribe politics in the country and the ambiguities of the Santos government. In the Paraguayan case, while I did not initially intend to analyze the Cartes government, I present a detailed reconstitution of the motivations and events that led to the preceding impeachment. I note that this text, which points to Lugo's successor as being the prime articulator and main beneficiary of the coup, was written in August 2013, long before Cartes was elected. This is not a prophetic talent, but an indication that the politically informed Paraguayans understood quickly what had happened and why.

The historical timelines adopted in the chapters are also not uniform but examine essential facts in order to contextualize the contemporary dilemmas in each case. However, there is a relative symmetry between the analyses that address countries of similar socioeconomic background and whose recent political orientation has been remarkably different: Venezuela and Colombia; Bolivia and Peru; Argentina and Chile. Those who wish to deepen the comparative analysis can collate these chapters.

One last observation about the final reflections: The fundamental hypothesis of the book is enunciated in this introduction and underlies the different chapters: i.e., the establishment as a permanent counterrevolution and the infeasibility of reform as a path to change. With these issues in the background, the final reflections delineate the meaning of history in the period, pointing to relevant relations or contrasts between countries. The aim is to reconstruct the general picture in thick strokes, placing national peculiarities in dialogue as a means to see similarities or differences. It is an essay exercise, for I was not convinced that it would be fruitful to detail the comparisons between the countries, which in any case would be beyond my means.

So, this is not a book in which arguments contained in the successive chapters converge in a conclusion that proves the thesis. But it is a book in which, similar to its object, the thesis of the permanent counterrevolution is everywhere; except in the third section of the final reflections, where I advance nine propositions around the response needed for the permanent counterrevolution: a Latin American revolution.

CHAPTER 1

Venezuelan Revolution: Underdevelopment despite an Abundance of Foreign Exchange

> It is a bit what I said about the third way proposed by Tony Blair, the British Prime Minister. A model that is neither socialist nor communist, nor the wild neoliberalism that generates unemployment and instability. That there is employment, work, fair salary, social security. A humanistic economic model, that is the solution.
>
> *Hugo Chávez, 1998*

> You remember, and the country remembers, on some occasion naively sketched that thesis of a third way, on some occasion I even got to read the thesis of the so-called Rhenish capitalism or with a human face, but I came here and began those dynamics around my person, around my management, I was learning in reality, I was studying, I went around the world and in a few years, and especially after the coup of April 2002, after the imperialist onslaught with that savage action of economic sabotage, terrorism, I realized that the only way for us to be free, for Venezuela to be free, independent, is the way of socialism.
>
> *Hugo Chávez, 2008*

1   Introduction

The election of Hugo Chávez in 1998 was the first victory of an alternative to conventional neoliberal politics in South America. During the previous four decades, Venezuela was commanded by two parties that took turns at power under a political arrangement known as the 'Punto Fijo Pact'. Dependent on oil exports, the country experienced a remarkable economic expansion in the 1970s, with the sudden dramatic rise in the price of oil. In the following decade, however, the debt crisis together with a fall in oil prices plunged the country into a protracted recession. The application of the neoliberal recipe by successive governments was at the root of a popular uprising in 1989 known as the *Caracazo*, as well as the attempted coup led by Chávez in 1992 and, finally, his election. Despite the moderate initial orientation of the new government, the intention to regain state control of oil income polarized the country. Faced with an attempted coup in 2002, followed by an oil lockout promoted by the opposition, the government responded by radicalizing its positions. A dynamic process that brought the prospect of radical change back to Latin America, the self-styled 'Bolivarian revolution' faced the challenge of a situation described by Celso Furtado as 'underdevelopment with abundance of foreign exchange reserves', which has framed both its achievements and its limits.

2　Underdevelopment with Abundance of Foreign Exchange Reserves

As one of the main insurgent centers in the war of Hispano-American independence, and the birthplace of the iconic figures Francisco de Miranda, Simón Rodríguez and Simón Bolívar, Venezuela's trajectory throughout the nineteenth century reveals similarities with the other countries of the region, where the geographical, social, political and economic barriers to the affirmation of the national state were expressed in recurring civil conflicts. In the Mexican manner, the efforts of capitalist modernization in the last quarter of the century were guided, directly or indirectly, by the modality of the 'civilizing autocrat'. General Guzmán Blanco, who provided the political line of the regime even after he stepped down from the Venezuelan presidency in 1888, would not be the first or the last ruler to identify his modernizing project with the independence movement of Simón Bolívar, who died in 1830, isolated and embittered by the fragmentation of his regional unity project, but was subsequently elevated to the status of a national icon (Carrera Damas 2006).

When, in 1899, the regime was overthrown by an Andean military force led by Cipriano Castro, the new government was different, not because of its dictatorial political methods but through its nationalist orientation. Thus, when a coalition of European powers blocked Venezuelan ports in 1902 on the pretext of collecting foreign debt, the president condemned the aggression in a statement that began: 'The insolent plant of the foreigner has desecrated the sacred soil of the motherland'. The outcome of the episode, which imposed mediation by the United States in favor of foreign powers, revealed what the intercession of this country in the eastern border dispute with British Guiana a few years earlier had already announced: that the US had displaced Britain as the discretionary power in the region. The US claimed control over the Caribbean as a kind of internal sea in the wake of the American Hispanic War of 1898, when it occupied Cuba and Puerto Rico (LaFeber 1963). The US intervention in the Colombian civil war, which resulted in the territorial division that gave birth to Panama in 1903 and the construction of the canal that began in the following year, consolidated this trend.

When a conflict broke out between the Venezuelan government and an American mining corporation in June 1908, leading to the rupture of diplomatic relations between these countries, a military coup took place a few months later. The coup led to the presidency of Juan Vicente Gómez, who recognized American demands, opened the doors to foreign capital and commanded the country until his death in 1935. Venezuelan history did not differ from that of other Central American and Caribbean countries except in degree, in a region where the US intervened in an increasingly explicit way, shaping political institutions and the economy.

At the turn of the century the export of Venezuelan primary products did not show the dynamism of other South American economies. Venezuela's slow development is exemplified by the fact that after the eighteenth century no new cities were founded, in a country where 85 per cent of the population lived in rural areas and most of them in cities of between 5,000 and 10,000 inhabitants. Even Caracas did not exceed 100,000 residents (Carrera Damas 1997: 129). This situation changed in 1917 with the discovery of oil, a product that by 1926 had already become Venezuela's main export. Despite meager taxation, fiscal revenues from oil multiplied by 50 in six years, jumping from 6 million bolívares in 1924 to 300 million in 1930, in a development that Maza Zavala synthesized in the following words:

> Castro was the last ruler of an agro-exporting country, fragmented by the dominance of the *caudillos*, indebted to the outside, poor in fiscal, financial and monetary resources, still moved by the agonizing slices of internal wars. Gomez was the first ruler of an oil country, with a predominance of foreign capital, without the fierce traditional *caudillaje*, without the 'historical' parties (different shades of conservatism and liberalism), with an increasing fiscal, financial and monetary potential, solvency reestablished in terms of public debt and relative public peace under the slogan of 'union, peace and work'.
> MAZA ZAVALA 1984: 477

Originally run as a private business ('managing the country is like managing a hacienda', said the dictator), Gómez distributed concessions among his relatives and favored people through the Venezuelan Petroleum Company (CVP). The beneficiaries in turn re-negotiated them, arriving at a situation in which Standard Oil and Shell controlled 85 per cent of the business (50 per cent and 35 per cent respectively) in the late 1930s. In a phenomenon that later literature would describe as 'Dutch disease', the appreciation of the bolivar from oil exports caused a rise in agricultural prices, aggravating the sector's critical situation at the time of the inter-war world depression. The country gradually became a food importer, which has resulted in a process of 'de-peasantisation' and urban migration, revealing one characteristic feature of contemporary Venezuela: the emptying of productive activities as a result of how the revenue generated by oil reinforces the social relations bequeathed by the country's history.

The consolidation of Venezuela's identity as an oil country had fundamental consequences in the way the population related with the state, and nationalism itself. Oil income was identified as a natural wealth belonging to the Venezuelan people that should be managed by the state. The different political groupings in the democratic field that were consolidated in the years after Gomez's death agreed on the importance of the distribution of oil income, as opposed to private appropriation by the dictatorship. In this way, individuals benefitted through the effective performance of the state as mediator between transnational corporations and the population as a whole.

This identification of democracy with the distribution of oil income resulted in an ambiguity of Venezuelan nationalism. On the one hand, the growth of national income depended on the appropriation of oil revenue by the state from the transnationals that dominated the business. On the other hand, since the nation's revenue was tied to the oil business, the profitability of foreign companies was a necessary condition of its expanded reproduction. According to Miguel Tinker Salas, 'employees of foreign oil companies and sectors of the middle class created a vision of a modern Venezuelan nation rooted in political and social values promoted by the industry' which had as its main line the idea that 'the interests of the industry were the same interests of the nation' (Tinker Salas 2013: 22–23).

The perception of Venezuela as an oil nation unfolds in an association between democracy and distribution of oil income, whereas the nation's progress is identified with the prosperity of the oil business. This ideology underlies the slogan of strong resonance in contemporary Venezuela: 'to sow oil'. Originally formulated by the intellectual Arturo Uslar Pietri in the 1930s, when a formerly agrarian country had become dependent on food imports, the text denounced, in a premonitory way, the risk that the oil wealth would turn Venezuela into a species of parasite feeding on nature.

Turned into the slogan of political projects that sought to break the country's dependence on oil revenue through the diversification of production and industrialization, the idea of 'sowing oil' has been present since the first political programs of AD (Acción Democratica, originally of social-democratic inspiration), founded in 1941, until the Bolivarian process in the twenty-first century. It has informed the analysis of critical thinkers such as Juan Pablo

Pérez Alfonzo, the architect of the Organization of Petroleum Exporting Countries (OPEC) and Brazilian economist Celso Furtado, who, in the face of high oil prices, diagnosed in 1975 that 'there is a possibility in this country of modifying it [underdevelopment] without major social upheavals' (Furtado 2008: 122).

This identification of nation with oil business exemplifies the influence of the rentier economy in all spheres of Venezuelan society (Tinker Salas 2013: 344). Since the state is the intermediary between the oil revenue and the national interest, the dispute over oil surplus materializes as a dispute for the state. Thus, if the common denominator of the democratic organizations that emerged after Gómez's death in Venezuela was the social distribution of oil income, the political instability of this period – in which a succession of military coups placed and removed the AD from government until the Punto Fijo Pact in 1959 – is linked to concluding a satisfactory arrangement of the privileges associated with oil revenue for the different sectors of the ruling class. The infamous Punto Fijo Pact implied sharing the state between the two dominating parties, AD and Copei (the Christian Democracy, founded in 1946), which reserved the alternation of executive power; the integration of the armed forces in oil concessions; the control of trade unions including the Confederation of Venezuelan Workers (CTV) which was mainly linked to the AD; and the repression of dissenters, especially communists.

The pact was based on the premise that oil business would be managed in association with international capital which, because of the geopolitical reality of the day, led to the country's alignment with the US. The Punto Fijo Pact corresponded internationally to the Betancourt Doctrine, which, under the rhetoric of an uncompromising commitment to democracy unpleasant to dictators like Trujillo in the Dominican Republic or Duvalier in Haiti, revealed militant hostility towards the Cuban Revolution. Internally, the limits of political tolerance were defined by the foundations of the Pact itself, resorting to the repressive techniques characteristic of Southern Cone dictatorships against those who questioned the status quo (Defensoría del Pueblo 2013).

Despite the coups that deposed Medina Angarita in 1945 and Romulo Gallegos in 1948, as well as the 'little coup' that consolidated the dictatorship of Perez Jimenez in 1952 or the mobilization that overthrew this same regime in 1957 giving place to the Punto Fijo Pact, analyses that focus on the rentier state emphasize continuity as the hallmark of Venezuelan history. Looking from the angle of oil policy, Bernard Mommer locates a key modification when the oil nationalization commanded by Carlos Andrés Pérez amid the Punto Fijo Pact changed the petroleum policy practised until then:

> Oil history can be divided into three periods. The first, the Period of the Concessions (beginning of the century until 1975) was characterized by a

continuous progress of the state as owner of the natural resource and as sovereign owner. It culminated with the nationalization of industry in 1975 and the creation of Petróleos de Venezuela SA. The second period, the Period of the National Petroleum Company (1975 to 2003) was characterized by a contrary movement to annul, one by one, all the achievements of the first period ... The third period of our petroleum history that began in 2003 can be called the Epoch of Confrontations between the two opposing policies already mentioned – national the first and anti-national the second – under the motto of Full Oil Sovereignty....
    MOMMER 2013a: 23

As with Mommer, the work of Fernando Coronil draws attention to lines of continuity in Venezuelan history beyond alternations of government, and even regime. Mommer focuses on the sense of oil policies, while Coronil highlights the multiple social, political and cultural consequences, for Venezuelan society, of petroleum rentism. It is possible to situate the crisis that projected Hugo Chávez into power in the convergence between these two issues in a society marked, in all social spheres, by underdevelopment despite an abundance of foreign exchange.

According to Mommer, the reversal of petroleum policy practised since the 1930s was paradoxically signaled by the creation of the state owned Petróleos de Venezuela (PDVSA) in 1976 in an operation that merely nationalized the transnational capital but kept untouched control over the commercial dimension of the business – as it was carried out in the main countries associated with OPEC in the period (Mommer 2013a). In Venezuela, the new company was driven by a mercantile rationality impervious to state policies. Therefore, the PDVSA consolidated itself in the following decades as a kind of 'state within the state', in a trend that deepened in the 1990s in light of the liberalization of oil policy (Parra Luzardo 2012).

Analyzing the consequences of oil nationalization, Coronil points out that this separation of oil income and the national interest came hand in hand with corruption and delinquency in a country where the use of public office as a means of private enrichment was common practice. Parallel to the euphoria of the boom in revenues resulting from the oil shock of 1973 (which resulted in numerous public works and a sophisticated pattern of consumption based on imports and public indebtedness secured by the certainty of future revenues), the sensation spread that oil was corroding the social fabric of the country. This perception was summed up in the title of the book published in 1975 by Juan Pablo Pérez Alfonzo (2011): 'Sinking in the excrement of the devil'.

The structural roots of this malaise are linked to the peculiarities of class struggle in an oil rentier economy. According to Coronil, in a society in which the primary source of wealth is associated with distribution, the dispute over economic surplus does not take place in production but is expressed in a dispute for the state or – more specifically – for the way the state distributes oil revenue. In this perspective, the Punto Fijo Pact implied an uneven but comprehensive division of state revenue, including to the direct beneficiaries of the oil business: the state bureaucracy comprising the army and contractors – but also segments of workers, whose unions often push for a greater distribution of oil income rather than wage increases. In short, the petroleum business, civil service, infrastructure works, social programs and direct and indirect subsidies for consumption constitute a network that extends the benefits of oil income to different strata of the population, albeit unevenly. According to Coronil, the nature of this relationship results in a fetishistic perception of the state as 'a place endowed with the alchemical power to transmute liquid wealth into civilized life', which he dubs the 'magic state' (Coronil 2013: 294).

Owing to the socio-economic distortions associated with the 'Dutch disease' and its impact on the productivity of the non-oil sectors, consumption subsidies translate into import stimuli, spreading a standard of living detached from the productive structure. Since the vital sap of the national economy comes from oil income, which drives imports, bourgeois strata thrive by links to trade instead of production. In addition to the economic hindrances to 'oil sowing' (such as internal market, technological dependence and capital investment), multiple obstacles to a national bourgeoisie arose in a reality in which industrial initiative was perceived as a mere extension of commercial activity.

This means that industrial investment – when, for example, the government implemented protectionist tariffs for the manufacture of certain products – often aimed to preserve an advantageous commercial position. The case study of the FANATRACTO tractor factory in the 1970s shows that the company's shareholders were linked to trade in imported tractors, so that when the government, as it adopted liberalizing policies, gradually withdrew its support for the initiative, the factory was closed without protest and its owners went back to importing tractors. This pattern, where distribution of oil profits prevails over value production, leads Coroníl (2013: 470) to suggest, reversing Marx's assertion, that in Venezuela circulation has absorbed production as a phase of circulation.

The malaise derived from the perception that oil income spread corruption and 'parasitism', rather than sowing industrialization and sovereignty, turned into social indignation in the 1980s when the combination of the debt crisis and the fall in international oil prices caused a lack of foreign exchange which dissolved the power associated with the 'magic state', putting Venezuela on the neoliberal rails. The first unmistakable symptom of the crisis was the devaluation of the bolivar in 1983, on a day that became known as 'black Friday', at the same time that the exchange system was changed. The headline of a national newspaper synthesized the state of mind of the moment: 'The party is over' (Lopez Maya 2006: 23).

The first package of neoliberal measures was implemented the following year. However, the crisis came to the fore when a popular rebellion was triggered by the increase in the price of petrol in 1989 – affecting the cost of public transport – as part of fiscal adjustments implemented by the government of Carlos Andrés Perez (1989–1993). The president, who, ironically, had commanded the country from 1975 to 1979 in the midst of the 'oil euphoria', now administered a state that directed more than half of its revenue to the payment of creditors. The *Caracazo* was the most violent rebellion against the neoliberal agenda in Latin America in the late twentieth century, leaving an unknown number of dead (but said to be in the hundreds) after five days of fighting.

As it explained the autocratic nature of the Venezuelan state, the episode is considered a milestone in the corrosion of the Punto Fijo Pact, underpinned by its economic degradation. According to Mommer, during the period of the so-called anti-national petroleum policy (between 1975 and 2003), there was a decrease of 1.5 per cent of GDP per capita, in contrast to growth of around 4 per cent in the previous period (Mommer 2013b). The negative rates between 1980 and 1984 were followed by abrupt fluctuations, reflecting the country's dependence on oil exports.

The neoliberal program had corrosive effects on the world of work. Between 1983 and 1998 there was a decrease in formal employment in the public sector (22.67 per cent to 16.33 per cent) and private sector (36.03 per cent to 35.47 per cent), corresponding to an increase in informal work (41.3 per cent to 48.2 per cent). This reduction in formal employment was accompanied by attacks against workers' rights, resulting in a decrease of the purchasing power of the population as a whole, and exacerbated by inflation. Between 1980 and 1997, the percentage of households in poverty rose from 17.65 per cent to 48.33 per cent, and in extreme poverty from 9.06 per cent to 27.66 per cent. The homicide rate multiplied by four in Venezuela as a whole, and by six in Caracas between 1986 and 1999, while vehicle robberies tripled between 1990 and 1996 (Lopez Maya 2006).

This is the background against which the political leadership of Hugo Chávez came to the fore. The military coup he led in 1992 failed, but the unpopularity of the government of Andréz Pérez resulted in popular identification with the leader of the uprising, who assumed responsibility for the defeat on national television, underlining that he yielded 'for now' (*por ahora*). Affiliated with the AD, Andréz Pérez prevailed at that moment, but was demoralized. He was dismissed in the following year for corruption and placed under house arrest. His successor was another emblematic figure of the Punto Fijo Pact, the former president and founder of Copei, Rafael Caldera, who was elected by announcing a break with the policies of his predecessor, seeking to disassociate himself from the political arrangement he had helped to build. In spite of its original intentions, this government soon capitulated to neoliberal constraints, consolidating, in full view of the population, the bankruptcy of conventional political alternatives. It was in this context that Hugo Chávez, pardoned at the beginning of the Caldera government, was elected president in 1998, facing an unprecedented coalition between the groups that had alternated in power for forty years.

3   Bolivarian Revolution

From a continental perspective, Chávez's election refers to a pattern in which the implementation of the neoliberal agenda wore out conventional parties, providing room for the election of alternative candidates, historically identified with the left in some situations (such as Tabaré Vazquez in Uruguay and Lula in Brazil) or simply with an alternative to prevailing politics (such as Morales in Bolivia and Correa in Ecuador). Against this background, the singularity of the Venezuelan process was the determination with which its president faced the constraints to social change, responding with a progressive radicalization of the self-styled 'Bolivarian Revolution' when his counterparts often legitimized neoliberalism (Webber and Carr 2013). Chávez himself was aware of this dynamic, which he described as a 'question of theoretical maturation and eminently dialectic practice'.

> You remember, and the country remembers, on some occasion naively sketched that thesis of a third way, on some occasion I even got to read the thesis of the so-called Rhenish capitalism or with a human face, but I came here and began those dynamics around my person, around my management, I was learning in reality, I was studying, I went around the world and in a few years, and especially after the coup of April 2002, after the imperialist onslaught with that savage action of economic sabotage, terrorism, I realized that the only way for us to be free, for Venezuela to be free, independent, is the way of socialism.
> RANGEL 2014: 274

Although for most Venezuelans Chávez suddenly emerged in national politics with the frustrated uprising of 1992, he traces his original revolutionary commitment to the late 1970s, and the beginning of a military movement claiming the constitutional right to rebellion to the founding of the Revolutionary Bolivarian Movement-200 (MRB-200) in 1982, the year that preceded the bicentenary of the birth of Simón Bolívar.

A lieutenant-colonel influenced by progressively-oriented military such as the governments of Velasco Alvarado in Peru (1968–1975) and Omar Torrijos in Panama (1968–1981), Hugo Chávez Frías's political formation is also a strand of the Venezuelan left linked to armed struggle in the 1960s and coupled with a nationalism that claims the legacy of the nation's founders and of Latin American unity (Gott 2004). This conjunction is evident in the program that guided the 1992 uprising, known as the 'Blue Book', probably an allusion to the 'Green Paper' prepared by another nationalist military in an oil country, Muammar Ghaddafi. In this booklet a tree with three roots is described, in the manner of the three sources of Marxism popularized by Lenin: 'it is the project of Simón Rodriguez, the master; Simón Bolivar, the Leader, and Ezequiel Zamora, the General of the Sovereign People' (Chávez 2013). In concrete terms, political reform based on the convening of a constituent assembly was proposed as a path to refund the country and construct a 'participatory and pro-active democracy' – a veiled criticism of the institutionalism consecrated by the Punto Fijo Pact.

In fact, this was the script followed by Chávez when he was elected. Once he was sworn in, he convened a constituent assembly, but maintained the previous government's minister of the economy, signaling moderation, although in previous years he had suggested a moratorium on debt and the establishment of a 'postwar economic model' (Rangel 2014: 107). In an interview months before the election, he described his economic proposal in these words:

> It is a bit what I said about the third way proposed by Tony Blair, the British Prime Minister. A model that is neither socialist nor communist, nor the wild neoliberalism that generates unemployment and instability. That there is employment, work, fair salary, social security. A humanistic economic model, that is the solution.
> RANGEL 2014: 217

The result of intense constitutional activity in its first year of government, the new 'Magna Carta' approved through a plebiscite changed the name of the country to 'Bolivarian Republic of Venezuela' and created new 'citizen' and 'electoral' powers as indicated in the 'Blue Book'. Among other changes in the political arena, it expanded and updated human rights, incorporating indigenous and environmental rights, and pointed out various forms of direct political participation as well as the possibility of repealing mandates. The constitutional mobilization was accompanied by a strengthening of the parliamentary base linked to the process, which was then called the 'Bolivarian Revolution'.

However, what outraged the opposition was not the constitutional process but the set of 'enabling laws' announced at the end of 2001 emanating from the executive. Among the enacted laws were the Law on Land and Agrarian Development, facilitating the expropriation of areas larger than 10,000 hectares without regular documentation; the Fisheries and Aquaculture Law defending fishing by traditional means in relation to industrial fishing; and especially the Hydrocarbons Law that signaled a re-appropriation of oil revenues by the state for public policy purposes (Maringoni 2004: 57).

This set of measures triggered a conspiracy that culminated in the coup d'état of 11 April 2002, orchestrated with decisive media support, as the documentary 'The revolution will not be televised' reveals. Reversed by the convergence of mass popular protest and the intervention of loyal military, a few months later the opposition offensive took the form of a 'national civic strike' – a lockout, aimed at interrupting oil exports with the shutdown of PDVSA.

Despite the success of destabilizing the economy, leading to a 27 per cent fall in GDP in the first half of 2003, the political balance of the clash tilted the correlation of forces in favor of the government. Determined to reverse the anti-national petroleum policy practised since 1975, the government carried out a purge at PDVSA, dismissing about 18,000 employees out of a total of 42,000. At the same time, social policies were intensified, mainly through the so-called 'missions', which responded to the double challenge of meeting popular demands and stimulating organic bases of support for the regime. This process counted on the decisive participation of the army, against the obstacles that the state bureaucracy placed in the relationship with Chavism.[1] According to López Maya:

> It was after this political victory that the government appeared to be clearly aware that its survival, not only in the medium and long term, but in the short months to come, was intrinsically linked to the possibility that it should undertake as soon as possible in a tangible manner, the

---

1 'Was it politically feasible to start the government already with a deeply revolutionary project? Was there political viability? How!? With almost all the state against' (Rangel 2014: 408). Monedero records a graffiti in Caracas these days: 'Chávez is our infiltrator in this shitty government' (Mondero 2013: 18).

participatory and proactive democracy that he enunciated from the beginning of his administration, and which until then had advanced only timidly.

LOPEZ MAYA 2006: 276

Chávez summed up the dilemma of these early years: 'Either I let myself be dragged or I stand firm' (Rangel 2014: 313). The triumph over the opposition in Venezuela coincided with Lula's assuming the presidency of Brazil, followed by the victory of Néstor Kirchner in Argentina a few months later. This auspicious regional convergence stimulated Bolivarian radicalization and marked the take-off of the process described retrospectively as a 'progressive wave' in South America.

Determined to stand firm, the Venezuelan government articulated initiatives in several dimensions, aiming to consolidate the bases of change. In the economic field it encouraged productive activities on different fronts, including the nationalization of companies, incentives to national entrepreneurs (the so-called '*boliburguesía*'), stimuli for cooperatives in the countryside and in the city such as social production companies (EPSs) and, later, the proposal of special zones of industrialization (ZEIs). In ideological terms, there was a radicalization, revealed by the incorporation of anti-imperialist rhetoric in 2003, leading to the proposal of a Bolivarian socialism that has been aired since 2004, which some would describe as 'socialism of the twenty-first century' (Dietrich 2005) and which would be furthered by the proposal of the communal state from 2006 onwards. At the international level, an alternative policy flourished, emphasizing regional integration as part of a multipolar strategy. It was signaled by the launch in 2004 of ALBA (originally the 'Bolivarian Alternative for the Americas') as opposed to the FTAA (Free Trade Area of the Americas); the constitution of Petrocaribe in 2005; the entry into Mercosur in 2006 and consummated in 2012, as well as deepening relations with countries such as China, Iran and Russia. In the social field, it invested in a multitude of programs, ranging from a comprehensive food security policy between food production (Gran Mision AgroVenezuela) and its distribution in state markets (Mercal), to massive popular education programs at different levels (Bolivarian Schools, Misiones Ribas and Sucre, Bolivarian University), through medical assistance plans (Misión Barrio Adentro, with the outstanding participation of Cuban doctors), and an impressive program of housing construction (Gran Misión Vivienda).

Confirmed by 17 elections over 14 years, in which it suffered only one defeat in a popular referendum, in 2007 (to which we will return later), the government was acutely aware that the 'tangibility of participatory and protagonist democracy' referred to by López Maya implied consolidating organized bases of support as opposed to the context when Chávez was elected for the first time. In a word, the Bolivarian Revolution would have to overcome Chavism to advance. Hence, the multiple organizational initiatives, from the Bolivarian circles and the missions in the polarized context of the first years. Hence the emergence of the Bolivarian Fuerza de Trabajadores within the CTV, which had supported the lockout in 2002–2003 and the creation in 2003 of the National Union of Workers. Hence the CTUs (local urban committees) in places where there was a need for urban land regularization, as well as the OCAS (self-managed community organizations) in the first Chávez government; the formation of the PSUV (United Socialist Party of Venezuela) in 2007; the commitment to the communal councils and communes, especially from the Law of Communal Councils of 2006, (López Maya 2011). Obviously, these initiatives have faced the dilemmas inherent in organizing the population by the state, which threatened their autonomy.

Proposals in the political arena were accompanied by initiatives concerning the press and propaganda, in order to counter-balance the hostility of the corporate media, which denounced supposed limits to the freedom of expression with a histrionic rhetoric. Research indicates that, out of the 90 national and regional newspapers, about 80 pursued opposition lines with the capacity to influence public opinion broadly, as many radio stations use them as a source for their news programs. In addition, most media outlets are in private hands; among the television channels, 65 were commercial and six were state-owned (Diaz Rangel 2012: 40). Faced with this impressive power, the government invested in Telesur, a regional channel funded by Venezuela, Cuba, Bolivia, Ecuador and Uruguay, as a press sympathetic to its policy. But perhaps the main channel of communication with the population was Chávez himself. He turned out to be a talented mass media communicator, live or on television, as in the Sunday program '*Aló Presidente*' in which he starred.

But charisma could hardly sustain a process that lasted for almost 15 years under Chávez. The social investment policy based on the oil income, which benefited from high prices, registered undeniable social advances. Between 2002 and 2010, the poverty-stricken population in Venezuela fell from 48.6 per cent to 27.8 per cent, a figure that would fall to 21.2 per cent in 2012. Similarly, there was a reduction from 22.2 per cent to 10.7 per cent of people in extreme poverty, reaching 6.5 per cent in 2012. These figures placed the country in third place, after Argentina and Uruguay, regarding poverty within continental Latin America. In addition, Venezuela had the lowest Gini coefficient in the region (0.394), an index that shows the degree of income concentration. In the labor field, unemployment fell from 14.6 per cent in 1999 to 6.4 per cent in 2012, while formal employment rose from 53 per cent to 57.5 per cent in the period. Enrollment at all levels of education rose sharply, as did the extension of the retirement system (from 387,000 beneficiaries in 1998 to almost 2.5 million in 2012), while infant mortality and malnutrition declined. As a result, the country registered a consistently higher position in the Human Development Index (HDI), reaching position 63 among 187 countries, and in the section considered as 'high' on the scale (Plan de la Patria 2013).

These numbers, based on a re-appropriation of oil income in the public interest, suggest that the Bolivarian process had begun to overcome the nefarious legacy of neoliberalism, placing the country back on the road to building a nation. However, the persistence of high crime rates, corruption and state inefficiency, clientelism, a rentier culture, dependence on oil, lack of food security and a pattern of consumption based on imports indicate the boundaries between what was accomplished and what the revolution aspired to.

4 Dilemmas of the Venezuelan Revolution

Since Nicolás Maduro was elected with a narrow margin of votes in April 2013, the biggest challenges facing the government have been in the economic arena, mainly increasing inflation, supply problems and a currency mismatch, in which there is a notable disparity between the different exchange rates practised and the dollar price in the parallel market. The disorganization of the economy had disintegrating effects on the social fabric and there are indications that the abovementioned advances have reversed (conversation with Lander 2015).

I will detail the mechanisms and effects of the crisis later – at this point I draw attention to its structural dimension, while at the same time delineating the contours of what appears to have been the Chavista strategy to overcome these constraints. The central hypothesis is that the emphasis on political dispute over economic contradictions was a symptom of the weakness of Bolivarianism to produce change. This analytical approach diminishes the weight of Chávez's death in the current crisis, suggesting the limits of the process in its entirety.

The structural root of inflation in Venezuela is the discrepancy between consumption patterns mediated by imports frequently subsidized by the state, and the country's productive base, a characteristic feature of underdevelopment. The Venezuelan peculiarity is to rely on what Furtado described as a 'stable liquid flow of foreign capital' from oil revenues, signaling the possibility of dodging capital shortages, one of the barriers to peripheral industrialization

(Furtado 2008: 46). However, by engaging in the structures of underdevelopment this 'abundance of foreign exchange' generates the socio-economic distortions associated with the 'Dutch disease' – an appreciation of the national currency that discourages local production vis-à-vis imports – and that in Venezuela resulted in social relations subsumed to petroleum profits, anchored on a pattern of consumption based on imports and state subsidies. Far from being restricted to an economic question, overcoming oil dependence implies changing the social relations crystallized by underdevelopment, whose origins go back to colonization, as Coronil notes:

> Paradoxically, money from oil, which was the result of the activities of some of the most dynamic transnational corporations, reinforced in Venezuela concepts and practices arising from the discovery and colonization of the Americas, which considered wealth not so much a result of productive labor, but rather as the reward for activities not directly related to production, which included conquest, plunder, or pure luck.
> CORONÍL 2013: 470

Theoretically, 'sowing oil' is not an end in itself, since a hypothetical equitable distribution of oil revenue would sustain a rentier nation, or at least a 'rentier socialism' as provocatively suggested (Álvarez 2012). However, beyond the existential question about the meaning of a society that reproduces itself as a 'parasite of nature', the overcoming of oil dependence is a condition for taking control of one's destiny and, in this sense, a premise of the Venezuelan revolution. In other words, oil income is the Venezuelan expression of the problem of dependence, which is inseparable from the pattern of class struggle that reproduces underdevelopment (Fernandes 1968, 1975).

In this perspective, the slogan 'to sow the oil' revived by Chávez suggests the economic content, but omits the class dimension of the Venezuelan revolution. It focuses on the distribution, not the production. This ambivalence can be observed in Chávez himself. On one hand he clearly envisages the character of the Venezuelan bourgeoisie ('imagine that I had ended making a pact with the Venezuelan right, with the capitalist bourgeoisie, I would have already been politically liquidated') and therefore radicalized the process. At the same time, he made a call to class collaboration ('there is no other way than to achieve the greatest possible social consensus') and to a loyal opposition, which would observe a 'code of ethics' (Rangel 2014: 378, 361). The ambivalence between the implications of radicalization and the aspiration to class conciliation was most clearly expressed in an interview given in September 2012, during his last presidential campaign:

> Our victory suits the owners of Televen, it suits the owners of Venevision, it suits the owners of large private companies, it suits the great bourgeoisie of the Lagunita Country Club. Why? Because with Chávez here, tranquility in the country is guaranteed, the peace of the country and the development of the country ... I am a guarantee for you, a stability insurance; What else do you want me to tell you?
>
> RANGEL 2014: 465

And yet, whenever a critical situation emerges Venezuelan capitalists demonstrate that they have no organic ties to a national project. In addition to the contradictions inherent in the promotion of a national industry when the interest of the dominant classes is linked to imports, neoliberal openness has increased financial speculation and sharpened the volatility of the national economic space. It is estimated that between the oil boom and the economic liberalization of the 1990s there was capital flight of US$60 to 90 billion – that is, between two and three times the external debt of the period. In the months of the 'oil strike' in 2003, capital flight was already estimated at US$7 billion. In the recent crisis, there is a convergence between financial speculation which puts pressure on the dollar by betting on a devaluation of the bolivar, and commercial speculation which imports commodities at the official dollar to resell them at the parallel price.

Given this reality, and assuming that the Bolivarian process involved a genuine commitment to consummating the Venezuelan revolution, how can we explain the conciliatory stance of Chávez?

It is possible to interpret his statements as a tactic to minimize social contradictions, due to a perception that the correlation of forces discourages open confrontation. A similar rationality can be thought of in the context of international relations, in which Chávez frequently criticized the neoliberal orientation of MERCOSUR (which he ended up joining) while he defended UNASUR as a route to an anti-neoliberal integration, although what was imposed was the Brazilian form of an umbrella organization with an eminently political character (Sanahuja 2012). In both cases, Venezuela accepted the limited benefits these initiatives offer as a counterweight to US virulence, in a world context hostile to projects alternative to neoliberalism, let alone of socialist inspiration.

In an international context unfavorable to change, confronted with a bourgeoisie detached from a national project and the production of wealth, inheriting an 'ineffective, corrupt, authoritarian, indolent and wasteful state' (Monedero 2013: 18), hopes of a revolution could only rest with the Venezuelan people, to whom Chávez gave testimonies of fidelity.

And yet, in this front too the starting point was not auspicious. As noted, Chávez was elected at a time of the fraying of political parties and working-class weakness, mobilizing a broad but diffuse base of popular support. Faced with a corrupt state, oppositional trade unions and an incipient peasant movement, he initially relied on the army to launch the missions. However, the goal of radicalizing change motivated a strategy of transition to another Venezuela, which Chávez described as 'Bolivarian socialism', thus signaling that its horizon would not be capitalism, nor the Soviet paradigm. In this regard, he liked to cite Fidel Castro, who said that his biggest mistake was to believe that there were people who knew the way to socialism. Hence the motto of Simón Rodríguez embraced by Chávez: 'either we invent, or we err'. The terrain of invention chosen by Chávez was politics, a field in which he had his greatest successes – and the method was the communal state.

The communal state was conceived from the articulation of various instances of popular power – between the communal councils, the communes, the communal cities and, finally, the communal state – culminating the ideal of 'participative and protagonist democracy'. Initially receiving political attributions, several communes were grouped around productive activities, especially in the countryside. For projects of similar economic orientation, a 'motor district' was established, linked to the 'Strategic Regions for Defense and Integral Development' (REDI) promulgated in the 'Plan de la Patria' of 2013–2019, a government program left by Chávez and incorporated by Maduro (Plan de la Patria: 2013). In mid-2014, there were more than 48,000 communal councils and more than 2,000 communes, of which 754 were registered as such, and a process of transfer of competences and resources to these communal bodies was being carried out, mediated by the Ministry of Communal Power, an organ that, according to its deputy minister, 'must have a finite existence' (conversation with Toledo 2014).

The proposal of the communal state as an instrument toward socialism flourished in a reality in which even opponents of the regime recognized that 'participatory innovations promoted by the government over 12 years have rooted the conviction that the problems of Venezuelan democracy can be resolved with the participation and efforts of all' (López Maya 2011: 113). However, this emphasis on the political path was not without its contradictions. As Victor Álvarez points out, throughout the Bolivarian process the economy became 'more capitalist' in the sense that private sector participation increased, from 64.8 per cent to 70 per cent between 1999 and 2008–2009, a phenomenon that he explains:

> Bolivarian economic policy, concentrating on the reactivation and not on the transformation of the existing productive apparatus, contributed to

the growth of the capitalist sector of the economy at a faster rate than the public economy and the social economy.

ÁLVAREZ 2012

Dependence on oil also increased, accounting for almost 95 per cent of exports of the Maduro government, which still had the United States among its main buyers, despite growing Chinese participation. Beyond these challenges, there were modest reforms that signaled a disciplining of wealth and consumption that Chavism resisted. For example, in Venezuela there is no tax on financial gains, while neighboring Colombia has a rate of 25 per cent; the tax burden in the country is between 9 per cent and 12 per cent of GDP while in Brazil it reaches 35 per cent. Finally, the government resisted tinkering with the price of petrol, which is the cheapest in the world, but whose subsidy bleeds public coffers.

This subsidy condenses the contradictions inherent in the pattern of distribution of oil income that characterize the 'magic state'. First, it produces inequality, since the subsidy to those who enjoy cheap public transport is tiny compared to the owners of cars, whose consumption increases according to the size and sophistication of the model. Consequently, this issue refers to another dilemma of the Venezuelan revolution, involving the need to change a pattern of consumption mirrored in the societies of central capitalism. As Furtado pointed out, in the Venezuelan case 'disciplining consumption is at least as important as guiding production' (Furtado 2008: 126).

Chávez was an attentive reader and a voracious intellectual with the humility to learn from books and from life. The motto 'either we invent, or we err' translates into an awareness that 'revolution is an eternal review'. The Venezuelan leader was also a dedicated strategist[2] and Ramonet draws attention to his tendency to be underestimated, related to his poor background (Ramonet 2013: 21). It is plausible that the communal state emerged inspired by the Cuban Defense Committees of the Revolution (CDRs), in a strategy that associated direct democracy and territorialization of power (Briceño Méndez 2014) with the intention of overcoming obstacles to the radicalization of the Venezuelan process:

> I believe that this is the best fight against bureaucratism, against State inefficiency, against corruption. Empowering the people, there are the

---

2 'In the Academy I learned what Napoleon calls the "arrow of the tempo". When a strategist plans a battle, he must think beforehand about the "historical moment", then the "strategic hou", then the "actical minut" and finally the "second of victory". I never forgot that scheme of thought' (Ramonet 2013: 20).

communal councils and their laws, they are already institutions; there are the communes that are forming; there are social comptrollers and the law just approved, these are examples ... They are a general strategic configuration, much more complicated, much more laborious.

RANGEL 2014: 333

The proposal of the communal state was part of a strategy of consolidation of the Venezuelan revolution, conceived as a long historical process whose axis was not the relations of production, but the construction of what Gramsci conceptualized as 'hegemony'. Viewed from this angle, Lopez Maya's criticism of instrumentalisation of communal councils by the PSUV should be qualified, as it expresses the deeper contradiction inherent in the role of a state that intends to dissolve its power (López Maya 2011). As Azellini records:

> The challenge of transformation in Venezuela means that many institutions have to work to tend to overcome their own existence (eg, the Ministry of the Communes), or at least to completely change their functions and reduce them in favor of the leading role of the people organized. And no institution, by inherent logic, does that by itself.
>
> AZELLINI 2012: 119

The resistance that this process aroused in the Bolivarian field itself was predictable, because it conflicts with interests associated with the prevailing institutionality. After all, Bolivarianism became the established power. Communal power was perceived as a rival by cadres linked to different instances of state power, who did not like the idea of a 'finite existence' of their positions. Many have evaluated this as the reason behind Chávez's only electoral defeat, in a consultation that sought, inter alia, to confirm the communal power and the socialist orientation of the process. It is plausible that Chávez himself cultivated an ambiguous relationship with the communal proposal, divided between the demands of state power and the utopia of popular power, a familiar dilemma of the Cuban revolution with which he established strong ties.

5   Crisis

The watershed of Bolivarian fortune was the parliamentary election of December 2015. At that point, economic imbalances grew worse. Inflation was estimated at 150 per cent according to unofficial data (the government did not disclose figures during the year). There were shortages in various sectors, including basic foods, medicines and medical supplies, as well as productive inputs and spare parts. The currency mismatch took off: in the official exchange the dollar was quoted at 6.30 bolivars, while in the parallel market it surpassed 800 bolivars per dollar, a phenomenon that encouraged speculative practices of a different nature. As a result, there was shortage of foreign exchange, making it difficult to travel abroad. The country's level of international reserves was low, around US$16 billion and with low liquidity, since more than 80 per cent was in gold. The International Monetary Fund envisaged a recession of around 10 per cent for the country. Faced with this disheartening economic scenario, President Maduro's popularity was estimated at around 25 per cent and the loss of the majority in the congress was predictable, although few imagined the magnitude of the defeat (conversation with Ramos 2015).

The contours of the process leading to this situation are known. Against the background of an overvalued fixed exchange rate, the price of the dollar in the parallel exchange started from 12 bolivars in October 2012 to reach the peak of 88 bolivars at the end of February 2014. This jump was linked to a shortage of foreign exchange in dollar terms in mid-2013, coupled with the sharp increase in public spending as of 2010, after five quarters of recession following the fall in oil prices. The main investment went to the construction of houses in the program Gran Misión Vivienda, launched in response to a natural catastrophe that left thousands of homeless in the state of Vargas. Beyond its social motivation, the program signaled a new round of grassroots action in the wake of a run-of-the-mill electoral campaign that ended up consuming public finances and the health of its top leader.

The scarcity of foreign exchange led to a spike in the price of the parallel dollar, burdening imports, which had inflationary repercussions, affecting the purchasing power of wages. The shortage of some products that followed generated nervousness and intentions to stock up, which in turn aggravated the scarcity. The drop in the ratio between the parallel dollar and the official dollar, whose difference was double but jumped more than tenfold, spread opportunistic attitudes in which traders importing at the official exchange rate readjusted their prices according to the variation of the parallel, increasing the inflationary pressure. The government launched an intermediate exchange band known as SICAD 2, aiming at lowering the demand for the dollar in the parallel and breaking the cycle of depreciation and inflation. As of February 2014 there were different exchange rates: the dollar at 6.3 bolivars for the importation of essential goods; Sicad 1 at the range of 10 bolívares at the time for secondary items and international travel; Sicad 2 – following the system of supply and demand with intermediation of the Central Bank – at around

50 bolivars; and, finally, the parallel dollar, which at that moment fell below 70 bolivars (Ramos 2014).

In the second half of 2015 the explosion of the difference between the official exchange, frozen at 6.30 bolivars and the parallel, which surpassed 800 bolivars, had become an irresistible impulse to speculation, in various ways and scales. In retail, there were multiple speculative activities such as the phenomenon of *'raspacupos'* who bought tickets on international flights to access dollars at official prices and later resold in the parallel, exhausting the virtual seats of planes that in fact took off empty (Ramos 2014); or, the smuggling, on small and large scales, of everything imaginable – from petrol to diapers, to food and medicine, especially to Colombia.[3] The government's commitment to preserving basic necessities boosted this illegal trade, benefiting corrupt border officials. On a larger scale, there are controversial accounts of manipulation by companies, such as in the field of civil aviation, generating constant friction with the government. More serious for the legitimacy of the process, there was evidence of corruption scandals involving public officials, including allegations of smuggling on oil ships with the complicity of members of the government and the armed forces. When one recalls that Chávez turned to the army, especially in his first years in office, to counterbalance the difficulties in implementing a program of change in the face of the inherited 'ineffective, corrupt, authoritarian, indolent and wasteful' state, one can sense the depth of the dilemmas.

The detachment between the exchange rates, combined with rising inflation, resulted in practice in the dollarization of the price of imported items. A bottle of ketchup marked at 3,000 bolivars would correspond to almost five hundred dollars at the official exchange rate. The other side of this situation is the real devaluation of wages, accentuated in comparison to activities involving access to dollars: someone selling a Venezuelan tank of petrol in Colombia, once a day, five times a week, would earn more than a university professor (conversation with Ramírez 2015).

The conjunction of the reference to the dollar in an import-based economy, and the fall in the purchasing power of wages despite continued increases granted by the government, forced Venezuelans to seek dollars to survive. From a situation in which larger and smaller owners handled the crisis as a

---

3   It was in this context that the Venezuelan government deported 1,532 Colombians in August 2015, according to United Nations data, and decreed the closure of the border, causing the return of at least 18,377 citizens to their country of origin for fear of the unfolding of the situation, described by the Colombian state as a 'humanitarian crisis'.

mercantile opportunity, profiting from the exchange gap, they moved into a reality in which many supplemented their incomes, or even left their jobs in search of foreign exchange, aiming to maintain their standard of living. Frequently, the means of access to foreign exchange involved illicit activities, and juggling with exchange rate disparity was ethically questionable. This phenomenon, which has a formal resemblance to the so-called 'special period' in Cuba following the collapse of the Soviet Union, signals an ethical corrosion of the Bolivarian process, insofar as social reproduction based on work is not enough (conversation with Lander 2015).

Faced with the progressive deterioration of Venezuelans' everyday conditions, observers sympathetic to the process questioned whether political wear and tear would not outweigh the onus of shifts that discipline the economy. Even measures whose needs were widely recognized, such as the readjustment in the price of petrol, were resisted. The memory of *Caracazo* intimidated the leaders. Meanwhile, at a price of 10 cents per gallon, a dollar could buy 8,000 liters of subsidized petrol by the end of 2015, bleeding public coffers.

Operating deficits were covered by issuing currency and by loans, mostly of Chinese origin, and by mortgaging future oil production. Simultaneously, Maduro's international efforts to negotiate an increase in oil prices with producer countries were fruitless but revealing, as it demonstrated that the way out of the crisis was envisaged within the frame of the rentier state. In fact, the only point on which the Chávez 'Plan de la Patria' resembled the electoral program of opposition leader Capriles was the commitment to double oil production by 2019.

This explains the limits of the Bolivarian process: after almost 20 years Venezuela has become a country more dependent on oil exports. Government efforts to materialize the utopia of 'sowing oil', using the 'steady net flow of foreign capital' from oil revenues to dodge capital shortages have failed.

Although a balance of the efforts made in this direction requires consistent field research that empathizes with the obstacles encountered, it is possible to observe that, in general, rent-seeking behavior prevailed over production. An investigation of a group of small and medium-sized nationalized companies between 2002 and 2009 showed devastating results from the point of view of productivity (Obuchi 2011). Large companies also did not present satisfactory results, although there are always exceptions such as CANTV, a telephone company re-nationalized in 2007 and still profitable. As a rule, state-owned companies suffered from political factors, such as the nomination of favored people, internal strife, or even the suspension of union elections, when a left-wing opposition critical of Chavism won elections at Sidor, the country's largest steelmaker.

There have been, and are, ongoing attempts to strengthen the power of workers through social production. However, the structural obstacles to change in the relations of production, added to the rentier culture that permeates social relations, has proved an extraordinary obstacle. In 2008, the nationalization and surrender to workers' control of the country's largest steelmaker, Sidor, in the context of a large strike demanding higher wages, did not alter labor relations in the company, nor did it prevent conflicts with the state in the following years. Similarly, there are numerous labor disputes in companies linked to CVG (Venezuelan Corporation of Guyana), a public conglomerate that employs more than 20,000 workers in the region (Posado 2013). Despite the intention of the Guyana Socialist Plan 2009–2019, which aimed to convert the country's heavy industry into a 'laboratory for the new role of workers in the control and management of production', President Maduro suggested in a speech shortly after being elected that the model of worker control in Guyana did not fail, because in reality it had never existed (Maduro 2013).

Meanwhile, in the countryside, experienced militants with the Brazilian Landless Rural Workers Movement (MST) on a technical cooperation mission witnessed a unique reality, in which there was a government that expropriated land, but there was no one to work them. On the other hand, the subsidized importation of agricultural products hampered profitable production, and the state ended up banking many of the companies of social production, in order to avoid returning the land to the landowners. In short, the culture prevails that 'it is easier to harvest in ports than to harvest in the fields' (conversations with Micilene and Derli 2014).

Altogether, the approximately US$23,377 million invested in nationalizations in the period between 2007 and 2009, when the Bolivarian process radicalized in a socialist direction, was unable to alter the productive structure of the country. From the point of view of the relations of production, the hierarchies of labor did not change either. Álvarez, on the other hand, saw an upsurge in the exploitation of workers by observing that in 1998 the 'labor factor' absorbed 39.7 per cent of the value created, surpassing the 36.2 per cent that belonged to capital. Ten years later the share of labor fell to 31.69 per cent, while that of capitalists rose to 49.18 per cent, according to data from the Central Bank of Venezuela (Álvarez 2012).

Despite what the Bolivarian process represented for the history of Venezuela and its importance in reinstating radical change as a possibility on the continent, the process was unable to consistently challenge rentier logic. And at a time when the death of its uncontested leader and the international fall in oil prices would require a solid basis to overcome adversity, contradictions arose, related to the very circumstances that had allowed Chávez to rise.

First, the organic weakness of the Venezuelan social movement led Chávez to lean on the army as a party, a situation that was sharpened in response to the failed coup in April 2002 and was evidenced in the role of the institution in the implementation of the missions. However, the centrality of the army contradicts the pressures of democratic sense embodied in the ideals of the communal state from 2006. Strengthening local powers parallel to the state is antagonistic to the military rationale, where autonomy is identified as a threat to sovereignty.

Second, the militarization of the state, which has been exacerbated by Maduro, reinforces a dilemma that accompanied the process: how to establish organic links between the Venezuelan people and the Bolivarian state without instrumentalizing this relationship for political or, more precisely, electoral purposes. The tensions between state power and popular democracy have had important consequences in the productive realm since valuable initiatives for the democratization of ownership and control of production have often suffered from the distortions typical of hierarchical processes

A third question concerns the timing of social change. Despite revolutionary rhetoric, Chávez's rise was consummated by the electoral process, and the Bolivarian process compensated for its organizational fragility and its economic weakness with recurring legitimation at the polls. However, the timing of elections presses for immediate answers, which inhibits the implementation of radical changes that may be unpopular, as is the case with the petrol subsidy, or even with measures that would not be radical or unpopular (such as the taxation of financial gains) but that run into the fear of stirring up opposition feelings. Electoral dynamics conditioned the reach of Chavism to democratizing redistribution of petroleum revenue, in which the extension of subsidies under a universalist perspective reinforced rent-seeking behaviors and patterns of consumption typical of central societies. There is a correspondence between the difficulties of developing a national productive sector and the adoption of economic and cultural standards adequate for the reality of the country.

Of course, the development of an industrial base in the twenty-first century faces numerous economic challenges that would be difficult to address on a national scale – hence the emphasis given by the Bolivarian project to regional integration. However, as we will see later, its most daring initiative in this direction, expressed in the ALBA proposition, was neutralized in practice by Brazil, whose regional project obeyed a mercantile rationality aimed at its national projection. On the other hand, the policies pursued by Venezuela through ALBA and Petrocaribe resented reciprocity, and when the crisis intensified the country felt forced to sell Jamaica and Dominican Republic debt bonds with substantial discounts (conversation with Cerezal 2015). Even the two countries with progressive projects in the region, Bolivia and Ecuador, established an instrumental relationship with ALBA, benefiting from the mercantile advantages that this approach offered them, but showing little interest in other dimensions of the proposal (conversation with Villegas 2015).

Recognizing the limits of the international context in which Chávez moved does not imply ignoring a terrain of fundamental agreement, synthesized in the illusion of progress, or, in Furtado's terms, the 'myth of economic development' – the idea that economic growth is a way out of underdevelopment. In the Venezuelan case, the paradigm of progress translates into the reproduction of dependence on oil. Although economic diversification driven by oil income is theoretically conceivable, history has shown that the problems are inseparable: to change the country's economic structure it is necessary to face the link between dependence and inequality.

Petroleum rent-seeking behavior is the way in which underdevelopment is expressed in Venezuela. And just as the overcoming of underdevelopment is not limited to the equation of its economic variables, rent-seeking behavior demands to be faced in its totality, covering the economic obstacles to productive diversification and self-determination; the social distortions that militate against a society based on work; political aspects as relations of dependence and clientelism affect popular organization; and cultural aspects promoting a subjectivity referenced on patterns of consumption unrelated to Venezuelan reality.

6 Final Thoughts

Faced with the constraints to promote change within the order, Chávez led a progressive radicalization of the Bolivarian process. The broad popular support secured by the loyalty of a section of the armed forces ensured the government's victory in decisive clashes in its early years. As a result, the opposition was disbanded and Chavism was strengthened at a time when presidents identified with the progressive camp were elected in Brazil and Argentina. Anchored in the re-establishment of PDVSA's public role, the undeniable social advances of the government reinforced the legitimacy of the process, reaffirmed in numerous popular elections and consultations that buried the political foundations of 'Punto Fijismo'.

However, the pretension of deepening the popular conquests encountered structural obstacles, rooted in the ways that oil income was coupled to a society forged as a colony, engendering the peculiar situation of 'underdevelopment with an abundance of foreign exchange'. Faced with national and international imbalances of power unfavorable to anti-capitalist projects, the self-proclaimed 'Bolivarian revolution' chose the terrain of politics, in which it achieved its greatest successes, as a route to a projected radicalization.

Its most daring proposal formulated as the communal state, faced obstacles and contradictions, between the resistance of chavista sectors encrusted in the state and constraints to the autonomy of the popular field. Conscious that this was, as Chávez put it, 'a general strategic configuration, much more complicated, much more laborious', the strategy seems to have been a lengthening of revolutionary time, with the intention of solidifying the subjective conditions for later radicalization. However, the commitment to spread a positive identification between national revolution and socialism contradicts the limits that capitalist reproduction in Venezuela imposes, resulting in paradoxes such as increasing the share of capital in total wealth produced, an intensification of labor exploitation, dependence on oil and cultural mimicry.

Without the presence of its undisputed leader, facing economic problems characteristic of 'underdevelopment with an abundance of foreign exchange' at a time when the accumulated gains seem smaller in the face of everyday difficulties, the vulnerabilities of a courageous process committed to change appear. After more than 15 years, the constraints of the structure have overwhelmed the conjuncture, putting in check the Venezuelan revolution.

Faced with the erosion of a state permeated by corruption, increasingly supported by military personnel who often do not recognize Maduro's leadership as they did Chávez's, in a context of public insecurity and economic unpredictability that constrains citizens to day-to-day acts of survival, the rhetoric of 'economic war' (although real) has proved insufficient to renew votes for the process. The staggering electoral defeat in December 2015, when the opposition elected over two-thirds of the parliamentarians, led the government into a controversial reaction, resorting to political juggling and ideological euphemisms to elude the ballot upon which it had relied in the past. The Congress was disregarded, the convocation of a referendum called for in the Constitution was undermined and elections for governors were postponed. The bourgeoise institutionality that underpinned Bolivarianism up to that point became a hindrance to its survival, already deprived of any revolutionary potential. Against this background, the convening of a constituent assembly elected on the basis of specific criteria favoring the government in 2017 was interpreted as a means of strengthening executive power and scorning the elected parliament. On the whole, this path has divided the left in relation to Bolivarianism among those who consider it legitimate to defend it against the reactionary alternatives that present themselves – albeit by questionable methods – and those who identify unsustainable contradictions between the means and ends of such politics, compromising any aspiration to progressiveness. In any case, the process is on the defensive and the seeds sown will not blossom into popular power.

Venezuela's evolution shows in a paradigmatic fashion the limits of progressivism. Powerless to overcome primary commodity exportation, establish a new pattern of accumulation, or undertake a social revolution that modified power and property structures, the Bolivarian process stalled midway. In Latin America there is no room for half terms; since 2014 a vortex has consumed past conquests at the same time that it threatened Venezuela's social fabric, bringing the worst of Bolivarianism to the surface. Unable to promote the change that it once symbolized, Bolivarianism focused on blocking opposition, in the process becoming a conservative power, while the country faced degradation at an accelerated pace.

As Lander noted, the fundamental difference in relation to the most difficult times under Chávez's leadership, which had run through very serious economic problems in the aftermath of the oil strike of 2002–2003, is that the population then believed they were living in a temporary situation, in transit to something better. Under Maduro, the prevailing feeling is that the Bolivarian process has simply run out.

CHAPTER 2

Conciliation and Order under 'Lulaism' in Brazil

> Will the PT maintain its nature of a historical necessity for workers and radical social movements if it prefers the 'occupation of power' to the Marxist revolutionary view?
>
> *Florestan Fernandes, 1991*

> I've never made a political concession. I make accords ... If Jesus came here, and Judas had a vote in some political party, Jesus would have to call Judas to make a coalition.
>
> *Lula, 2009*

1 Introduction

The election of Luis Inácio Lula da Silva to the presidency of Brazil in 2002 sparked expectations of change in the region and beyond. Arising at the end of the dictatorship (1964–1985), the Workers Party (PT) consolidated itself in the struggle for democratization in the 1980s and in the resistance to neoliberalism in the 1990s. By the time it reached the presidency, the PT had adopted a conciliatory discourse and practice. During the next decade, which coincided with economic expansion, the party achieved notable success in pacifying the country and won three more presidential contests. However, in 2016, President Rousseff suffered a controversial impeachment and two years later, Lula was imprisoned. Progressive expectations gave way to a reactionary offensive, which had been unthinkable years before. The PT option to address Brazilian misery through its symptoms, while avoiding its roots, revealed its limits and contradictions. The defenestration of the party from the circles of power marked a reflux to the progressivism with which it was identified: the bells that toll in Brazil, toll throughout the region.

2 Preamble

The last country to abolish monarchy and slavery in the Americas, Brazil has been a conservative reference on the continent since its emancipation. In the century that followed, it became the principal Latin American economy, in the midst of an accelerated industrialization. Like Argentina and Mexico, it went through an experience described as populist, revealing fissures in the oligarchic pattern of domination in the interwar years. However, the military coup of 1964, the first of a repressive sequence in the Southern Cone, asserted the bourgeois option of dissociating development and national integration. Despite industrial progress and natural wealth, the country is still one of the most unequal in the world today.

The PT emerged in the throes of dictatorship (1964–1985) with a commitment to change this reality. Unions, popular movements, grassroots ecclesial communities and progressive Brazilian intelligentsia converged in its origin, constructing an original political instrument. Created as a mass party and not a vanguard, the PT intended to surpass what had, until then, been the main historical vehicles of popular politics in the country: on the one hand, the populist demagoguery associated with labor and Getúlio Vargas,[1] which presumed a guided integration of the people with mass society; on the other communism, plagued by dogmatism and fratricidal disputes, which hindered its ability to root itself at the base. At the same time, the PT emerged in the shadow of guerrilla groups decimated under the dictatorship, while Eurocommunism was asserting itself in Europe. In this context, although socialism and anti-imperialism were not absent, strategic formulations asserting 'democracy as a universal value' prevailed and crystallized in what became known as the 'popular democratic project' (Coutinho 2005). In other words, the PT emerged as a party of reform, not revolution.

Quickly, the new organization brought together those who identified with social change. The PT engaged in the last years of the struggle against the dictatorship and played an important role in broadening the debate around the transition, pushing for direct elections and social reforms. This role was consolidated with the influence, disproportionate to their representation, exercised by the party's members of Parliament in drafting the Constitution, adopted in 1998 and still in force in the country, known as the 'Citizen Constitution'. Significantly though, the party voted against the final text, because it considered the social advances of the fundamental document of the 'New Republic' that was at that time unfolding as insufficient. At that time, the PT had already accumulated important local electoral successes, and Lula emerged as a strong presidential candidate.

---

1 Twice at the head of the Brazilian state (1930–1945; 1951–1954), the leadership of Getulio Vargas was associated with a combination of national industrial development through state intervention and advances on work legislation. Both were responses to popular pressures, which he tried to patronize, while repressing dissent.

For many, the electoral defeat to Fernando Collor de Mello in 1989 by a narrow margin was a turning point in the trajectory of the party. Faced with a sordid campaign, in which conservatism united around a hitherto unimpressive politician, but marketed as a savior of the system, the defeated party faced a dilemma: to prepare to confront those opposed to change, or resign itself to policies tolerated by the system. The choice of the second option was evident in the following years. To the extent that the party accumulated electoral successes elsewhere, its political originality was being lost. Practices identified with the 'PT way of governing', such as self-managed community projects or participatory budgeting, gave way to the ideology of efficient management that colonized the public sphere. In campaigning, militant excitement was replaced by marketing and corporate donations. In short, the party was converted to the ends and means of conventional politics.

Despite this conservative inflection led by the PT leadership, the triumph of Lula's presidential candidacy in 2002 after three consecutive defeats sparked hopes for change. The union leader was reelected in 2006, and in 2010 was succeeded by his ally Dilma Rousseff, also re-elected in 2014. However, in 2016, Rousseff's second term was shortened by a controversial impeachment process and two years later, Lula was imprisoned. Progressive expectations gave way to a reactionary offensive, which seemed unthinkable a few years earlier.

To understand this shift we will look at the PT's various administrations in the entirety, as a premise to understand critical recent events. To begin we will approach the strategies of accumulation promoted by the PT presidencies, to then analyze the adopted forms of political legitimation. In this respect, my hypothesis is that Rousseff's impeachment is part of the crisis of the so-called 'Lulaist' mode of regulating social conflict that weakened the functionality of PT presidencies. This loss of functionality, evident from the days in June 2013, which saw the largest social upheaval since the end of dictatorship, was sharpened in the following years by the combination of economic crises and corruption scandals.

3   Strategies of Accumulation: Neodevelopmentism or Neoliberalism?

3.1   *Conciliation and Order*

PT administrations relied on the conciliation of classes as a method to reform Brazilian capitalism. It was a reasonable premise that, given the acute inequality that characterizes the country, much could be done to solve it without facing the structures that reproduce it. The 'Zero Hunger' program, whose leadership was initially given to a Catholic friar, summed up this approach: who would be opposed to ending hunger?

But if bread would appease the poor, conciliation with the rich demanded a commitment to so-called economic stability. In the Brazilian case, the founding milestone of such a commitment is the 'Real Plan', implemented by then-Minister of Economy Fernando Henrique Cardoso in 1994 who was later elected president. The main lines of the plan refer to ongoing monetary stabilization programs in the neoliberal world and provide for the commercial and financial opening of the economy, reduction of the state through privatizations, rigid monetary and fiscal policy and high real interest rates. As in other situations, it succeeded in containing inflation but worsened structural imbalances in national accounts, while at the same time irreparably reducing the State's maneuvering room to deal with them.

Exchange appreciation (i.e., parity of the Brazilian real against the US dollar) and trade liberalization stimulated imports and helped to curb prices, but compromised domestic industry, causing increasing trade deficits. Initially, this imbalance was mitigated by privatizations and foreign investment, mainly to acquire domestic assets, while increasing the pressure and incentives to export. However, the main mechanism to compensate for trade imbalances was the attraction of speculative capital, which required a series of measures that preceded the Real Plan, in order to make Brazil an attractive destination for international finance. In particular, the opening of the Brazilian public securities market, converted the country into an issuer of fictitious capital (Paulani 2008).

The other side of this story is the disciplining of the State as an instrument to transfer national wealth to international financial circuits. The logic of structural adjustment was imposed, ending with the fiscal responsibility law negotiated with the International Monetary Fund (IMF), implemented in the context of the crisis that preceded the devaluation of the real in 1999 when Cardoso began his second term. This anti-social law was then denounced by the PT for establishing a hierarchy in public spending, giving top priority to financial creditors at the expense of social policies and public investments.

In sum, the adoption of the Real Plan in 1994 culminated a process that converted Brazil into a platform for the valorization of international financial capital. This meant that, at the same time that the country consolidated itself as a destination of speculative capital, the flow of this capital became indispensable from the point of view of the orthodoxy now implemented. Permanent fiscal adjustment, high interest rates, contractionary monetary policy, floating exchange rate and free movement of capital are the pillars of this macroeconomy.

It is this commitment that the then presidential candidate Lula secured when he released the 'Letter to Brazilians' during the 2002 campaign. It was actually a letter to capital, responding to the specter of capital flight that loomed large just as Brazil was about to elect a worker president.

Once inaugurated, the PT government proved faithful to its commitment, espousing all the aspects of neoliberal adjustment consolidated in previous administrations: liberalization processes, deregulation and privatization, currency stability, implementation of the Fiscal Responsibility Law, primary surpluses, limits to the indebtedness of the public sector, flexibile labor relations and, the reduction and removal of acquired rights among others. This commitment to international credibility required further antisocial reforms, such as the new Bankruptcy Law, which put workers on an equal footing with other creditors, running counter to the premise that business risks fall on the employer.

But the main issue that surfaced in Lula's first term was the reform of public service pensions. The shift from a social security model to a private pension system broke with the idea of generational solidarity, in which the contribution of young people assures the pension of the elderly. This was done in the name of a model in which each worker has an individual account, managed as an investment fund. Generational and class solidarity gave way to a partnership in the mechanisms and risks associated with financial capital.

This reform was emblematic for two reasons. First, because it revealed the PT's functionality from the point of view of the system: the prestige of the president vis-à-vis workers was fundamental to enable, in the first year of his term, a reform that his predecessor had failed to pass due to strong opposition. Second, it follows an individual and commercial logic, transforming a social right into a financial product. Beyond the macroeconomic options that led Paulani to describe the first Lula government as 'the most complete incarnation' of neoliberalism (Paulani 2008: 10), it revealed that the party's civilizing horizon was in perfect harmony with the neoliberal world vision (Dardot and Laval 2010).

3.2 *Neodevelopment*

Regardless of the historical reality, PT policy has never assumed itself as neoliberal. On the contrary, in Lula's second term, when there was a surge of growth brought about by the increase in commodity prices associated with Chinese expansion, the proposition that a 'neodevelopmentalist' project was in progress circulated widely. After decades of stagnation, the slow recovery of the purchasing power of wages, the reduction of unemployment, a slight improvement in the distribution of income, the reduction of extreme poverty through targeted policies, the expansion of consumption that accompanied the abundance of credit, in addition to the perception that the country was going through the world economic crisis unscathed, supported the discourse that Brazil was undergoing a period of development, whose parallel with the post-Second War national developmentalism justified the neologism.

The common denominator between the different neo-developmentist formulations is the diagnosis that the country should seek an alternative route between financialization, which characterizes neoliberalism, and nationalism, which is associated with developmentalism. This route proposed returning to the emphasis on productive activities to the detriment of rentism, but without incurring inflation, fiscal populism, nationalism and other elements related to national-developmentalism. Sampaio Jr. has described such a neodevelopmental ambition in the following terms:

> The challenge of neodevelopmentism, therefore, is to reconcile the 'positive' aspects of neoliberalism – unconditional commitment to currency stability, fiscal austerity, the search for international competitiveness, the absence of any kind of discrimination against international capital – with the 'positive' aspects of old developmentalism – commitment to economic growth, industrialization, the regulatory role of the state, social sensitivity.
>
> SAMPAIO JR. 2012

The yearning to reconcile an 'external element, liberalism, with an internal element, Brazilian developmentalism' (Cervo 2003), materialized in support for the internationalization of large companies of national capital or based in the country. These were seen as vectors of national capitalist development policy: it is this policy of 'national champions' which we will examine in more detail in a later chapter. Its main vehicles were business diplomacy practiced by the Brazilian Ministry of Foreign Affairs, mainly in South America, and the credit policy of the National Bank for Economic and Social Development (BNDES). At its peak in 2010, the Bank's loans for this purpose exceeded the sum of resources handled by the World Bank and the Inter-American Development Bank (IDB) by 250 per cent.

The bank's action intensified the concentration of capital in sectors of the Brazilian economy considered internationally competitive, notably in the field of primary exports and construction. To give some examples: the bank provided R$ 6 billion[2] to the JBS corporate group for acquisitions in Brazil and abroad, which made it the largest meat producer in the world; R$ 2.4 billion for Votorantim Celulose to acquire Aracruz Celulose, also resulting in one of the

---

2   R$ stands for 'real', the Brazilian currency, while $ stands for the US dollar

largest pulp producers, Fibria; and, more than R$ 1.5 billion for the Sadia-Perdigão merger, making the Brasil Foods group the world's largest chicken exporter (Garcia 2012).

However, the key protagonist of Brazilian mercantile expansion was civil construction, a sector that did business in all Latin American countries, from Colombia to Cuba as well as in other parts of the world, especially in Portuguese Africa. Odebrecht, a corporation that symbolizes this trend, presented the city of Lima with a replica of the Rio de Janeiro Jesus Christ Redeemer, at a moment when it called itself the 'construction company of regional integration'.[3] The sector also benefited at the domestic level with the Growth Acceleration Program (PAC) which provided for an infrastructure work agenda and the 'Minha Casa, Minha Vida' ('My home, my life') program, which extended housing credit to the grassroots.

On the whole, this internationalization of Brazilian corporations, mainly in South America, corresponded to a political project of regional leadership. The strategy foresaw that the economic expansion of Brazilian businesses would serve as a foundation for the country's political projection onto the world stage, a process we will analyze in another chapter.

An argument can be made, that during the cycle of economic expansion, which lasted until Rousseff's first term, this proposal progressed with relative success. The expansion of Brazilian business corresponded to a recognition of the country's international prominence, personified in the figure of President Lula, who in 2009 was considered by Obama as the most popular politician in the world (Newsweek 2009). At the same time, the cover of the conservative publication 'The Economist' showed the Rio de Janeiro Christ the Redeemer rising like a rocket, with the caption: 'Brazil takes off' (The Economist 2009).

However, the combination of an economic slowdown and corruption scandals, which escalated from 2014, put this project on the defensive. While the Brazilian economy was entering a recession, numerous exposés revealed corruption schemes involving contractors and other national champions, both at home and abroad. The combined result was a critical questioning of both the PT government and its developmentalist proposal.

At that point, BNDES investment leverage was severely reduced, as budget cuts added to the decline in revenues from the Worker Support Fund (FAT)[4]

---

3 In 2017, when corruption scandals hit Odebrecht in Peru and former President Alan Garcia, who devised the monument, the statue was nicknamed 'Christ from the robbery'. In April 2019 Garcia killed himself to prevent his arrest on that case.
4 FAT is a special accounting and financial fund linked to the Ministry of Labor to cover the Unemployment Insurance Program, the Salary Bonus Program and the financing of Economic Development Programs. [N.E.]

reduced the amount of capital available for long term investment. Several indicators questioned the effectiveness of the 'national champions' strategy in any case. First, some companies that received large contributions from BNDES, soon after came under international control. This was the case with: the beverage conglomerate Ambev, which merged with a Belgian corporation and moved its headquarters to that country; of the Santa Elisa ethanol plant, acquired by France's LDC Dreyfuss; of EBX that associated with Chinese and Korean capital companies after receiving large volumes of public credit for its projects; and, of Alunorte and Alumar, companies sold by Vale[5] to Norwegian Norsk Hydro, among others (Tautz et al. 2010).

There have also been situations such as the Odebrecht operation in Peru, which have become autonomous: i.e., legally registered as a local company no longer supported by the BNDES and no longer collaborating in exporting Brazilian products or services. Overall, there is scant evidence that BNDES support for these businesses corresponded to neodevelopment expectations. At the same time, there is evidence that the 'national champions' engaged in long-term borrowing to reduce capital costs and benefit from interest rate arbitrage profits while investing the borrowed money in government bonds, which paid higher interest rates (Bonomo et al. 2014).

If the strategy of the national champions yielded dubious results, the expected association between neodevelopment and industrialization did not occur. On the contrary, during the PT administrations the disarticulation of Brazilian industry, a phenomenon that preceded it, was accentuated. Since 1985, industrial participation as a portion of GDP has declined, from 35.88 per cent to 13.13 per cent in 2013. Similarly, during the mid-1980s Brazil accounted for 2.8 per cent of world industrial production, a figure that fell to 1, 7 per cent in the 2000s (Unido 2011).

The dismantling of the Brazil's industrial fabric is supported by several indicators, such as the increase in participation of primary components in industrial production, the increase of imported inputs used in the manufacturing of industrial goods, and a higher concentration of added value in a few segments. All of this suggests a weakening of the links that allow industry to function as an organic whole (Carneiro 2008). In this context, the share of consumption served by imports roseby 6 per cent from 1996, reaching 21.7 per cent in 2014, while non-industrial exports doubled their share of total exports. In 2010, a Ministry of Finance report classified 64.6 per cent of Brazilian exports as

---

5 One of the largest mineral corporations in the world with businesses spreading over five continents, Companhia Vale do Rio Doce was created in 1942 as a state enterprise focused on iron mining; it was privatized in 1997.

commodities, a figure that in 1994 was around 50 per cent (Esposito 2017). Here, it should be remembered that a substantial part of Brazil's industrial exports are carried out by multinationals, as is the case of automobile assemblers operating in the country.

Despite these regressive tendencies, Lula's first term was bestowed with a rare five-year sequence of positive balances in current transactions, which inflated the neodevelopmental illusion. However, since 2008, the balance became increasingly negative, surpassing US$ 100 billion in 2014 – or 4.3 per cent of GDP. In practice, the perennial demand to increase exports resulted in unconditional support for agribusiness and mining, fueling numerous social and environmental conflicts and disasters, such as in Belo Monte and Mariana.

The percentage of imports and exports in relation to GDP increased during successive PT governments, reflecting a greater degree of openness of the economy, but also of dependence. Equally significant, average capital mobility rose from 5 per cent in the period 1986–1990 to 37 per cent between 2006 and 2010, a period when external liabilities also multiplied, indicating an increase in the country's vulnerability to crises caused by the flight of capital (Machado and Sampaio Jr. 2012). In sum, the convergence between the disarticulation of the industrial system, the displacement of the dynamic axis of the economy to outside the country, and the erosion of internal decision-making centers in the face of international finances, all point to a de-industrialization of the country.

These findings explain the ideological character of the neodevelopmentalist proposition. In suggesting a contradictory association between the supposed salutary aspects of neoliberalism and those longing for the old developmentalism, the neo-developmentist pastiche (Fiori 2011) ignored the nexus between the different dimensions inherent in both ideas. Two good examples are the antithetical relationship between restrictive monetary policy and economic growth that characterizes neoliberalism and, the protection of national capital that conditions industrialization in the perspective of development. Even more so, the proposition abstracts the historical conditions that pointed to the national-developmentalist utopia as a way for the humanization of peripheral capitalism, since at present, the possibilities of a national horizon for development are constrained in a world ruled by a regime of global accumulation.

Under this rhetorical veneer, referring to an ideology that once tried to conciliate capitalism and nation in the periphery, a conservative economic policy that accepted the parameters of neoliberalism took hold. In practice, the Brazilian economy continued to operate as a platform for valorization of international financial capital, in a context in which banks made money as never before; through financing the export of raw materials, including in sectors that have internationalized operations such as meatpackers, mining companies and agribusiness; and further backed by multinational corporations that exploit the domestic market but also export, although less and less in the manufacturing sector. Indeed, the prevailing economic trends have intensified: denationalization, deindustrialization, environmental devastation and overexploitation of labor, as well as the opening up of the commercial and financial sectors. With this have come an intensified vulnerability to crisis and its counterpart, the dominance of international finance.

According to Sampaio Jr., the neodevelopmentist ideology served a dual function: 'it distinguishes the Lula government from the Cardoso government, classifying the latter as 'neoliberal', and reinforces the myth of growth as a solution to the problems of the country, deceiving the masses' (Sampaio 2012). Neodevelopmental rhetoric fulfilled a regressive ideological role by narrowing the economic debate, dominated by microeconomics and by shortening the scope of political discussion, limited to the conjuncture. By reducing the horizon of social change to the parameters accepted by neoliberalism, politics was confined to a discussion about the pace and intensity of structural adjustment, distinguishing itself only in ancillary aspects such as: the intensity of the cash transfer policies emanating from the World Bank; the strategy to deal with social pressures; the role assigned to the regional environment; and, the marketing for internal and external consumption, among others. The PT strategy under such parameters is what we will call the 'Lulista' way of regulating social conflict.

4 The Lulista Way of Regulating Social Conflict

4.1 *Articulation of Two Consensuses*

The Lulista way of regulating social conflict can be summarized as a combination of modest gains for the lower ends of the Brazilian social pyramid with the dominance of banks and international capital, who, as always, continued to handle the country like merchandise. The combination of small gains for the poor, pursued either by the extension of cash transfer policies or by a slight evolution of the minimum wage, with the usual profits for the upper class, created a relative social pacification of the country for more than a decade.

According to Ruy Braga, the Lulista hegemony relied on the articulation of two distinct but complementary forms of consent. First, was the passive consent of the subaltern classes. In general, the semi-rural subproletariat benefited from the Bolsa Família Program, moving from extreme poverty to official poverty, while the urban precariat benefited from increases in the minimum wage above inflation and the creation of formal jobs. Finally, in the context of a heated labor market, the trade union organized proletariat succeeded in getting advantageous collective bargaining pacts, both in terms of wages and in terms of labor benefits (Braga 2014, 2016). In a country reputed for its abysmal inequalities, these discrete advances were enough to seduce the consent of the subordinates to the Lulist regulation.

At the same time, the government concretely articulated the interests of the trade union bureaucracy as well as the leaders of the social movements and intellectual sectors, creating the base for an active consent to Lulism (or Lulaism) whose locus was the State apparatus.[6] By occupying posts on the boards of pension funds and public banks, the high-level trade union bureaucracy became 'financialized', that is, it merged its interests with financial capital. Chico de Oliveira denounced the symbiosis between 'technicians and economists *doublés* of bankers, who formed the nucleus of the Brazilian Social Democracy Party (PSDB), and workers transformed into pension fund operators, the nucleus of the PT', that controlled access to public funds (Oliveira 2003). Significantly, the profitability of such funds is often linked to processes of productive restructuring that generate unemployment: thus, creating a situation where a privileged stratum of workers makes money from the precariousness of the others.

The adhesion of the Central Workers' Union (CUT) to this project revealed the philosopher's stone of Lulism: the main social organizations that once resisted the advance of neoliberalism now supported a government committed to the deepening of the same. The relationship of trust built up over the years between the party and social organizations was used to neutralize them, facilitating the neoliberal push. Lula's personal charisma was also manipulated for this purpose. As part of this mode of regulation, public policies and participatory bodies multiplied, innocuous to modifying social structures but effective in diverting social activism. Militants were converted into managers of government projects when they did not simply become government officials. Altogether, this arsenal of practices and strategies consolidated an active consensus around the PT project, weakening the autonomy of social movements.

Initially, leaders and organizations justified their support with the argument that the government was contested. However, the argument that it was possible to bring the government to the left was wishful thinking. Since Lula's first victory in 2002, the party had never considered seriously constructing a correlation of forces to change the Brazilian State. On the contrary, it embarked consciously on practices associated with professional politics, characterized by venality and opportunism. If there was an illusion that the PT governments

---

6   That is to say, PT politics that increasingly gravitated around Lula. For more on Lulism and its contradictions, consult Singer: 2012; Loureiro; Singer: 2016.

handled the State by obscure means for legitimate ends, what happened was the reverse; the PT machine was absorbed by conventional policy, of which it became an integral part.

As is often the case with individual people, movements got 'married' to the government believing they would change it, but it was they who eventually changed. In turn, the government discovered in this marriage that despite numerous public betrayals, divorce was not one of the partner's considerations. Thus, the use of sordid alliances and immoral practices had no limit. Vulgarizing the analogy; while the government felt that it did not need to cultivate the spouse, who could accept everything, it worked to please lovers, among them the voluptuous Party of the Brazilian Democratic Movement (PMDB) – a physiological party[7] to which then vice-president and coup organizer, Michel Temer belonged.

Political crises accentuated the distance between the fidelity of the movements and the venality of the government. Since the first serious crisis around the monthly payment scandal in 2005[8] the PT base brandished the threat of a coup, despite the consensus against impeachment among the bourgeoisie at this time. Instead of considering that the PT, then implementing conservative politics in all spheres, also maneuvered the parliament in a conventional way, even resorting to bribery, social movements closed ranks with the government: 43 organizations signed a 'Letter to the Brazilian people', a homonym to the 2002 document, labeling the denunciations as coup-like maneuvers. Meanwhile, the government responded by reinforcing PMDB participation in government, alongside intensified commitments to financial capital and targeted welfare policies.

Ten years later, the *Lava Jato* (Car Wash) scandal that exposed promiscuity between companies and politicians, would also be reduced to political persecution, despite the arrest of entrepreneurs whose innocence few believed. Echoes of the rhetoric of a 'contested government' were still proclaimed, implying that the social movements had been defeated in all battles throughout that period. The discourse of some leaders was framed by the idea that a fence was being built against the left. Few have suggested the hypothesis that, at this point, the PT was part of the fence, not part of the left.

To summarize, the convergence between the PT's strategies of neutralizing criticism and the inability of many militants to separate from the party

---

7 The term for a political party that has no ideology but only exists to participate in power, a sort of chameleon that changes its beliefs and tactics according to the conjuncture.
8 So-called *'mensalão'*, a scandal involving the buying of parliamentarians' votes with monthly deposits.

provoked a kind of kidnapping of the left. Paradoxically, the main legacy of active consensus to PT hegemony was immobilism, which has had devastating consequences since the sinking of Lulism.

4.2 Conservative Modernization

The Lulista mode of regulating social conflict was successful during the expansionary cycle of the economy, which encompassed Lula's presidencies and Rousseff's first term. In order to understand its later downfall and the reaction that followed, one must analyze the dynamics on which the passive consensus of the masses was based. Specifically, we will examine job creation, the raising of the minimum wage and the expansion of university education, three elements in the universe of the key participants in the protests of June 2013, when the contradictions of Lulism came to light. The failure of urban reform, encouraged by early PT administrations in the 1980s and which then became a 'way of governing', along with the regression in agrarian reform, which mobilized the most powerful Brazilian social movement under neoliberalism, complemented a panorama of conservative modernization by these PT administrations.

The denouement of the passive consensus to the Lulist pact became evident from the protests of June 2013, the largest cycle of popular mobilizations since the end of the dictatorship in 1985. Field investigations indicate that the protests were carried out by young working students and young workers who study. This segment was doubly affected by the PT project, since more than 60 per cent of the jobs created during these administrations were occupied by young people between 18 and 24 years old, who were also the main beneficiaries of the expansion of higher education in the country (Braga 2014b).

Contrary to the mythology surrounding a 'new middle class', studies show that what happened under the PT administrations was an extension of the base of the Brazilian social pyramid. Nine out of every ten new jobs generated during the 2000s paid less than one and a half times the minimum wage. In 2014, when the effects of the economic downturn were accentuated, about 97.5 per cent of the jobs created were in this pay range. This is not surprising given that the engine of expansion was the service sector, such as telemarketing, encompassing segments of society that historically receive lower wages and are more discriminated against in the labor market: i.e., women, blacks and young people (Braga 2014a, 2014b; Pochmann 2012).

From the point of view of economic dynamism, Marcio Pochmann points out that 'this movement of expansion of low-paid jobs proved compatible with the absorption of the enormous surplus of labor power previously generated by neoliberalism'. Reflecting on the subsequent impact of this on the social structure, the economist notes that, 'whether by income level, occupation type, or personal profile and attributes, the bulk of the emerging population does not fit into any serious and objective criteria that could be clearly identified as middle class'. On the contrary, they reveal a profile characteristic of the popular sectors, which in the context of a rise in income, do not focus on savings but immediately increase consumption (Pochmann 2012).

For this social group, the recovery of the purchasing power of the minimum wage is crucial. Despite a slight evolution in respect of labor's share of the total social wealth created during the Lula governments, the scope of the policy of recovering the value of the minimum wage should be nuanced. First, it must be recognized that this trend preceeds the PT governance cycle: during the eight years of Fernando Henrique Cardoso, between 1994 and 2002, there was a recovery of 42 per cent in the real value of the minimum wage, while between 2003 and 2014, the increase was 76.5 per cent. The so-called minimum wage appreciation policy, which has been in effect since 2008, linked salary increases to inflation and to GDP growth at a time of economic growth. This policy had some effect during the rise of commodities, but became neutered under conditions of recession (Krein, Manzano and Santos 2015).

Secondly, it is necessary to contextualize the results achieved in relation to previous periods. The more recent increase in employment is referenced to the mass unemployment of the 1990s. Correspondingly, it was only in 2013 that the increase in the average real wage of the worker reached a level similar to that at the beginning of the Real Plan. However, its purchasing power remained inferior to the one verified in the early 1980s, which in turn reflected the depletion resulting from two decades of dictatorship.

Similarly, the increase in labor's share of the total social wealth created between 2002 and 2009 from 42.4 per cent to 43.6 per cent according to data from the Institute of Applied Economic Research (Ipea), was still at a level below 1994, when it reached 48 per cent – and much lower than the 1959–1960 biennium when it reached 57 per cent. Above all, the deplorable distance between the minimum wage established in the Constitution and the minimum wage actually paid was perpetuated. According to calculations by the Inter-Union Department of Statistics and Socioeconomic Studies (Dieese), the ideal minimum wage in June 2013 should have been more than four times the real minimum wage in order to cover the elementary expenditures of a decent social reproduction (Dieese 2016).

If the quantitative advances are meager, the qualitative data indicates a regression in working conditions. During the period, there was an increase in the rate of outsourcing of enterprises, a greater flexibility in working hours, an increase in the rate of job turnover and an increase in accidents and deaths at work – all indications of a deterioration in the quality of the jobs created. When we consider that the driving forces of the economy in the period were civil construction, agribusiness and the services sector, we could hardly expect another result. It is evident that the ensuing economic growth was based on the super-exploitation of workers, making more explicit the contradiction between mercantile interests and popular aspirations.

In short, the world of work under the PT advanced, in rapid steps, in line with the global movement of increasingly precarious work. Ruy Braga refers to this historical subject as the Brazilian 'precariat', variningly, 'that mass formed by disqualified and semi-skilled workers who enter and leave the labor market very quickly, by young people looking for their first job, by workers who have recently left the informal sector and by underpaid workers' (Braga 2014a). It is a social group stripped of labor guarantees, subject to uncertain income and lacking a collective identity rooted in the world of work.

Many of these young people enter higher education expecting to compete for above minimum wage jobs with the middle class, to leave behind the uncertain and low-paid world of the precariats. They thus become the main clients of expanding private universities that offer courses of very poor quality at low prices. While it is true that under the Federal University Restructuring and Expansion Plans Support Program (Reuni), which ran from 2003 to 2012, 14 new federal universities and 100 new campuses were created, increasing enrollments in undergraduate courses, the precariousness associated with this expansion is notorious. The deterioration of working conditions and the career of technicians and teachers, aggravated by violent cuts in education funding, resulted in two major strikes in 2012 and 2015.

The main component of the expansion of higher education was private, not public. Between 2003 and 2014, the offering of undergraduate courses in the country spread from 282 to 792 municipalities and 78.5 per cent of vacancies in higher education were new. However, out of a total of 8 million spaces, 90.2 per cent belonged to private universities. Strictly speaking, this is a subsidized expansion, since the federal government disbursed, through the Student Funding Fund (Fies) and the University for All Program (Prouni), large amounts of public funds for private education. In 2013, the Ministry of Education gave R$ 5.8 billion to Fies and R$ 12.3 billion the following year. While the 2015 budget cuts removed R$ 12 billion from education, the federal government released $ 17.7 billion for Fies and waived R$ 970 million in taxes for Prouni (Zagni 2016). The underlying logic is that it is cheaper for the state to subsidize students in a private college than to maintain a public institution to educate them.

Once out of university, many find that the path to social ascension is narrower than promised. Precarious work, originally envisaged as a temporary engagement, becomes permanent. The precariousness stops being a step and becomes a wall. Passages get narrower in a room with increasingly lower ceilings. Life becomes anguish, in the etymological sense of the term: compressed, narrow and stressed. Those who achieve some success realize that the labor market demands the daily sacrifice of ethics to secure a place in a world marked by competition, despotism and fear. And yet there is no certainty about the future, for they are all expendable. In short, it is discovered that being less poor does not make existence more stable.

For the most part, this anguished and unstable existence takes place in the city, between home, study and work. Locomotion is at the center of life and Brazilian cities have ceased to exist as sites of positive social interaction, which can nurture a meaningful and civilized life.

To trace the roots of the failure to stop this process, Pedro Arantes analyzes the trajectory of the struggle for urban reform in Brazil and its connection with federal urban policies (Arantes 2014). Drawing on an analogy with the Brazilian trade union movement, which has hardly questioned private ownership of the means of production, Arantes points out that, housing movements never transcended the threshold of private land ownership. Thus, insofar as the 'democratic-popular' urbanism practiced by PT municipal administrations in the 1980s declined – a process involving the urbanization of slums, the production of housing by self-help and self-management and practices such as participatory budgeting – conditions for forging a consensus on market-based solutions were created, with the ideology of home ownership as its landscape.

Treating cities as a brand or as a business the PT administrations increasingly turned to international urban consultants, while defending and introducing postmodern mechanisms of privatization of cities such as urban operations, sales of certificates of additional construction potential, major urban projects and mega-events. Emptied of their original transformative potential the practices that characterized the 'PT way of governing' became technologies for the management of impoverished urban masses.

Consistent with the political and ideological inflections embraced by the PT, urban reform was no longer seen as a totality to the point that it could be conflated with 'practices of the real estate sector, right-wing governments and the World Bank', as Arantes points out. Along this path, substantive thinking about the city, which is the very objective of urban reform, has stalled. Mobility understood as a fundamental urban right because it is a means of access to other rights, was one of the casualties. Just as the ownership of land was not questioned, the urban turnstile, which symbolizes paying for public transport, was not problematized.

Reaching the presidency, the main form of PTism social dialogue between capital and workers in the area of popular housing was the Minha Casa Minha Vida program. From the point of view of government rationality, the challenge was to convince real estate capital to serve the poorest, which meant turning the homeless into consumers of housing, and turning popular housing into a profitable business. The era of self-construction and of joint efforts gave way to an alliance between workers and real estate owners guaranteed by public funds. In this arrangement, every dimension of the construction process is controlled by the private sector: from land policy to the pattern of urbanization, site selection and construction technology. The complementary identification between the right to housing and the right to property is completed in a process that Arantes interprets as a 'compensatory solution to the urban reform that did not occur' (Arantes 2014).

The agrarian question under PT presidencies was addressed in a similar way, with equally frustrating results. According to Ariovaldo Umbelino de Oliveira, it was evident from the beginning that agrarian reform under Lula would be marked by two principles: 'Do not do it in the areas dominated by agribusiness and only do it in the areas where it can 'help' agribusiness. That is, agrarian reform is definitely coupled with the expansion of agribusiness in Brazil' (Oliveira 2013). A set of measures adopted during successive PT administrations established this anti-popular orientation, such as: the Biosafety Law, which regulated the production and commercialization of transgenic seeds; the Legal Land Program, which legalized land grabbing in the Amazon; the renegotiation of debts of large land owners; the dismantling of the Forest Code; and, the development of infrastructure aimed at strengthening agribusiness related to the PAC and the Initiative for the Integration of Regional Infrastructure in South America (IIRSA).

This reality confronted rural organizations such as the Landless Rural Workers Movement (MST), with a difficult situation. Support for the government contradicted the defense of agrarian reform, which gave the movement its raison d'être. On the other hand, federal management offered practical linkages, from the nomination of movement militants to low-ranking government positions to the expansion of assistance policies at the grassroots of the movement, such as Bolsa Família. It was a striking contrast to the repression of previous management.

In terms of production, the government increased the allocation of resources to the National Program to Strengthen Family Agriculture (Pronaf), something that has been emulated by the World Bank and implemented in the country during the Cardoso administration. More than a credit line, the design of the program implied a social engineering oriented to transform family agriculture into a cog in the gears of transnational agribusiness. From a political point of view, this incentive spoke to one of the bases of the movement: already settled families. However, this was done at the expense of the landless campesino families, the impoverished farmers, and agricultural worker in general.

As a rule, incentives to family farming tend to dispense with the involvement of social movements and almost always foster monoculture; for example, half of the credits released between 2003 and 2011 went to corn and soybean plantations. As a result, according to Alex Hilsenbeck, in the Northeast and South of the country there were settlements of the MST dedicated to the monoculture of castor bean or sunflower, in initiatives facilitated by agreements with Petrobras,[9] to the detriment of the polyculture of foodstuffs (Hilsenbeck 2013).

The manner in which PT presidencies have dealt with agrarian reform and the urban question – two areanas that have seen the most combative mobilization of popular movements in Brazil since the end of the dictatorship – reveals much about the political economy that has been proposed. In the countryside the contradiction between family farming and export monoculture was diluted, at the expense of agrarian reform. In the city, the contradiction between the right to housing and the city was dealt with as a business, at the expense of urban reform.

Covering both the countryside and the city the aim was to alleviate the contradictions between social integration and overexploitation of labor, replacing the struggle for rights with the capitalization of the poor. The expansion of the Bolsa Família and cheap jobs was directly linked to the expansion of popular credit and private higher education to outline a horizon of individual insertion, mediated by consumption. The dream of social mobility encouraged the precariat as a temporary condition, which had as a floor the Bolsa Família and private higher education as its ceiling. Popular credit fueled dreams of consumption and professional growth, as well as home ownership and mercantile farming (Minha Casa, Minha Vida and Pronaf). While some families ate more, others had a child at university for the first time. They all dreamed of leaving the slave quarters, though not together.

In its effort to alleviate the excruciating miseries that have afflicted Brazilian society since colonial origin, PTism provisionally mitigated some of the

---

9 Founded in 1953 as a state oil enterprise, Petrobras is now a publicly traded company, which still has the government as its main shareholder and is the largest company in the country.

symptoms. But the root causes have worsened. Modest advances corresponded to a deepening of structural problems, evidenced by the generalized deterioration of working conditions and regression in urban and agrarian issues, both set against the background of an economy increasingly dependent on the exports of primary resource commodities. At the political level, the focus on class reconciliation has nurtured conservative business interests – between financial capital, agribusiness, corporate media, neo-Pentecostalism, and physiological parties – while many of those who pushed for change in the past accommodated themselves to the system, through concessions and privileges.

This effort to circumvent the contradictions that strain Brazilian society, as if it were possible to eradicate its miseries without touching their roots, proved to be a chimera, with things beginning to fall apart in June 2013.

5   Lulism in Crisis

5.1   *From the June Days to Mobilizations for Impeachment*

The contradictions of the conservative modernization associated with the Lulista mode of regulation of social conflict emerged in the mass mobilizations of June 2013, although the government itself did not interpret the events in this way.

For those who looked at Brazil through the spectacles of Lulism, the popular revolt appeared like a bolt of lightning in a clear, blue sky. It was believed that the country was not affected by the global crisis and had been reunited with economic growth after three decades of stagnation. The real minimum wage had grown and consumption had increased, giving rise to a new middle class. The formalization of work had been boosted and domestic maids had gained labor rights. Absolute poverty had declined, in line with comprehensive policies of cash transfers. The country had broken records in both mineral and agricultural exports, while the discovery of the pre-salt petroleum pointed toward even greater prosperity. Brazil had gone from being a debtor to a creditor of the International Monetary Fund (IMF), from a student of to an advertorial for, the World Bank.

With Brazilian leadership, new forums of articulation for South American countries such as UNASUR were formed. This international role was recognized with the chairmanship of the World Trade Organization (WTO) and the Food and Agriculture Organization of the United Nations (FAO) and legitimized the request for a permanent seat on the UN Security Council. As the cherry on top of the cake, the country would host the World Cup in 2014 and the Olympics in 2016, a tacit recognition of its competence and modernity.

The protests of June were a multifaceted movement, which generated various readings. There were Lulists who argued that the achievements of previous years raised social expectations, which then overflowed on the streets. To the extent that reactionary slogans began to project themselves on posters and through megaphones, it was suggested that the demonstrations were the expression of a middle class troubled by the rise in the cost of services which made domestic servants more expensive, and increased competition in the labor market due to the increase in the number of university students from the lower classes; in short, the protests were seen as a reaction against the democratization of Brazil.

Although the second point is relevant to the anti-PT demonstrations that grew in 2015 and 2016, the participation of an angry middle class in June 2013 was late and minor, as was the participation of key unions and other government partner organizations, including the PT. Those who were on the streets from the outset were movements and parties to the left of the political spectrum. From their initiative, they mobilized a troubled and willing youth, but with little political experience, and it was they who set the tone for the June days. The slogans centered around three fundamental questions: democratization of cities, universal public policies and a reaction to parliamentary cretinism – i.e., the illusion that parliament represents a nation. In spite of the fact that it did not target a particular government, the rebellion challenged the conservative modernization of the PT.

The initial demonstrators that numbered around six thousand people in São Paulo on June 6, 2013, protested against a hike in public transportation fares. Police repression catalyzed a doubling of the protester numbers in the days that followed. During the same week, the mayor of Sao Paulo, Fernando Haddad, and an ascendant star in the PT was in Paris, defending the candidacy of the city for Expo 2020 in the company of Governor Geraldo Alckmin, one of the main national leaders of the PSDB. In tune with the Toucan colleague, Haddad condemned the protests and praised the behavior of the Military Police.[10]

But the protests continued. And when the military police adopted more brutal tactics, arresting more than 200 people and wounding hundreds of protesters, as well as two-dozen journalists, the demonstrations escalated. Soon they reached national scale and could no longer be repressed by the police. For the next three weeks a social earthquake shook the Brazilian political scene. At its height, it is estimated that two million people took to the streets in more than 120 cities and that about 80 per cent of Brazilians supported the protests.

---

10   Both were candidates for the Brazilian presidency in 2018; in the case of Haddad, due to Lula's candidacy being disallowed.

The agenda of claims transcended the theme of collective transportation, including other public services, notably health and education. The extension of the original scope of the protests was summed up in the slogan: 'It's not for pennies, it's for rights!'

Coinciding with the Confederations Cup, a test event for the World Cup facilities, the protests of June captured – in FIFA's relations with the country – a synthesis of the PT's conservative modernization. The parody 'It was a very funny country, had no schools, had only stadiums' summed up this malaise, in which sophisticated patterns of consumption coexist with the primitive reproduction of existence. The World Cup stadiums – made possible by population removal, the overexploitation of labor and armed with public money – the product of spurious international business deals that enriched politicians and contractors, as well as amusing a few regulars who were able to pay for the tickets, emerged as authentic monuments to underdevelopment.

In sum, while it is true that the demonstrations did not target the PT government in particular it is also a fact that the contestation against the system included it. It is only possible to argue that the malaise on the streets was not directed to the federal government and PT if we consider that, ten years after reaching the presidency, they had nothing to do with where the country was. The opposite is more likely: that the demonstrations translated, albeit diffusely, an enormous frustration.

However, the government's reaction revealed that the frustration would continue. If the demonstrations succeeded in suspending tariff hikes throughout Brazil, the national political agenda remained unchanged. Cents were won, but not rights. The Rousseff government staged scenes and gave rhetorical promises, but soon announced a new round of privatizations, raised the interest rate and further tightened fiscal adjustment by cutting public spending and increasing the primary surplus. Instead of listening to the demands of the demonstrators, she accelerated an anti-terrorism law to intimidate them, aiming to keep the masses away from the World Cup in 2014 and the Olympics in Rio de Janeiro in 2016.

In the October 2014 presidential elections, the public agenda shouted on the streets the previous year was also ignored. Government priorities are illustrated by data from the Citizen Debt Audit, indicating that for 2014 45.11 per cent of the entire national budget was committed to interest payments on and amortizations of, the public debt; constituting twelve times that invested in education, eleven times the health spending and more than double that of social security (Fatorelli and Avila 2015).

However, the election witnessed a political polarization that did not correspond to what was actually in dispute: managing the crisis that was looming.

A climate of visceral hostility intoxicated the electorate and the Brazilian people witnessed a reactionary radicalization. In this context, many of the best militants adopted a passionate defense of PTism, despite seeing no real potential for social change. On the other pole, a dominant class always averse to popular protagonism felt that the Lulist momentum had passed and went on the offensive. Without programmatic alternatives to present, this criticism quickly slipped into prejudices, revealing intolerance of the existence of a workers' party, though devoid of class autonomy.

Reelected by a small margin, Rousseff was confronted by a different scenario in her second term. The reversal of favorable international commodity prices, inflationary pressures, the advance of unemployment, high interest rates, a fall in exports, and a collapsing industrial sector, all in the middle of a succession of corruption scandals, accentuated the fragility of the Executive, assiduously exploited by a Congress whose profile reflected the degradation of the Brazilian social fabric. In this context, Rousseff immediately abandoned her campaign program and adopted the defeated candidate's agenda, implementing a draconian fiscal adjustment, which entailed cuts in all socially-oriented ministries. Haunted by the specter of impeachment the government would be pressured to give way more and more, hoping to placate the voracity of the PMDB and big capital.

Regardless, the economic slowdown which led to negative growth rates in 2015 and 2016 compromised the government's bourgeois stance. In turn, cuts in federalspending aggravated the effects of the recession on employment, harming workers. According to the Monthly Survey of Continuous Domicile Samples, the unemployment rate for the quarter ended in November 2016 reached 12.1 million workers, compared to 9.1 million in the previous year. At the same time there was a resurgence in the hostility of traditional middle sectors, bothered by the increased price for domestic workers, the influx of poorer strata into malls and airports, and increased competition for jobs paying more than one and a half times the minimum wage.

As denunciations of corruption around Petrobras began to monopolize the news, the dissatisfaction of this middle class exploded in a wave of demonstrations favorable to Rousseff's impeachment, which took to the streets of major Brazilian cities in March and April 2015. Marcelo Badaró points to the difference in the social base of demonstrators compared to June 2013. Instead of the workers who study, the 2015 demonstrators were mostly white adults between 30–50 years old who earned more than 5 times the minimum wage, with demonstrators from families earning up to 3 times the minimum wage, not exceeding 20 per cent (Badaró 2015). In addition, the protests received media support and were directed and funded by organizations with class ties and some with links to US think tanks. What this reveal is a twist but not linear continuity, between the cycles of demonstrations from 2013 and 2015.

However, there is at least one important relationship between the two waves of protest. June 2013 opened a new political conjuncture, marked by the exhuastion of the Lulist way of regulating social conflict. To put it graphically: the PT emerged into politics in the 1980s by putting people on the streets and then reached power in the following decades by taking the people off the streets. The June protests showed that the party had no more power to either put people on or take them off the streets, which for many put their role in question. Additionally, the economic crisis narrowed the scope for class reconciliation, thus creating more pressure for an updating of the accumulation regime. The PT version of inclusive neoliberalism gave way to social spoliation, while the era of conciliation slid into class warfare. Although initiated in the Rousseff government, this inflection was consummated with the process of impeachment.

5.2   *Impeachment*

Framed in this perspective, Rousseff's impeachment in 2016 did not reflect a substantive dispute of a country project, but a realignment of political forces and accumulation strategies, in a context of the exhaustion of Lulist social pacification. Initially, the strategy of the anti-PT right did not contemplate the coup but was 'to make the government bleed', as it was openly stated. However, as is often the case in history, politics acquires its own dynamism and the pace is accelerated accordingly. When the PT launched a party candidate for the presidency of Congress, the parliamentary base of the government cracked. The diabolical president of the House Eduardo Cunha, first accused in the *Lava Jato* operation which investigated the corruption associated with Petrobras, soon became the ruthless enemy of the presidency, instigating the conspiracy stirred by his party mate, vice president Michel Temer.

In April 2016, Rousseff was removed from office and when the Olympics ended in August, the act of deposition was consummated. The pretext was the so-called 'fiscal pedals', which were constituted by the practice of postponing the transfer of resources to be distributed in government programs, such as Bolsa Família to public banks, and which aimed to minimize imbalances in the state budget. In order not to delay the programs, banks use their own resources, which are subsequently repaid by the federal government. According to the opinion of the Court of Auditors of the Union, this practice constitutes a loan, which is prohibited by the Fiscal Responsibility Law. However, this has been a past and ongoing practice in Brazilian public management, used by previous presidents (Cardoso and Lula), as well as seventeen governors of the federation during the same year (2015). A political trial, in the guise of a judicial process, was therefore created: i.e., a coup d'état carried out by the Parliament in collusion with the Judiciary and large media.

However, this coup was not motivated by fundamental programmatic contradictions. Threatened by the conspiracy, the government welcomed the right-wing agenda, such as further pension reform, the freezing of public spending and the denationalization of the pre-salt oil reserves. Rather, the process was confined to a dispute within what Marx described as the 'party of order', averse to popular protagonism. Accordingly, the government tried to negotiate its salvation until the last moment with Cunha himself, always within an anti-republican praxis of horse-trading politics.

The loss of command over petty, horse-trading politics, which the PT had successfully managed for thirteen years, reflected the weakening of the Lulist way of regulating social conflict. When the party assumed the presidency in 2003, its prestige in the eyes of workers was fundamental to enable the pension reform that Cardoso had previously not achieved. By 2016, however, militancy was in the throes of dispersion and resignation. On the other hand, the reduction in household consumption, which was anticipated for the first time since 2004, suggested that the popular base of Lulism was at risk, while the economic recession (-3.8 per cent of GDP growth in 2015 and -3.5 per cent in 2016), compromised its bourgeois backing. The political functionality of Lulism was exhausted. The right arm of the system resumed the initiative and launched an offensive against its rivals. Lula's arrest in April 2018, in a markedly persecutory process and with no consistent evidence of corruption, was a complete demonstration of this offensive.

6   Final Thoughts

Conceived in the original sin of betrayal, the Temer government reflected the abandonment of the conciliatory strategy of the Brazilian bourgeoisie, in the name of open confrontation with the working class. The combination of a twenty-year freeze on public spending, labor reform, and proposed pension reform all pointed to a regression of workers' living conditions; akin to those that existed in the nineteenth century. Deeply antipopular, this process was accompanied by: the intensification of the repression and criminalization of social struggle; attacks on trade union organization and the right to strike; the advance of gag laws such as the 'school without party' law which limits professor's autonomy in many municipalities; and high school reform, among other measures aimed at neutering the insurgency of popular sectors, particularly among the younger generation. What all this represented was the requiem of the 'New Republic', founded in the 'Citizen Constitution'.

However, unlike the military coup in 1964, this assault did not translate into a major change in the direction of Brazilian history. Rather, it pointed to an acceleration in the rhythm and pace of prevailing politics. For example, the constitutional amendment that freezes public expenditures for twenty years radicalized the logic of structural adjustment, practiced by successive PT administrations. A month before she was dismissed, Rousseff surprised public servants with Bill 257, which was of more modest scope but of similar rationality. The change in the regime of oil exploration in the pre-salt layer, deepened by Temer, was also initiated by the deposed PT government, while the ongoing popular persecution was based on Rousseff's anti-terrorist law passed on the eve of her departure. The continuities are summed up by the figure of Henrique Meirelles, the Minister of Treasury in the coup government who had left his position as a PSDB federal deputy to direct the Central Bank during Lula's presidency (2003–2010).

From this point of view, the Temer government should be seen as a metastasis of the PT administrations, given that the anti-popular interests never previously faced had now spread unimpeded. In the same way, the corrupt professionals who secured the governability of the PT ceased to play the role of extras and took over the state. In short, the exhaustion of Lulism depleted the mediations between the predatory designs of the Brazilian bourgeoisie and the rights and aspirations of the workers. However, by demolishing the PT and arresting Lula in a kind of preventive coup in 2018, the elite showed a self-confidence that might well cost them dearly in the future, because they threw out their main card to tame the masses.

This assault on the country's institutions and workers' rights raises the question: why have the masses not reacted to the challenge? This problem requires a succinct examination of the legacy of Lulism in the area of popular mobilization and PT policy after the coup.

First of all, it is necessary to say that the PT in power collaborated to confuse, pacify and alienate social movements. By implementing a right-wing program but presenting itself as the left, PTism helped to confuse popular perceptions. The lack of difference between left and right fueled apathy, a form of depoliticization. However, in preserving its identification with the left, the party deepened popular disbelief in relation to politics in general and with the left in particular. It is in this light that one can understand the high abstention rates in the municipal elections in October 2016. When combined with spoilt and blank votes, the number of abstentions surpassed the number of those who voted in the two largest cities.[11]

The other side of the policy that integrated the PT into the system was to distance itself from its grassroots. As we have seen, rather than neglecting the historically supportive organizations the PT administrations sought to involve them in public management, though not to fulfill their historical demands, but to neutralize them. Evidently, this is a two-way street: organized sectors of Brazilian workers identified with this policy, either because they believed in the possible advances or because of the material and symbolic benefits they accessed in the process.

The disjunctive between being a minority power partner and being in opposition provoked fractures in the trade union movement and popular organizations. The defense of an anti-popular government, however identified with the left, generated ambiguous situations for militancy at all levels. In some cases, contradictions alienated organizations from their bases. Only those most politically or emotionally committed to the PT were able to overlook what happened. Although these tensions did not converge in a left opposition, the disappointment reinforced the fragmentation.

Finally, PT policy contributed to alienating people instead of politicizing them, because it promoted popular consumption as a solution to social problems – an individual and non-collective approach which commodifies what should be considered rights, such as health, education and social security. Instead of encouraging class responses to Brazilian problems, the PT cultivated variants of liberal ideology and practice: focused policies, class reconciliation, and inclusion by consumption.

It is under the prism of promoted confusion, domestication and alienation that one understands the fickle popular reaction to critical recent events: the impeachment, the antipopular assault led by Temer and the arrest of Lula. During these moments, the PT's position was ambiguous, since the idea of mobilizing the population was subordinated to electoral calculations, whilst projecting the return of the party's maximum leader. In this context, it is

---

11 In the case of São Paulo, the only candidate who was not associated with professional politics overcame three former mayors elected by the PT, even in the first round – including the one seeking re-election. In Rio de Janeiro, a former minister of the Rousseff government and also minister of the Universal Church defeated a peripheral leftist candidate in the second round, waving the spell of faith as a substitute for disenchantment with politics. Indeed, the right-wing candidate beat his left wing opponent ones with a landslide of votes from the poor in the favelas, mostly because of his evangelist background.

difficult to say whether the party did not appeal to the masses for fear of opening a Pandora's Box, or because it estimated it would be a fiasco. The fact is that at the time the former president was taken to prison, his eternal leadership in presidential polls did not turn into solidarity on the streets.

Between the coup in August 2016 and the arrest in April 2018, any expectation of party self-criticism was frustrated. On the contrary, the gap between the indignation of the popular bases and party practice continued to grow exponentially: two months after the impeachment, the PT was united with parties directly involved in the coup in about 1500 campaigns for mayor around Brazil, in many cases with Toucans and with the DEM party, its nemeses in congress. The trade unionist and former Minister of Labour Luis Marinho justified such approaches with the argument that, 'the majority of the people also supported impeachment and we want to recover the majority of the people', while Lula spoke of 'forgiving the coup makers who made this disgrace in the country'. In the municipal elections, party candidates avoided using the term 'coup', such as the then mayor of Sao Paulo, Fernando Haddad, who considered the word a 'little harsh' in public debate. Shyness showed up in popular protests. In the general strikes carried out the following year (2017) many shouted 'out with Temer' but spared criticism of the dictatorship of structural adjustment, with which a re-elected Lula would not have broken.

Among the left, the notion that it was necessary to attract PTism limited the breadth of criticism, driven by the aspiration to form a front with a party that for thirteen years had formed fronts with capital. In general terms, the dilemma that other left parties faced in the presidential elections in 2018, which had its main political expression in the form of the Socialist and Freedom Party (PSOL) was to pursue a broad front candidacy, thereby risking a moralized PTism, or to overcome this political horizon in the name of a revolutionary project, which may have little immediate resonance. In the internal left dispute, the candidacy of the homeless leader Guilherme Boulos pointed to the first path while the other pole, incarnated by the economist Plínio Sampaio Jr., was defeated.

The dilemma of a left that struggles to free itself from the magic lamp of Lulism was re-created: in 2016, the challenge was to oppose impeachment without endorsing the Rousseff government; in 2017, to build an 'out with Temer' rather than a 'come back PT' campaign; in the 2018 elections, to pursue a campaign that does not make Lula's liberation its axis, even while condemning the associated injustice. In short, the Brazilian left still has to settle its score with the PT, a necessary premise for creating policies that surpass it. Meanwhile, the country is now even more deeply submerged in the reactionary wave that characterizes world politics.

Post-scriptum: the 2018 Brazilian Presidential Elections

On the surface of things, the Brazilian presidential election seemed complex. Despite the coup and arrest, the PT reached the second round and faced a fearsome creature of the dictatorship – former Army Captain Jair Bolsonaro. What was in dispute in this election? Who was capital's candidate? What was the strategy of the ruling class? And, what was the answer from the left?

1. For the ruling class, the economy was not in dispute in the elections. The winner would confront the problems of neoliberalism with more neoliberalism, whether through the utopian way of an 'inclusive neoliberalism' preached by the PT, or through the ultraneoliberalism of the Toucans or Bolsonaro.

What the ruling class was contesting was the political form of management of the Brazilian crisis. In other words, the face of the institutional, legal and cultural arrangement to replace the New Republic,[12] now definitively condemned.

Immediately, two tracks were laid.

In his words, Lula offered credibility and stability. The credibility of which he spoke was not with those from above but with those from below. The message was simple; what Lula says, society will accept. In other words, Lulism offered its capacity for persuasion and popular neutralization, as a way to guarantee order. If Dilma Rousseff was Lula's shadow, Fernando Haddad projected himself as the avatar of this policy.[13]

At the complementary opposite pole was Bolsonaro, but how are we to understand him? Bolsonaro is the frightening response of a frightened society. Those who are out of work are afraid of hunger and those who work are afraid of unemployment. Everyone is afraid of violence, and also afraid of the police.

At a time when collective forms of struggle are discredited, Bolsonaro promises order through truculence. With Trump in the United States, Erdogan in Turkey, Modi in India, Uribism in Colombia or fascism in Italy – all in power at the time of the election – Bolsonaro was not alone: he is part of a trend, not an aberration.

---

12 The New Republic is the period after the dictatorship and has the 1988 Constitution as its core reference point.
13 Haddad is the former mayor of Sao Paulo, the largest city in the country, and became the PT candidate after the candidacy of Lula was denied.

In summary, different ways were offered to manage the colossal Brazilian crisis: the PT offered order through conversation, while Bolsonaro proposed order through violence.

2. With the likelihood of electing any one of the other main presidential candidates – Alckmim, Meirelles or Amoedo[14] – almost impossibile, the question is which of these routes was preferable to capital?

If Haddad won, it would be a problem to govern. The dilemma of power would be how to get the snake of anti-PTism back in the hole. How to convince those who called for Lula's impeachment and imprisonment to accept that all of this would result in Haddad?

With Bolsonaro winning the problem is for the governed. His base among the powerful is fragile; his level of rejection is high and his character, unpredictable. The question is: who will discipline the disciplinarian?

Haddad and Bolsonaro are provisional and necessarily unstable responses of a ruling class in a state of reorganization.

3. The direction of the bourgeois movement is toward Bolsonaro. For the end of the new Republic also compromises the Toucans. This is what explains the New Party – as 'new' in politics as the DEM party is 'Democrat';[15] it expresses a ruling class sensing that new times demand new answers. It is Bolsonaro that has not yet come out of the closet; because the ideal for the ruling class is a Bolsonarism without Bolsonaro.

In France, the fascist Marine le Pen complains of those who came together to defeat her in the second round, because someone was elected who implements her policies but without bragging. Beneath the dust of the elections, the Brazilian ruling class forges its Macron. The intersection of Bolsonaro and Amoedo may be João Dória or Sergio Moro.[16]

---

14 Geraldo Alckmin was the candidate of the PSDB (known as 'Toucans'), the party that faced the PT in the last five Brazilian presidential elections. Formerly the President of the Central Bank under Lula, Henrique Meirelles was the candidate for the PMDB, Michel Temer's party. João Amoedo is an entrepreneur, one of the founders of the New Party that will be discussed later.

15 DEM, or Democrats, is the name adopted by the former PFL, a party that congregates heirs of the dictatorship.

16 Television communicator and entrepreneur, João Dória made his debut in politics in 2016, becoming mayor of São Paulo in an election in which he defeated three former PT mayors in the first round. In 2018, he became governor of the state of São Paulo for theToucans. Sergio Moro is the young judge that sent Lula to prison in April 2018, and became Minister of Justice under Bolsonaro.

4. Between the collapse of Lulaism, which began in the rebellion of June 2013, and a trustworthy Bolsonarism that is in the oven, the ruling class is updating itself. This reordering was expressed in the dispersion of candidates. As in 1989, when the New Republic began, the ruling class searches for a path, but this time to bury it.[17]

In this context, the Toucans conducted some self-criticism: it would have been better to let Dilma bleed than to conspire for the coup and compose a government with Temer. They tried to rush things, and now they are condemned to patience.

The ruling class and the Toucans calculate who is most useful to burn and to be burned, in the expectation that, on the subsequently scorched earth, they can create a new order in their likeness.

However, the future under Bolsonaro is imponderable. Many have supported him to get rid of the PT, but who will then free Brazil from him? The Christian-Democrats supported the 1973 coup in Chile in order to return to the presidency, which in fact happened, only 17 years later.

5. There is no novelty in the adherence of those from above to Bolsonaro. Although brute and vulgar, the violence he embodies is, first and foremost, a class violence.

The drama is the adhesion of lower classes. In the absence of the charismatic leader, the subproletariat that sustained Lulaism shifted to Bolsonaro, except in the northeast. Every Brazilian knows someone who voted for Lula but who ended up voting for the captain. Lula was in prison, but those who voted were not. What happened?

Discarding the hypotheses that all who voted for it are fascists or were manipulated against the PT, this result suggests the uncomfortable hypothesis that Bolsonarism is the complimentary 'opposite' of Lulaism – its B side, but not its contrary.

It is true that anti-PTism poisoned the debate, but several candidates wielded this banner. A man of old-time politics, Bolsonaro sold himself as new. The secret may have been form rather than content: the captain uses the language of brutality, which a brutalized people know and understand. In a perverse way he talks with the people, like Lula. In the process, he differentiated himself from the regular candidates.

If Lula emerged as a messiah, Bolsonaro became a myth.[18]

---

17   In the 1989 elections, there were 22 candidates, five of whom were considered competitive. Fernando Collor beat Lula by a small margin in the second round.
18   Bolsonaro came to be known as the 'Myth', particularly among the youth. In Brazilian popular talk, a 'myth' is someone who gains a reputation for daring deeds or behavior, thus singling him out from ordinary people.

6. Albeit in a fake fashion, Bolsonaro projected himself to be on the side of those who, like him, do not articulate ideas well or understand many things. He defended a specifically constructed set of values, not a program; hence the fluid dialogue with the evangelicals.

The PT campaign, in turn, bet on Lula's victimization and then on making him the candidate behind the candidate: i.e., 'Haddad in government, Lula in power'. One way or another, the campaign was shaped by Lulism until the start of the second round, without ever discussing the country's problems or the Temer government. Bolsonaro was not attacked either. In short, Lula intended to turn the elections into a plebiscite on himself; in the process, the party contributed to depoliticizing the dispute and displacing it onto moral grounds.

While the PT campaign branded itself around the concept of justice, the main value evoked by Bolsonaro was order, which for him means concluding the unfinished work of the dictatorship. Maybe this is, after all, his program.

Paulo Arantes suggests the following hypothesis: in the past, the military associated their power with the industrialization of the country, which started and consolidated between two dictatorships: Estado Novo (1937–1946) and the 1964 coup. Faced with industrial regression and social degradation, the military threw in the towel, giving up a powerful Brazil. Then they rolled up their sleeves for an armed management of social life, aiming to hold up a country falling apart. They placed their bets on a privileged relationship with the United States, in a context of a global 'save yourself if you can' trajectory.

Lula sent General Augusto Heleno to lead the UN mission in Haiti, thinking that this would make Brazil a 'global player'. The general returned to Brazil thinking about how to prevent Brazil from becoming a Haiti. Barred from being Bolsonaro's vice-President by his party, Heleno will now use this experience as director of the Institutional Security Office in the new government.

7. As in Colombia, the lies of the right intoxicated the campaign, locked-in the debate and targeted the left. First and foremost, they are lies because they accuse a left that is no longer there, as it has been consistently working in the opposite direction for a long time now. It was on its own initiative that the PT took the color red from its campaign materials. To show Brazilians what right politics is, Bolsonaro had to invent a left; if class struggle is not dead it is his fault, not Lula's.

The anti-PTism of the upper classes does not target what the party is, but what it represents historically: the PT emerged as the first autonomous political instrument of the Brazilian workers – a time when the senzala [slave quarters] raised its head and organized itself.

The anti-PTism of the lower classes is a complicated mix, which includes deep frustration with the PT transmuted into rage; it turns out after all, that hope has not overcome fear,[19] because it has never confronted it. Rather, fear has sequestered hope and it is now the left that has the task of freeing it.

8. And where is the left in all this?

Paradoxically, it reveals more difficulty in understanding what has changed. To the right, things are clear since June 2018: the time of inclusive neoliberalism is gone. There has been a shift from conciliation to class warfare; this is the background for Lulaist agony.

That Lula himself does not realize his anachronism is expected. That the PSOL is affected by this self-deception might be a tragic myopia, as its candidacy hesitated to differentiate itself from the PT.

Lulism is a politics that navigates the waters of the system and only the rise of the masses can resurrect it as a bourgeois alternative. The paradox is that this will only happen if the ties to Lulism are broken, as they were in June. But when that happens, the rioters will ask: would all this end up with Lula as president?

If the snake of anti-PTism is difficult to control, what comes after PT-ism will be much more so. This is why not not even Lula is interested in people on the streets.

Ambitioning to be a bridge between PTism and the left, the PSOL candidacy was embarrassed by the agenda of the first. In the process, it risked corroborating the kidnapping of the left in the magic lamp of Lulism. In addition to its internal contradictions, this policy has lost its bearer in history: therefore, it will not be repeated, except as a farce.

Lulism is not the antidote to fascism, but a drug that hinders the understanding of what is happening. Only with struggle, not morphine, will Brazilians escape barbarism.

9. Regardless of the final outcome, the winner of the election was already Bolsonaro because it was he who set the terms of the debate. The axis of the discussion shifted to the right, further insulating any structural debate. On the other hand, the left had already lost this election because it didn't even directly contest the imposed agenda.

---

19 After Lula's first successful campaign in 2002 the slogan 'Hope has overcome fear' circulated widely.

To go back to the major league of politics, the left needs to update its diagnosis and strategy. Until then, it will see defeats accumulate without even disputing the course of history.

São Paulo, 10/29/2018, the day following the election of Jair Bolsanaro as president of Brazil.

CHAPTER 3

Kirchnerism and Impasses of the Bourgeois Way in Argentina

> For us, Peronism was the most important and unique attempt of the bourgeois-democratic revolution in Argentina, whose failure is due to the incapacity of the national bourgeoisie to fulfill this task.
> *Silvio Frondizi, 1955*

> It is impossible to consolidate a country project if we do not consolidate a national bourgeoisie.
> *Néstor Kirchner, 2003*

1   Introduction

Strictly speaking, the election of Néstor Kirchner a few months after Lula's triumph in Brazil in 2003 marked the beginning of the South American progressive wave, when presidents identified with the left took command of the two largest countries in the region, in addition to Chávez. Among the ten largest economies in the world at the dawn of the 20th century, Argentina continued to dispute regional leadership even after World War II. However, the period since its most recent dictatorship (1976–83) has witnessed the impoverishment, deindustrialization and denationalization of the country. Neoliberal fundamentalism under the *Menemato*[1] deepened a crisis that eventually exploded at the beginning of the 21st century and set the background for the Kirchner governments that followed.

Although Néstor[2] had a conventional trajectory in the Peronist ranks, he was elected in the context of an extraordinary popular mobilization that overthrew presidents and imposed change. Benefiting from the end of the parity between dollar and peso as well as the default on external debt enacted in the

---

1 Refers to the presidencies of Carlos Saúl Menem during the period from 1989 to 1999.
2 I employ the first name to distinguish both Kirchner presidents, who were then husband and wife. It should also be noted that it became common practice in Argentina politics to refer to their leading politicians by their first name, so that 'Cristina' (Kirchner) was defeated by Mauricio (Macri) in 2015.

midst of the crisis, the Néstor government practiced a developmental resurgence that then faced obstacles of a different nature. As the international environment favorable to primary exports cooled, his successor (and wife) Cristina Kirchner adopted controversial measures, responding to economic difficulties with policies aimed at strengthening her authority over the state and the sectors that supported her. A more daring process than its Brazilian counterpart, Kirchnerism suffered the ambiguities inherent in the belief in a national bourgeoisie combined with the tutelage of the popular movement; all of which resonates from decades old Peronist politics with which the Argentine left still has accounts to settle.

2 Perón and Peronism

Projected onto the national political stage as minister of labor during the Second World War, Colonel Juan Domingo Perón (1895–1974) presided over Argentina on three occasions. He served two consecutive terms between 1946 and 1955, when he was ousted in a coup, and then returned to the presidency in 1974 after a long exile. However, it was the first period of his rule that captivated Argentine workers, sowing the foundations of Peronism. This political phenomenon, which transcended both the personal life and the various positions taken by the colonel himself, imprinted an indelible mark on the country's political culture; its reverberations still resonate today (Murmis and Portantiero 1972).

In the economic sphere, the first Peronist government fostered national industrial development, especially in light industries, while at the same time it impelled State presence in base sectors, although without the same success. In those years Argentina experienced a unique prosperity, supported by a favorable international environment, boosted by high exports of cereals and meat in the post-war period. Under Peronism, the Argentine economy continued to be larger than the Brazilian economy.

On the other hand, the government favored state intervention on behalf of workers on several occasions and promoted what became an unprecedented income distribution in the country's history. The share of wages as a percentage of the country's GDP reached 50 per cent, a level that continued in subsequent years. Political successes, such as labor legislation, the right to trade union organization (although tied to the state) and the universal vote among others, were added to the economic success (Kaplan 1984; Romero 2001). In the memory of many Argentine workers, these were the years in which they became citizens.

Ideologically, Peronism referred to three slogans: 'social justice', understood as an elevation of the standard of living of workers, but which rejected the contradiction between capital and labor and the notion of class struggle; 'economic independence', identified with the autonomy of the country before the foreign monopolies; and the 'third position' at the international level, assuming neutrality in relation to the two blocs of the Cold War (Bobbio et al. 1983: 923).

The balancing act of reconciling capital and labor, industry and primary exports, national development and international capital, was possible while the international environment was favorable. However, a decline in primary exports coincided with increasing pressure from transnational capital, mainly of American origin, for economic liberalization. Faced with financial problems, the state lost the ability to subsidize the domestic market and decided to freeze wages, relying on the role of the General Confederation of Labor (CGT) and the adoption of coercive methods to contain popular demands. The repressive face of the government was evident in the control of the press, of party activity and the trade union movement. In this context, concessions in favor of international capital were insufficient to reverse the growing uneasiness, since for the opposition any political solution necessarily excluded the permanence of Peronism in power (Ayerbe 2002; Kaplan 1984).

The impasse was solved by a military coup in 1955. In the evaluation of Silvio Frondizi, the fall of Perón attested to the impossibility of consolidating the Argentine nation in bourgeois foundations: 'For us, Peronism was the most important and only attempt at realizing the bourgeois-democratic revolution in Argentina, whose failure is due to the inability of the national bourgeoisie to fulfill this task' (Frondizi 1955).

The period between the removal of Perón and the military dictatorship begun in 1976 was marked by political instability and social confrontations. Although outlawed, Peronism had more votes than competitors in the various elections that took place, in which it pushed for the blank vote. An expression of the prevailing instability is the fact that the two radical presidents[3] elected, Arturo Frondizi (1958–1962) and Arturo Ilia (1963–1966), did not complete their mandates.

The Ilia government was overthrown by a military coup in 1966 that tried to stabilize the situation by means of an 'Argentine revolution'. However, the subsequent military regime led by General Juan Carlos Onganía was confronted

---

3 Reference here is to the Radical Civic Union, a party that originated as an intra-oligarchic split in Argentine politics in the late 19th century and reached the presidency for the first time in 1916, attracting the vote of the middle class. For decades, it polarized institutional politics in opposition to Peronism.

with a sharpening of social confrontations, expressed in both university struggles and union strikes, whose combined efforts led to the 'Cordobazo' mobilization in 1969, when the city of Cordoba was briefly taken by workers. The insurrection was violently suppressed, but the regime was discredited, and several groups took up arms to confront the repression. The Montoneros Peronistas, the Revolutionary People's Army (ERP) and the Revolutionary Armed Forces (FAR) of Marxist reference emerged in this context. Challenged by those below him but also by his peers, Onganía convened elections in 1973 and a leader of the Peronist left, Hector Campora, prevailed. He immediately created the conditions for the return of Perón, who assumed the presidency months later.

By this time, Peronism had taken on a life of its own. Groups that assumed opposing political positions claimed themselves as such, while the leader himself manipulated everyone at his convenience. By inciting the armed left at the same time as it incited the reactionary sectors, the general contributed to a climate of confrontation and disorder which apparently, he alone could appease. The functionality of Peronism for the reestablishment of order was the passport for his return.

Back in power Perón disavowed leftist Peronism, while anti-communist para-militarism received government support to act. When he died, the General was succeeded by his wife Isabelita (1974–76), who intensified the repressive actions but showed little ability to govern. In 1975, a package of unpopular economic measures known as 'Rodrigazo' raised the cost of living and inflation, triggering the first general strike against a Peronist government in history (Sartelli 2007). Workers' insubordination was an indication that Peronism was losing its political function.

At the same time, political violence became an everyday occurrence. While the Triple A (Argentine Anti-Communist Alliance) articulated by Perón's personal secretary and minister, José López Rega targeted selected victims, guerrilla actions multiplied. Faced with this climate of civil war, a military chaplain pontificated in early 1976 that 'the Argentine people committed sins that can only be redeemed with blood' (Novaro and Palermo 2007: 87). This was the mission undertaken by the armed forces in the following years.

3 From the 'National Reorganization Process' to Neoliberal Democracy

The dictatorship inaugurated in 1976 unified the ruling class around the reestablishment of order, a process which counted on the population's benevolence and/or indifference. 'Silence is health', proclaimed regime posters. To achieve this goal, the so-called 'National Reorganization Process' sought to reconfigure social relations in the country, in a reaction to the Marxist left but also to Peronism. It was a more ambitious and radical project than all previous dictatorships, including the Argentine Revolution of 1966, which in the evaluation of those who now assumed command had failed because of its moderation and weakness (Novaro and Palermo 2007: 30).

Based on the extermination of a generation of militants, this 'national reorganization' changed the prevailing pattern of accumulation, which had industry as a dynamic nucleus. In the process it created the conditions for the implementation of neoliberalism, which the dictatorship began to execute itself (Basualdo 2001). The social relations of production, the function of the State, and the insertion of the country into the international economy changed substantially, in parallel with a continuous degradation of the population's standard of living, which would extend for decades. Although this process was not completed under military auspices, the regime laid the groundwork for the economic and social regression that would occur later.

The strategy to restore order was to expand terror, linking kidnappings, clandestine detentions and disappearances in a massive and systematic manner. The 30,000 fatalities, encompassing those murdered and disappeared, denote an unprecedented and qualitatively different scale of repression (conversation with Hourcade; Tufró 2017). At the same time, the regime sought to extricate itself from political responsibility, avoiding the international pressures suffered by the Chilean experience. Disappearances as a method fulfilled this double role of extending the mantle of suspicion and uncertainty while preserving public opinion, since the government did not have to justify what it claimed to be unaware of.

On the economic level, the regime disrupted the two core pillars of Peronist political economy, industrial development and the working class. The state regulation that had protected industry from agricultural exports and financial capital was dismantled in favor of the latter two, and its weight in the economy has since declined. At the same time, the combination of state reforms and repression devastated worker resistance.

Some argue that the fundamental goal of the regime was political rather that economic, inducing a change in power relations intended to have structural effects on social morphology: i.e., the dictatorship asserted itself against an 'undisciplined' working class but also against an 'inefficient' business community. To achieve this objective, it mixed neoliberal, conservative and developmentalist recipes (Novaro and Palermo 2007: 56, 79). However, the general direction of these pursuits was determined by the 1977 financial reform that was deepened in 1979, when a monetary approach to balance of payments was adopted, reversing the subordination of the financial system to the real economy (Basualdo 2009: 329).

The further opening of the market to goods and capital raised commercial and financial imbalances, which were resolved with increasing indebtedness until the country succumbed to a crisis similar to Chile in the early 1980s. In the Argentine case, the dictatorship sought to overcome problems with a political exit and attacked the Malvinas (Falkland Islands), which the British had occupied since 1833. They planned for a national victory that would support General Galtieri's candidacy, thus paving the way for a return to elections that would crown the military's 'national reorganization'.

Even though the issue of the Malvinas is an injustice recognized by the UN since at least 1965 and serves to mobilize Argentine nationalism like no other, the results of the campaign were disastrous. Margaret Thatcher also faced a critical domestic moment and seized the opportunity to become popular, engendering a massive British counterattack. Because Argentina had advised U.S. counter-insurgency in Central America, the Argentine military assumed the support of the United States, in the process revealing a deep-seated ignorance about contemporary international relations. The ephemeral popularity of the adventure vanished with defeat and many lives lost, precipitating the end of the regime.

The socioeconomic record of the dictatorship was discouraging. In 1982 per capita GDP was 15 per cent lower than in 1975; the industrial GDP had decreased by 25 per cent since 1970; real wages fell by 40 per cent and wages' share of GDP declined from 45 per cent (1974) to 34 per cent (1983). It is estimated that social spending shrunk by half (Novarro and Palermo 2007). The convergence between the brutality of the repression, the Malvinas disaster and economic failure demoralized the Argentine military and the regime itself, which few would later defend. The Argentine dictatorship was the first in the Southern Cone to lose power, and the military suffered pressures for justice and reparation at a level unmatched in the continent.

In spite of these peculiarities, the Argentine transition also involved negotiations between civilian and military leadership of the dictatorship and the political leaders of the opposition, who agreed to discard the use of popular mobilization. In the elections that followed, Peronism was defeated for the first time in history. The radical Raúl Alfonsín (1983–1989), who identified with the center-left and the defense of human rights, won the election. From the point of view of order, his main task was to recompose the political system, putting Argentina back on the track of bourgeois normalcy.

The boldness with which he initially confronted the military yielded to moderation and then resulted in capitulation, as expressed in the laws of Final

Point and Due Obedience, which as their names describe, aimed at absolving those who fulfilled orders. The same dynamic was observed on the economic plane, in which a developmental beginning soon translated into submission to the IMF and adjustments to pay the debt. Pressed between the expectation of change that he fed and the conservatism he endorsed; between civil disappointment and military revenge; between Peronism and the painted faces (*carapintadas*);[4] and, between the IMF and hyperinflation, Alfonsín resigned before finishing his term, and the Peronists returned to the Casa Rosada (Presidential Offices).

In the year that Carlos Saúl Menem (1989–1999) assumed the presidency inflation was close to 5000 per cent. The 'Productive Revolution' that he promised during the campaign but failed to create, became a program of radical structural adjustment, consolidating the neoliberal path inaugurated by the dictatorship. If the military put the country on the path of deindustrialization, the *menemato* deepened denationalization. Seen as a whole, this movement of history eroded the nation's foundations, resulting in the degradation of the Argentine social fabric and the impoverishment of its population.

As in other situations in the subcontinent, the drastic reduction of inflation provided popular ballast to implement the prescriptions of structural adjustment. With the support of all justicialists (as the Peronists are officially known), but also of radicals from the 'Radical Civic Union' (UCR), Congress ceded power to the executive to enact the Emergency Economic Law and subsequent State Reform. 'Reduce the State to enlarge the nation' was the motto of the reform that privatized telecommunications, commercial aviation (*Aerolíneas Argentinas*), electricity, the social security system, transportation, distribution of gas, subway lines, a third of the road network, ports, railways, airports, real estate, iron and steel, oil and gas (YPF), petrochemicals, sanitation companies, racetracks, post offices, and nuclear power plants among others. The privatization process entailed the largest reduction of external debt in the region, since the State accepted debt securities, which accounted for about 1/3 of the amount collected as payment (Aspiazu and Basualdo 2002: 24; Cano 1999).

In the monetary sphere, the minister Domingo Cavallo executed a plan of convertibility in 1991 that, in practice, dollarized the Argentine economy. The '"carnal relations" with the United States' called for by the Chancellor Guido di Tella came to an apex. In addition to trade liberalization and the liberalization of a significant part of the production of goods and provision of services, the chosen path contained inflation while it exponentially increased dependence on foreign capital flows. As in the case of Brazil, this policy tilted the balance of

---

4 Radical right-wing military groups who engaged in a failed coup d'état in 1987.

trade. The surplus of US $ 4.6 billion recorded in 1990 turned into a deficit of US $ 12.2 billion in 1998, a hole covered by the inflow of foreign capital, which in turn saw a doubling of the external debt during the same period (Cano 1999: 140–142). This architecture stood still as privatizations thickened external flows of capital, facilitated by the increase in international credit supply and the surge in export prices (Kosacof 2010: 29). However, when these favorable aspects dissipated, the country was faced with a monumental crisis, with scarce resources to confront it. At the end of Menem's second term, the country plunged into recession.

His successor kept the commitment to convertibility, which vetoed the possibility of managing the currency to mitigate growing trade deficits. In a country where the rich save in dollars stored overseas the situation was exacerbated by capital flight, contributing to the scarcity of currency in a dollar-indebted state. This reality effectively forced the government into successive renegotiations of debt to access new credit, which implied unpopular measures that drained resources from the State. The situation came to a head in November 2001, when capital flight accelerated, triggering a run on the banks. The former minister of economy of the *menemato*, now back at his post, decreed the freezing of bank deposits, known as '*corralito*'.

What was happening in the world of work during all of this? Unemployment, which was high in 1998 (14.8 per cent), jumped to 22.5 per cent in 2001, while 48 per cent of the workforce was informal. Poverty more than doubled in the period, jumping from 25.9 per cent to 52 per cent and then reaching 57.5 per cent of the population in 2002 – a year in which there was an 11 per cent fall in GDP. Between 1998 and 2002, GDP declined by one-fifth while industrial production of the economy as a whole declined by 135 per cent between 1995 and 2001. The labor share of GDP also declined to the lowest level in Argentine history in 2005, when it stood at 20 per cent (Basualdo 2009: 355; El Descamisado 2015).

Beyond statistics, poverty and hunger haunted large numbers of people in a country with little experience of these phenomena in the twentieth century. There are numerous testimonies of schools that became 'popular soup kitchens', where women partnered to feed the neighborhood children (conversations with Isacovich 2017; MTL 2017; MOI 2017). Unemployed workers swelled the ranks of the picketers' movements, consisting mostly of people fired from jobs in production, who now stopped the circulation of goods by blocking streets and roads. On the other hand the middle class became proletarianized, while public servants and pensioners suffered cuts in their incomes to meet the requirements of the IMF. In addition, public workers were paid with public bonds, such as the famous '*patacones*', resulting in further wage reduction and monetary confusion. Regardless, the IMF announced in December 2001 that it would no longer help the country because the commitments made were insufficient.

In this scenario, the *'corralito'* provoked a strong reaction also among the middle class, because it made clear that convertibility was wrecked, foreshadowing the devaluation of their blocked savings. A wave of mobilizations, looting and strikes rocked the country. Unexpectedly, picketers were welcomed by the middle class who beat pans, both demanding *'que se vayan todos'* (that all go away). President Fernando de la Rua faced the situation by declaring a state of siege, a measure that had the opposite effect and set popular protest on fire. The crackdown on protests in December 2001 claimed 39 lives; the President resigned and escaped the *Casa Rosada* by helicopter, while four potential successors fell under popular fury the following week.

In those days Argentina experienced unprecedented levels of popular mobilization, characteristic of a revolutionary situation. Hundreds of neighborhood assemblies were held every day throughout the country, with massive participation. In these meetings of popular initiative, the problems of the nation were discussed, and concrete actions carried out. In the capital, assembly representatives gathered on Sundays in Buenos Aires' Parque Centenario in an attempt to articulate joint actions. Organizations of the Argentine left joined but did not lead the process. It could be argued that the strength of the movement was that it transcended bureaucratic ties, interstitial quarrels and petty calculations; but these were also a weakness, since the absence of direction hindered its efficacy.

Successive maneuvers to restore order resulted in a parliamentary arrangement that led to the Menem's former deputy, the Peronist Eduardo Duhalde becoming President, tasked with completing the deposed president's term. Although conceived as a buffer government, there were at least three events under Duhalde that were decisive for the future of the country. First, a debt moratorium was enacted even before Duhalde took charge, initiating a process of renegotiation that would be continued by the next government. Second, convertibility was abolished in January 2002, which led to a significant depreciation of the Argentine currency. These two measures were fundamental to the economic growth that followed, as the peso devaluation favored domestic production and exports, while the moratorium provided large amounts of public funds for purposes other than debt service. In this context, two million people benefitted from the 'Program for Unemployed Heads of Households' designed to mitigate unemployment and poverty, and which was a response to picketer demands (conversation with Gambina 2017; Sartelli 2007).

The third determining element was political in nature. The assassination of two young militants at a demonstration on the Pueyrredón Bridge in Avellaneda in June 2002 was a turning point in the extraordinary popular mobilization. The ensuing public uproar led to the announcement of presidential elections, from which Duhalde withdrew to support his co-religionist Néstor Kirchner. Between the repression and disorder, pressures from above and below intensified for the return to normality, translated as a bourgeois normality. Again, Peronism would fulfill this role.

4 Kirchner Governments

A prosperous lawyer and former governor of the southern-most petroleum province of Santa Cruz, Néstor Kirchner had a conventional political career in the Peronist ranks. Supported by Duhalde in 2003, he faced two other Peronists in the presidential elections, among them the veteran Carlos Menem, who won the first round. However, the former president withdrew from the election in the second round, bequeathing to Argentina a president voted in by 22 per cent of voters.

Néstor's initially modest legitimacy grew in years to come, and his wife Cristina became president twice with increasing support each time: 45 per cent of the votes in 2007 and 54 per cent in 2011. Over the twelve years that they were at the helm of the country, the Kirchners mobilized a rhetoric that referred to historical Peronism but gradually gained a life of its own. 'Kirchnerism' renewed its political impetus after Néstor's death in 2010, intensifying in Cristina's second term. Although it failed to win a third consecutive term when its candidate was defeated in the 2015 polls, Kirchnerism has since circulated the slogan 'Volveremos' ('we'll be back'), with an obvious Peronist resonance.

But what is the concrete base of this remission to Peronism, historically associated with national industrialization, the integration of workers and sovereignty? The meaning of the Kirchner governments is a matter of dispute: some interpret *Argentinazo*[5] in 2001 as a historical inflection, which modified the pattern of accumulation in a national-developmental or neo-developmental direction pursued by the government (Basualdo 2009; Schincariol 2013). Others emphasize situational aspects that allowed a partial recovery of the economy while structural continuities were not challenged (conversations with Gambina 2017; Gallo Mendoza 2017).

This dispute had political consequences since the stance toward the government fractured popular movements and unions, in addition to dividing the progressive intelligentsia. Divisions amongst the Argentine left are not

---

5 As some refer to the social upheaval triggered in December 2001.

unprecedented, but they were deepened by Kirchnerism, especially when it sought to monopolize progressive identity in more recent years. As in other countries of the subcontinent, the government captivated parts of the social movements and was intolerant of those who preserved autonomy. In the Argentine case, different interpretations and approaches to Kirchnerism are complicated by disputes of feelings around Peronism; although inconclusive these seem far from being exhausted (conversations with Movimiento Emancipador Peronista 2017; CTEP 2017).

Although some of the aspects described above indicate formal similarities with the PT presidencies, the Kirchner governments engaged in fights that Brazilians never dreamed of: the renegotiation of foreign debt which involved taking on a relative isolation from international finances; the repeal of laws that acquitted the military, who were again tried and imprisoned; the proposal of a media law that attacked the largest media group in the country; and, the attempt to increase the soybean tax, causing an agribusiness rebellion. In addition, privatizations were reversed, changes were made to the Supreme Court of Justice, egalitarian marriage was approved (the first country in the region to do so) and television broadcasting of all football matches was permitted.

However, the Kirchner governments continued to participate in IMF meetings, enacted an anti-terrorism law modeled by the U.S. State Department, defamed and repressed dissidents, froze communal media licenses and failed to carry out tax reform. All the while, inequality remained unshaken while the concentration and denationalization of the economy increased.

Elected in the midst of a revolutionary situation, the character of the Kirchner governments was related to the scope and limits of the rebellion that preceded it. From the point of view of order, Peronism reemerged as an effective political resource for removing politics from the streets and returning it to institutions. On the other hand, the *Argentinazo* stopped unpopular policies that had been imposed since the dictatorship and undergirded by State terrorism. Popular mobilization did not succeed in getting 'everyone [to] leave' ('que se vayan todos') as had been sung in hope, but buried neoliberalism as an uncontested ideology in the country (Sartelli 2007: 171). At this juncture, Kirchnerism can be interpreted as the most basic possible denominator between popular fury and the demands of the system.

The margin of maneuver of the Kirchner governments was related to trends in the economy. Initially, accelerated economic growth made Néstor's government popular, but in the following period, between 2007 and 2013, there were oscillations that canceled each other out. In this context, fiscal pressures led Christina to adopt controversial measures which reduced her support amongst sectors of the bourgeoisie and the middle class while strengthening it among other segments of the middle class and popular strata. Starting in 2014 there was economic stagnation, which persisted in the early years of the ensuing Macri administration.

The resumption of economic growth preceded the election of Néstor. As noted, it resulted from the convergence between the peso devaluation, the debt moratorium and the commodity boom which set the stage for the prosperity that sustained the government's popularity. The debt moratorium of 2002 was fundamental to the recovery of the financial capacity of the State, as confirmed by the drastic reduction of its interest expenses, from US $ 12 billion in 2001 to US $ 3.5 billion in 2002 (conversation with Gambina 2017).

However, a significant portion of the debt continued to be paid. Of the U.S. $ 140 billion the country owed, U.S. $ 40 billion was paid to international financial institutions. The rest was restructured by the Kirchner government according to parameters of the international financial system. Debt negotiations, which were completed in May 2005, can be considered successful from this point of view, as they achieved a discount of 75 per cent, although some argue the real discount ended up being between 15 per cent and 20 per cent. On the other hand, pressure to denounce the loans negotiated by the dictatorship, in order to render them illegitimate – as was attempted in the Iraqi case after the fall of Saddam Hussein, failed (El Descamisado 2015). Creditors who did not accept the terms of the bond exchange offered by Néstor had a second chance in 2010 under the Cristina administration. However, about 7.5 per cent of these debt funds remained irreducible, constituting what Argentine journalists nicknamed 'vulture funds'. As a result, debts with these creditors hindered access to international financial markets during the Kirchner governments, both of which counted on loans from Venezuela at first and then from China.

The second important measure that preceeded the Néstor administration was the end of convertibility. While the immediate consequences were an increase in prices and confusion around contracts previously set on dollars (Kosacof 2010: 33), in following years the competitiveness of local manufacturing increased and imports became more expensive. In turn, this boosted industrial recovery and added to the appreciation of primary exports, lifting the country out of recession. Between 2002 and 2007, industry grew by 73.5 per cent and GDP rose by more than 50 per cent, with an annual average increase of 8.5 per cent. Further, employment levels rose, misery declined, and consumption heated up. The population below the poverty level, which reached 52 per cent during the years of the crisis, retreated to 20.6 per cent by 2007. Popular leaders recall that between 2005 and 2006 soup kitchens were no longer needed and schools were once again just schools (conversation with MTL governista 2017).

The Kirchnerist rhetoric that espoused the reconstruction of a national capitalism found its bearings in this process. In contrast to the speculative frenzy of foreign capital during the *menemato* which led the country to disaster, the president preached capitalism in earnest, projecting the development of national industry and its social counterpart, a national bourgeoisie: 'The plan is to build in our country a serious capitalism, with clear rules in which the State intelligently plays its part to regulate, to control, to make itself present where it is necessary to mitigate the evils that the market does not repair, providing a balance in society that allows for the normal functioning of the country' (Kirchner 2003).

The gradual evolution of industry's share of GDP during the tenure of the Kirchner governments did not justify the enthusiasm of the original project. Data indicates an increase from 14 per cent to 17 per cent in the Kirchner period, returning to the situation prevalent in 1994 but at a much lower level than the 25 per cent registered in 1973 (Basualdo 2009: 337). Industry was far from resuming the productive centrality that it had in the years before the dictatorship in a reality in which 'there was no productive development strategy in general, nor industrial in particular' (Aspiazu and Schorr 2015: 101).

A detailed investigation of economic power during Kirchnerism discredits the ideology of Argentine neo-developmentalism, according to which the national bourgeoisie regained a dominant position under the protection of the State, an argument repeated by Cristina until the end of her term. Instead, this research reveals a high level of concentration and de-nationalization of the domestic economy: 'There is a remarkable confluence of interests in the national project of foreign businessmen and different sectors of local capital. The result is the deepening of a regressive international specialization and a type of passive and subordinate insertion in the world market' (Gaggiero, Schorr and Wainer 2014: 7). In short, the existence of Argentine capitalist groups that profit from the model did not translate into the expected dominance of a national bourgeoisie (Varesi 2012: 248).

It is possible to observe a similar dynamic in the world of work. The recovery of the economy and increasing employment helped unionism regain a certain combativeness assisted by the generalization of collective agreements of work endorsed by the government. Initially, this favoring of workers also involved a political calculation, as it was intended to weaken the picketer movement. At the same time, the increase in labor productivity in the Néstor government did not correspond to an increase in wages, which indicates an expansion in the margin of exploitation (Aspiazu and Schorr 2015: 102).

More significant from the point of view of the world of work are reports that those who prefer to work informally would rather continue receiving government aid of about 4000 pesos per month instead of the minimum wage that reached 9000 pesos in 2017. For example, a militant who works as a domestic worker reported that she did not want to be legally registered as a house cleaner, so as to preserve her access to the 'child allowance' grant, which is topped with a small income from a cooperative in which she participates (conversation with MTL 2017). Symptomatic of this reality is the rise of the 'Confederation of Workers of the Popular Economy' (CTEP), one of the main popular movements that arose during the Cristina government (and from which it distanced itself). The CTEP started from the diagnosis that even if the economy grows, there will be no work for everyone and this is a permanent situation. As its leadership put it, 'We are the refuse of the market economy', whilst referring to the unemployed as 'workers of the popular economy' (conversation with Gringo 2017). In this context, the CTEP agenda includes basic income modalities similar to those that the picketers demanded and received during the 2001 crisis. Even a trade union official believes that in Argentina today, 'the new factory is the neighborhood' (conversation with CTA 2017).

In summary, analyzing the profile of the economy and labor relations during the Kirchner governments shows that the pattern of accumulation bequeathed by the structural reforms going back to the dictatorship continued, despite improvements that emanated from the most serious crisis the country has experienced. The other side of this marginalization of industry and degradation of work is the deepening of the 'regressive international specialization profile' mentioned above. Under Kirchnerism, the engine of the Argentine economy was primary exports, notably soy, accompanied by hydrocarbons and an unprecedented growth in ore exploration.

As in other countries in the region, soybean planting in Argentina expanded dramatically after the release of the genetically modified variety in 1996. By 2002 the area under cultivation reached its limit, such that any further expansion involved the appropriation of lands already occupied, leading to conflicts. While soybeans took off, the production of industrial goods in relation to the economy as a whole declined 135 per cent between 1995 and 2001 (Basualdo 2009: 355). At the beginning of the 21st century, the end of convertibility cheapened Argentinian commodities in international markets and the rise in prices further boosted their expansion. By the end of the Kirchner era agribusiness occupied 22 of 33 million arable hectares, of which 90 per cent were dedicated to soybeans. At the moment, soybeans and its derivatives account for about one third of the country's exports (conversation with Palmisano 2017; Petz 2017).

In addition to regressive specialization, the production process associated with transgenic soy implies a cultural, social, technical and economic system that transforms the physiognomy of the Argentine countryside. The domination of this productive system, which has been described as 'extractive agriculture' or 'agriculture without farmers', causes a significant loss of economic, social and ecological diversity, transforming the country into 'a laboratory where one experiences the elimination of rural life' (GRR 2003: 40). The commitment to this model was reaffirmed by the Cristina Kirchner administration in 2010 in its *'Plan Estrategico Agroalimentario 2020'*, which projected a 60 per cent increase in the export of transgenic grains, mainly soybeans and corn.

At the same time, the pressure on the environment and rural populations was intensified by the expansion of mining, an activity that has no tradition in the country. Technical developments and rising international ore prices have stimulated international investment over the last twenty years. The first open pit mine in Argentina was opened in 1997 and the Kirchner governments cultivated a mining policy by stimulating the exploration of gold, silver, copper, and more. By the beginning of the 21st century, the sector had grown by 20,000 per cent in ten years, a trend that caused numerous socio-environmental conflicts. By 2017, popular resistance had succeeded in driving 6 mining multinationals out of the country (Varesi 2012: 152; conversation with Palmisano 2017).

Argentina has the second largest reserves of shale gas in the world and the fourth largest reserves of unconventional oil. There are indications that the partial nationalization of 'Fiscal Petroleum Fuels' (YPF) in 2012, the largest company in the country, is related to this business. Privatized under Menem in 1999, the company had been controlled by Spain's Repsol with the huge profits from its Argentine operation financing the expansion of the company across Latin America and Africa, with little being reinvested in the country. In this context, Argentina is now no longer self-sufficient in oil, with reserves having fallen and import expenditures having risen. In 2011, Argentina imported more gas and oil than it produced, a fact unheard of before privatization. The following year, the state took control of 51 per cent of the company, divided between the provinces and the national government; in the process, Repsol was indemnified to the tune of US$ 5 billion. YPF then signed a secret agreement with Chevron (formerly, Rockefeller Standard Oil) that opened the doors to US backed unconventional hydrocarbon exploration; a development informed by the assessment that the agreement would be very unpopular if it had been signed with the Spanish Repsol company (conversation with Marcos 2017). Since then, the exploitation of unconventional hydrocarbons has grown in the country.

Just as the industrial outbreak did not change the productive structures, nationalizations did not signify a reorientation of the State's role in the country. The nationalizations focused on companies that presented problems, such as

Aerolíneas Argentinas, the post office, the water company and YPF itself. Meanwhile the most profitable ones, such as the telephone and power companies, remained under private command receiving million-dollar subsidies, partially reduced by Macri.

5   Cristina Kirchner

When Cristina Kirchner was elected in 2007, the economic expansion that took place under her husband's previous administration slowed at the same time that inflationary pressures intensified. Further, there was a growing fiscal deficit, which was a direct result of the resumption of the country's renegotiated debt in 2005 following a three-year grace period.

The government reacted in a different and controversial way to this new scenario. On the one hand it intensified social spending to sustain employment and income levels. The basic income program, the 'universal child allowance' exemplified this course, which in turn aggravated fiscal problems. In response, the government sought to raise its revenues, but without implementing any major tax reform. An example was the attempt to increase withholding taxes on exports and the nationalization of the pension system. More controversial with those on the left was the intervention in the INDEC (National Institute of Statistics and Census), a move that de-structured the statistical reference agency of the country.

A watershed in Cristina's presidency was the attempt to establish a mobile system for agro-export taxation, increasing the rate in situations of high international prices in order to tax surpluses. The measure was not unprecedented in Argentine history, although the proposed increase from 35 per cent to 44 per cent was relatively high (Palmisano 2017). The proposal provoked an en bloc reaction of Argentine agribusiness, in which large and small owners mobilized to bring the country to a halt. Over a period of four months the rural landholders incited various forms of direct action such as the blockading of roads and bridges, protests and marches. While the issue divided the country, the controversy was restricted to its distributive dimension: the question of dependence on primary exports was rarely questioned. At the end, the relevant bill was approved by the lower house of Congress, but the senate vote was tied. The tie-breaking vote fell to Vice President Julio Cobos, who aligned himself with the ruralists and defeated the government he represented.

This conflict and defeat affected the latter part of the government's tenure. The loss of allies within the ruling class led Kirchnerism to strengthen its support amongst other social segments. In this endeavor, the rhetoric of conflict which provided the tone for the agrarian strike was intensified with Peronist motives being frequently used. The overall purpose was to solidify an identity between government and national interest in opposition to its detractors.

The controversy surrounding the media law passed in 2009 is part of this scenario. Relations with the Clarín group, the largest media conglomerate in the country, suffered during the confrontation with agribusiness, which was defended by mainstream media. In retaliation, the government passed a law limiting the concentration of radio and TV licenses, a measure that directly affected the group. Clarín responded with lawsuits that restrained the law's enforcement and provided journalistic coverage viscerally hostile to the law's proponents until the end of the President's term. More recently, the Macri government has been tasked with emptying the law of its most democratic aspects.

Two other important initiatives that followed the agrarian conflict were the nationalization of the social security system (AJFP), against which no bank protested, and the universal child allowance, a cash transfer program implemented in 2010. To a certain extent, these measures complemented each other, since nationalization provided the State with social security revenues which it unduly used to pay current expenses, including social programs, in a context of fiscal tightening (Katz 2012: 234).

The cumulative impact was that the country's economic situation deteriorated. The policy of mitigating the social effects of the economic downturn by raising public spending already under pressure by spending on services inherited from the 2001 crisis, aggravated inflationary pressures and the fiscal deficit. At this juncture, government intervention in the national statistics agency, INDEC, was interpreted as a maneuver to conceal rising inflation and impose a kind of inflationary tax, which would reduce debt service expenses but also affect savings (Altamira 2009: 130). Since then, INDEC statistics have lost their reliability and economic problems have worsened.

As we have seen, the failed attempt to raise taxes on soy also had political effects, prompting the government to intensify confrontation with the opposition as a strategy to strengthen presidential authority. This rhetorical amplification of conflict as a tool to strengthen Cristina Kirchner's identity was increased after the death of Néstor Kirchner in 2010. According to Maristella Svampa's reading, this unforeseen event 'opened the floodgates to high-intensity populism', synthesized in three points: the claim of the state as the builder of the nation; the exercise of politics as a permanent contradiction between two antagonistic blocks; and, the centrality of the leader (Svampa 2017: 216, 230).

Initially Cristina's leadership strengthened, resulting in her victory in the 2011 presidential elections with the highest vote received by the Kirchners until then. In contrast to historical Peronism, Kirchnerism cultivated the middle sectors as its main base of support, which has been described as a 'middle class populism' (Svampa 2017: 232). In 2012 Kirchnerism broke with Hugo Moyano, leader of the General Confederation of Labor (CGT), its main support base in the labor movement. As a result, Kirchnersim's support was reduced to a fraction of the Central de Trabajadores de la Argentina (CTA) which was composed of civil servants and teachers. The CTA, which emerged as a dissident group to the CGT that remained docile to Menem, had divided internally, one part faithful and another critical of Kirchnerism, a cleavage that was repeated in numerous popular movements.

But the main vulnerability of the government was the economy. The swings that marked Cristina's first term in office gave way to stagnation after 2014. The combination of inflation, of increased private unemployment (partially offset by public employment), fiscal and financial problems aggravated by capital flight and the country's financial isolation, ultimately eroded Kirchner's prestige.

In this context, the government tried to return to international financial circuits by repaying the debt with the Paris Club and approving a sovereign payment law aimed at better negotiating with the vulture funds. The preamble of this law stands as a proud affirmation of the country's financial discipline that framed debt payments of US$ 190 billion between 2005 and 2013, contradicting the discourse that Argentina was debt free. However, access to new lines of credit would only be consolidated under Macri who quickly resolved the debts in favor of the vultures, with the country increasing its debt at a runaway pace. This situation, in which the government neither broke with international finance nor regained its confidence, is illustrative of the impasses of the 'serious capitalism' to which it aspired.

Kirchnerism arrived in the 2015 elections partially discredited for various reasons: the middle class was bothered by inflation and corruption scandals; the business community called for an end to populism and enhanced market confidence; the people felt the effects of the crisis; and, the left resented intolerance of dissent and the contradictions within government. However, Kirchnerism was also partially popular in all these sectors, because it was identified with the recovery of Argentine society that followed the crisis: the middle class reigned again; capitalism resumed growth; the people had food and work; and, the left had concrete achievements to show. For instance, of the 2489 members of the armed forces and 343 civilians accused of crimes against humanity under the Kirchners, 616 had been condemned by 2015.

This contradictory terrain foreshadowed tight elections, in which any of the major contenders could win; and that is exactly what happened. The idea to reform the constitution allowing Cristina to contest a second re-election was aborted by the defeat of the government in parliamentary elections in 2013. Then, internal disputes in the governing coalition resulted in the candidacy of Daniel Scioli, a representative of the right Peronists who had become known in politics with Menem in the 1990s. As a result, the vote for Kirchnerism on the left became more difficult, but not impossible. The opposition clustered around the candidacy of Mauricio Macri, the son of a family that was enriched under the dictatorship. Macri became famous as President of the Boca Juniors football club, projecting himself onto the national political stage as mayor of Buenos Aires, where he completed two terms.

Scioli won the first round but Macri took the second with just over half the vote. He was the first President elected in 100 years who was not affiliated with radicalism or Peronism, in a political situation increasingly characterized by names such as 'Mauricio' and 'Cristina', rather than by disputes over policies. A few days later, Bolivarianism suffered a resounding parliamentary defeat in Venezuela, signaling that the progressive wave was entering a hangover on the subcontinent.

6   Final Thoughts

In the midst of the extraordinary dynamism of the Argentine economy at the beginning of the twentieth century, a combative workers' movement with various trade union and partisan expressions was consolidated; ever since, it has been pressuring for the democratization of society. On the opposite pole of workers' vitality, the country's history was traversed by the military's intervention in politics, including when it moved to bourgeois reformism under the leadership of Perón. In his personal trajectory, the general gravitated towards anti-popular positions, showing the limits of the ideology he embodied. However, the penetration of Peronism in the popular sectors has endowed this political phenomenon with a unique longevity, morphing into a multifaceted ideology that was at the service of multiple agendas and hindering autonomous working class politics.

Political instability in the period between the presidency of Perón and the dirty war was related to the impasses of a bourgeois revolution within dependent capitalism, with which Peronism was originally identified. The military coup of 1976 buried this historical possibility and began to turn in a neoliberal direction. But unlike Chile, in Argentina this change was not immediate despite the devastating effects of state terrorism on popular resistance. The lack of cohesion of the dominant classes around this project, in addition to a relatively weaker state, limited the reorientation of society in this direction.

On the other hand, the economic failures of the dictatorship led to the disastrous Malvinas war, which precipitated the end of the military regime. Pressed between the changes that elected him and the continuities that sustained him, Alfonsín succumbed in the midst of coup attempts and hyperinflation. It was then time for Peronism, disguised as *menemismo*, to solve the ambivalences that remained, which it attempted to do by implementing a radical neoliberal agenda that culminated in the dollarization of the economy. At first, tamed inflation, parity with the dollar, access to credit and cheap imports made the government popular. But when the favorable environment faded, growing trade and fiscal deficits showed that the model was unsustainable. The economy went into recession and the country's social indicators, into free fall. The next government quickly surrendered to the logic of structural adjustment, which was only restrained by a popular rebellion that while threatening to destroy existing institutions, only succeeded in toppling some presidents.

Once again, Peronism found a role to play, cooling the politics of the streets by reframing it in institutions. The Néstor Kirchner government was conditioned by the extraordinary popular mobilizations but also by two crucial measures that preceded it: the end of convertibility and the debt moratorium. The state quickly regained fiscal capacity, while the commodity boom put the economy back on track.

In this context, Kirchner flirted with the idea of a national capitalism, recycling motifs of the original Peronism. However, this proposition found few objective and subjective bases upon which to materialize regardless of which, did not prevent sectors of the business community from approaching government, earning money in the process. Industry did not return to the centrality it once had in the economy, nor did national capital. On the contrary, the intensification of soybean planting, coupled with the exploitation of hydrocarbons (including non-conventional ones) and ores, deepened the primary export orientation that has prevailed since the dirty war, at the same time that socio-environmental conflicts have intensified.

At the political level, sectors of the social movements 'fell in love' (se enamoraron) with the Kirchner governments, some because the soup kitchens were emptied, others because the military were arrested (conversations with MTL 2017; MOI 2017). However, those who preserved their autonomy risked defamation and repression, and in many cases, ended up divided into parallel organizations.

When favorable economic conditions cooled, the government tried to raise more money without disturbing the structures, while at the same time spending to preserve employment and income. This policy course stressed the limits of the strategy adopted, evidenced in the defeat the government suffered over the issue of agro-export taxes, decided by the vice president himself. At this point, the rhetoric of conflict became more pronounced as a resource for confronting new enemies (such as Clarín), strengthening Cristina's authority and intimidating the left-wing opposition. Kirchnerism consolidated its allies but also deepened opposition and did not solve the economic problems. This project of power was defeated at the ballot little by little: first in the legislative elections of 2013 that prevented the attempt to institute a third consecutive candidacy of Cristina; and then, with the defeat to Macri in 2015 presidential elections.

In the first year of his administration, Macri disarmed the media law, made peace with the vulture funds, resumed indebtedness, cut subsidies and fired officials according to political criteria, among other measures that contrasted with the previous government and which exacerbated national problems. It is estimated that in Macri's first year in power the number of poor has increased by 1.5 million people (conversation with Gambina 2017). The specter of unemployment and hunger again haunts the peripheries of a country that only understood what Latin American underdevelopment was at the end of the last century.

On the other hand, popular organizations have mobilized with tenuous unity and relative success against the new government, imposing limits on the anti-popular offensive. On the propositional level, it seems necessary to settle accounts with Kirchnerism, the 21st century version of the Peronist utopia of a bourgeois reformism. Kirchnerism bet on rebuilding Argentine capitalism based on a national bourgeoisie. In this process it went further than Uruguay or Brazil, carrying out concrete measures and genuine, albeit moderate, struggles. However, it did not build the correlation of forces necessary to overcome the confrontations that emerged within the framework of the ruling classes, nor did it favor popular power to sustain the intended advances. The result of this timid bet on a national bourgeoisie in the 21st century reveals, once again, the insufficient and provisional status of any change that does not affect the structures of dependence and social asymmetry in Latin America. The advances that the earlier crises did not undo, are being undone by the Macri government.

As Cristina struggles to return, those who desire different politics are challenged to settle accounts not only with the recent, but also with a more distant, past. An evaluation of Kirchnerism implies adjusting accounts with Peronism, which translates into a belief in bourgeois reformism and the conciliation of classes as a way forward for the Argentine nation. This utopia had some bearing on reality in the national-developmental years, when social democracy seemed a historical possibility in the country. Since the dirty war however, this ideology has lost its material basis. Today, overcoming it implies confronting the legacy of the dictatorship deepened by *menemism* and a return to the unfinished agenda of the rebels of 2001: i.e., 'that all go away', to begin with.

CHAPTER 4

The Process of Change in Bolivia: Creative or Destructive Tensions?

> This process of change is without return; whatever they say, whatever they do. Neoliberalism will not return to Bolivia.
> *Evo Morales on the referendum for a new constitution, January 2009*

> Its function ('strategic ethnicity') is to do as if the Indians governed, as if the country were Plurinational (...), as if the Armed Forces could be intercultural and democratic allies of the Indians. This 'as if' was updated through a discourse and a performative identity, which ended up covering up the (neo) colonial continuities of the past, under the label of 'process of change'.
> *Rivera Cusicanqui, 2015*

1   Introduction

The election of Evo Morales in 2005 in the wake of a popular mobilization that opposed neoliberal measures and overthrew two presidents promised new horizons to the progressive wave. Unlike the Venezuelan context, the Bolivian President relied on a powerful popular movement, tempered and radicalized in successive struggles. The country with the highest population percentage of indigenous people on the subcontinent, Bolivia was founded upon a form of social apartheid of the white minority in relation to the indigenous mass. This variegated society ('*sociedad abigarrada*') as described by Zavaleta Mercado, produced in 1952 a nationalist revolution led by workers in reaction to a ruling class that had led the country into wars and territorial losses. With revolution tamed, as a result of American pressure and the fear of popular autonomy by those who took charge, the country went through a series of military regimes until it confronted the debt crisis and hyperinflation in the 1980s. The neoliberal spiral and political degradation that followed were only halted by a popular revolt, resulting in a situation with characteristics of a revolutionary conjuncture at the beginning of the 21st century. Paradoxically, Morales' election in this context restored politics to institutionality. After overcoming the threat of secession and civil war, the so-called 'process of change' gravitated in a conservative direction in all dimensions, provoking a split with its popular base. The government has responded to dissent with intolerance, while the intensification of 'Evoism' and extractivism question the nature of the envisaged change. The question to be asked is: are we facing a neoliberalism with an Aymara[1] face?

2 The Variegated Society between Revolution and Dictatorships

A core component of the Castilian colonial enterprise, the territory that comprises present-day Bolivia, is populated mainly by descendants of the original population, a situation shared by neighbors Peru and Ecuador. Despite independence in the nineteenth century, this population continued to be exploited while its cultural references were discriminated against and marginalized, conforming to a rigid pattern of social segregation that resembles caste stratification. Underlying this domination however, economic, political, and cultural forms that favor diverse social relations and often fuel forms of resistance continue to exist.

This pattern of segregation was conceptualized by Zavaleta Mercado in the Bolivian case as '*sociedad abigarrada*' – a variegated society. This refers to a social formation in which different historical times overlap, corresponding to different relations of production that are little articulated at the political and cultural levels, and expressing itself in various forms of government, justice, languages and other factors.[2] It differs from socioeconomic formation because it is a 'partial and apparent domination of the dominant mode of production, not the rearticulation of the rest of the modes of production to the new dominant organic principle' (Urquidi 2007: 46).

According to Zavaleta, the state corresponding to this historical formation seeks to make diversity invisible instead of representing it, thereby exacerbating contradictions that emerge in moments of crisis in all their concreteness: they are moments of tearing (as opposed to variegation) and universality (Zavaleta Mercado 1988: 20). For this, the Bolivian intellectual advocates the

---

1 Aymara refers to the principal indigenous people in Bolivia.
2 Tapia reworked this notion referring to Bolivia as a 'multi-societal' country, which is not the same as a multicultural society where 'people may have different identities, but it does not have a different form of government identification and is part of the same economic and political structures' (Tapia 2011).

study of the 'general national crisis as a method of knowledge': as Bolivian society advances by spasms, the methodological proposition of 'constitutive moments' emerges as a reference for analysis (Zavaleta Mercado 1988: 2007).[3]

The national revolution of 1952 is one of these constitutive moments, a fundamental reference in the constitution of contemporary Bolivia. Its origins go back to the Chaco War (1932–1935), an episode that made clear the lack of ruling class commitment to the country, while at the same time projecting a national-popular horizon in a geographically and culturally fragmented society. The popular uprising of 1952 was the culmination of two decades of political instability and social conflict, overthrowing not only the government but the State itself.

One of the region's most notable events in the twentieth century, the trajectory of the Nationalist Revolution of 1952 illustrates the overlap between national revolution and democratic revolution in Latin America. The core of the issue is to understand how a process that begins with the taking of the State under a popular insurrection, in a circumstance in which even the army dissolved, capitulates before the establishment of a military dictatorship in 1964, the same year as the military coup in Brazil.

Some elements are essential to understand this trajectory. The revolutionary government lived in permanent tension between the radicalizing pull of the workers, the counterrevolutionary pressures of the United States, and the very moderate nature of the leadership of the Nationalist Revolutionary Movement (MNR), which took over the State. From the workers point of view, the relationship with the party that assumed the government strengthened its political role, expressed in the appointment of several workers as ministers. At the same time, however, the impossibility of an autonomous class policy condemned the working class to constant vulnerability. In the synthesis of René Zavaleta, it was a class 'as victorious as it was impotent' (Zavaleta 1998: 70).

In the countryside, the acceleration of social struggles forced the government to enact an agrarian reform with the intention of controlling a process that it could not contain. The intention was to channel it politically through unions that, despite different regional situations, often established a clientelistic relationship with the revolutionary state (Rivera Cusicanqui 1984). The expansion of rural schools and the universalization of voting, both important

---

3 According to Zavaleta; 'From a methodological point of view, it is a matter of isolating certain events, by circumscription in time, or regional situations, by circumscription in space. This is a response to the scarcity of information and is undoubtedly a symbolic selection. In defense of the method it must be said that no social science is otherwise possible in a country with the characteristics of Bolivia' (Zavaleta Mercado 2007: 9).

advances of the revolution, also lent themselves to an instrumentalization with the aim of building the hegemony of a reluctantly revolutionary party.

It is also possible to analyze the evolution of the revolutionary process through the prism of a progressive submission to the United States. The turning point was the adoption of an International Monetary Fund (IMF) program of economic stabilization in 1956, which froze wages, cut public expenditures and rendered unfeasible any industrialization around mining. This submissive trend caused a gradual alienation of the workers' movement, which in turn opted for a reformist policy under the leadership of Juan Lechín, in the process moving away the support of anti-imperialist sectors such as the Trotskyists of the Revolutionary Workers Party (POR).

Regarding international affairs, the vision of President Víctor Paz Estenssoro was summed up in a statement to Congress, which opined that it was prudent to avoid Iran's fate – a reference to the CIA-contrived overthrow of Iranian Prime Minister Mossadegh a few years earlier (Hylton and Thomson 2007: 81). Faced with the suspension of 70 per cent of tin exports, as a result of the refusal of tycoon Simón Patiño and the United States to refine the mineral due to partial nationalization, the government opted to indemnify the 'tin barons', who in any case faced difficulties with the depletion of mineral reserves. Meanwhile, international capital maintained control over central operations, such as smelting and transportation.

The docility of the new government was rewarded by the United States, which proceeded to give Bolivia the most economic aid of any country in Latin America. In 1958, about one third of the national budget was funded in this way, making Bolivia the recipient of the highest level of per capita aid in the world. At the same time, the U.S. refused funding for the state-owned company, Bolivian Fiscal Oil Fields (YPFB). For these reasons, President John F. Kennedy (1961–1963), who agonized over Cuban radicalization, referred to the Bolivian process as a 'great revolution [which] has blazed a path for others to follow' (Kennedy 1961: 184). Not surprisingly then the country, alongside Venezuela under Rómulo Betancourt (1959–1964), became a showcase of what would be the 'democratic revolution' embraced by the Alliance for Progress.[4]

In parallel, the United States played a direct role in 'advising' on the reconstruction of the Bolivian army. The new state was faced with the need to contain the masses in a country where the working militias maintained their weapons and the miners handled dynamite. When Paz Estenssoro began his

---

4   The 'Alliance for Progress' was a short-lasting policy adopted by the J.F. Kennedy administration in 1961 in response to the Cuban Revolution. It emphasized economic development and social reform fueled by US aid as a way to prevent revolution.

third term in 1964 he faced growing opposition from the working class movement, including the moderate sector led by Lechín, while at the same time being harried by the right. The November 1964 coup that abbreviated his mandate was led by an officer in the air force, a force that had barely existed during the Chaco War, providing confirmation of the key role played by the United States in reconstituting and re-integrating military forces into Bolivian politics and society.

The dictatorship that followed rested on the solid nationalist base built in rural areas to support the so-called Military-Peasant Pact. In gaining rural sympathy, the regime neutralized the previously existing links of solidarity among workers when it brutally repressed resistance by workers in the mines. US intervention in the country reached extreme levels, as witnessed in the events surrounding the 1967 assassination of Che Guevara's (Gott 1971; Agee 1976).

The death of the dictator General René Barrientos in a helicopter crash in 1969, allowed for the rise of a military still motivated by nationalism. The ascension to power of General Juan José Torres shortly thereafter was supported by the mobilization of workers, a development that prevented a reactionary conspiracy. On this occasion the workers refused to take part in the government and created a Popular Assembly, which was accepted by the general, who nevertheless made little effort to strengthen ties with the broader left. Placed with the continental context, these were the days of the Revolutionary Government of the Armed Forces in Peru, commanded by Velasco Alvarado and, of the triumph of Unidad Popular in Chile, under the presidency of Salvador Allende.

The specter of a duality of powers precipitated a military backlash backed by Brazil and led by another cadre trained in the United States, Colonel Hugo Banzer (1971–78). Banzer established a dictatorship friendly with similar regimes in the Southern Cone, while General Torres was assassinated in Argentina under Operation Condor (Dinges 2004). At the political level, the new regime relied mainly on agribusinesses that flourished in the east of the country where the dictator came from, in the process consolidating what Vice-President García Linera later described as 'business-haciendal power', a reactionary bastion in contemporary Bolivia (García Linera 2013c).

Simultaneously, the social and economic policies that underpinned the Military-Peasant Pact were abandoned. The turning point occurred in the valleys of Cochabamba in 1974 with the massacre of rural workers, who had been protesting against the increase in the price of basic goods. The resurgence of an autonomous peasant movement had been nourished by a political current that recuperated the Aymara martyr Tupac Katari as a symbol of the Aboriginal legacy.[5] The so-called 'katarismo' in the Bolivian highlands was fed by an urban subculture of indigenous traits, fermented in the heart of migration to La Paz. This new syndicalism, led by young people who were born after the period of agrarian reform, had a critical vision in relation to para-state syndicalism. It played a fundamental role in mobilizing for democracy, converging in the Single Trade Union Confederation of Bolivia's Peasant Workers (CSUTCB) founded in 1979 (Rivera Cusicanqui 1984).

The overthrow of Banzer in 1978, when economic expansion slowed, generated a period of political instability with nine successive governments over a period of 4 years, until the reestablishment of electoral democracy in October 1982 (Mesa and Gisbert, Mesa Gisbert 1999: 671). A rising popular movement overthrew three dictatorships (Banzer in 1977, Natusch in 1979 as well as García Meza and successors in 1982), despite the unprecedented repression practiced by the latter, who murdered more than a thousand militants in less than a year. García Meza defended the interests of another economic sector that prospered in the east under Banzer, drug trafficking, whose importance would grow extraordinarily in the 1980s.[6]

3 Democracy and Neoliberalism

The general contours of the Bolivian trajectory since 1982 resemble those of several South American countries in the period, albeit with a singular intensity. After an ephemeral attempt by a center-left government to confront the economic problems left by the various dictatorships, a neoliberal project was implemented in the country. From then on, there was a succession of rulers with different shades of post-revolutionary politics, ranging from the leader of the MNR to a former dictator. Accompanying this, there was a progressive corrosion of the country's socioeconomic fabric within the framework of a weakening of conventional class organizations.

In turn, this accentuated the vulnerability of workers, while new social movements slowly matured. This process resulted in the decreasing popularity of parties identified with conventional politics, who were unable to offer an alternative to the rationality of multilateral organizations who proposed to confront the problems of neoliberalism with more neoliberalism. This spiral of

---

5 The associated intellectual reference can be found in the work, 'Indian Revolution' by Fausto Reynaga.
6 García Meza was serving a 30-year prison sentence when he died in April 2018.

degradation, which culminated in the election of the dictator Hugo Banzer in 1997 as the successor to a millionaire who spoke Spanish with an English accent, was only stopped by a marked rise of new social movements. This opened up another chapter in the history of the country, of which the eventual election of Evo Morales is part.

In 1982, the end of the sequence of military dictatorships was precipitated by intense social mobilizations in the countryside and in the city. In an indirect election held by the Congress, Siles Zuazo, a former post-revolutionary president (1956–60) who abandoned the MNR dominated by Paz Estenssoro to join a coalition of center-left parties, Democratic and Popular Unity (UDP), was elected. Facing a difficult economic situation inherited from the dictatorship, which included recession, currency depreciation, trade imbalances, inflationary pressure and the explosion of external debt, Siles Zuazo faced problems typical of a centrist government in Latin America. Confronted in the streets with the trade union movement he resorted to printing more money, exacerbating inflationary pressures. In congress, he encountered stiff opposition from his former colleague Paz Estenssoro, who allied himself with the newly founded organization of the dictator Banzer, the Nationalist Democratic Alliance (ADN). Isolated in a context of hyperinflation and widespread social discontent, Siles anticipated the end of his term, which came in 1985.

Significantly, the fourth government of Paz Estenssoro (1985–1989) dismantled the economic framework of Bolivia's post-1952 nationalist politics which had been maintained by successive dictatorships, implementing neoliberal policies that were contrary to the project embodied by the revolution. The notorious Decree 21.060, designed by Minister Gonzalo Sánchez de Lozada with advice from Jeffrey Sachs,[7] was successful in controlling inflation but the cost was a notable deterioration in the social fabric of the country. It was in this context that the firing of 23,000 miners from the state-owned Mining Corporation of Bolivia (COMIBOL) provoked the March for Life, which ended up being crushed by state repression and marking a turning point for union power in the country from which it would not recover. Many miners who lost their jobs in these years migrated to the Chapare region where coca cultivation flourished, taking their experience of struggle to one of the few unions that gained strength under neoliberalism, coca leaf cultivators (conversation with Vadillo 2015).

Paz Estenssoro's successor was Jaime Paz Zamora (1989–1993), a figure linked to the Movement of the Revolutionary Left (MIR), an organization that

---

7 An influential, neoliberal and market-friendly US economist and academic, who later advised the governments of Poland and Russia along similar lines.

was part of the UDP. In spite of having said in earlier times that 'a river of blood' separated Banzer from the MIR, he ruled in alliance with the former dictator. In the process, the Zamora government ended up reproducing neoliberalism. At the same time, the US intensified its pressure to combat coca, something that the president did not have the courage to implement. Neither did his successor, Sánchez de Lozada (1993–1997), architect of Decree 21,060. Lozada, who grew up in the United States and went by the nickname 'Goni', had an important Katarista leader, Victor Hugo Cardenas, as vice president.

Beyond the rejection of Cardenas' participation in the government by a significant sector of the indigenous movement, the alliance was symptomatic of new social configuration where the ethnic question assumed a central role. At the political level, Loayza Bueno's research shows that the preference for parties or candidates with ethnic discourses increased notably after 1991 (Loayza Bueno 2011: 104–105). Thus, the radicalization of neoliberal policies, which involved the privatization of the country's state-owned companies under the euphemism of 'capitalization', proceeded simultaneously with the indigenist policies of a multiculturalist matrix. This multicultural neoliberalism was embodied in the 1994 constitution.

More important than the promotion of bilingual education and the constitutional recognition of the multiethnic and plurinational character of the country was the regulation of land of community origin (TCO) – autonomous and communally owned indigenous lands. Another initiative that sought to give a democratic veneer to the government was the 'law of popular participation', which expanded the possibility of union participation at the municipal level, generating the expectation of rural workers occupying different levels of government. According to Almaráz, who participated in the first leadership of the Movement for Socialism-Political Instrument (MAS-IP), the MAS originated with this objective and did not have a national program (Almaraz 2015). Also the organization of the National Council of Markas and Ayllus of Qullasuyu (CONAMAQ) surfaced during this time, although from a distinct perspective, since it fostered the logic of the ayllu[8] as a form of organization (Schavelzon 2015).

Meanwhile, the radicalization of the privatization project catalyzed a social crisis. For example, YPFB was divided and auctioned and royalties paid by multinationals that took on new contracts were reduced from 50 per cent to 18 per cent. As a result, the $ 350 million a year that the YPFB passed on to the national treasury between 1985 and 1996 was drastically cut such as within a few

---

8   Ayllu refers to an extended family group with a common origin who, whether holders of a territory or not, use it in a communal way for the subsistence of its members.

years the payment was seven times lower (Hylton and Thomson 102). The consequent rise in unemployment was accompanied by a reduction in government revenues, which further reduced the state's margin for public policies and increased the country's dependence on international loans. As a percentage of GDP, such loans rose from 3.3 per cent to 8.6 per cent between 1997 and 2002. Like the growing US aid, the loans were tied to the further deepening of neoliberalism and the policy of eradicating coca.

This perverse situation would only be changed by the influx of social protest starting with the Water War in 2000 and culminating in the Gas War of 2003, the overthrow of two presidents and the election of Evo Morales. While I will not go into detail about these events (Crabtree 2006; Hylton and Thomson 2007; Dangl 2011; Webber 2013), I will argue that Bolivia crossed a revolutionary conjuncture in which popular insubordination made the country unmanageable to its ruling classes until the election of Morales in 2005 and the inauguration of the constituent assembly, processes that contained the possibilities of systemic change in this extraordinary context.

4   Revolutionary Conjuncture

At the political level, the degradation of the country under neoliberalism reached its lowest point with the election of former dictator Hugo Banzer in 1997. Unlike former presidents, his mandate was marked by adherence to the US policy of coca eradication, a policy that was continued and intensified by vice president Tito Quiroga (2001–2002) after Banzer died in 2001. In the face of evident foreign interference in the country, the escalation of the conflict with the *cocaleros* (coca cultivators) provided national projection to the movement led by Evo Morales, who associated the coca leaf with ancestral practices and Bolivian nationalism.

The rise of the mass movement in this conjuncture had as its initial reference the Water War, which broke out in Cochabamba in 2000. The seed of the confrontation was the World Bank's 1997 commitment to forgive $ 600 million of the country's debt if the Cochabamba water system was privatized, which it was in 1999. As in the case of the *altiplano* (highlands), where a similar conflict erupted autonomously, the idea of paying for the use of water was in violation of customs and practices associated with deeply ingrained community values. In both cases, state repression provoked an escalation of the conflict and the popular camp became radicalized. In Cochabamba, popular assemblies (*cabildos*) saw more than 50,000 people gather to reject multinational control over natural resources, and air the proposal of a constituent assembly. The government was forced to retreat.

In the *altiplano*, the Aymara peasants led by Felipe Quispe at the head of the CSUTCB blocked the main roads of the country, resurrecting the ghost of the indigenous siege of La Paz by Tupac Katari in the 18th century. The state employed the army and air force in its repression, destroying houses and torturing people. Food was flown to the capital by order of Banzer, while peasants held mass assemblies in Achacachi, marking the resurgence of Aymara radicalism. Even though the government agreed to a long list of demands, which included the suspension of Decree 21,060, the protests returned the following year.

The new protagonists of social struggles in Bolivia were described as 'unstructured, varied in their composition (neighbors, guilds, coca growers, teachers, peasants, indigenous) and in their demands, but all similar for their high intensity and emotionality, an expression of historic fractures in the country' (Lazarte 2015: 5). They replaced the traditional strike that restrained the production of goods, with radical forms of direct action such as blockades that impeded their circulation. They also cultivated forms of direct democracy, such as the large open *cabildos* or town halls that encouraged fractions of the movement to radicalize their critique of the state in following years.

Other sectors were pushing for a reform of the state. In 2002, a political rights march was not immediately successful but it spread the proposal of a constituent assembly in the popular imagination. This demonstration conflicted with Morales' interests, which were focused on the elections that would take place in June of that year. In the end, 'Goni' was re-elected with a small margin of victory over the MAS candidate (22.5 per cent versus 20.9 per cent). However, Morales' campaign received a push when the US ambassador declared that the country's economic aid would cease should the *cocalero* leader be elected (Stefanoni and Alto 2014: 56).

The country that 'Goni' took over in 2002 was different from the one he encountered as minister in 1985. One of the countries in Latin America which previously had the largest state presence in the economy was now one of the most open economies in the region. The informal work force had reached 68 per cent and unemployment had tripled since 1990. After Brazil, Bolivia was now the most unequal country in the region. Historical poverty had not diminished: 41.3 per cent of the population lived in extreme poverty and infant mortality and life expectancy rates only outperformed Haiti. The economy had low or negative growth rates for the fifth consecutive year as well as a large deficit in the balance of payments, while data from the Ministry of Labor revealed a significant increase in strikes and social protests.

The decision to implement a 12.5 per cent tax on all wages above $110 per month, a policy required by IMF conditionalities, triggered a new wave of protests in February 2003. Lower-level police officers went on strike and the army's savage repression triggered grassroots riots in different sectors, which spread to other parts of the country, forcing the government to retreat. A few months later however, a plan to export Bolivian gas to California through Chilean ports was leaked, revealing that the president had been negotiating this in secret since his previous term. The plan offended the national sensibility of the people because it echoed the historical foreign exploitation of natural resources in the country, as well as the delicate relationship with Chile ever since the loss of access to the ocean in the Pacific War (1879–1883).

In the following months, demands of a diverse nature converged around this nationalist outrage, engendering an extraordinary sequence of social struggles which had as its epicenter El Alto, a municipality on the outskirts of La Paz occupied and controlled by the organized population. Again, the ruthless repression of the State, which resulted in the deaths of dozens of people, only served to intensify the levels of protest. Subsequent clashes reached epic proportions, such as the night when thousands carried and positioned train cars to close the bridge connecting La Paz to El Alto, preventing even the passage of tanks. At the political level the demands were condensed into what was known as the 'October agenda', which demanded: the industrialization of gas instead of its export through Chile; a rejection of the Free Trade Area of the Americas; the annulment of the law of 'protection and security to the citizen', which legitimized state repression; and, the resignation of the president. The last demand was realized with the intensification of protests that saw more than 300 thousand people gather in La Paz.

Vice-president Carlos Mesa (2003–2005), a historian and television communicator and son of prestigious intellectuals who appeared like a calming figure in the middle of the storm, assumed the presidency. It was a controversial arrangement endorsed by MAS, which defended institutional solutions throughout the crisis. In retrospect, it is evident that the party calculated an electoral triumph in the following election and was interested in appearing as a guarantor of order.

Mesa's brief presidency witnessed a sharpening of social contradictions. These were polarized between the return of popular protest due to the frustrated nationalization process and the resurgence of the claim of autonomy by the Media Luna, a region with Santa Cruz de la Sierra as its epicenter and in which Bolivia's hydrocarbons and agribusiness are concentrated. The *Cruceños*[9]

---

9   Those from the city of Santa Cruz de la Sierra.

in particular nourish a regionalist sentiment anchored in a racist ideology, defining themselves as '*cambas*' against the natives of the altiplano (the '*kollas*') – despite the existence of indigenous peoples in the East (Soruco 2008).[10] As Zavaleta points out, the cumulative result is a regional cleavage mixed with ethnic and class tensions bringing to light the contradictions of the country's formation amidst the crisis.

On the popular level, the resurgence of mobilizations was a response to the government's refusal to consider the nationalization of hydrocarbons. With the support of the MAS, Mesa offered up a complex plebiscite with five questions, but eluded the fundamental one: the expropriation of multinationals by the State. Notwithstanding the boycott of significant popular sectors, the result of the vote opened up the possibility of modifying the terms of the State's relationship with the multinationals, which in turn was interpreted as a threat to private property and foreign investment, especially by the eastern elite. As mobilizations intensified at both poles, Mesa aligned himself with Santa Cruz and his 'January agenda' in defense of business autonomy, which forced a reluctant MAS to distance itself from a government it was allied with informally. The demonstrations began to reach massive proportions, bringing together half a million people in La Paz alone. While Mesa did not call on the military to repress the protest he was harassed in the congress and on the streets and resigned soon thereafter.

Despite indications that popular mobilization was growing, becoming more radicalized and strengthening its autonomy, again Morales interceded to limit the unfolding of the process to the political level. The end result was that in December 2005 he became one of the few presidents in Bolivia to be elected with a majority of votes (54 per cent). The so-called 'process of change' had begun.

5   The Process of Change

From the outset, the Morales government was perceived internationally as a progressive administration, adding to the wave of presidents elected across South America in reaction to neoliberalism. His credentials were strong: of poor origin and with indigenous features in a country marked by racism; the

---

10   *Cambas* and *kollas* are popular terms that imply a racial bias emanating from those of white background against those of native roots in the Eastern part of Bolivia, which has Santa Cruz as its main city.

association with the coca leaf, which has become a symbol of cultural self-determination; the antagonism to the United States; the identification with the 'mother-land', the embracing of 'Living Well' (*Buen Vivir*) and other values of native origin; the historical trajectory as a rural union leader; and, the context within which he rose to the presidency, allied with powerful mobilizations that reversed neoliberal measures and overthrew two presidents. The diffusion of this image can be attested to by numerous examples, of which I will cite two.

In 2009, Morales proposed to the United Nations that 'Earth Day', celebrated on April 22, be changed to 'Mother Earth Day', an attribution that 'links original conceptions that until recently were considered primitive with sophisticated and modern conceptions that consider human life as a further step into the life of the entire cosmos' (Albo 2014: 20). This resulted in the president of the UN general assembly, Miguel d'Escoto, declaring Morales 'World Hero of the defense of Mother Earth'. More recently, during the G77 + China Summit in 2014, d'Escoto convened the Summit of Heads of State and Government 'for a new world order to live well', and included in its resolutions the themes of Mother Earth, 'Living Well' and the Andean principles of '*ama suwa* (do not be a thief), *ama lulla* (do not be a liar) and *ama qhilla* (do not be lazy)' (Guevara 2015: 8).

A second example comes from an article that circulated in Brazil at the beginning of 2016, written by Leonardo Boff, an internationally known proponent of liberation theology. The article, entitled, 'The misconceptions of the PT and Lula's dream', offers a strong critique of the Workers Party in which Boff evokes the Morales government as a counterpoint to the trajectory of the PT under Lula:

> In Bolivia, Evo Morales Ayma sought support in the vast network of social movements, from where he came as a strong leader. He got that support, fighting against the parties. After years, he built a base of popular support, of indigenous, women and young people to the point of giving a social course to the State and making more than half the Senate today composed of women. Now the main parties support him and Bolivia enjoys the highest economic growth on the Continent.
> BOFF 2016

This is the image spread by the president himself, who announced that he would govern according to the Zapatista principle of 'leading by obeying'. The international impact of this image of Morales was confirmed when Bolivia was chosen to host the second world meeting of Pope Francis with popular movements in July 2015.

The notion that Morales' administration is a 'government of social movements' has, like many others, found its main ideologue in vice president Alvaro García Linera, a respected intellectual with previous militancy in Katarism.[11] García Linera coined the term 'Andean-Amazonian Capitalism'[12] to describe the possibilities and limits of the government in 2006 but has more recently referred to 'community socialism' (García Linera 2015). Underlying these concepts is the proposition that the strengthening of community processes in a country with the economic and cultural characteristics of Bolivia is the way to overcome capitalism in the long run.[13] The vice president refers to the obstacles that this process faces, especially in the popular field, as the creative tensions of 'our revolution', among which he stresses 'the creative contradiction between the necessity and will to industrialize raw materials, and the essential need for Living Well' (García Linera 2011: 62).

In this chapter it will not be possible to discuss the rhetoric that adorns the 'process of change' emanating from the vice-presidency.[14] However, I would like to point out that on the eve of a referendum proposing a fourth term for Morales in 2016, the country's leading indigenous and environmental leaders as well as numerous left-wing intellectuals and advisors to social movements sustained a rather different view of this government. To understand the critical point of view, I will outline the evolution of the government, framed by the disputes to approve a new constitution, the affirmation of MAS in power in the 2009 elections and, the demand for a fourth term for Evo Morales by referendum in 2016.

The MAS government faced a crucial challenge in its early years. In keeping with popular demand, Morales followed the path taken by Chávez and

---

11 Referred to by Cusicanqui as 'the best student of the worst Bourdieu', García Linera actually studied mathematics, although it was recently revealed that he did not finish his degree.
12 Defined as, 'the construction of a strong state, regulating the expansion of the industrial economy, extracting its surpluses and transferring them to the community to promote forms of self-organization and mercantile development, specifically Andean and Amazonian' (García Linera 2006a).
13 Such a reading also emerges from the notion of an 'integral state', understood as the place where the state 'begins to develop a lengthy process in society and where the latter begin to increasingly appropriate the decision-making processes of the State' (García Linera 2014: 29).
14 I was struck by the fact that Ramiro Saravia, who has been doing outstanding teaching work for years in the central square of Cochabamba repeated in his expositions several motives emanating from the vice-presidency (conversation with Saravia 2015). A critique of García Linera's view on the Bolivian identity can be found in Cusicanqui 2015: 23–30.

convened a constituent assembly. In advance though, the decision that congressional participation would only be through political parties, thus interdicting representation by indigenous movements or nations, was interpreted as a setback for the popular forces. The practical result was compulsory membership of MAS. However, the results of the national election in 2006 only gave a simple majority to MAS in the congress (54 per cent), far short of the two thirds necessary to advance without allying with other forces. The hopes for change that came from the congress plenary were met with decided opposition to prevent the new constitution, on the pretext of a demand for decentralization and autonomy articulated from Santa Cruz. Banzer's vice-president, Tuto Quiroga took over the leadership of this bloc, and thought it fit to change the name of the late dictator's party to 'Social Democratic Power' (PODEMOS).

The opposition's intransigence triggered a climate of permanent tension between the separatist threat and the imminence of civil war, since the MAS base in the highlands was considering surrounding its enemies. It was in this context that the American ambassador Philip Goldberg, a veteran of the Kosovar secession and accused of financing the Santa Cruz autonomists, was expelled from the country, as well as the US Drug Enforcement Administration (DEA). The denouement of the impasse demanded prolonged negotiations. Despite the government giving in to most of the demands of the opposition, they nonetheless rewrote 130 articles of the agreed text. The new constitution was only endorsed in 2009, which in those circumstances was interpreted as a political victory for MAS.

In fact, in the 2009 general election that followed, Evo was re-elected with 64 per cent of the votes and the MAS won a two-thirds majority in the congress and the senate. The constitutional opposition articulated around PODEMOS largely dissolved, in a scenario in which the traditional parties were liquidated. On the other hand, the MAS had a solid popular base around the Pact of Unity, sealed in 2004 between the main organizations of the country: CSTUCB, Bartolina Sisa,[15] CONAMAQ, *cocaleros* and the lowland Indians gathered in the Confederation of Indigenous Peoples of Bolivia (CIDOB). The situation that García Linera described as a 'catastrophic tie', referring to the impasses that prevailed since 2003, was broken; and, it was a thrashing. In these circumstances, the risk was that Morales would feel like the 'monarch of the country' (conversation with Ávila 2015).

Contrary to what one might expect, in the following years there were continued defections amongst the grassroots, and important adhesions amongst the oligarchy. The first march against Morales took place in 2010, demanding

---

15 Known as 'Bartolinas', it is the National Confederation of Peasant Native Indigenous Women of Bolivia.

territorial autonomy. This was a central demand for indigenous peoples, associated with the plurinationality consecrated in the new name of the country: 'Plurinational State of Bolivia'. In contrast to the multiculturalist policies implemented by Sánchez de Lozada, territorial control implies political sovereignty, which in turn signals separate legal systems and different economic relations. However, the regulation of the law imposed a set of limitations on the ability to realize this constitutional right, resulting in practice in districts and indigenous municipalities becoming part of the structure of the State that the policy was intended to modify. Schavelzon synthesizes the paradox: 'autonomy was born as a slogan to weaken the state. Now the state has become "indianized" and the autonomy loses the force that it had before' (Schavelzon 2015: 53).

A second antagonism between the government and its base surfaced in protests that were a response to a decree promulgated on Christmas day 2010, instituting a tax that would raise the final price of fuels by more than 70 per cent. Though presented as a measure necessary to curb public spending on fuel subsidies, research revealed that the initiative actually spelled out the limits of the nationalization of hydrocarbons.

Announced on May 1, 2006 in the midst of intense national emotions, nationalization translated into a deepening of the tax reform begun in 2005 under Mesa, when taxes on the sector rose from 18 per cent to 50 per cent. The revision of the contracts between multinationals and the State raised taxes to 62.5 per cent, while simultaneously breathing new life into YPFB through the purchase, at high prices, of half plus one of the shares of five companies which in the past were state-owned (Arce and Gómez 2013: 78). However, this did not translate into command of the sector by the state, since the multinationals retained control of the reserves and the extraction process, including in the so-called *megacampos* (huge oil fields), on which the production of the country's gas and oil depends. Although the profit rate of companies decreased their total profit increased, as evidenced in the almost three-fold increase in the value of production between 2004 and 2010. In 2010 the multinationals controlled more than 80 per cent of the production, a percentage that has since grown, while the share of Brazilian Petrobras rose from 56.7 per cent in 2005 to 63.7 per cent in 2010 (Arze, Espada, Guzmán, Poveda 2011; Rodríguez Cáceres and Gandarillas undated).

Far from full-scale expropriation or state monopoly of the sector, the 'nationalization' fully respected the rights of foreign companies, under the logic that foreign investment is essential to develop the sector. However, the volume of hydrocarbon production has not grown significantly under Morales in a country where private investment has been less than 10 per cent of GDP (Molina 2015: 27). The increase in profits and taxes collected reflects the rise in international prices of these raw materials in an economy increasingly dependent on hydrocarbons: between 2001 and 2005, they accounted for 47 per cent of total exports, increasing to 69 per cent between 2010 and 2015 (Requena 2015: 21). On the other hand, imports of gasoline rose from 3 per cent to 9 per cent of total imports in the same five-year period. In spite of an overall increase in fiscal revenues, the central government suffered recurrent deficits under Morales. These were mainly the result of increases in expenses related to the expansion of the state bureaucracy, whose personnel quintupled. In this context state-owned enterprises played a key role supporting so-called fiscal surpluses (Arze, Espada, Guzmán and Poveda 2011: 24).

Facing a scenario of stagnation in the production of hydrocarbons, the Bolivian state was faced with two choices: generate new taxes or resort to external indebtedness. As it was powerless to confront the multinationals, it opted for a new tax proposed in 2010 in order to create a fund that would realize an additional $ 32 per barrel and in the process raise corporate profits by about 400 per cent with the aim of encouraging them to increase production. Protests known as *gasolinazos* forced the government to reverse the measure. However, in April 2012, an incentive of $ 30 per barrel was decreed, which constituted a subsidy twice the size of income obtained through the Direct Tax on Hydrocarbons (IDH) and the royalties on the price of $ 27.11 then in force (Arze, Vargas and Gómez 2013: 84). What this revealed was the government's ongoing determination to intensify primary exports, including hydrocarbons, minerals and agribusiness, in response to fiscal pressures.

One result of this trend has been the progressive lowering of socio-environmental requirements for the expansion of extractivist activities in the country, in direct contradiction to the country's constitutional precepts and the image of motherland protector. The conflict surrounding the Indigenous Territory and Isiboro Sécure National Park (TIPNIS) that surfaced in 2011, has condensed these tensions and is considered a turning point in the government's relationship with indigenous movements.

As its name describes, TIPNIS is an indigenous territory and an environmentally protected area that has existed since the 1960s; both of these legal realities are supposed to protect it from development. However, the Morales government began building a highway through the park, awarding the contract to Brazilian contractor OAS. The project was immediately associated with the controversial Initiative for the Integration of Regional Infrastructure in South America (IIRSA), which will be analysed later (conversation with Villegas 2015). Beyond the business contracts, the motivations underlying the highway were the exploration of oil and the expansion of the *cocaleros* within the park.

Although the indigenous population of TIPNIS is relatively small, estimated to be around 2000 families, it was argued that the construction work would jeopardize all territories in a similar manner (conversation with Paz 2015). On the other hand, the government argued that one cannot risk the future of the country for only a few people. As Morales suggested in opening the meeting of popular movements with the Pope in 2015, when the law contradicts the 'interests of the people', it is necessary to change the law (Morales 2015).

Under the leadership of CIDOB and lowland indigenous people several protest marches were organized in a tradition that stems from the original mobilizations of the 1990's. The eighth march, held in 2011, had international repercussions. On this occasion, the government brutally suppressed the demonstrators in Chaparina. Adults were kidnapped, families were dispersed in the jungle, children disappeared for days and a few deaths were reported. There are records of pregnant women who lost their children due to beatings. The repression generated popular solidarity and the burning of tires at a nearby airport prevented the departure of imprisoned leaders. At the end of the march demonstrators were welcomed by a crowd in La Paz, while CIDOB and CONAMAQ withdrew from the Unity Pact (Fundación Tierra 2012; Cusicanqui 2015: 48–49; conversations with Ávila 2015; Chávez 2015; Paz 2015). At the same time a group of intellectuals, some of whom held high positions in government, circulated a 'Manifesto for the recovery of the Process of Change for the people and with the people'. Morales's base of support had fractured.[16]

The reaction of the government to popular sectors that gravitated towards the opposition was targeted and relentless. CIDOB and CONAMAQ were divided and their headquarters were occupied by allied sectors. The government created an alternative organization to organize a counter-march, the Indigenous Council of the South (Conisur). And, the leadership of dissenting social movements was slandered and criminalized.[17] Organizations that supported

---

16 The position of Osvaldo Peredo, a former guerrilla leader whose brothers fought and died with Guevara, is significant: a supporter of a government that he rarely criticized, Peredo acknowledged that the situation of TIPNIS 'puts me in dissidence with myself' (conversation with Peredo 2015).

17 There are two examples from the TIPNIS involving CIDOB leader Adolfo Chávez: a boat motor stolen from a congressional representative that was in conflict with indigenous communities resulted in an aggravated robbery charge being laid against Chávez even though he was not on the scene; another case involved a cacique (indigenous leader) of the Conisur, Gumercindo Pradel, condemned by community justice to 12 lashes. In response, Chávez was placed under an arrest warrant for three months, although he successfully escaped. Both cases highlighted conflicts between the constitutionally recognized community justice system and the Bolivian state (conversation with Chávez 2015). Further, in

the government received money while the financing of opponents was stifled. A good example was the hotel that was under construction in the backyard of the headquarters of the Departmental Labor Coordinator (COD) in Santa Cruz, in contrast to the small garage on the outskirts of the city where the autonomous sector of CIDOB would meet. In Cochabamba, the expansion and renovation of the headquarters of the government-allied Six Federations of the Tropic of Cochabamba was completed at the end of 2015, celebrated with a party that had a cake with the president's face.

The persecution extended to those who supported these dissident groups: Ibis, a Danish non-governmental organization (NGO) that funded the organization of indigenous groups was expelled from the country, and several others faced problems, including domestic NGOs. In 2015 three well-known centers of investigation and support to popular movements – the Center of Studies for Rural and Agrarian Development (CEDLA), the Fundación Tierra and the Bolivia Documentation and Information Center (CEDIB) – faced a defamatory campaign launched by the government under the leadership of García Linera, which threatened their activities (Fides 2013, 2015).[18]

The vice president smeared all opponents with notable virulence: in a pamphlet in which he defended the TIPNIS highway he accused the movements that marched of 'defending the interests of conservative right-wing forces, undermining their own revolutionary process'; said that NGOs 'reproduce mechanisms of clientelistic cooptation and ideological subordination to the financing agencies, most of them European and North American'; and excoriated critics on the left as, 'organic intellectuals of the restoration of "coloniality"' (García Linera 2012: 14, 26, 84). A group of notable former government officials who signed the manifesto for the 'the recovery of the Process of Change' were labeled as 'political resenters' in the vice president's response, a pamphlet entitled 'NGOism, childish illness of the right' (García Linera 2013a).[19] The simplistic crudity of the accusations is analogous to the logic of the Cold War, in which every opponent is a rightist at the service of imperialism.

	December 2015, Chávez was issued with an arrest warrant while attending the UN climate change conference in Paris, accused of misappropriating the Indigenous Fund.
18	The Millennium Foundation, an outfit aligned with neoliberalism also became a government target.
19	The people mentioned included: the former Deputy Minister of Land, Alejandro Almaráz; the former General Director of Standards and Public Management of the Ministry of Economy and Public Finance, and former Deputy Minister of Strategic Planning, Raul Prada; the former ambassador to the United States, Gustavo Guzmán; and, the former Superintendent of Hydrocarbons, Hugo Sainz.

Therefore, the self-assigned label of a 'government of social movements' needs to be, at a minimum, qualified. His home base, the *cocaleros* unconditionally support Morales. But, contrary to what might be imagined, it is not an indigenous organization from the socioeconomic point of view, but a peasant one. Because in a country like Bolivia, where the vast majority of the population has an indigenous phenotype, it is necessary to differentiate at a number of levels: between urban Indians, who may be rich as are the Aymara commercial bourgeoisie, and the majority poor; between indigenous peasants, who conceive of the land as a commodity to be exploited, as is the case of the *cocaleros* and of Morales himself and the indigenous community, whose way of life is linked to an organic relationship with the territory (conversations with Ávila 2015; Vadillo 2015; Ribera Arismendi 2015).

These differentiations help explain the tensions between the lowland Indians and the *cocaleros*, who in their colonizing expansion became the 'spearhead of the anti-community project' (conversation with Ávila 2015). Another cleavage to be taken into account is that the majority of peasants and urban Indians are from Quechua or Aymara extraction, while dozens of other peoples of little demographic relevance are not. It is in this perspective that the CIDOB leader, Adolfo Chávez, complains that under the MAS government, 'decolonization would make us Quechua or Aymara' (conversation with Chávez 2015).

In spite of the international sympathy that the decriminalization of the coca leaf mobilizes, something that is identified with indigenous rights when it actually antagonizes these rights in Bolivia, coca leaf production and distribution is a nebulous economic activity. Bolivians say that coca for domestic consumption is the soft leaf produced in the Yungas, near La Paz. Hence the widespread suspicion that the *cocaleros* of Chapare, Morales' original base, are involved in drug trafficking, earning much higher yields per hectare than soy. Indeed, there are indications that the country currently not only plants the leaves but processes Peruvian cocaine, half of which is sold to Brazil, the second largest market globally (conversation with Almaraz 2015). The Chapare region's producers are organized and unconditionally loyal to 'brother' Evo, and consider it a duty to defend him. With some irony, some comment that Chapare is the only truly autonomous territory in the country (conversation with Vadillo 2015). Although there is little research on this subject, as researchers report a fear of getting involved with the topic, there is a perception that the role of the coca leaf in the economic performance of the country is not insignificant, generating resources that are not accounted for in the GDP but which enter the economy through civil construction and imports.

There have been several drug trafficking scandals involving high-ranking government officials. In 2011 in Panama, the DEA – the same body that was expelled from Bolivia by Morales, arrested Rene Sanabria, director of Bolivia's Special Drug Trafficking Force (Felcn); in other words, the country's anti-drug tsar. Extradited and sentenced to fifteen years in prison, the general issued a letter when his son was later arrested in Bolivia for illicit enrichment, accusing the government of covering up for several officials involved in corruption and drug trafficking. Additionally, the head of the General Directorate of the Coca Leaf and Industrialization (Digcoin), Luis Cutipa, was arrested in 2013, accused of reselling the cocaine he had seized. However, he was released after only two weeks, a development that exposed another democratic vulnerability of the government: the lack of judicial autonomy.

Cumulatively, the conjunction between: the state-supported *cocalera* expansion in TIPNIS; scandals involving authorities of the highest level; and, numerous indications of money laundering, such as buildings in Cochabamba being bought with cash, led the renowned intellectual Alejandro Almaráz, the government's Deputy Minister of Land until 2010, to describe it as a 'drug-trafficking government', a suggestion endorsed in recent writings by Rivera Cusicanqui (Rivera Cusicanqui 2015; conversation with Almaráz 2015).

The peasant base of the government, which had in the *cocaleros* an unconditional ally, was reinforced by other movements that were integrated into the Unity Pact, in addition to the faithful factions of the fractured indigenous organizations. Many of them accessed the so-called 'Indigenous Fund' ('*Fondo Indígena*'), made up of a fraction of the hydrocarbon revenues, to finance development projects. But the fund eventually became a source of allegations of corruption, affecting the movements and the government, until it was closed down by the president in August 2015. By the end of that year a report by the country's attorney general found that there were 49 ghost projects diverting US$ 6.8 million, resulting in the indictment of 205 people and the arrest of 24 other figures. These included the former Minister of Rural Development and Land and leader of the peasant organization Bartolina Sisa, Julia Ramos, two senators, and other social leaders such as the head of the government-friendly CIDOB (BBC 2015).

Miners' unions also form a key component of the government's base, although the sector is only a shadow of what it was in the past (conversation with Campos, Tosito and Romero 2015). One of those unions, the Central Obrera Boliviana (COB) had earlier broken away from the government, but resumed ties in 2013, after the 'defeat of the ultra-left in the miner unions' (Rada Vélez 2015: 4). In fact, the mining cooperatives are small and medium groups of capitalists known for their overexploitation of labor, while large scale mining is commanded by international capital. Also in this sector, where only two mines are operated by the state, there was no intention to affect the operations of transnational corporations. The government limited itself to imposing a 12.5 per cent tax on the extraordinary profits of the companies and although the collection of this tax has doubled in the last decade due to rising commodity prices, the political power of the cooperatives keeps the taxation far below that imposed on hydrocarbons (conversation with Escobar 2015).

During this period, the tax contribution of the mining sector was around one seventh of that paid in relation to hydrocarbons, although its share in the GDP was 1.7 times greater (Arze and Gómez 2013: 105). The importance of the mining and hydrocarbon sectors to the country's income has relegated socio-environmental concerns to the margins. In 2014 the government decreed the Mining and Metallurgy Act, authorizing exploitation in protected areas and glaciers, critical sources of water supply in the highlands. Subsequently, Decree 2366 of May 2015 authorized the exploration of hydrocarbons in eight protected areas. Not surprisingly then, there is no reason for these sectors to oppose the government.

Another social group that supports Morales is the so-called 'Aymara bourgeoisie', migrants of rural origin who have risen up the socio-economic ladder through import trade, whether legal or not. Many boast about their culture and economic power, symbolized in the buildings of peculiar architecture that are common in El Alto and are known as '*cholets*', alluding to their '*chola*' origin.[20] The paradox is that the general direction of government policy, which relies on this Aymara pride while repressing plurinationalism, has had a negative effect on the broader self-identification of the indigenous population, which reached 62 per cent in the 2001 census and fell to 40 per cent in 2011 (Cusicanqui 2015: 38).

It is a commercial bourgeoisie because despite the official discourse, industrialization has not been a priority of the government. In 2012, only three of the nine state-owned manufacturing plants planned in 2007 were in operation. And although the constitution speaks of a plural economy, providing for four sectors (community, state, private and social-cooperative), the emphasis on primary exports inhibits the diversification of production. From the point of view of labor relations, García Linera himself has acknowledged that in stimulating the community economy, the objective is not to compete with the private sector but to provide palliative help to rural producers (García Linera 2013b: 46). Indeed, as the country's dependence on commodity exports has increased, the share of the so-called community sector has declined: from 7 per cent in 2005, to 6 per cent in 2010, while the social sector grew from 2 per

---

20 A word with multiple meanings, '*chola*' popularly alludes to the poor urban population of indigenous roots.

cent to 3 per cent in the same period. Similarly, state participation in the economy, leaving aside that of the public administration, rose from 4 per cent to 10 per cent – far from the 34 per cent claimed by the government (Arze and Gómez 2013: 100–102).

The government has also imported various products, mainly food, as part of a social policy aimed at simultaneously containing inflation. Anchored in a currency that has appreciated against the US dollar, this policy discourages local production whilst creating expanded profit opportunities around extractive income, whether through the service sector or imports. Bolivia's is an increasingly consumerist economy, which is becoming less and less productive.

Perhaps the greatest impact of this economic orientation is in rural areas. The per capita value of food imports has tripled in the last decade, from US$ 24 to US$ 70. This is in addition to a government subsidy estimated at 800 Bolivians per family per month related to the price of sugar, bread, milk and chicken (Urioste 2015: 22). Today Bolivia imports vegetables, fruits and even potatoes (and Andean heritage) from Peru (Escobar 2015).

As a result, the peasant way of life that has always centered on an organic relationship with the land in contrast to the mercantile mentality of the rural mono-producer, is in accelerated decomposition. It is estimated that 79 per cent of the food consumed in rural areas is currently purchased from agro-industries. At the same time, more profitable export-oriented activities, such as quinoa, are thriving. Many peasants have stopped being farmers and are engaging in the burgeoning transport sector in cities, are selling their labor in construction, or are emigrating (Urioste 2015: 22).

When MAS initially came to power it seemed that things would be different. Speaking of a second Agrarian Revolution, MAS's first government (2006–9) accelerated the land titling process initiated in 1996, covering about 20 million hectares between 2005 and 2010. In reality though, there was only an effective change of property involving about 4 million hectares (Almaraz 2015: 23; Arce and Gómez 2013: 92). Most of the land distributed or incorporated as TCOs belonged to the government itself (*tierras fiscales*), with only 821,000 ha being redistributed, up until 2011, for not fulfilling its economic function (Ormachea and Ramírez 2013: 82). After 2011 even this process was stopped, with land policy focused mainly on titling the properties of the rural oligarchy.

In the second MAS government, the rapprochement between the government and agribusiness in the state of Santa Cruz intensified. In 2011, the Productive Revolution Law liberated transgenic crops, which had been banned since 2008. The government then agreed to two explicit demands from the agribusiness sector. Although the country deforests about 200,000 ha per year and has one of the largest per capita CO_2 emissions in the world (Requena

2015: 21), in January 2013 the government passed the Law for Support of Food Production and Restoration of Forests. Nicknamed *'perdonazo'*, (huge pardoning) this law amnestied more than 2 million hectares of deforested land that should have reverted to the state. At the same time, in an act that constitutes another barrier to land expropriation, the government agreed to a five-year pause in verifying compliance with the social function of land envisaged in the constitution.

But in the clearest indication of its commitment to the oligarchy of Santa Cruz, the government announced in 2014 its intention to extend the agrarian frontier by 10 million-hectares by 2025 on the pretext of securing food sovereignty. Shortly afterwards, the National Association of Producers of Oleaginous and Wheat (ANAPO), an organization of Oriental agribusiness, assumed responsibility for outlining a strategy for this purpose, creating one of the objectives of the 2025 Patriotic Agenda launched by Morales (Condori 2015). In short, 'the MAS, naturally and vertiginously, is becoming the party that represents the general interests of "business-hacienda power"' (Ormachea and Ramírez 2013: 98).

This reality points to one of the main causes of the dissolution of the opposition and the appeasement of the autonomist agitation; that the government stole their political agenda and base of support. Partisans of the late Hugo Banzer joined the MAS, while Santa Cruz civic leaders placed candidates in the party. Embarrassed about these alliances made by the party, the historic guerrilla leader Osvaldo Peredo commented, that, 'guests should be received in the living room' and not in the bedroom (conversation with Peredo 2015).

While it is true that a histrionic right wing opposition persists, it is motivated more by openings in positions of power rather than by a dispute over the country's political project. Those in opposition also risk facing the long arm of the MAS, which controls the electoral bodies, the judiciary, and the media. There is widespread recognition that regional elections held in Beni and Chuquisaca in 2015 were manipulated. To give one example: in Beni 228 candidacies were rejected, all from the opposition. The trigger was the mention of a poll by an opposition spokesman when electoral law forbids referring to unofficial polls. The legal personality of the 'guilty' party was removed even though the two polls that take place during elections are sponsored by government (conversation with Almaraz 2015).

Politicized judicial decisions have also become naturalized, on both the left and right of the political spectrum. Almaraz cites the case of the son of a reactionary politician from Santa Cruz who in 2015 was jailed for seven years, accused of plotting a coup based on a 17-second telephone call. In a country where the police are free to act as they please, the political goal of the arrest was to discipline the father (conversation with Almaraz 2015). Some people even suggest that 'one is more afraid now than during the dictatorship' (conversation with Gandarillas 2015).

Regarding the press, contrary to what might be expected there is no consistent opposition. As one journalist has noted: 'After a wave of changes of owners, the new owners stopped their previous critiques of the MAS. ATB, La Razón, PAT and the Extra[21] changed ownership and shareholders. Unitel and the UNO network radically softened their editorial lines. In 2013, the president told El Deber newspaper that only 10 per cent of the media were confronting his administration' (Archondo 2015: 34). While there are suspicions that García Linera has played a central role in the creating this situation, the vice president denies any attempts to control of the media and says he only has books.

However, the undisputed political leader of the government is Evo Morales. His leadership is becoming more and more like a personality cult in a party in which there is no internal democracy and, in a government committed to not casting shadows on its largest star. This may explain the nomination of ministers who appear to meet advertising resonance criteria, such as the search for an indigenous woman trained in law for the Ministry of Justice. Another possible reading is that the appointment of young people with little political experience facilitates the management of the public machine to meet the tastes of Morales. Health Minister Ariana Campero, who was 29 in 2015, describes the president's calls in the middle of the night to request her intercession in personal situations. In her view, this illustrates the humanist concern of the leader, but it can also be interpreted as clientelism (conversation with Campero 2015). The ideological veneer of this personalization of politics, which materialized in the attempt to give Morales a fourth term, was anticipated by García Lineira in the notion of 'evismo, the popular-national in action' (García Linera 2006b).

Beyond the ideological and political disputes, the macroeconomic orientation of the project led by Morales has been to increase state revenue through the intensification of primary exports, in order to boost public investment, all of which has happened in practice. In contrast to the low level of private investment, public investment has quadrupled in recent years, mainly oriented towards highway infrastructure (conversation with Escobar 2015). Because productive projects geared towards economic diversification and industrialization have been pushed to the background, growth has been boosted by primary exports, construction, public administration and a criminal economy.

---

21   These are all names of media networks.

As has been the case in many countries in the region, the increase in fiscal revenues has facilitated conditional monetary transfer policies aimed at reducing poverty. In Bolivia, there are three core programs: the Juancito Pinto program targeting children of school age, who receive U$ 30 per year; the Juana Azurduy program aimed at pregnant women who are entitled to receive U$ 7 each time they attend a medical appointment; and, the Renta Dignidad program in which the elderly receive about U$ 1/day and that moves more resources than the first two combined. This last program aims to improve an initiative launched in 1996, under the impact of a social security reform more brutal than the Chilean one. It is difficult to assess the impact of these programs on poverty alleviation in the country but data indicates that the volume of expatriate remittances is at least three times higher than the total spent on the three programs (Arze and Gómez 2013: 117).

According to official statistics there has been a reduction in poverty. In 2008 these showed that poverty had fallen by almost 30 per cent due to a change in the methodology of the World Bank. This led Bolivia to be considered a 'middle income' country, qualifying for non-concessional loans at market prices. However, there was no parallel change in the world of work to endorse this promotion, more especially in a country where half of the urban population still lives in subsistence conditions (conversation with Escobar 2015).

Considering that international indices generally refer to poverty as an income of less than US$ 2/day, and to extreme poverty as an income of less than US$ 1/day, it is necessary to take into account exchange rate appreciation in a context in which the Bolivian currency has remained stable in recent years despite inflation. The data indicates that increases in wages have been unable to respond to increases in the cost of living, except in the public sector. In 2004, the minimum wage bought 99 per cent of a family's basic food basket but by 2010 it covered only 74 per cent, which shows a loss of purchasing power. In 2010, the income of about two-thirds of employed workers was lower than the cost of a basic family basket. The share of national income going to labor fell from 36 per cent in 2000 to 25 per cent ten years later, while the share going to capital rose from 47 per cent to 55 per cent, revealing an economy that grows by exploiting labor (Arze and Gómez 2013: 133–142).

The other side of the coin when it comes to conditional income transfer programs is that public social spending has not been prioritized. State spending on health and education is lower than private spending. Only 35 per cent of salaried employees are covered by the health system and 38 per cent by the pension system, which corresponds to between 13 and 14 per cent of the economically active population. The precariousness of the health system, in a country where a child dies every half hour and a woman in childbirth every three days, contrasts with the very high defense budget and benefits for the military – such as full retirement in a country where pensions are very low and where the tripartite contribution (employers, employees and the state thus enhancing available funds) has been abolished (conversation with Saucedo 2015). In short, the neoliberal approach remains in force, despite the symbolic and partial exemption of Decree 21,060 in 2011.

6   Final Thoughts

Emerging on the crest of the sub-continent's most radical popular mobilization of the early 21st century, Evo Morales' 2005 election sought to return street politics to parliament. While some anticipated the frustration of a process that, at the time, threatened the structures of the State, the feeling prevailed that it would be possible to modify Bolivia substantively through the parliamentary route. In other words, that it was practically and politically necessary for reform to be imposed on the revolution. The inauguration of the constituent process sharpened the social contradictions of the country, exposing cleavages based on class, ethnicity and region. Confronted with an agenda emanating from the popular bloc, the reaction was articulated around the Media Luna, threatening the very unity of the country. The outcome of what García Linera has described as a 'catastrophic tie' implied significant concessions from the popular camp, signaling what was to come. But in 2009, many interpreted the approval of the new constitution as a victory.

At that time there were many signs that a process of change was underway: Tiwanaku's tenure,[22] the defense of Pachamama, the plurinational state, the ancestral claim of the coca leaf, the nationalization of hydrocarbons and the resurrection of the YPFB, the expulsion of the US ambassador and the DEA, alignment with Chávez and the ALBA, the sudden international projection of the country, the reorganization of land, the prohibition of transgenics and, the implementation of social programs. It was because of this that Morales was re-elected in 2009 with 64 per cent of the votes in an election that gave him an absolute parliamentary majority.

Paradoxically, the dismantling of the political right corresponded to a rightward turn by the government, intensifying relations with the 'hacendal-patrimonialist power' while deepening the commitment to primary exports. This articulation proved to be incompatible with the expectations of plurinationality, sovereignty and defense of the environment, which emerged in the

---

22   An archeological site that evokes the native, pre-colonial past of Bolivia.

indigenous march of 2010, in the *gasolinazo*, and especially in the conflict around the TIPNIS. Anchored in the conservative alliances that were solidified, the government confronted growing popular dissent with intolerant rhetoric and political repression.

From then on, disillusionments have accumulated: plurinationalism dressed itself as the Aymara bourgeoisie, while references to Tupac Katari adorned the *cholets* and planes of LATAM airlines; community justice was criminalized by common justice; territorial autonomy only happened in the Chapare region; the coca claim was overshadowed by the suspicion that the social base of the government and authorities were involved in drug trafficking; the government of 'social movements' corrupted the faithful, while crushing dissidents, extending its domination to electoral organs, the judiciary and the press; 'hacendal-patrimonial power' composed the base of the government, together with the party of the ex-dictator; the soybean thrived while the peasantry died; 'nationalization' was powerless to meet basic national needs; opposition to the United States coexists with the defense of international capital, alongside emulation of Brazil; engagement in the ALBA was instrumental, with the main interest being Venezuelan resources; and 'Living Well' has been massacred by extractivism. In short, one cannot look at the MAS of 2016 with eyes of 2006.

In this context, the project underpinning a fourth term for Morales was a distant cry from, 'moving from the democratic and cultural revolution to the economic and social revolution, in a process that allows for the beginning of the construction of community socialism under the paradigm of 'Living Well' (Rada Vélez 2015: 4). Analysis shows that, in a process analogous to the PT's in Brazil, MAS has used the knowledge and confidence it has of social organizations to overcome obstacles to the further exploration of hydrocarbons and the expansion of agribusiness,[23] engaging in regional competition to offer the best judicial guarantees to international capital and thus ignoring all socio-environmental obligations. This is exactly the opposite of 'Living Well', unless it is identified with the practices and interests of Latin American ruling classes, where the most sophisticated patterns of consumption are combined with cheap domestic labor, based on an obscene concentration of wealth. In short, Morales' Bolivia has engaged in a reproduction of underdevelopment with an Aymara face.

It is undeniable that Bolivia has changed in the last ten years. Travelers no longer find the tortuous bumpy roads that were impassable in the rain and the

---

23 Many government ministers and advisors come from social movements that they now criticize, such as the minister Carlos Romero, who was an advisor to CIDOB and now confronts it on the TIPNIS issue.

country is no longer a cheap destination. The economy has been monetized, there are indigenous people and women in power and there is more consumption. But there is also more abandonment and more violence.

The more 'modern' the country seems to become, the more it ceases to be the 'variegated society' as analyzed by Zavaleta, but not for the sake of a sovereign nation integrated around an internal market as revolutionary nationalism intended, or through the equitable coexistence of different visions of the world, as plurinationalism hoped for. Rather, what we have witnessed is the capitalist mode of production subsuming community lifestyles in the bosom of a project that reedits the political style of the old MNR, where power has become an end in itself.

The fact that a significant part of the international left still identifies this government as progressive provokes reflection. Discarding the barrier of disinformation, which is not insignificant, there are the remnants of 'wishful thinking' – i.e., believing in what you want, not what you see. Many however, support the government based on geopolitical considerations that ignore the dynamics of class struggle in the country (Borón 2016), or on a binary reasoning that the alternatives would be worse, a practice that fits well with TINA's ideology ('There is no alternative').

It is necessary to enlarge the horizon, to break with immobility. The fact that relations with the United States are not friendly or that indigenous faces predominate in the congress is inconclusive. Internationalism must overcome the logic that the enemy of my enemy is my friend, a kind of thinking that would lead the international left to support repressive regimes in Syria and Iran. It also needs to clarify the ties between class and ethnicity, the 'two eyes' of Katarism. The relationship between development and ecology, and the articulation of the class dimensions of racial and gender issues are among the challenges that revolutionary politics must address in an original way in the twenty-first century. In the Bolivian 'process of change', the creative aspect of these tensions only survives as ideology.

CHAPTER 5

Ecology versus Capitalism: Dilemmas of the Citizen Revolution in Ecuador

> The greatest danger for our country project is leftism and infantile environmentalism. I fear that I was not mistaken, although perhaps I forgot to add infantile indigenism.
>
> *Rafael Correa at the National Constituent Assembly, 2008*

> There is no other possible conclusion: this is a citizen revolution without citizenship.
>
> *Ospina Peralta, 2013*

1 Introduction

Rafael Correa's election to the presidency of Ecuador a few months after the 2006 victory of Evo Morales in Bolivia signaled the peak of the progressive wave which eventually elected Fernando Lugo in Paraguay in 2008. In these Andean countries, the electoral triumphs seemed to crown years of popular insubordination which overthrew several presidents, paving the way for constitutional processes that promised new forms of government. Ten years later, Morales and Correa remained in the presidency, but were leading power projects far removed from the expectations of change with which they were originally identified. In Ecuador, the Venezuelan challenge of overcoming oil dependence and the Bolivian need for integration of the indigenous population converge as a synthesis of the dilemmas of progressivism. On the one hand, the constraints to overcoming dependence faced by a meager primary export economy based on oil exploration are exacerbated by the absence of a national currency since dollarization in 2000. On the other hand, the degrading social and environmental legacy of the ephemeral petroleum wealth of 1970s is at the root of a keen sensibility in the present for the renewed exploitation of natural resources, where indigenous and peasant resistance joins the environmentalist argument in pressing for an alternative pattern of development. As in Bolivia, these ideals converged, albeit diffusely, on the notion of '*Sumak Kawsay*' or 'Living Well' consecrated in the 2008 Constitution. The conflicts between the affirmation of this principle and the simultaneous deepening of primary exports are at the root of the contradictions lived by the self-proclaimed 'Citizen Revolution' that in 2017 appeared to have gained an electoral afterlife.

2   Ecuadorian Formation

The advertisements showing Ecuador as a tourist destination highlight the impressive diversity of landscapes concentrated in a small country. A territory smaller than Poland, it is crossed by the Andes Mountains – punctuating the landscape with snowy peaks and volcanoes – which separate the Amazon in the east from the Pacific coast, where the ecological sanctuary of Galapagos, a tourist attraction of world appeal, is located. If its geography displays a diversity of landscapes in a small space, the impasses of the recent political situation merit a political analogy, where the aim of reconciling sovereignty, economic development and ecology points toward an alternative civilizing pattern, exhibiting, in a concentrated fashion, the dilemmas underlying continental politics in the twenty-first century.

Viewed in historical perspective, this rugged geography has impeded the national integration of the country which, since independence, has faced internal and external obstacles to consolidation. At the international level, Ecuadorian borders suffered recurrent harassment from its larger neighbors, Peru and Colombia, which materialized in several armed confrontations, mainly with the former, resulting in significant territorial loss. At the domestic level, the insertion of the country into the world market as a primary exporter, especially cocoa from the mid-nineteenth century, has sharpened regional disparities. The opposition between the interests of a commercial and financial bourgeoisie based on the export dynamism of the Guayaquil-centered coast, and a mountain oligarchy focused on land ownership and exploitation of indigenous labor based in Quito, was expressed in conflicts of regionalist hue that sometimes gave an ideological tone to mere disputes of power.

Vulnerability to international market flows and corresponding political instability characterized Ecuadorian history in the twentieth century. The fall in international cocoa prices in the face of African competition, combined with plagues that affected local production and the effects of the 1929 crisis, plunged the country into a period of economic stagnation and political alternation: between the 'Julian revolution' in 1925 and the presidency of Galo Plaza in 1952 there were 26 variations of leaders and regimes. The rise of banana exports from the 1950s uprooted the country from economic lethargy within primary export milestones, favoring political appeasement. However, the unprecedented succession of three constitutional presidents was broken with the overthrow of President Velasco Ibarra and his successor through a military coup supported by the United States, in the context of the triumph of the Cuban Revolution. The five-time president of the Republic, Velasco Ibarra, was elected president for the last time in 1968 and again did not complete his term, interrupted by another military coup in 1972, the moment when large-scale oil exploration began in the country (Cueva 1984; Hurtado 1988; Maiguhasca 1991).

Oil extraction in Ecuador received a decisive boost from the rise in international prices triggered by the 1973 Yom Kippur war in the Middle East which made investment in the country an attractive alternative. Although Ecuador has never been a major world producer, the relative size of the oil business has had an extraordinary impact on the national economy: the country's total exports grew from less than US$190 million in 1970 to US$2,500 million in 1981, an increase of more than thirteen times, while GDP in this period grew at an annual average rate of 8 per cent (Acosta 2006: 117).

However, the influx of oil resources was ephemeral and left a devastating environmental and financial liability. Ecuadorian oil is concentrated in the Amazon region and its exploitation has caused irreparable ecological damage. In 1993, natives and settlers from the Amazon filed a lawsuit against Chevron-Texaco, the leading multinational in the area for 28 years (from 1964 to 1992), in a process known as 'the trial of the century'. The compensation estimated by the expert appointed by the court reached US$27 billion (Acosta 2009a). In 2015 the action was still underway, but the wounds opened by this predatory action have had repercussions on the unique projection that the ecological issue has in the country.

On the economic front, the nationalistic inclinations of the military resulted in investments in infrastructure and industrial development related to state planning. In this perspective, the objective was to nationalize oil, and similarly to what happened in Venezuela in those years, a state company was created: the Ecuadorian State Oil Corporation (CEPE). During the dictatorships (1973–79), the industry's average rate of expansion was 10 per cent and the share of industry in the economy rose from 14.3 per cent to 20 per cent of GDP, while investment measured as fixed capital formation grew on average by 21.8 per cent per year (Dávalos 2014: 70). At the same time, a pattern of income concentration has remained untouched, fueling import-based consumption of goods and deepening the determinants of underdevelopment.

> The oil-fueled bonanza, bringing the largest amount of foreign currency ever received by the country to date, has emerged in a massive and relatively unexpected form, accumulating on existing structures and reproducing, on a larger scale, much of the old social and economic differences.

> The quantitative leap led Ecuador to another level of economic growth but, as there was no corresponding qualitative transformation, it soon crystallized into the 'development myth'.
> ACOSTA 2006: 117

In an international context of capital availability, the oil income financed an escalation of external indebtedness, also similar to what occurred in Venezuela: the value of Ecuadorian debt grew almost 22 times between 1971 and 1981, going from US$206.8 million to US$5,868.2 million, from 16 per cent of GDP to 42 per cent. Viewed from another angle, debt servicing committed 15 out of every 100 dollars exported in 1971 and grew to the ratio of 71 per cent ten years later (Acosta 2006; Correa 2009).

The outbreak of the debt crisis from the Mexican default in 1982, coupled with the drastic drop in oil prices in the following years, highlighted the vulnerability of the country's economy. In this context, the Ecuadorian state was forced to progressively give up its participation in the oil industry due to the implementation of neoliberal policies, whose social effects provoked an intense popular response.

3   From Re-democratization to Alianza País

Ecuador's economy between the debt crisis and dollarization in 2000 is marked by stagnation, in a context where the shift in international credit flows aggravated the difficulties stemming from the fall in oil prices. The country's weak position vis-a-vis financial capital forced the progressive adoption of neoliberal policies, despite the diverse political affiliations of presidents-elected. The narrow margin of maneuver to manage the crisis within the limits imposed by international organizations is at the root of the problems suffered by the successive rulers, evidenced by the fact that, from the military exit in 1979 to Correa's re-election in 2009, no president elected his successor to the presidency.

This inflection begins with the signing of the letter of intent with the International Monetary Fund (IMF) in 1983, signaling the abandonment of the prevailing national developmentalist orientation, including under the military. In the following years, the country would sign five other letters of intent, until adopting in the 1990s the structural adjustment policies characteristic of neoliberalism, affecting the role of the national state. The political outcome of this process was the massive discrediting of conventional parties, exacerbated by corruption scandals that have plagued more than one government, generating the favorable environment for affirming Correa's candidacy in 2006 against what he called 'partidocracy'.

In the 1980s, the expectations of change brought about by the end of the dictatorship were thwarted by the imperative of managing the crisis according to the limitations imposed by the order that had been inherited. The antipopular responses to economic stagnation had devastating social consequences, especially when contrasted with the prosperity of the previous period. Helped by the oil boom, per capita GDP rose from US$375 in 1973 to US$1,668 in 1981. On the eve of the debt crisis, the minimum wage surpassed – for the first and only time in the country's recent history – the estimated cost of the basic basket (Dávalos 2016).

In the following years, however, gross income per inhabitant fell by almost half, to US$951 in 1989. The formal employment rate, which was at 65 per cent at the beginning of the decade, declined to 40 per cent, a ratio that remained in following decades. The share of wages in national income declined steeply, falling from 35 per cent at the end of the dictatorship to 12 per cent in 2007. External debt servicing captured an extraordinary share of public spending, reaching 28 per cent of GDP in 1986 and 25 per cent in 1988, while social spending on health and education averaged 4 per cent of GDP. Between redemocratization and Correa's rise, poverty had always reached at least 60 per cent of the population, while social indicators associated with poverty such as child malnutrition, maternal and child mortality, mortality due to diseases, and dropping out of school registered a substantial increase (Dávalos 2016: 72–74). The degradation of the living conditions of workers that fermented the rise of social protest is summarized in two figures: the purchasing power of real wages fell by almost a quarter between 1980 and 2000, while in the same period the number of emigrants working abroad, which was less than 1 per cent of GDP, jumped to 7.8 per cent, becoming the country's main source of foreign exchange after oil (Acosta 2009a: 286–89).

The impact of this formidable social regression on popular forces in the country was heterogeneous. The workers' movement faced a severe decline in the number of affiliates, which affected its capacity to fight, a reflection of the precariousness of labor relations and unemployment. In this scenario, indigenous organizations that converged in the formation of the Confederation of Nationalities and Indigenous Peoples of Ecuador (CONAIE) in 1986 assumed the leading role in popular struggles: in 1990, they led an uprising of national impact, and five years later they organized a political party (Pachakutik). In 1997, they played a central role in the overthrow of President Abdalá Bucaram, less than six months after his inauguration. A charismatic and corrupt figure, this president had begun a radical structural adjustment program advised by the Argentinean Domingo Cavallo, a former Menem minister, an indication that dollarization was already considered as a response to the crisis.

The country's economic difficulties were worsened by a new military conflict with Peru in 1995 and by the natural devastation brought by El Niño in the years 1997–99. After almost two decades of stagnation, the crisis peaked in 1999, when the country's GDP fell by 7.3 per cent in sucres, and GDP per capita in dollars declined by almost 32 per cent. In these years the country suffered the most rapid impoverishment in Latin American history, according to the United Nations Children's Fund (UNICEF): the number of poor increased from 3.9 million to 9.1 million, jumping from 34 per cent to 71 per cent of the population, while those in extreme poverty rose from 2.1 million to 4.5 million, or from 12 to 31 per cent of the population. This process was accompanied by a higher concentration of income, as the richest 20 per cent increased their share of wealth from 52 per cent to over 61 per cent, while the share of the poorest 20 per cent decreased from 4.6 per cent to 2.5 per cent (Acosta 2006; Correa 2009).

In this recessive scenario, the government abruptly decreed the dollarization of the economy, extinguishing the sucre as the national currency in January 2000, in a process marked by unpredictability, lack of transparency and promiscuity with the financial sector (Correa 2009). Immediately, the macro-devaluation reduced the minimum wage to US$4 per month, while national income fell by about 30 per cent in nominal terms. The measure also affected the purchasing power of the middle class, fracturing confidence in the state and its institutions. On the whole, far from averting the crisis, the measure accentuated social problems, causing a rise in the cost of living, with growing unemployment, while at the same time exposing the country's vulnerabilities to the dynamics of international capital.

The popular reaction to the policy implemented pointed in two different directions. On the one hand, there was an intensification of emigration: a search for better material conditions of life at the cost of affective and cultural ties. It is estimated that more than one million people left the country at that juncture, bringing the total number of emigrants to about 3 million, of a total population of almost 14 million (Acosta, Olivares and Villamar 2006; Eguez 2001). On the other hand, dollarization triggered a vigorous popular rebellion led by the indigenous movement, which won the sympathy of a sector of the military. Mass pressure precipitated the fall of President Jamil Mahuad in January 2000. However, the alliance's relationship with the military dissolved when the commander betrayed his commitment to popular leadership and handed the government over to the vice president, who ratified the dollarization.

In the ensuing elections, however, the whole social movement, headed by indigenous organizations, supported the candidacy of Colonel Lucio Gutiérrez, who had emerged as a radical nationalist leader in the uprising. Gutiérrez's victory at the end of 2002, at the same time that Lula triumphed in the Brazilian elections, excited South American progressives, who applauded both candidates at the World Social Forum in Porto Alegre in January of that year.

However, the new Ecuadorian president quickly undid any expectation of change, committing himself to neoliberal austerity and the United States – which embarrassed his indigenous supporters, at the time occupying various ministries. Driven by denunciations of corruption and selling out the country that quickly placed him in opposition to popular forces and the middle class, Gutiérrez's mandate was disastrous for the indigenous movement, which was left demoralized and divided by its brief participation in a government that also did not survive until the end of its mandate, beset by the rebellion of the *'forajidos'* (outlaws). If Domingo Cavallo showed the way to dollarization, the shouts of *'que se vayan todos'* (that all go away) from the Argentine streets in 2001 also arrived in Ecuador four years later.

It is in this context that the economist Rafael Correa emerged in politics, minister of finance in the remaining term fulfilled by Gutiérrez's vice president, Alfredo Palacio. Referring to a discourse critical of neoliberalism and conventional politics, nicknamed 'partidocracy', his candidacy was supported by parties considered to be left-of-center, such as the Democratic Left (ID) and the Popular Democratic Movement, but also by the Socialist and Communist Parties as well as the Pachacutik movement, the political arm of CONAIE.

However, it is wrong to see a line of continuity between the rise of Ecuador's indigenous and social organizations and Correa's mandate. At a time when the combativeness and legitimacy of the indigenous movement had declined, Pablo Dávalos considers the way in which the middle class joined the Alianza País, a vehicle for partisan politics, to be decisive. The 'citizenization of politics' proposed meant 'not only establishing a radical distance from existing political parties, but also the cooptation and confiscation of the history of resistance and social mobilization that had the working class and indigenous movements as its most important historical subjects' (Dávalos 2016: 246).

Rejection of political parties is part of this ideology of 'citizenization of politics', which would unfold into the slogan of the 'Citizen Revolution'. True to this perspective, the young Guayaquil teacher won at the polls without belonging to a party or supporting candidates for Parliament. However, the anti-party commitment posed a concrete problem: the new government had no representatives at the congress, though the congress had little social legitimacy. To overcome this dilemma, Alianza País placed its chips on the convening of a

Constituent Assembly, which was only feasible when the 27 deputies of the Partido Sociedad Patriotica, led by former president Lucio Gutiérrez, surprisingly adhered to the proposal after long negotiations (Muñoz Jaramillo 2013: 185).

Drawing inspiration from the path opened by Chávez in Venezuela and followed by Morales in Bolivia, Correa set up an assembly that wrote the twentieth constitution of the country's history, using a combination of media management and the ballot box to initiate, in only 28 months, the self-described Citizen Revolution. As in neighboring countries, the route was turbulent from the start. On the same day that the constituency was inaugurated in the city of Montecristi, the new government brutally suppressed a protest in Dayuma, in the Amazonian province of Orellana, when the population closed access routes to the Auca oil field operated by state-owned Petroecuador. It was a significant harbinger of the confrontations to come, in the assembly and on the streets.

In Montecristi, the tension between the aspiration to a constitution based on the concept of Living Well, as expected by popular movements, and the imperative of primary exploitation, imposed by capital, caused the resignation of the president of the Constituent Assembly, Alberto Acosta, at the request of Correa. In addition to differences regarding the sense of the Constitution, Acosta advocated an in-depth discussion of sensitive issues embedded in popular participation, as opposed to the immediate political demands and verticalism of the presidency.

In spite of the setbacks and contradictions, the perception prevailed that the approved text distanced itself from constitutional liberalism in important aspects, incorporating notions such as plurinationality, *Pachamama* (Mother Earth); *Sumak Kawsay* (Living Well), community democracy, indigenous justice and interculturalism, as well as becoming the first country in the world to adopt the concept of Rights of Nature (Ávila Santamaría 2013: 70). The fact that this Constitution had undergone 23 changes as of 2017 is an indication of the sense in which Alianza País has evolved since then.

4 Political Economy of the Citizen Revolution

Despite his resounding criticism of the interference of multilateral organizations such as the IMF and the World Bank in South American countries, as well as Ecuadorian dollarization, President Correa did not propose to reverse the measure. In concrete terms, his nationalism endorsed an audit of the foreign debt that led to the revision of parts of contracts and did not renew the transfer of the military base of Manta to the US army, fulfilling a campaign promise. Similar to Morales, the Ecuadorian president renegotiated contracts with oil companies, aiming to invest in conditional cash transfer programs and infrastructure. This policy benefited from the rise in international oil prices, so that Correa had more resources than all his predecessors. There is a consensus among critics of dollarization that this is the main one of a series of factors that sustained the inherited architecture:

> Dollarization was supported by exogenous factors and not by its own merits. Remember the contribution of remittances, rising oil prices, the boom for many exports, and access to cheap external credits by private economic agents. To this, we must add the income of dollars coming from 'narcolavado' or other criminal activities, encouraged by dollarization itself.
> ACOSTA, OLIVARES and VILLAMAR 2006: 117

This situation put the government in a dilemma: the resources derived from primary exports, especially oil, facilitate social spending without facing the structural constraints of Ecuadorian society. This immediate benefit entailed a further investment in the extraction of the product, when estimates indicated that the country's reserves had already reached their peak and were decreasing irreversibly, explaining the provisional nature of the current arrangement. As a result, there is a contradiction with the extractivist orientation of the economy that is intended to be overcome within the framework of the constitutional precept of *Sumak Kawsay* (Benalcázar 2008).

The contradiction between state-mediated pressure on natural resources and the constitutional precept of *Sumak Kawsay* became paradigmatic in the negotiation of the Yasuní-ITT initiative. In a nutshell, this initiative proposed to keep untapped a potential 850 million barrels of oil that occupy about 200,000 hectares of tropical forest in the Yasuní National Park, in exchange for an estimated contribution of US$350 million per year over ten years to be donated by the international community. This money would be administered by a commission supervised by the United Nations Development Program (UNDP), with the intention of investing it in social programs, renewable energy, reforestation or energy efficiency.

Beyond the ambiguities of a proposal based on the goodwill of the 'international community', the initiative has been treated in a contradictory way by Correa since its launch. Even when the government signed a protocol with UNDP in 2010, supporters of the proposal felt that it was a staged game, and that the government would not invest its efforts in raising funds and would therefore drop the initiative as unfeasible. When this scenario materialized in 2013, the Yasunidos[1] movement proposed a national referendum to decide the issue. The president replied, 'if you want a consultation, do not be vagabonds, collect the signatures if you have so much support' (*El Universo* 17 August 2013). Months later, the 'vagabonds' delivered a number of signatures higher than necessary, but the referendum was never held, claiming problems in the signatures presented.

At this point, this did not surprise anyone in the country. It had long been clear that Alianza País would solve the contradiction between extractivism and Living Well by supporting the first and confronting the second.

Since the approval of the Constitution in a referendum in October 2008, leftist figures who joined Alianza País were left out. For example, the candidacies of former ministers Alberto Acosta and Gustavo Larrea in the parliamentary elections in February 2009 were made unfeasible. This letting-go of the sector permeable to popular pressures corresponded with a strengthening of the style of Correa, whose temperament many Ecuadorians would describe as 'authoritarian, intolerant and personalist' (Ospina Peralta 2013b: 27).

At the same time, the government advanced, in 2008, a mining law antagonistic to the spirit and norms of the Constitution. The text of the law contradicts the affirmation of collective rights, the right to prior consultation, the pre-legislative consultation and the territorial ownership of indigenous nationalities, which triggered protests by the indigenous movement against a government closed to dialogue. The following year, water and land laws motivated the resumption of mobilizations by CONAIE, which announced: 'We did not swallow the story of the citizen revolution, we resumed our political project' (OSAL 2008). In 2010 the National Confederation of Peasant, Indigenous and Black Organizations (FENOCIN), an organization allied with the government, surprisingly added to the struggle triggered by the water law, underlining the detachment between Alianza País and social movements.

The pattern of relations between government and popular movements was cooptation mainly through the Secretariat of Peoples, Social Movements and Citizen Participation, as well as repression. According to a study carried out by the Ecumenical Commission for Human Rights (CEDHU), the Regional Human Rights Advisory Foundation (INREDH) and Acción Ecológica, an organization that had its legal persona provisionally revoked, between 2008 and 2010 the government proposed 41 politically motivated judicial processes, including 31 criminal cases, involving 199 persons, a number that grew in following years

---

1 A pun is implied as 'Yasuní' refers to the protected area while 'Unidos' means united: Yasunidos implies 'united for Yasuní'.

(Acción Ecológica, CEDHU and INREDH 2011). In 2011, the arrest of Shuar leaders accused of sabotage and terrorism provoked widespread outrage. At that time, organizations such as CONAIE, the Congress of the Confederation of Peoples of the Kichwa Nationality of Ecuador (ECUARUNARI), the Confederation of Indigenous Nationalities of the Ecuadorian Amazon (CONFENIAE) and the Confederation of Nationalities and Indigenous Peoples of the Ecuadorian Coast (CONAICE) demanded amnesty for almost 200 activists who were being politically persecuted, in their view, for 'defending life and Pachamama' (Batista 2010). The protests were not restricted to the indigenous movement: the government proposed an Organic Law of Higher Education that was interpreted as an attack on the autonomy of universities, provoking demonstrations and conflicts in the main cities of the country.

Despite the intolerance shown, Alianza País was faced with high levels of conflict. In 2010 there were around 900 conflicts, the next year there were around 800, and in 2012 the estimate was 700 events, including the March for Water, Life and Dignity, the most important popular mobilization under Alianza País until then. As a benchmark for comparison, at the height of the economic crisis in 1999 there were 750 conflicts. Based on this data, observers noted that 'The Citizen Revolution is the period of greatest social conflict since the return to democracy in 1979' (Ramírez Gallegos 2013).

This level of conflict contrasts with the way the government settled issues with the bourgeoisie, evidenced in the negotiations around the Productive Code mediated by minister Nathalie Cely in 2010, later named ambassador to the United States. Upper-class support for the Alianza País was demonstrated by a controversial episode that same year, qualified by the president as an attempted coup d'état. On 30 September, police officers rebelled against incorporating their careers into the recently approved Public Service Law. Correa went personally to the main focus of the protest and soon argued with the rioters. The mood escalated, and the president, who was recovering from knee surgery, was taken to a military hospital, which was then surrounded by demonstrators. In the ensuing clash with elite army squadrons in charge of the president's protection, there were five casualties – one civilian, two military and two policemen.

In this context, the business community positioned itself unanimously, through its representative institutions, in favor of political stability and order, in marked contrast to the performance of the Venezuelan Fedecamaras in 2002, led by Pedro Carmona. In Ecuador, it was explained that there was no class articulation supporting an alleged coup – just the opposite. In the face of the facts, a consistent investigation concluded: 'Among the policemen acting in the event there was no will to carry out a coup, that is, the overthrow of

Rafael Correa and the formation of a de facto government, through the formation of alliances of parties, movements or specific groups, with the rebel police and necessarily with military forces. Ecuador has a long and illustrative history of coups d'état, in the light of which the 30-S does not fit except as a police protest' (Muñoz Jaramillo 2014: 232).

Bourgeois support for Alianza País had been woven at least since the Constituent Assembly, when differences related to labor relations, the development regime and the requirement of prior consent for extractive projects forced Alberto Acosta to leave. The government's commitment to the new mining code, which resulted in confrontations with social movements, strengthened this affinity, especially with the segments of the bourgeoisie linked to globalization, as is the case of primary exporters.

In the context of the 2010 military uprising, this complicity had been sealed by the government's relatively successful reaction to the effects of the global crisis. With the fall in oil prices in 2008, the country's trade balance has been negative since 2009, and this persisted even as the barrel rose to almost a hundred dollars (from 2011 to 2013). Between 2009 and 2015, the trade deficit totaled US$7 billion, while migrants' remittances fell from over US$3 billion in 2007 to just under US$2.5 billion in 2015. Banana exports doubled in the period (from US$1.3 billion to $2.8 billion) but were insufficient to cover the difference. To mitigate the trade imbalance, the government resorted to external indebtedness. In 2009, public foreign debt reached a historical low of US$7 billion (12 per cent of GDP). In 2016, foreign debt had tripled to over US$22 billion (22 per cent of GDP). Relations with China were intensified, including trading future oil with this country (Ospina Peralta 2013a; Acosta and Guijarro 2016).

In general, data indicates that the economic policy practised favored large conglomerates that concentrate the country's wealth and endorse the government. By 2015, revenue from the top 20 economic groups was equivalent to 24.48 per cent of GDP, while the extractive sector, construction companies and financial groups recorded the highest levels of profitability. In spite of the rhetoric of a 'change in the productive matrix', intensified since the decision to exploit oil at Yasuní-ITT, the country's productive structure and international insertion pattern remained unchanged. The share of manufacturing in GDP between 2007 and 2015 was around 12.5 per cent, while the share of primary exports rose from 74 per cent to 79 per cent of the total. Instead of favoring industrialization, the drop in the weight of oil exports, which declined from 52 per cent to 35 per cent in the period, accentuated pressure for the export of other primary products (Ospina Peralta 2013a, Acosta and Guijarro 2016). The intensification of agri-business and mining, until then a marginal activity, are among the factors that have boosted social conflict in the 'Citizen Revolution'.

In the area of work, the employment rate of the economically active population was around 40 per cent between 2007 and 2015. There was a modest improvement in wages, while GDP and consumption grew, following a trend that dates back to the beginning of the decade, when the crisis was reversed. This trend was not unique to Ecuador, as the recessive pattern prevailing in the 1990s was reversed throughout the subcontinent. The pace of recovery in the second half of the decade declined for understandable reasons: cyclical recovery would need to be deepened with structural changes that did not occur (Ospina Peralta 2013a: 226).

The wage gains of the minority in formal employment were eroded by the cost of the basic basket, which rose from US$427 in 2007 to US$683 in 2016, while the minimum wage covered, on average, 51.7 per cent of this cost. In a country where there is no unemployment benefit, cash transfer programs have played a fundamental social role, as well as consolidating the support of impoverished sectors to the government. The most important of these programs is the Human Development Grant, raised from US$35 to US$50 per month in the middle of the presidential campaign of 2013 (Acosta and Guijarro 2016; Muñoz Jaramillo 2014). However, Dávalos considers it wrong to establish direct links between the increase of primary exports and social programs. The Ecuadorean economist says that the institutional architecture that guides public spending in the country, designed with input from multilateral agencies, prevents exports from financing social programs: 'Extractive income can allow the construction of hospitals and schools, but prohibits the recruitment of health personnel or education staff necessary for these new hospitals and schools' (Dávalos 2016).

These expenses are funded by taxes, whose revenues grew under Alianza País through economic growth, the modernization of the state apparatus and the increase in taxes themselves, including on financial returns. This revenue, which accounts for three-quarters of state collection, finances social programs, while exports finance fuel subsidies, infrastructure investments and international reserves deposited in foreign banks (Dávalos 2016: 146). Illustrative of this trend, while more than 50 per cent of public investment between 2008 and 2013 focused on transport and roads that benefit the export sector, investment in irrigation and water management, which is fundamental to the peasant economy, has been reduced from 7.5 per cent to less than 2.5 per cent (Muñoz Jaramillo 2014: 61).

As in Bolivia, the harassment of traditional ways of life and peasant agriculture correspond to a greater commodification of the economy. Alianza País reinforced this movement on the subjective level, by spreading consumption as a value in a context of economic growth and popularization of domestic credit, in which levels of family debt have risen. Since the beginning of dollarization, there has been an increase in household consumption, a deepening trend under Alianza País since 2000, household consumption has gone from US$11.83 million to US$33.2 million in 2007, rising to US$61.51 million in 2015. Although statistics indicate a reduction in poverty, which reached 57 per cent of the population in the midst of the crisis in 1999, falling to 26 per cent in 2013, the precariousness of workers is suggested by the centrality of emigrant remittances: between 2000 and 2015, it is estimated that US$35.27 billion was sent to the country, an amount three times higher than the direct foreign investment in these years, which reached US$11.33 billion (Dávalos 2016: 126, 151).

Alianza País endeavored to recover the agency of the state in the economy and politics. In their governments, there has been a notable expansion of non-financial public sector participation in GDP, from less than 25 per cent in 2006 to almost 50 per cent five years later, while payroll more than tripled between 2005 and 2015 – from US$2.9 million to US$9.9 million (Ospina 2013a: 199). Supporters of Correismo point out that public employment was an important inducer of consumption, while its critics claim that the state machine was used as an instrument of the party: 'the public servants mimicked the militancy of the pro-government movement and vice versa' (Machado 2013: 17).

There is a consensual perception that Alianza País carried out successful modernization of the Ecuadorian state. However, the conservative nature of this modernization was recognized by the president himself: 'We are basically doing better with the same model of accumulation, rather than change it, because it is not our desire to harm the rich, but it is our intention to have a more fair and equitable society' (Correa 2012).

However, in the process of doing 'better things with the same model of accumulation', the government has taken on an anti-democratic disposition that has been denounced by leftist movements and personalities in the country. Similar to what happened in Bolivia, there are indications that institutions such as the Constitutional Court, the State Attorney's Office, the Attorney General's Office, the State Comptroller's Office, the Courts of Justice, the Ombudsman's Office, among others, act with limited independence. On the whole, opponents find that the only criticism accepted by Alianza País is that coming from the traditional right, because it allows it to legitimize itself (Dávalos 2016: 65).

Rendered to the 'same model of accumulation', the original creative potential of the 'Citizen Revolution' waned. The challenge of reconciling development, ecology and sovereignty gave way to trendy politics. The intensification of extractivism alienated the support of organized popular sectors, which the government intended to compensate with the extension of welfare policies to the unorganized poor, stimulated by economic growth, the expansion of credit and the illusion of consumption, amidst a massive propaganda campaign. In the field of ecology, the dropping of pioneering proposals such as the Yasuní-ITT initiative or the constitutional idea of the 'rights of nature' corresponded to the adoption of the *SocioBosque* and *Socio Páramo* programs which are part of the carbon market logic and the financialization of nature favored by the World Bank (Houtart 2014: 167). In the area of regional integration, the country that hosts the Union of South American Nations (UNASUR) and is part of the Bolivarian Alliance for the Peoples of Our America (ALBA) sealed a trade agreement with the European Union in 2014, within the framework of what had previously been negotiated with Peru and Colombia, governments that favored multilateral liberalization.

In short, the Alianza País project implied an effective strengthening of the state for extractive businesses and *Correista* politics, but that distanced itself from the democratic expectations that promoted its ascent. The dynamic that was imposed is summarized in the following words:

> In the disjunctive of having to choose between democracy and effectiveness, the government has chosen the second. Its priority is not to democratize the State but to strengthen it, and that means strengthening the Executive; ... In this sense, public unions, indigenous organizations and ecologists and local organizations are above all obstacles to an efficient State and a disciplined society.
>
> OSPINA PERALTA: 2013a, 263

By denying the utopia of conciliating development, ecology and sovereignty that had propelled it since its origin, Alianza País resigned itself to a conservative modernization of the state and business in Ecuador. In this process, 'leftism', 'infantile environmentalism' and 'infantile indigenism' became enemies of a regime that replicated the characteristic intolerance of Latin American bourgeoisie, although 'disguised in the skin of socialism' achieving, at best, 'a citizen revolution without citizenship' (Acosta and Guijarro 2016; Ospina Peralta 2013a: 263).

5 Final Thoughts

Emerging in a context of crisis and rebellion in which several presidents were deposed under popular pressure, the consolidation of Alianza País under the leadership of Rafael Correa opened a new era in Ecuadorian politics. Initially thought-of to run for president in 2006 in a solo candidacy, his victory transformed the convening of the Constituent Assembly from a campaign promise into a political imperative, aiming to lay the foundations of support for the new government. In this process, party factions permeable to popular aspirations were removed from important positions, while relations with bourgeois sectors deepened. Intolerance of popular protest contrasted with the fluid dialogue with capital.

The core of the discord was synthesized in the worldview of Living Well. Features of Ecuadorian socio-economic formation, coupled with recent history of environmental depredation, have forged a singular sensitivity to the ecological theme, in which indigenous, peasants and environmentalists converge around a vision of an alternative modernity, opposed to the interests of international capital and to the rationality of the bourgeois state.

If the Constitution drafted in Montecristi contemplated aspects of these aspirations and was incorporated in the rhetoric of Alianza País, its practice went in the opposite direction. The repression in Dayuma and the imposition of the mining code gave the initial tone of the administration. Since then, the ambiguities in negotiations for the Yasuní-ITT initiative have evaporated amidst aggressive scorn for its proponents as the government embarked on carbon market policies in tune with 'green capitalism' that it rhetorically denies. Constitutional rules that impede extractivism have been altered or ignored, as is the case with the ban on transgenic agriculture.

Modified 23 times in seven years, the Constitution of Montecristi reminds us that the parliamentary arena often serves for the counter-revolution to circumvent change. In a situation that synthesizes the trend of the period, in 2014 the indigenous Amazonian community of Sarayacu granted asylum to three politicians persecuted by Alianza País, including a Pachakutik deputy: the Constitution supported, through plurinationality, the freedom of those who were impotent to defend the Constitution itself.

It is indisputable that Alianza Pais led a re-foundation of politics and a modernization of the national state. The parties that have alternated in power since the end of the dictatorship, such as the Social Democratic Party (PSC), the Democratic Left (ID), the Popular Democracy (PD) and the Ecuadorian Roldosist Party (PRE) have lost relevance. In contrast to the neoliberal rhetoric of the minimal state, the centrality of the state to the economy and politics was regained. However, the sense of this re-foundation contradicts the popular aspirations that initially propelled it. Alianza País has advanced a modernization functional to capitalist reproduction, combining new and old businesses, all of which are compatible with the peripheral international insertion of the country: oil income, large-scale mining, agri-business (including transgenics), major infrastructure projects and growing consumption of imported products.

This conventional economic policy corresponded to a conventional political economy. Alianza País used state power to suppress dissent and gain the loyalty of the masses, in the midst of permanent propaganda that flattered its leader. Economic growth, rising consumption, cash transfer policies and infrastructure works sustained the popularity of the government, which triumphed in ten consecutive elections.

In 2014, Alianza País was defeated in municipal and provincial elections, and the opposition took over 19 of the country's 20 major cities. The fall in oil prices from this year has challenged the regime's political economy. The traditional right retook the initiative, even in the streets, forcing Correa to back down on the proposal of a tax on inheritances – the first time he had had to do so.

Although his term had ended, Correa elected his successor in a tight election in 2017, countering successive defeats of so-called progressives in the region. He soon quarreled with the new president, Lenin Moreno, while the vice president was arrested for corruption. In an effort to 'unCorrear' the country, Moreno leaned to the right, seeking to strengthen his position in an internal dispute that cut off Alianza País, foreshadowing the melancholic degradation of a revolution that never happened.[2]

---

[2] Rafael Correa left the Alianza País in January 2018 to create a new party, the National Agreement for the Citizen's Revolution Movement. In July 2018, a judge ordered him to be remanded on suspicion that the former president was the intellectual mentor to the kidnapping of former congressman Fernando Balda in Colombia in 2012. The arrest of Correa, who currently lives in Belgium, did not take effect. In April 2019 the Ecuadorian Embassy in London turned Julian Asange to the British Police after hosting him since 2012, in another clear sign of the right turn of the Moreno government.

CHAPTER 6

The Deposition of Lugo in Paraguay and the *Brasiguayo* Question

> In an interview he gave to Folha, at the HQ of his business group in Asunción, this Santa Catarina man born in the small town of Videira called the peasants who surround his farm 'delinquents', praised the dictator Alfredo Stroessner's government ('At that time you could sleep with the window open and no one stole from you, we've only been getting worse since then') and said that it is useless to deal with the landless on the basis of diplomacy, that they have to be treated 'as a bad guy's woman, who only obeys the use of a stick'.
>
> *Interview with Tranquilo Favero, Paraguay's largest soybean planter, 2012*

> I want you to feel at home; beyond the protocol, I will repeat what I already said: use and abuse Paraguay ... everything with Brazil, nothing against Brazil.
>
> *Horacio Cartes to Brazilian entrepreneurs, 2014*

1   Introduction

Paraguay has been briefly touched by the progressive tide but has also suffered from the contradictions inherent in the process. The election of Fernando Lugo in 2008 was the first political alternation in the country after six decades of Colorado rule, including the region's longest dictatorship, from 1954 to 1989. Identified as a progressive, Lugo's main electoral promise was agrarian reform. However, the government faced stiff obstacles to advancement on that front, hardened by the recent prosperity of soybean agri-business of Brazilian origin known as *brasiguayos*.

Although the presence of Brazilians in the country is not recent, their central role in soybean expansion has given it another dimension. During the governments of the Workers Party (PT), the Brazilian state encouraged *brasiguayos* progress through lines of credit and political support, but this helped to stiffen the opposition faced by Brazil's ally, the Lugo government in Paraguay, and affected its ability to democratize access to land. As a result, the position of the

Lugo government was weakened in the face of interests that started the impeachment, which Brazilian diplomacy was then unable to stop. It is a paradoxical situation: Brazilian government support for economic sectors that oppose desired political change ends up reversing that change. Viewed from the prism of the *brasiguayo* issue, the impeachment in Paraguay explains the contradictions of Brazilian regional policy and South American progressivism, inherent to the pretence of articulating political change and economic conservatism.

2   The Agrarian Question and Brazilian Presence in Paraguay

The *brasiguayo* issue is rooted in the confluence of two aspects of independent Paraguayan history: the agrarian question and the influence of Brazil. In historical perspective, both are related to the outcome of the War of the Triple Alliance (1865–1870), a decisive episode in the formation of contemporary Paraguay that affected social relations in rural areas as well as the country's international position. In its present form of expression, the consolidation of *brasiguayo* power arises from the convergence of economic and geopolitical interests between the dictatorship of Alfredo Stroessner from 1954 to 1989 and Brazilian foreign policy in that period.

Although the nature of the relations of production prevailing in Paraguay before the War of the Triple Alliance is a controversial subject, in the country and abroad (Pastore 1949; Rivarola 2010; White 1984), an understanding that the war drastically altered the existing relations of production prevails among scholars of the agrarian question. Until then, peasant-oriented ways of life were dominant, in a country where state ownership of the land predominated and there was no oligarchy linked to the *latifundia* – a unique case on the continent. The outcome of the war aborted the relatively autonomous course of the Paraguayan state, which was then incorporated into the sphere of influence of its neighbors, starting with Argentina. In the process, the mercantile conversion of land use backed the formation of a ruling class analogous to that of other countries in the region, as well as the massive acquisition of land by foreigners.

From the point of view of relations with Brazil, historiographic consensus points to a change in the orientation of Paraguayan foreign policy by the Alfredo Stroessner regime (1954–1989), which would progressively strengthen ties with its Portuguese-speaking neighbor to the detriment of Argentina (Moraes 2001). American interference in the 1954 coup was reportedly to prevent an undesired rapprochement between the Paraguayan president Frederico Chaves and his Argentine colleague Juan Domigo Perón. In the following years, the establishment of a trade route linking Paraguay to the Atlantic Ocean through the port of Paranaguá (thus erasing the century-long dependence in relation to Buenos Aires); the construction of the Friendship Bridge between Foz do Iguaçu and the new city of Puerto Stroessner (now Ciudad del Este), begun in 1956; the establishment of this new city as a commercial center oriented to the Brazilian market; are indicative of this change in Paraguayan foreign policy, which echoed the interests of the Brazilian state at that time.

These ties became closer with the military coup in Brazil in 1964, when geopolitical and economic concerns led to projects of common interest such as the colonization of the border region (the 'March to the West' in the Brazilian case, and to the east in the Paraguayan case); the construction of the Itaipu hydroelectric power plant, the largest in the world at the time; and complicity around social repression, backed by Operation Condor (Albuquerque 2000, Menezes 1987, Laino 1979).

Regarding the agrarian question, in 1963 the dictatorship created the Rural Welfare Institute (IBR) and promulgated an agrarian statute, signaling its intention to expand the agricultural frontier, promoting the colonization of areas mainly in the east of the country, with the dual goal of relieving social pressure in the central region and preventing the forming of guerrilla groups in border regions. Designed as a mercantile development strategy for Paraguayan agriculture, the colonization promoted by the IBR was out of character with its official purpose of rooting out workers in the countryside, distributing areas to those favored by the regime and practising a prosperous commerce in lands originally intended for agrarian reform.

Throughout the 1970s, this policy of colonization of eastern Paraguay converged with the expansion of the Brazilian agricultural frontier, intensified in the border region with the construction of the Itaipu hydroelectric plant. The combination of the relatively low price of Paraguayan land, soft fiscal pressure, and the permissiveness of the state in relation to legal, labor and environmental issues produced a significant flow of Brazilians across the border. Immigrants found favorable credit conditions in the new country, where the National Development Bank (Banco Nacional de Fomento) provided funds from the World Bank and the IDB, lending at 13 per cent interest with repayment terms of eight years with a three-year grace period (in Brazil the rates ranged from 22 per cent to 24 per cent, with a five-year repayment term and one-year grace period). Andrew Nickson (1981) points out that these loans mainly benefited Brazilians, who bought their land in cash, as the requirement of a definitive land title excluded the majority of Paraguayans – who parceled the acquisition of their lots – from access to credit.

> In conclusion, there is much evidence to suggest that since its formation in 1963, the IBR has operated in a way that facilitates the penetration of capitalist agriculture in Paraguay under Brazilian control. Its policy of not expropriating existing *latifundia* and decision to sell the region's virgin lands contributed to the subsequent transfer of most of the RFO (eastern border region) to Brazilian hands within little more than a decade.
>
> NICKSON 1981: 240

The migration of Brazilian landowners and farm workers to expand the agricultural frontier, and the expulsions caused by the construction of Itaipu, converged with the policy promoted by the regime of colonizing the Paraguayan east. This trend responded to the geopolitical interests of both dictatorships. Stroessner was firmly in line with Brazil, establishing the Paraguayan position as subaltern beneficiary of the neighboring country's economic growth while joining the ideas of settlement and territorial development as an antisubversive policy within the framework of the Cold War. The Brazilian dictatorship, on the other hand, encouraged the occupation of the border region backed by its ideologue Golbery do Couto e Silva through the concept of 'living frontiers', prescribing that the area of state influence extends to the territory occupied by its citizens (Couto e Silva 1967). At the same time, official agreements involving the Itaipu hydroelectric dam, or tacit arrangements stimulating the colonization of the Paraguayan east, favored not only this geopolitical strategy, but also the economic interests behind the Brazilian state.

The massive penetration of Brazilian rural producers attracted by the opportunities they glimpsed across the border was one of the results of this confluence of interests. It is this migratory movement that is at the root of what the French geographer Sylvaine Souchaud called '*brasiguayo* space' – distinguished by the predominance of the Brazilian language, culture and political and economic power in Paraguayan territory (Souchaud 2002). This is a unique phenomenon in that immigrants discriminate against native workers, echoing stereotypes conveyed by the national ruling class itself:

> The universal rule is usually that the one who arrives is discriminated against, in some places that discrimination reaches incredible limits. But in Paraguay the opposite is true: the one who arrives appropriates what we have and discriminates against us. That is unique.
>
> FOGEL: 2011

Although most of the migrants were rural workers and current Brazilian immigrants include all social classes, the conflicts involving rural owners of Brazilian origin popularized, in recent years, a kind of synecdoche, in which *brasiguayo* became synonymous with soybean entrepreneur. At the political level, the local economic hegemony of Brazilians forms a kind of parallel power to the weak Paraguayan state, which in turn is uninterested in or incapable of integrating these immigrants into national society. *Brasiguayo* dominance is reinforced by the election of Brazilian residents as councilors and mayors in municipalities in areas where their presence is dominant. Where most Brazilian workers are still undocumented, speak Portuguese and watch Rede Globo, the impermeability of Brazilian power in local institutions is, according to some analysts, a reality recognized and endorsed by Brazilian diplomacy (Fogel 2005: 95).

A central dimension of the *brasiguayo* issue is that the occupation of Paraguayan soil carried out by Brazilians in recent decades has been based on irregular practices of land distribution since the dictatorship, which is the origin of the so-called 'ill-gotten lands' (*tierras mal habidas*). Clientelism and corruption in the management of the country's land patrimony continued after the fall of Stroessner in 1989, when Paraguay was entering democracy, led by the same party that commanded the dictatorship.

Throughout those decades Brazilians have been involved in these irregular practices in two main ways: negotiating the lands given to the favored ones of the dictatorship, but also acquiring lots distributed to the genuine beneficiaries of the colonization. These lands are called *derecheras* (righters), since they consist of the *derecho* (right) to occupy a piece of land granted by the state and which, therefore, may not be sold. As an aggravating circumstance, Brazilians have acquired land in the border region, a situation that the government has sought to regulate by means of a law in force since 2005, which creates a 50-kilometer security zone along the border in which foreign ownership is prohibited – an initiative that, despite its limitations, is severely criticized by the ruling classes of the country (Programa 2012: 8). Finally, owing to the precariousness of the cadastral situation where the state does not have reliable records on the titling or measurement of properties, there are so-called 'surplus lands' (*tierras excedentes*), where the extent of the land actually appropriated is greater than that registered in title – and often of questionable legitimacy.

3   Soy and *Brasiguayos*

Although the substantial Brazilian presence in Paraguayan territory is not a recent phenomenon, conflicts involving *brasiguayos* have multiplied with the expansion of soybean cultivation in the twenty-first century, within the framework of a productive model dominated by transnational corporations. It is estimated that in 1973 oil seeds occupied 40,000 hectares in the country. In

1996, the planted area was close to 1 million hectares. With the introduction of transgenic seeds at the end of the century, the soybean frontier advanced by an average of 125,000 hectares per year, reaching 2.8 million hectares in the 2010–2011 agricultural cycle (Palau 2012: 33, 347). Throughout this period, the country maintained high growth rates, breaking with the lethargy prevalent since the construction of Itaipu: in 2010, for example, the pace of expansion of the Paraguayan economy was only behind that of Qatar. Paraguay has become the world's fourth largest soybean exporter and eighth largest beef exporter.

The expansion of soybeans, the country's primary export, implies the adoption of a business model associated with a technological package promoted by transnational corporations, which determines how the commodity is produced. As in Brazil, the market is dominated by transgenic seed resistant to the herbicide Roundup (glyphosate), patented by Monsanto. This technological package is tied to the technique of no-tillage, in which the ploughing and cleaning processes are replaced by the application of chemical products whose effectiveness requires their use in increasing quantity. No-tillage can reduce manpower, estimated at two people per thousand hectares per year, in a productive model viable for large-scale cultivation alone. This intensification of agriculture is compared by some authors to 'an extractivist agriculture, a mining in agricultural soil', in a reality in which 'the soy package implies absolute "depeasantisation", it is agriculture without farmers' (Rulli 2007: 18–20). At the other end of the process, transnational companies such as Cargill, ADM and Bunge take over and export the soybeans produced, which led one author to conclude that 'in practice, producers are only a cog between the process of supply and the collection of production' (Rojas 2009: 73).

The socio-environmental impacts of the expansion of soy in Paraguay are documented and reported regularly by organizations linked to peasant and indigenous movements. The consequences include: expropriation of small-scale farms through multiple mechanisms; serious damage to health and the environment through the use of pesticides; increased unemployment, rural exodus and emigration; greater concentration of land; threat to food sovereignty; deforesting of virgin areas, worsened by the displacement of the cattle frontier; potential desertification of the soil through sowing; and contamination of the Guarani aquifer. In this context, soybean expansion faced the resistance of social actors identified with the democratization of the relations of production in the countryside and environmental preservation, and which oppose the interests of transnational corporations (Palau 2007; Fogel 2008; BASE IS 2010; Benitez Leite et al. 2011)

The role of Brazilian rural entrepreneurs in the expansion of agri-business in Paraguay is notorious. Although there are no precise statistics, Marcos Glauser (2009) analyzed official data from the National Institute of Rural

Development and Land (INDERT) to estimate the amount of foreign owned land. His work revealed that about one-fifth of Paraguay's land, equivalent to 4,792,528 hectares, was in foreign hands, of which about two-thirds belonged to Brazilians. Since the country had 24 million hectares of arable land, it is estimated that Brazilians own about one-fifth of the best land, within which about 40 per cent of the country's soybeans are planted. Large-scale land grabbing was also recently reported in Argentina and Bolivia (Klipphan and Enz 2006; Urioste 2011), but the unique role that the vindication of the defeated in the War of the Triple Alliance had for the affirmation of Paraguayan nationalism in the twentieth century makes Brazilian preponderance particularly sensitive.

According to Paraguayan analysts, the specificity of the country's situation lies in the minimal integration of agri-business into other national production chains, which is accentuated by the characteristics of the *brasiguayo* insertion. In general, the low tax rates on agri-business, which additionally benefits from a subsidy on fuel used in agriculture, minimizes the possibility of state intervention in a redistributive sense (Fogel 2005: 69). The export of a high percentage of soybeans, including to Brazil, reduces the potential economic dynamism of processing the commodity in the country.[1] An aggravating circumstance is that the production of soybeans controlled by *brasiguayos* involves large-scale smuggling operations, mainly through the dry frontier where their presence is dominant, negatively impacting the country's tax collection and trade balance.

> In this dynamic that could be classified as clandestine, Brazilian entrepreneurs come with their own machinery, their own tractors that they later take back to Brazil, so technically there is no investment. The ridiculous taxes on exports are also evaded, with some sources estimating one million tons of soy smuggled in the last agricultural season.
> FOGEL and RIQUELME 2005: 68

The ties that connected the *brasiguayo* economic space to agri-business dynamics in Brazil were related by Luis Rojas, who analyzed a sample of the main companies in the country. Emphasizing that 'the backbone of agri-business in the country is constituted by transnational corporations … that ultimately determine what and how to produce…', Rojas describes the performance of nine

---

1 Paraguay is one of the few countries that recognize Taiwan, which prevents direct exports to China. This situation intensifies the flow of Paraguayan soybeans into Brazil.

other foreign companies, of which three are Brazilian, in addition to analyzing another 28 companies considered to be Paraguayan. He concludes: 'Of the 28 companies named, at least 14 are wholly or partially owned by Brazilians (or *brasiguayos*), representing 50 per cent of this sample of local companies' (Rojas 2009: 52–53). Considering links established between Brazilian land owners and the Paraguayan economic space, analysts consider that soybean production is a modality of enclave economy in Paraguayan territory (Fogel and Riquelme 2005). In this sense, Fogel states:

> ...it should be emphasized in the analysis of the expansion of Brazilian soy growers, that the dynamics of the border space centered on the *brasiguayo*, responds more to the relations and patterns of Brazil on which it depends, than of internal relations to our nation-state (Paraguay).
> FOGEL 2005: 97

In this perspective, the evolution of *brasiguayo* agri-business is related to the dynamics of corresponding Brazilian governments. In the case of the PT governments, there was a clear commitment to support and defend their businesses, not only in Paraguay but also in other countries in the region. In fact, the expansion of soybeans by Brazilians in Paraguay is part of a larger expansive movement of oil seeds in a transnational region, which includes territories of Paraguay, Bolivia, Brazil, Argentina and Uruguay. This region was described by an advertisement for the transnational Syngenta as the 'United Republic of Soy'. The announcement reminds us that if the Brazilians constitute an economic enclave in Paraguay, the global business is still controlled by the transnationals.

As with construction, soy was boosted by Brazilian National Economic and Social Development Bank (BNDES) credit policy and defended by the business diplomacy of the Brazilian Ministry of Foreign Affairs.[2] This can be seen by the two antagonists: agri-business entrepreneurs and those who struggle for agrarian reform. Nilson Medina, considered the largest Brazilian rural entrepreneur in Bolivia, refers to this support in an interview:

---

2 In May 2007, the visit of President Lula in the framework of the Brazil-Paraguay Agrofuels Seminar concluded with the signing of a memorandum of understanding. The Brazilian president was accompanied by 30 businessmen and encouraged them to invest in Paraguay. The Brazilian National Economic and Social Development Bank (BNDES) announced at the Seminar that it will have a specific line of credit to finance Brazilian entrepreneurs who decide to invest in agribusiness in Paraguay (Socio-environmental impacts of soy in Paraguay. Asunción: BASE IS, 2010: 10).

> Now, we, Heloisa, have the guarantee of the Brazilian government, you know, I think that, just as the *'brasiguayos'* are guaranteed by the Brazilian government, when something happens there is an intervention, I believe we will have the same attention. The government, Celso Amorim, he came exclusively to talk to us; Celso Amorim,[3] who I think is spectacular this Celso Amorim, so I think that if something happens here in Bolivia, the government will immediately intervene, and then Lula calls Evo and says: 'Look, the property of Nilson Medina was invaded, he is all right, he fulfills the social function and everything...'.
>
> GIMENEZ 2010: annex

Since the most important Brazilian soybean planter in Bolivia evokes the example of the *brasiguayos* as a precedent that guarantees its situation under the government of Evo Morales (a situation certainly more conflicted than the Lugo government's), it is inferred that Brazilian diplomacy in defense of its interests is seen as a fact of life by businessmen in the sector.[4] Medina himself recounts an episode in which, during Morales's presidential campaign, he expressed concern to Roberto Rodrigues, then minister of agriculture in the Lula government, about the possibility of expropriation of Brazilians. A few days later the Brazilian ambassador in the country telephoned to reassure Medina, who would later receive personal guarantees from Morales himself (Gimenez 2010: annex).

On the other side of the political spectrum, former directors of agrarian reform agencies in Bolivia and Paraguay report pressures exerted by Brazilian diplomacy to defend Brazilian rural entrepreneurship.[5] Observers of the agrarian question in Paraguay also recorded Brazilian intercession in the Ñacunday land conflict, an episode that explained the impasses faced by the Lugo government in its last year.

---

3   Brazilian minister of foreign affairs under Lula, from 2003 to 2010.
4   In the same interview: '... in the Fernando Henrique government, we were a little forgotten in Bolivia, in the Lula government, Lula gave us spectacular assistance, right. I am a fan, particularly, of the Lula government, because it was a government that always helped us. It was in the Lula government that we had the concern of the Brazilian embassy with the Brazilian producers in Bolivia' (Gimenez 2010: annex).
5   For the report by Alcides Vadillo, former director of the INRA (National Institute of Agrarian Reform), see the annex of the dissertation of Heloísa Gimenez cited. In an interview with the author in August 2012, Alberto Alderete, former director of INDERT in Paraguay, said that he had been under pressure from the Brazilian government during his term.

4 The Lugo Presidency (2008–2012)

The election of Fernando Lugo as Paraguayan president in 2008 represented the first reversal of power from Colorado domination in Paraguayan politics since Alfredo Stroessner's accession to power in 1954. The dictatorship commanded by the general came to an end in 1989 through a military coup led by his subordinate, General Andrés Rodríguez. Dramatic events that animated national politics in the following years – such as the assassination of vice-president Luis María Argaña in 1999 and the subsequent resignation of Cubas Grau in the face of popular pressure (the so-called 'Paraguayan March'); the misfortunes that led General Lino Oviedo to exile and imprisonment (and the dissidence he led within the Colorado party) – did not overstep the boundaries of Colorado's domination. Although state management after the dictatorship involved, to some extent, the sharing of the state apparatus with the conservative opposition, the Paraguayan transition was carried out by the same party that sustained the dictatorship – a unique case on the continent. In this context, the liberals, rivals of the Colorados in the realm of conservative politics since the end of the nineteenth century, saw in the Lugo candidacy nothing more than a path to regaining executive power.

On the other hand, popular forces had identified in this political novelty an opportunity to advance long-rejected demands. In a low-industrialized country with the lowest Human Development Index (HDI) in South America, together with one of the highest levels of wealth concentration on the continent, the focus of social tension since the end of the dictatorship has been the agrarian issue. It is reported that on the day after Stroessner's deposition three land occupations were carried out (Riquelme 2003).

Tensions in the Paraguayan countryside have intensified since the 1990s. The expansion of soybeans and livestock where the availability of state land (so-called 'fiscal lands') was exhausted has exacerbated the contradictions between agri-business and peasant-oriented ways of life, as well as causing environmental devastation in the eastern part of the country and in the Chaco, where one of the last aboriginal groups on the continent living in voluntary isolation, the Ayoreo, is threatened. As a response, the organized resistance of peasants and indigenous people in the only officially bilingual country of the Southern Cone has been intensified, expressing itself in a dynamic of struggle for land and state repression familiar to most Latin American countries.

Fernando Lugo, although not a recognized activist of the left, was projected as a political figure through an episcopal performance in tune with the social sensitivity characteristic of liberation theology, exercised in the interior of the country in this context of sharpening tensions in rural areas. As a candidate, he made agrarian reform his main campaign promise, garnering the support of those who empathized with social change.

Backed by the popular sectors, but based in the liberal party structure, Lugo's candidacy was a marriage of convenience in which disparate yearnings converged under the common aim of defeating the Colorados. As a result, his electoral triumph can be interpreted as a rejection of the prevailing situation rather than as a triumph of the left, in a country where popular forces – suffocated by half a century of Colorado domination, mostly under the dictatorship – encountered difficulties in strengthening autonomous organizations. In this sense, Lugo's election parallels other cases on the continent, in which unknown people were elevated to executive power by means of ad hoc political arrangements, in a context of discredited parties and conventional politicians weakened by the unpopularity of their neoliberal policies. Asked about the new president's political beliefs, a future member of the government summed up the prevailing spirit: 'Do not ask me about who comes in, but about who goes out' (interview with Wehrle 2012).

Among those who sympathized with Lugo's victory there are doubts about the political will of the government to transform reality, but there is consensus about the obstacles it has faced (interviews with Bordenave 2012; Flecha 2012). Elected with 40.9 per cent of the votes in an alliance with the Liberals, who nominated the vice president, the left-wing organizations that integrated the coalition elected 3 out of 80 deputies, and an equal number of senators out of a total of 45. In order to constitute a majority in the chambers, the executive would need to join not only with the Liberals, who elected 29 deputies and 14 senators, but also with the Colorado dissidents commanded by Lino Oviedo under the National Union of Ethical Citizens (UNACE). The president's fragile autonomy is highlighted by the Constitution, which comes from the transition, and which accentuates the executive's dependence on Parliament. The constraints to proposing substantive changes through existing legal channels are evident, considering the profile of the parliamentarians in question.

> The most obvious thing to note is that they are almost all large rural landowners, with titles held either directly or in the names of friends and family. In 2008, a former head of the World Bank in Paraguay expressed his shock at discovering that virtually every member of congress that he met fitted this description. Many were also beneficiaries of the illegal transfer of large tracts of state lands (typically 2,000 hectares and above) to military and civilian supporters of the Alfredo Stroessner dictatorship, a process that continued through the subsequent two decades of Colorado governments.
>
> NICKSON 2012

Unlike others in the subcontinent, Lugo did not consider convening a Constituent Assembly – which would require a political force that he apparently did not have to lead the process. In any case, this was not his proposal and Paraguayan analysts consider such analogy to be wrong in light of what the government had effectively set out to do (interviews with Rivarola 2012; Rojas Villagra 2012).

In an arrangement reminiscent of the first Lula administration, the most important ministries (such as the ministries of the economy, public works, and agriculture and livestock) were allocated to personalities trusted by capital, while space was opened to the popular field in health and in smaller organisms (such as the Ministry of Culture, the Indigenous Secretariat, the Environmental Secretariat and INDERT). Social welfare programs were implemented and multiple spaces for citizen participation were opened; however, this did not signify any structural change.

Despite the modesty of the social policies advanced, the main rural workers' movements adopted a sort of 'truce' with the government: moderation, but not the cessation of occupations and marches. It was understood that social pressure could destabilize a mandate that, despite its weaknesses, opened the presidential doors to them for the first time (interview with Aguayo 2012). To some extent it was not a misreading, considering the subsequent events.

The goodwill expressed by popular movements towards government was not reciprocated. On the contrary, matters related to national security commanded by the Ministry of the Interior resulted in various training and advisory services akin to the notorious Plan Colombia. Lugo also approved an anti-terrorist law along the lines propagated by the US and voted by the Parliament, in addition to allowing the establishment of the Northern Zone Initiative, providing for the installation and exercise of US troops in the eastern region of the country (interview with Mendez 2012).

The repression of social movements in the countryside has not slowed, with dozens of cases of violence in line with the pattern during previous governments, including the assassination of militants. According to observers of human rights, the culmination of this security policy occurred in mid-2010, when the government declared a state of siege in five departments of the country. Under the pretext of eradicating a small guerrilla movement called the Ejercito del Pueblo Paraguay (EPP), numerous violations of the civil rights of peasant militants have been committed. Many feel that the EPP, an obscure organization consisting of a handful of members who performed sporadic acts of social banditry, played a functional role in a discourse that, molded in the ideology of combating terrorism, endorsed policies of social policing such as in Colombia (Palau 2009). In any case, the opposition to Lugo, in an attempt to impair the government, systematically sought to link the president to the EPP.

5 The Agrarian Question in the Lugo Government

It is against this background that the Lugo government faced the agrarian question. In the early days of his presidency, agrarian reform activists diagnosed the ambivalence of the government, interpreting its efforts as lack of political will to transcend the rhetoric:

> It is easy to see that this large number of plans, programs, projects and initiatives of different government departments, many elaborated in parallel (at best) or in an antagonistic way when conflicting interests were or are politically different, can not but offer a bleak picture: it is the clearest expression that nothing will be done.
> RIQUELME, ROJAS and PALAU 2010: 31

According to experts, there are three legal ways to proceed with the distribution of land in Paraguay: purchase, expropriation or land reclamation. Apparently less conflictive, the purchase of land is impracticable to the extent that legislation requires that the acquisition of any property must be submitted to public bidding. Only land that is unsuitable for cultivation, or is remote and hard to reach, is offered. In practice, state action boils down to buying land already occupied, where there is no prospect of repossession. Expropriation is also discarded because of the very low levels of productivity required by the Agrarian Statute, as well as the lack of resources that would allow INDERT to buy land at market prices. Finally, there is the possibility of recovering irregularly acquired plots – the so-called ill-gotten lands, the origin of which, as we have seen, is closely linked to the Stroessner dictatorship and to the *brasiguayo* problem (interviews with Fogel 2012; Riquelme 2012).

The first director of INDERT in the Lugo government, Alberto Alderete, had worked on an extensive investigation with the objective of mapping the ill-gotten lands, work promoted by the Commission of Truth and Justice, whose purpose is to ascertain the legacy of the dictatorship in different spheres. The result showed that of a total of 12,229,594 hectares of land distributed throughout the dictatorship, 64.1 per cent were appropriated illegally, which constitutes about one-fifth of the area of the country. In other words, there were 7.8 million hectares of land illegally appropriated and therefore open to expropriation by the government. A list of 3,336 names relating to 4,232 properties, topped by Stroessner himself and Andrés Rodriguez, the military officer who overthrew him, was publicized. According to the sociologist Ramón Fogel (also in charge of the investigation), 90 per cent of the ill-gotten lands would currently be in possession of *brasiguayos* (Program 2012: 24).

Despite the public dissemination of Alderete's report and his profound knowledge of the situation, his brief management (August 2008 to March 2010) of the small and corrupt INDERT was unable to produce any significant results – it collided with the legal blockade to land reclamations, financial sabotage of the institution and political dismissal conducted by the press.

In fact, the crisis that brought about Alderete's downfall was triggered by an episode incomparably lesser than the expropriation of one-fifth of national territory. In an attempt to promote some land distribution, INDERT negotiated the purchase of 22,000 hectares from a Brazilian, Ulisses Rodriges Teixeira, for about US$30 million, with the intention of settling 2,000 families in the area. However, Congress vetoed the operation, which turned into a campaign led by the country's leading newspaper, ABC *Color*, against the incumbent INDERT and the president of the Republic, accused of overvaluing the land for obscure purposes. It seems that the campaign intended to avoid the precedent of distributing lands that could serve soy interests. It was at this juncture that the first serious threat of political judgement of Lugo occurred. Alderete resigned shortly after the lockout to the purchase culminated in a significant cut in the funds allocated to the INDERT by Congress. It was at this same time that the National League of Carperos, alluding to the *carpas* (tents) used by campers, was created (interview with Alderete 2012).

In April 2011, about 500 landless people occupied an area in Ñacunday, on the border with Brazil, triggering a conflict that would last till the following year and would reverberate in the neighboring homeland, since the area in question was appropriated by the icon of Brazilian power in the country, Tranquilo Favero. Paraguay's largest soybean grower, Favero is also known for his racist disdain for Paraguayan workers, counterbalanced by an undisguised admiration of Stroessner – in fact, both traits are common to many Brazilian owners in the country who, for the most part, identify themselves politically with the Colorado.

The occupation was carried out precisely by the segment of landless rural workers who radicalized their methods of struggle after the failure of the acquisition of the Teixeira area. There are indications that the government itself favored the occupation, with the intention of carrying out an expropriation loaded with symbolic value that would strengthen it politically for future elections, fomenting the perception that agrarian reform was advancing. In this circumstance, the newly constituted movement of *carperos* was described as opportunist by organizations of the peasant movement considered 'historical', who opposed the adopted methods (interview with Aguayo 2012).

The land in question had fragile documentation of dubious origin. But the central argument of the rural workers was that they were surplus lands, that is, that the area covered by the property would be larger by at least 12,000 hectares than that registered in documents. INDERT decided on measurement of the terrain, but there was resistance from the *brasiguayos*. With the backing of a judicial warrant and troops, work began, but shortly afterwards a second magistrate rescinded the original mandate and the judge who initially granted it was punished.

Faced with this intransigence, Lugo retreated. It was not the first or the last time he reacted like this, which led one analyst to describe his social policy as 'one step forward and two back' (interview with Rivarola 2012). The Ñacunday case provoked not only the unified reaction of the soybean business but the Brazilian government also intervened.

> The Brazilian government was interested in the Ñacunday case in response to the insecurity that families of brasiguayos could encounter. The government's interest manifested itself in several actions: the Deputy Consul of Brazil in Ciudad del Este, along with producers' lawyers and a legal adviser of the Brazilian Consulate, toured the area of Ñacunday in order to internalize the situation and the ambassador of Brazil paid a 'courtesy' visit to the president of INDERT.
>
> Program 2012: 5

In the end the lands were not recovered, the national government intervened in the INDERT amid allegations of corruption of its third director (close to the Liberals), and the peasants withdrew. Some of them moved to Curuguaty, the stage of the tragic events that served as a pretext to trigger the Lugo trial.

6   The Political Judgment

In the popular camp, there is a common perception that the events that resulted in the death of 6 policemen and 11 peasants on 15 June 2012 in Curuguaty were triggered by snipers. After the policemen were shot, 11 of the more than 50 peasants on the site were executed. The land in question was an old claim of the peasant movement, which had occupied and vacated it several times, appropriated by a well-known businessman and ex-senator, Blas Riquelme. The consensus regarding the illegality of the property is such that Frederico Franco, the president following the coup, wanted to produce a popular political fact by proceeding with the expropriation – which, incidentally, confirmed the irregularity of the eviction that caused the tragedy.

Although the removal of Lugo was made possible by a convergence of varied interests, the immediate articulation of the coup is attributed to two characters: Aldo Zucolillo and Horacio Cartes. The first is an influential businessman who has, among other businesses, a partnership with Cargill in the country and owns the leading national daily, ABC *Color*. Zucolillo is also reputed to be a top-level lobbyist for multinationals operating in Paraguay, as well as for the US government. Horacio Cartes is considered by his peers as one of the most successful entrepreneurs in the country, while his opponents describe him as one of the most powerful Mafiosi of the South Cone. His businesses are involved in the financial sector, beverages, cigarettes, farms, and even a football team. Cartes intended to be the next president of Paraguay representing the National Republican Association, official denomination of the Colorado Party.

However, analysts indicate that the Cartes candidacy found it difficult to transcend the scope of Coloradism, which was subject to ongoing internal disputes. President Lugo's popularity, which was estimated at over 40 per cent despite the limitations of his government, was not a minor obstacle. It is thought that Zucolillo, politically close to the Colorados, would have sensitized Cartes to the urgency of radical action to save his political project. Earlier in the year the publication in ABC *Color* of a story insinuating that Cartes's ties with illegal deals, cigarette smuggling to Brazil and drug trafficking, may have contributed to persuading him into action (interviews with Lovera 2012; Méndez 2012).[6]

After the massacre, the opposition increased its condemnation of the president, accused of being responsible for events because of his presumed inability to deal with the country's problems. Lugo's reaction was defensive. He expressed solidarity with the dead policemen, not with the peasants. And he replaced interior minister Carlos Filizzola with Rúben Candia Amarilla, a Colorado notoriously linked with anti-communist groups of Stronismo and detested by social movements for his role as state attorney general. In fact, once he was inaugurated the new minister's first announcement was the end of the 'protocol' established to deal with land occupations, which had provided for initial dialogue with demonstrators.

By naming a Colorado as a minister, Lugo incurred the contempt of the left as he deepened the gap that separated him from the liberals, his support base in Parliament. The probable reasoning behind this appointment is political:

---

6 This material is available at http://www.abc.com.py/edicion-impresa/opinion/el-lado-oscuro-de-horacio-cartes-207834.html [accessed on 7 August 2012].

Candia Amarilla was a Colorado close to the party's president, Lilian Samaniego, who in turn was opposed internally to Cartes's candidacy. His relationship with the Liberals worn out after almost four years of spurious coexistence, Lugo would visualize his political future in an approach to sectors of this party.

However, the game turned when the Liberals, who did not need many reasons to take over the state machinary within a few months of the election, reached an agreement with the Colorados, who had opposed Lugo from the beginning. The impeachment process took place after 23 previous threats of impeachment during his mandate. It was the eighth time that a Paraguayan president was ousted at the end of his term of government.

7   Final Thoughts

A cursory observation of Franco's first actions reveals other interests that yearned for a change of government. In the week following the coup a variety of genetically engineered cotton seed produced by Monsanto was released and, shortly thereafter, four more varieties of corn. Negotiations with the multinational Rio Tinto Alcán to build a gigantic aluminum plant on the banks of the Paraná River were accelerated. Although Paraguay does not produce bauxite, it is a process of intense energy consumption, which intends to benefit from proximity to the Itaipu plant. According to Ricardo Canese, who advised the Lugo government in negotiations with Brazil regarding Itaipu, the conditions placed by the Canadian[7] multinational implied a subsidy in the order of US$14 billion over the next 20 years – equivalent to seven times the amount of Paraguay's external debt (Canese 2012). Finally, there is an expectation that Paraguay will receive industries from neighboring countries, especially Brazil, replicating Mexican *maquiladoras* (assembling industries) in the Southern Cone.

In terms of international relations, the idea circulated that the US supported the coup, which is consistent with the role attributed to Zucolillo. Lugo's removal was a setback for Brazilian diplomacy, and the government moved swiftly to avoid it. On the other hand, *brasiguayo* power immediately aligned with Franco (ABC 2012).

The fundamental motive of the maneuver was, however, internal: the constraints against change in the country. Although political circumstances illuminate the way Lugo was deposed, the causes of the uncompromising

---

7   Canada was the second government, after the Vatican, to recognize Franco.

opposition he faced are structural. The episodes involving the purchase of land from Teixeira, Ñacunday and Curuguaty illustrate, on the one hand, the tenacious resistance of the ruling classes to any change in the countryside, where agri-business expels the peasant population, provoking the growth of cities and emigration, besides attacking those who remain on the land and aggravating environmental devastation. On the other hand, they reveal the strength of the *stronista* legacy in the state apparatus, as well as its reverse, the impotence of a government of ambiguous character to advance even minimal changes despite the individual commitment of many militants.

The backbone of agri-business in the country, *brasiguayo* power embodies resistance to any disciplining of land issues and to agrarian reform as an instrument to democratize Paraguayan society. *Brasiguayo* power is part of the interests of agri-business multinationals, Rio Tinto Alcan, the US Department of State, *maquiladoras*, ranchers and various traffickers in favoring the tactical alliance between Liberals and Colorados who carried out the coup. In this perspective, the Paraguayan dilemma reflected the paradox of Brazilian influence in the region, insofar as the support to Brazilian rural entrepreneurs stiffened the obstacles faced by the Lugo government in order to advance towards the democratization of access to land, weakening its position in the face of interests that unleashed a process of impeachment that Brazilian diplomacy was unable to stop.

Associated with Stroessner's dictatorship, the multiple illegalities that mark the country's agrarian question, the conflicts arising from the expansion of agri-business and the intermittent Brazilian threat to Paraguayan autonomy, the question of *brasiguayos* problematizes the articulation between the economic and political dimensions of Brazilian regional projection: agri-business reveals itself as a modality of capitalist expansion that combines socio-environmental violence and dependence supported by Brazilian diplomacy, signaling that Paraguayan sovereignty is subordinated to the power of the agri-business lobby in both countries. As a result, regional economic growth is strengthened within the framework of an international insertion based on the export of commodities, perpetuating fundamental conditions that impede a democratic and sovereign integration.

CHAPTER 7

Brazil and the Political Economy of South American Integration

> There are a lot of people who say 'ah, because American imperialism, imperialism, we are poor because of imperialism…' People never realize that American imperialism only had a harmful influence in some countries because their elites were disastrous. If people were honest and dignified and had an elite fighting there for sovereignty … it would not have happened.
> *Lula 2009*

> That's my man right there. I love that guy. He is the most popular politician on Earth.
> *Barack Obama referring to Lula before a G-20 meeting in London, April 2009*

1 Introduction

Elected for the first time in 2002 in reaction to the neoliberal agenda, the Workers Party (PT) won four consecutive presidential elections in Brazil. However, to the extent that macroeconomic continuity restricted the possibility of change in all its dimensions, from the point of view of the left the arguments for voting in the PT grew fewer and fewer. PT's foreign policy, widely perceived as progressive, particularly in its regional environment, was one of the last bastions to fall before submission to the idea of voting for the lesser evil. During this period, Brazil claimed a leading role in promoting numerous regional integration initiatives such as the creation of the Union of South American Nations (UNASUR) in 2008. The friendly relations cultivated with leaders such as Hugo Chávez and Fidel Castro, particularly under the presidencies of Lula, furthered the perception that the country had challenged the historical domination of the United States on the subcontinent.

This chapter questions that perception, proposing a critical review of Brazil's role in the South American integration process under the progressive wave – an approach that complements the analysis of national dynamics, since the possibilities of synergy converge in the sphere of integration. But so do the constraints on change in any regional process, in which Brazil necessarily has a decisive weight. My hypothesis is that despite the rhetoric of the PT government's calling for a 'neo-development' project that would support 'post-neoliberal' regional integration, the structural continuities imposed by neoliberal economic policies have limited the possibilities for change in the country and in the region.

2   Open Regionalism versus Developmental Regionalism

Although elected in a context of rejection of the neoliberal agenda implemented by Cardoso from 1994 to 2002, the Lula government honored the commitment to economic orthodoxy made explicit in the 2002 electoral campaign. The deliberate subordination to the logic of structural adjustment was consummated through a macroeconomic regime grounded on the standard neoliberal tripod that included a target inflation rate, a target primary surplus to reduce the debt-to-GDP ratio, and a floating exchange rate. Furthermore, the social security reform and a new bankruptcy law approved in Lula's first mandate corroborated the view that his governments constituted 'the most complete incarnation' of neoliberalism (Paulani 2008: 10). In spite of this evidence, the political economy of successive PT governments was often characterized as neo-developmentalist, an ideology that intended to reconcile the supposed beneficial aspects of neoliberalism with the positive traits of the old developmentalism.

The neo-developmentist ideology corresponds in international relations to the proposition that PT governments have implemented a 'developmentalist' or 'post-neoliberal' regionalism. Despite the recognition of lines of continuity with previous administrations, and despite the priority in relation to South America preceding the election of Lula in 2002, the reading prevails among analysts on opposite sides of the political spectrum that the foreign policy practised by the Lula governments represents a turning point from previous governments. In order to differentiate themselves from the previous administration, supporters of PT policy attribute the project of regional integration to a change in Brazilian diplomacy, in tune with the rise of progressive governments of different shades, questioning the prevailing domestic and regional neoliberal policies (Cervo 2003; Vizentini 2008; Vigevani, Cepaluni 2011).

In this context, it is argued that the Brazilian state has abandoned the orientation of previous administrations, aiming for a multilateral commercial opening in the framework of what the Economic Commission for Latin America (ECLA) has described as an 'open regionalism' (ECLA 1994), in favor of a policy that emphasizes South American integration as a path for 'developmentalist regionalism' or 'post-neoliberalism' (Serbin et al. 2012). It is suggested that this modality of integration will promote 'the physical integration between the interiors of the countries, a fundamental step for the integration of productive chains of suppliers and related producers, aiming at the formation of economies of scale and the very integration of South American societies' (Desidera Neto and Teixeira 2012: 32).

The need to reorient prevailing foreign policy parameters, giving priority to South America, emerged in the last years of the Cardoso administration (Silva 2010). In 1994, the implementation of a free trade agreement between the US, Mexico and Canada sealed the linkage of Mexican foreign policy to the US, at the same time that the Bush administration launched the idea of a Free Trade of the Americas (FTAA) at the first Summit of the Americas in Miami. Given this scenario, Brazilian diplomacy envisaged South America as a geographical reference for a regional leadership project, a perspective that materialized in an approximation between MERCOSUR and the Andean Community of Nations (CAN) as a strategy for the constitution of an economic bloc in South America (Funag 2012).

It was in this context that the South American Regional Infrastructure Integration Initiative (IIRSA) emerged during the Cardoso administration. Established as an institutional coordination mechanism for the twelve countries of South America, its objective is to build a common infrastructure agenda for transport, energy and communications. The fulfillment of the more than 500 projects foreseen in the portfolio would change the physiognomy of the subcontinent, besides causing considerable environmental impact.

Proposed at a summit of South American presidents in Brasilia in 2000, IIRSA was thought of as the infrastructure dimension of an integration project based on open regionalism. The initiative's portfolio of projects was designed by the Inter-American Development Bank (IDB), which divided the subcontinent into ten integration and development axes conceived as primary commodity export corridors. In territorial terms, it was intended to overcome two 'natural' obstacles to subcontinental integration, the Andes and the Amazon, strengthening the links between the Atlantic coast (Brazil) and the Pacific, in a context of world economic dynamism gravitating toward Asia.

In the year following the launch of IIRSA, the Mexican president, Vicente Fox, announced the Puebla-Panama Plan (later called the Mesoamerican Plan), which followed a similar but smaller-scale rationality and had the backing of the same multilateral financial organizations, notably the IDB. In the circumstances, IIRSA was interpreted as an infrastructural expression of the Free Trade Area of the Americas (FTAA), universally repudiated by the popular movements of the continent.

The FTAA did not take off, not only because of the multiple resistances it aroused in populations but also because it did not obtain consensus between sectors of the Latin American bourgeoisies. Equally important, the proposal was not consensual in the US, and the Bush administration was unable to obtain fast track authorizations to expedite negotiations. The failure of the initiative, defined at the IV Summit of the Americas in Mar del Plata in 2005, is celebrated as a victory for progressive governments in Latin America.

On the other hand, IIRSA was embraced by the regional integration project advanced by the Lula government. With the creation of the Union of South American Nations (UNASUR) in 2008, the initiative was incorporated into the Council of Infrastructure and Planning (COSIPLAN) of this organization, consummating a paradoxical situation: the initiative became the mainstay of an organization identified with 'developmental regionalism' which proposed to reverse the premises that guided the original constitution of IIRSA itself, under the umbrella of 'open regionalism'. The argument is that it would be possible, and desirable, to integrate the technical framework of the initiative, but to give it different political meaning within the framework of the Brazilian leadership under the aegis of UNASUR. To understand this paradox, it is necessary to analyze the economic rationality and the political objectives of the Brazilian integrationist project.

3   Political Economy of Developmental Regionalism

The economic substrate of the PT's regional integration policy was the strategy of Brazilian government to support the internationalization of large companies of national capital or headquartered in the country, understood as a vector of national capitalist development – the policy of 'national champions'. This support materialized mainly through the business diplomacy practiced by Itamaraty (the Brazilian Ministry of Foreign Affairs), and the credit policy of the National Bank for Economic and Social Development (BNDES).

In 2003, the bank changed its statutes to offer a new special line of credit stimulating the external expansion of these companies, provided they promoted Brazilian exports. Between 2003 and 2009, credit granted for this purpose through the BNDES Exim program jumped from U$42 million to U$1.26 billion, an increase of about 3,000 per cent (Folha 2009). In 2010, the volume of credit handled by the BNDES reached US$96.32 billion, which was 3.3 times higher than the US$28.6 billion granted by the World Bank that year, and much more than the US$11.4 million moved by the IDB. This expansion was directly related to the growth of the Brazilian economy, whose GDP in that year had grown

7.5 per cent thanks to the commodity boom, placing the country as the seventh largest world economy (Estado 2011).

In addition to the return on operations, the main source of BNDES financing is at least 40 per cent of the compulsory deposits of PIS-PASEP (social contributions made by legal entities), according to article 239 of the Constitution. Furthermore, resources have been channeled through the National Treasury. In fact, National Treasury participation increased from R$3.8 billion (or 3.4 per cent of the total) in 2001 to R$450 billion (or 54 per cent of the total) in 2014. This policy would also have an anti-cyclical goal, aiming to mitigate the effects of the global crisis unleashed in 2008 (Pinto and Reis 2016).

However, these policies implied subsidized loans by BNDES. This is because the long-term interest rates known as TJLP practised by the bank for most of its funds are lower and less volatile than the federal repurchase agreements referred to as SELIC, since Brazilian interest rates are among the highest in the world: 5.64 per cent at the beginning of 2015, compared to 4.1 per cent for China, 3.6 per cent for Russia, 2.75 per cent for India, and 0.45 per cent for South Africa. At the end of Lula's second term, government bonds were issued based on the SELIC rate, which at that time was at 11.75 per cent, while BNDES loans were referred to the TJLP, quoted at 6 per cent. It is estimated that the fiscal cost of these loans in 2009 was around 85 per cent of the Bolsa Família budget in that year (Estado 2009). This difference between the costs to the government of raising money and the subsidized interest rates has of course a fiscal impact, affecting the national debt.

Concentrated and oligarchical sectors of Brazilian capitalism, which often operate as an extension of transnational-dominated businesses, benefitted from such support, notably in the field of civil construction and primary exports, for products such as soy, ethanol, ores, meat, oil and others. The rationale for this focus is the assessment that these are the sectors in which the country is most competitive internationally.

Another form of support for this internationalization is the BNDES Participações S.A. (BNDESPAR), which capitalizes companies through the acquisition of shares or debentures. In 2009, BNDESPAR had a stake in 22 Brazilian-based multinationals and investments totaling R$92.8 billion, corresponding to 4 per cent of the total Brazilian market capitalization (Tautz et al. 2010: 261). In 2012, 89 per cent of BNDESPAR's shares were concentrated in the oil, mining, pulp and paper, energy and meatpacking sectors (Garzón 2013).

The bank's actions intensified the concentration of capital in sectors of the Brazilian economy. This movement had accelerated with the global crisis beginning in 2008, and reached a record in 2010, when more than 700 merger and acquisitions of Brazilian companies were registered: JBS, Fibria, Vale Ambev and Brasil Foods are among corporations solidified in this process. The JBS case is emblematic: two years after financing the purchase of the largest beef company in Argentina, US Swift Armor, the BNDESPAR injected R$4.5 billion into the JBS-Friboi conglomerate for the purchase of Swift & Co. and Pilgrim's Pride Corp. in the US. In 2008, BNDESPAR held 20 per cent of the company's shares – which reached 35 per cent in subsequent years, as a way of eliminating debts and debentures. By 2010, BNDES had already invested more than R$7.5 billion in JBS, a corporation that in 2016 was at the center of a corruption scandal that shook Temer's presidency (Estado 2010).

JBS's trajectory also illustrates the flow of Brazilian capital toward Argentina, a country that suffered a severe crisis that culminated in the overthrow of four presidents at the end of 2001. In 2003 Petrobras acquired control of Perez Compac (an Argentine oil company), increasing its presence in the country since then; in 2005 Camargo Corrêa bought the largest cement factory in the country, Loma Negra; in 2010 Vale acquired the Argentine assets of the Anglo-Australian company Rio Tinto (Projeto Potássio Rio Colorado); and Votorantim, which already owned AcerBrag steelworks, acquired 50 per cent of Cementos Avellaneda. In the services sector, the Banco do Brasil acquired the Banco da Patagônia (Fundação Dom Cabral 2010; Luce 2007).

However, the key player in the international expansion of Brazilian business was civil construction, a sector that had strengthened under the dictatorship from 1964 to 1985 and diversified its activities by becoming involved in privatizations in the 1990s, also driven by the BNDES (Campos 2009). Between 2001 and 2010, the transfer of BNDES funds to works of Brazilian contractors abroad increased by 1,185 per cent, from US$72.897 million to US$937.084 million. During the two Lula administrations, between 2003 and 2010, more than US$10 billion was invested in financing construction in the region, much of it based on IIRSA. These works include the construction and expansion of the Argentine pipeline network (US$1.9 billion, Odebrecht and Confab); the Chaco aqueduct in this country (US$180 million, CNO companies, Techint, OAS and ISOLUX); the San Ignacio de Moxos-Villa Tunari highway (US$332 million, OAS company); the North-Rurrenabaque-El-Chorro Project (US$199 million) and the Tarija-Bermejo Highway (US$179 million, Queiroz Galvão), all in Bolivia; expansion of the Santiago subway (US$209 million, Alstom); the construction of the bridge over the Tacutu River in Guyana (US$17.1 million); the second bridge over the Paraná River in Paraguay (US$200 million) and the Assis Brasil-Iñapari bridge in Peru (US$17.1 million); in Uruguay, the Montevideo Gas Distribution Network with US$7 million (OAS); (US$943 million, Odebrecht) and the construction of the La Vueltosa hydroelectric plant (US$121 million, Alstom). To this list it is necessary to add large hydroelectric plants designed in Peru, Venezuela, Ecuador, Colombia and the Dominican Republic by Odebrecht, Camargo Correa and OAS (Saggioro 2012).

Many projects supported by the bank have a large socio-environmental impact, besides involving companies that systematically disregard labor laws. For these reasons, the bank performance was contested by social movements in Brazil and abroad. In 2007, a group of social organizations and popular movements, the 'BNDES Platform', pointed out contradictions between the bank's performance and its role as a public entity endowed with a social function.

Examples of this controversial action include the Usina São João of the Brenco group, which received a loan of R$600 million in addition to BNDESPAR as a partner and was assessed by the public prosecutor's office for having 421 workers in a situation analogous to slavery. The Bertin meat company, which received R$2.5 billion from the bank, guaranteeing BNDESPAR control of 27.5 per cent of the shares (before being acquired by JBS), was censured several times for keeping cattle in illegally deforested areas. In another case, R$500 million was lent to the Alcoa group for the exploration of bauxite in an area with an expired environmental license in Juriti, involving several conflicts with the local population (Tautz et al. 2010).

Two of these conflicts reached national visibility. In 2011, a revolt broke out among the 14,000 workers at one of the country's main hydroelectric plants under construction, the Jirau plant in Rondônia, on the Bolivian border. This conflict triggered a wave of revolts in similar situations. Generally removed from larger cities, from state presence and the eyes of public opinion, these construction sites often become machines for grinding people. The consortium responsible for the Jirau plant is led by Camargo Correa, a company associated with Eletrosul and the French transnational Suez and received R$13.3 billion from the BNDES. A second conflict with broad repercussions broke out around the Belo Monte Dam on the banks of the Xingu River in the Brazilian Amazon. Despite the dubious need for the project, its uncertain economic viability and the extraordinary socio-environmental impact foreseen, the power plant was inaugurated in 2016, including at least R$23 billion from the BNDES.

The questioning of BNDES performance has been replicated at the international level. In the context of labor relations, the best-known situation involved the workers of the International Nickel Company of Canada (Inco), acquired by the Brazilian giant Vale do Rio Doce in 2006, who faced the company's new management in a prolonged strike. In South America there are multiple controversies. In Ecuador, tensions between the Correa government and Odebrecht over irregularities in the construction of the San Francisco hydroelectric plant led countries to the brink of a diplomatic crisis in 2008. In Bolivia, conflicts surrounding the construction of a highway crossing the TIPNIS, an environmental park as well as an indigenous reserve, are considered a watershed in the Morales government's relationship with indigenous movements.

Despite brutal repression of the eighth indigenous march in 2011, the project awarded to the Brazilian construction company OAS, which had a US$332 million loan from the BNDES, was suspended. A similar situation involved the construction of hydroelectric plants in the Peruvian Amazon, hitherto impeded by popular resistance.

The Peruvian case illustrates Brazil's regional strategy. In 2010, presidents Alan García and Lula da Silva signed an agreement for the construction of five hydroelectric plants in the Peruvian Amazon, which would export 80 per cent of their production to Brazil. The first and largest of them, to be located in Inambari, was awarded to a consortium of three Brazilian companies, led by the construction company OAS. Beyond the project itself, the partnership was conceived as part of a strategy to link the Peruvian economy to Brazil's, as happened with the construction of the Bolivian gas pipeline in the late 1990s, a milestone leading to Brazil's becoming the main commercial partner of that country. In the eyes of Brazilian formulators, the goal was to strengthen regional economic ties, creating the material base for the region's political autonomy, under Brazilian leadership (conversations with Araujo 2015; Paloschi 2015).

In general terms, the PT understood that the internationalization of Brazilian corporations would serve as a material foundation to project the influence of the country regionally, modifying its international role. Or, to use the jargon of diplomacy, to make Brazil a 'global player'.

It was from this perspective that UNASUR was created in 2008. But why did Brazil work for the creation of this organization and not join the ALBA, launched in 2004?

The ALBA beckoned for integration not restricted to the commercial dimension, involving the fields of education, health, culture and communication, among others. The exchange of Venezuelan oil for the service of Cuban doctors and the creation of the television channel Telesur in 2005, although not directly linked to the ALBA, are emblematic of this intention. In the field of economics, innovative ideas were proposed, such as a single regional compensation system (SUCRE), aimed at mitigating regional dependence on hard currency; or the formation of joint investment companies, such as Petrocaribe. The intention of the initiative was described in the following words: 'ALBA opted for the logic of trade cooperation, solidarity exchanges and economic complementarity between the different national productive structures as general principles of its philosophy, in an effort to extend revolutionary solidarity across the continent' (Cerezal, Simarro and Soler 2013: 152).

Ultimately, in proposing a Latin American (and not South American) integration that transcended the mercantile dimension, ALBA signaled for a counter-hegemonic political project on the continent, with its first and main partner in Cuba. However, this logic found little resonance in the Brazilian government, for which the aspiration of a multipolar world did not translate into political radicalization. From the Brazilian perspective, the ALBA was of little economic interest, because it did not bring with it attractive business opportunities. On the political front, the initiative was interpreted as responding to Venezuelan rather than Latin American interests, and was seen as competing with Brazil's projection, in spite of the personal empathy between Chávez and Lula (conversations with Cerezal 2015; Parkinson 2015; Ramos 2015).

Thus, in opposition to the logic advocated by ALBA that aimed at a counter-hegemonic integration of Latin American scope, UNASUR was ruled from the start by the lowest common denominator capable of bringing together disparate policies in South America, such as those then practised by the governments of Venezuela and Colombia. The accession of the latter country was only assured when it was agreed that decisions in the organization would be unanimous and not by majority, which in practice granted veto power to its members.

In addition to welcome achievements (but with little structural impact) such as agreements for the recognition of diplomas and joint purchases of vaccines (conversation with Nascone 2015), it was hoped that the creation of COSIPLAN as a UNASUR body would reverse the original rationale associated with IIRSA. In economic terms, this challenge implied minimizing the role of the multilateral institutions that designed the initiative: the IDB, the Andean Development Corporation (CAF) and the Financial Fund for the Development of the Plata Basin (FONPLATA). This is because the strictly mercantile logic that drive these institutions prevented investment in works relevant to regional integration, but unprofitable. This presence should be counterbalanced with the performance of other funding agencies, notably BNDES (Barros 2015). Simultaneously, proposals emerged towards a new regional financial architecture, which resulted in the creation of the Bank of the South in 2009, with the formal adhesion of Argentina, Bolivia, Brazil, Ecuador, Paraguay, Uruguay and Venezuela.

From the Brazilian point of view, the integrationist movement broadened business possibilities and strengthened its political leadership. Other countries in the region had two fundamental motivations to participate. On the one hand, there are those who saw the opportunity to consolidate an alternative political field to US influence. This is the underlying motivation of the South American countries that are part of ALBA, a potentially more radical integration initiative that has been neutralized in practice by Brazilian conduct. On the other hand, there are countries such as Peru that do business with Brazil as they do with any country. Symptomatically, Venezuela and Peru were the two countries in which Odebrecht, a symbol of the expansion supported by PT governments, had higher levels of business activity at the end of Rousseff's mandate (conversation with Chan 2015).

In general, the countries with the greatest intensification of trade ties with Brazil are those with whom PT administrations maintained close political ties, such as, in Latin America, Argentina, Venezuela, Cuba and the Dominican Republic. Outside the continent, this association between political affinity and commercial intensification seemed less relevant, given the volume of business with the shadowy Angolan dictatorship. But it was the search for political allies that motivated the active support for Ollanta Humala's candidacy in Peru in 2011, even though the president turned his back on Brazilian supporters after his election.

4   Developmentalism in Crisis

How has this process of regional integration evolved? From the point of view of Brazilian foreign policy, which aimed at capitalist development supported by the internationalization of its corporations and, as a result, aspired to a leading role in international politics, it is possible to say that the project progressed successfully during the Lula administrations. In this period, the commodity boom sustained an unquestioned popularity that allowed the president to elect a virtually unknown successor. At the same time, there was evidence of a new role for the country, between the leadership in the United Nations peacekeeping mission to Haiti and the victorious campaign to host the World Cup and the Olympic Games in the country, all triumphs of dubious merit.

Throughout the first presidency of Rousseff from 2011 to 2015, the process still progressed, but intermittently. In addition to her profile as a president who did not prioritize an external agenda or regional integration, there were signs that the crisis had reached the country – for example, hampering the National Treasury's transfers to BNDES. In the political field, although the rebellion of June 2013 had no economic motivations, it brought to light a deep social malaise, and was an unmistakable sign that the social pacification produced by the PT was losing ground. As people's aspirations were again thwarted, the political initiative steadily gravitated to the right.

In 2014, when Roussef was re-elected, this project was already threatened on different fronts. Fundamentally, the economic conditions that shielded Brazil from the most destructive effects of the 2008 crisis were no longer present, and there were signs of economic recession. On the other hand, numerous scandals evidenced corruption schemes in the modus operandi of construction companies doing business in the country and abroad. These revelations undermined the trustworthiness of the government and the ruling party, but also threatened the foundations of the capitalist project they defended. Paradoxically, the requirement of transparency in the BNDES was no longer a slogan of popular movements and was appropriated by the right in the streets.

Fenced in on all fronts, PT members interpreted the difficulties experienced by the contractors and Petrobras as a threat to their national project. Powerless to deny corruption, they claimed that the country always worked that way, but it had only emerged now because the PT was in government. Connected to this argument, it was suggested that the extensive work of ongoing investigations inhibited the investment of construction companies, among other sectors, which put the country's economy at risk. In other words, it was made explicit that the project of regional integration presupposes an identification between construction companies (with their corrupt form of doing business and appalling working conditions) and the nation.

To recognize weakness in the premises of the PT project does not mean to deny the anti-PT right's political use of the investigations or the disturbing infractions of legality incurred for this purpose. But the scandals made corruption undeniable. And the combination of corruption and economic crisis put the PT administration on the defensive.

Even before the crisis worsened, the BNDES was more concerned with scandals than with investments, at a time when its funds were considerably reduced at any rate. Furthermore, several indicators questioned the effectiveness of the 'national champions' strategy: companies that received large contributions from the bank were soon afterwards sold to international control; enterprises with support to internationalize their operations then became autonomous, adding little to the export of Brazilian products and services; on top of that, there were indications that the 'national champions' invested their long-term loans (ostensibly destined to foster the exportation of goods and services) in financial products.

Added to the domestic difficulties of the PT government were obstacles to the proposition that COSIPLAN would give a different meaning to IIRSA. According to this perspective, the projected infrastructure would contribute to the endogenization of growth, environmental sustainability and social inclusion. At the core of the problem is that the set of banks at the origin of the initiative (IDB, CAF and Fonplata) preserve, in practice, the power to guide the project's agenda. For example, these banks finance the studies that precede the projects and the IIRSA technical committee continues to be composed of representatives of these three institutions.

On the other hand, the proposal of a new financial architecture aimed at reducing the region's dependence on international financial institutions was blocked by Brazil itself. Objections from the Central Bank and the Ministry of Finance prevailed against using international reserves to finance investments, while receiving interest of 1 per cent in US treasury bonds, although at the other end of this financial engineering they paid the highest interest rates in the world. Although one of the main proponents of the new architecture, the Ecuadorian economist Pedro Paes, minimizes this issue, arguing that the contribution of international reserves could be preceded by numerous measures that do not entail burdens of this nature, the prevailing perception is that the reason the Bank of the South has not taken off is political: the institution provides equal voting power to countries, regardless of their contribution, in a model different from that of the IMF. This arrangement would not interest intended Brazilian leadership, which evidences the power motivations underlying its regional integration discourse (conversations with Acosta 2015; Paes 2015).

The fragility of the integrationist proposal is also explained by the fact that in 2014, 477 Cosiplan projects were national, 95 binational, five trinational and only two multinational telecommunications projects involving Bolivia, Colombia, Ecuador, Peru and Venezuela. Furthermore, the IIRSA report showed that 89.1 per cent of the projects and 66.5 per cent of the investments planned corresponded to the transportation sector, of which almost half were highways, while energy projects accounted for 9.3 per cent of projects and 33.5 per cent of investments, and the communications sector did not reach 2 per cent of the number of projects. Data shows the affinity between IIRSA and Brazilian constructors' core business (Cosiplan 2014). Fifteen years after its launch, it was possible to affirm that the initiative had advanced slowly but successfully, yet without fulfilling the political function that the PT project assigned to it.

This finding problematizes the assumed links between neo-developmentism and developmental regionalism. Since the economic dimension of the process is limited to deals enhanced by works related to an initiative incubated within the scope of open regionalism, the proposition of a developmental regionalism involves a rhetorical maneuver, evoking an inflection in a project that, in substance, remains the same. In this perspective, the association between the works carried out and regulatory modifications associated with the IIRSA and a neo-developmental horizon has a doubly ideological character. It associates the expansion of oligopolistic Brazilian and multinational businesses with new developmentalism, and at the same time it identifies this new developmentalism with a post-neoliberal regional integration. In this operation, interconnection is confused with integration; growth with development; oligopolistic interests with national interest; business diplomacy with south-south cooperation; and the internationalization of Brazilian businesses with post-neoliberal integration.

5 The Petista Order in South America

Finally, the management of regional conflicts, the main virtue attributed to UNASUR, is often confused with sovereignty. According to this reading, the constitution of regional organizations not led by the United States is seen as an advance toward a multipolar world, which opposes the interests of this power. It is important to note that the State Department of this country has never had this reading. On the eve of UNASUR's formalization, Condoleeza Rice expressed support for the Brazilian role in the framework of a regional integration project (Rice 2008). Under the Obama administration, the under-secretary of state for political affairs, Wendy Sherman, emphasized, 'Today, Brazil is a strategic partner in addressing global – not just hemispheric – issues of common concern. And I want to be clear that the United States needs and welcomes Brazil's positive expanded role' (Sherman 2012).

In keeping with this perspective, Brazilian intercession in regional affairs has never antagonized the United States. Brazil intervened against the coup interests endorsed by the US in the recent political crises in Honduras (2009) and Paraguay (2012). However, in both cases it was powerless to reverse the course of events, despite intense efforts in the case of Paraguay.

The limits of the PT's progressivism were evidenced in its relationship with the Bolivarian process in Venezuela. Lula cultivated close relations with Chávez, while condemning to relative marginality his initiatives of innovative potential such as ALBA, Banco do Sul and Telesur. This Brazilian conduct strengthened the more moderate sectors of Bolivarianism, a dynamic process whose meaning was in constant dispute, at the same time that Brazilian businesses in the country multiplied.

Even outside the presidency Lula continued to put pressure on the Venezuelan government. A year after Chávez's death, the former president sent a letter, delivered by Marco Aurelio Garcia to Maduro, advising him to accept his role as a reformer of the Chávez legacy instead of pretending to be a second Chávez (conversation with Ramírez 2015). As UNASUL offered to mediate the dialogue with the opposition, Lula proposed conciliation and social pact for Venezuela, which until then had seemed a successful recipe in Brazil:

> Maduro should try to reduce the political debate to dedicate himself entirely to governing, establish a coalition policy, build a minimum program and reduce tensions ... Venezuela should have a five-year pact to work against blackouts, fight against inflation and be self-sufficient in food production.
>
> LULA 2014

When the Venezuelan crisis worsened and the Rousseff government was trapped in Brazil, the perception spread that the country had turned its back on the Bolivarian government (conversations with Constant 2015; Urbina 2015).

By neutralizing the more radical expression of the progressive wave that is now depleted in the subcontinent, PT governments have helped to delimit the scope and limits of change. In some situations, the political change was radical, as in Venezuela where the legacy of the Punto Fijo Pact was buried, or in Bolivia where indigenous protagonism eroded what Zavaleta Mercado described as a variegated society characterized by the social divide between Indians and non-Indians. In any case, there was an inability to generate alternatives to an economy anchored in the exploitation of primary resources for export, inherent to the logic of IIRSA, to which all adhered.

There is a correspondence between the scope and the limit of the processes identified with progressivism in the region, where there was a political change within the framework of economic continuity, and the dynamics prevailing in the regional integration plan, where UNASUR emerges as a political novelty based on IIRSA, whose logistic framework deepens the economic structures of dependency.

6   Final Thoughts

There is a similarity between neo-developmentism as the ideology of the economic policy of PT presidencies and the notion of a developmentalist or post-neoliberal regionalism as the ideology of the foreign policy practised by these governments. The political end in both cases was to establish a cleavage in relation to previous administrations, intending to differentiate itself from neoliberal orthodoxy, even if not corresponding to any substantive change – whether in the macroeconomic policy founded by the Real Plan or in the integration project based on works associated with IIRSA.

Both poles of the debate have a common foundation that refers, ultimately, to the myth of economic growth. This fake polarization fulfills a second political function, which is to keep the debate within alternatives that ignore the connections between economic growth and the deepening of dependence and inequality that characterize underdevelopment. Propositions that point to an alternative civilizational pattern, whether around Sumak Kawsay, Bolivarianism or socialism, have no voice in the country.

In the economy the debate is restricted to microeconomics, discussing, in the final analysis, the pace and intensity of the deepening of the neoliberal agenda. In the field of international relations, the relevance given to the South in general, and to South America in particular, is disputed, as a privileged space for expansion of Brazilian businesses. The parameters of the debate are established by the pondering of the burden and benefits of regional integration, according to a mercantile rationality. The counterpoint to the PT position, which emphasizes the strategic importance of the region, was summed up in the criticism of MERCOSUR by the former Brazilian mission advisor to the World Trade Organization (WTO), Vera Thorstensen: 'it is no use marrying the poor' (Thorstensen 2014). On the other hand, IIRSA is defended by diplomats who are in tune with open regionalism, such as the former Cardoso government minister José Botafogo Gonçalves, who complains that the initiative 'has received little praise, when it is perhaps the institution that can give more dynamism to South American integration', and defends the practice of 'infrastructural diplomacy' (Gonçalves 2013: 268).

Despite the differences in focus, the common goal is the insertion of the Brazilian economic space into the movements of contemporary capitalism, as an exporter of raw materials, a base for the expansion of multinational business and a platform for the valorization of financial capital. From this perspective, politics is always instrumentalized by the economy. Contrary to what the rhetoric of post-neoliberal regionalism preaches, the sense of the integrationist process did not change after the election of progressive governments imbued with a neo-developmental horizon, but there are indications that the interconnection of the subcontinent as a mercantile imperative led to an instrumentalization of political affinity between these governments in favor of local and international business.

From this point of view, the analytical incognito that tries to explain how a politically conventional, socially conservative and economically neoliberal government would practise an innovative foreign policy disruptive to US interests in the region is undone. Once the ideological nature of the articulation between neo-developmentalism and post-neoliberal regionalism has been clarified, the policy of the PT governments towards South America is no longer seen as what it would like to be, but as what it was: instrumentalization of regional integration in favor of the internationalization of oligopolized Brazilian businesses consonant with the prevailing international division of labor, which would secure the country a leadership position on the subcontinent circumscribed to the political sphere, to be exercised in moments of crisis according to the narrow limits tolerated by the hegemonic power.

CHAPTER 8

Chile and the Political Economy of the Real Neoliberalism

> The moral conscience of Chile requires that truth be clarified, and that justice be done, as far as possible.
> *Patricio Aylwin at the National Congress on 21 May 1990*

> Market plus State equals less democracy. This is the equation that rules the current Chile.
> *Alberto Mayol, 2012*

1 Introduction

When the socialist Ricardo Lagos was elected president of Chile in 2000 there was some expectation of a progressive turnaround in the country. It did not, however, materialize. Heir to a solid left-wing tradition dating back to the nineteenth century, contemporary Chilean history is marked by the coup led by General Augusto Pinochet, who aborted the 'Chilean way to socialism' under the leadership of Salvador Allende from 1970 to 1973. The dictatorship that followed, a pioneering experience of neoliberal fundamentalism, radically changed the country in all spheres. The constraints that marked the democratization of the late 1980s imply deep continuities, summarized in the Constitution still in force today. In this context, the alliance between socialists and Christian Democrats that has dominated national politics since then has established itself as a guarantor of the system left by the dictatorship, which remains unshaken. In recent years, however, the so-called 'duopoly' began to be contested by the left in the streets and at the polls, making explicit the contradictions and resistance to this incarnation of neoliberal social utopia: Chilean 'real neoliberalism'.

2 Between the Popular Front and the Chilean Way to Socialism

Chile's trajectory between the interwar depression and the 1973 coup is marked by national developmentalism and institutional stability. In economics, the prevailing notion borrowed from the United Nations Economic Commission for Latin America (ECLA), whose offices were set up in Santiago, was that national industrialization was a necessary premise for sovereignty. In politics, the Chilean presidents succeeded each other between 1932 and 1973 in accordance with the constitutional order, a unique phenomenon in South America. In a significant part of the period, the Communist Party was not considered illegal and, like the socialists, disputed the presidency and directed ministries, which led part of the left to uphold the myth of Chilean democratic exceptionalism (conversation with Álvarez 2017).

After participating in Popular Front governments between 1938 and 1952, the left, with the socialist Salvador Allende as its candidate, was defeated by a small margin in the presidential elections of 1958.[1] It was amid the rise of the left that the Chilean Christian Democracy (DC) was founded in 1957, presenting itself as an alternative to conservatism but with sensitivity to social issues. In the following elections, this party received support and financing from the US, as part of its Alliance for Progress. Faced with the right's demise at the time, the Christian Democrat Eduardo Frei gained massive conservative support in the 1964 presidential election. But to defeat the left he ended up absorbing its flags and rhetoric, including revolution. He incorporated the nationalization of copper and agrarian reform into his program, whose spirit was condensed into the campaign slogan 'Revolution in Freedom'.

In practice, the Christian Democrat government has faced the inherent contradictions of conservative reformism. The 'Chileanization' of copper consisted of creating joint ventures between the state and US companies through the purchase of 51 per cent of the shares of its Chilean subsidiaries. Often, the indemnities paid exceeded the corresponding value declared by the companies which, in several cases, maintained control of management, so that this policy's potential for conflict was substantially mitigated (Elgueta and Chelén 1984: 247). The case of agrarian reform was different, as 3.5 million hectares, corresponding to 1,400 properties, were expropriated in a process that would accelerate under Allende. The agrarian reform law also stimulated peasant unionization, which sharpened the hostility of the conservatives at the same time as it multiplied strikes and land occupations in the following years, unleashing dynamics that even the future Allende government was unable to control (conversation with Chonchol 2017).

---

1   Soviet politics urged the Communist Parties to ally themselves with anti-fascist forces in the 1930s, albeit in the bourgeois camp. Popular Fronts reached the presidency in Spain, France and Chile. In the last-named country, the presidency was exercised by a member of the Radical Party for three consecutive terms.

The results of the 'Revolution in Freedom' displeased the right and the left, adding to the polarization of politics in the country. A Brazilian integralist captured the alarm among the conservatives denouncing Frei as the Chilean 'Kerensky': one with the intention of appeasing social tensions through reform, who opens the way for revolution (Silveira 1967). On the other hand, the singer Victor Jara satirized the atmosphere of Christian democracy in the song '*Ni Chicha, Ni Limoná*' (not chicha, an alcoholic beverage, nor lemonade, a refreshing drink), announcing that '*la cosa va pa' delante y no piensa recular*' ('it goes forward and doesn't think about retreating').

It was in this context that Salvador Allende was elected president in 1970 as the candidate of Popular Unity (UP), a coalition composed mainly of socialists, communists, and Christian Democrat dissidents called the Movimiento de Acción Popular Unitaria (MAPU). It was the fourth time that Allende disputed the presidency, always affiliated to the Socialist Party (PS), proclaiming Marxism and revolution. In contrast to the Cuban route, which had as its starting point armed struggle and the destruction of the bourgeois state, Popular Unity sought to build socialism from existing institutions. This path from reform to revolution was idealized as the 'Chilean way' to socialism, in a process that aroused worldwide attention.

Despite the socialist horizon, the economic architecture of the UP project revealed strong inspiration from the ECLA. A key aspect was to regain sovereignty over copper, which accounted for more than 80 per cent of the country's exports. In what became known as 'national dignity day', the government nationalized the sector without compensation. That the measure was passed unanimously in Congress reveals the popularity of the cause. This policy was subsequently extended to iron, saltpeter and coal, expanding the nationalization of natural resources.

In other segments of the economy, the program provided for three areas: private, mixed and social. The last-named was initially formed by 91 basic companies, while the Corporación de Fomento de Producción (Corfo) promoted more than 500 companies under the aegis of the state (Sader 1992). Banks were nationalized through the purchase of shares, as well as foreign trade. The fundamental objective was to enable the state to control the economy.

Another pillar of the program was agrarian reform, consummated with the expropriation of about 4,400 properties – more than 6.4 million hectares. In just under three years the UP government ended the *hacienda*, the 'crucible of Chilean culture' (Bengoa 2009: 105). The political, social and economic power associated with the *latifúndio* was removed, leaving only the wineries (conversation with Chonchol 2017).

At the international level, the UP was guided by non-alignment, condemning the subservience of the Organization of American States (OEA) to the US at the same time that it was in solidarity with Cuba, and denouncing the interference of US companies in domestic politics (Carlos et al. 1970). The Soviets barely supported the UP, and when Allende, suffocated by economic problems, visited the USSR in 1972, his request for credit was denied by Leonid Brezhnev (Alvarez 2017).

Unsurprisingly, the UP project met with active congressional opposition, where the government did not have a majority: decrees were systematically blocked, charges were forged and ministers were dismissed. Christian democracy emerged as the tiebreaker, because their support would guarantee a majority for the government or for the opposition. In practice, its role was instrumental in thwarting government projects and, when the time came, in overthrowing him.

In the economic field, the positive results at the start of the mandate – when the economy grew, wages rose and unemployment fell – were eroded by the combination of falling copper prices, inflation and a shortage of primary goods, fueled by international and domestic boycotts. The UP faced a strike in the country's largest copper mine, owner lockouts and a shutdown of transportation, all supported by Washington.

This situation polarized Chilean society, which saw marches led by middle-class women hitting empty pots in reference to the scarcity, to be followed by multitudinous demonstrations of support for the government. To combat the black market, people formed and managed Supply and Price Boards (JAP). The owner lockouts, in turn, provoked the occupation of factories and the management of production by the workers, organized in '*cordones industrials*' (industrial lines). In the countryside, popular pressure accelerated agrarian reform, backed by the army. On the whole, social radicalization opened gaps for the strengthening of popular power.

Despite the social and economic wear and tear intensified by hostile media, votes for the UP rose in the March 1973 parliamentary election, frustrating the prospect of an institutional exit. At this point, it was clear that the opposition would have to resort to the military coup to overthrow the government, which occurred on the fateful 11 September 1973 under the leadership of General Augusto Pinochet, with strong support from the US (Kornbluh 2003). As Henry Kissinger said, 'I don't see why we need to stand by and watch a country go communist due to the irresponsibility of its people. The issues are much too important for the Chilean voters to be left to decide for themselves' (quoted in Peck 2010: 43).

The protagonists drew different lessons from this tragic outcome. Militants of the Revolutionary Left Movement (MIR) have rebuked the legalism of the government, which did not arm the people: 'a revolution must know how to defend itself', noted one activist (conversation with Mundaca 2017). On the other hand, cadres close to the president, such as Jacques Chonchol and Joan Garcés, believed that the government had bought too many fights while simultaneously facing internal opposition and hostility from the US. In particular, the nationalization of copper without indemnity and the difficulty of forming an accord with Christian democracts were subject to reconsideration (Garcés 1993; Chonchol 2017).

Christian democracy also carried out its own revision of conscience. Despite individual exceptions, the party created obstacles for the UP government – even supporting the coup – with the expectation of returning to the presidency. In fact, this occurred, but only 17 years later. In 1990, revisionisms converged, and Christian democracy returned to La Moneda hand in hand with the socialists. But in the meantime, the country bequeathed by the UP had been disfigured.

3   From Dictatorship to Protected Democracy

The military government junta commanded by Pinochet from 1973 to 1990 radically changed Chilean society in all its spheres. The caravan of death, in which the military crossed the country assassinating militants who had been identified and placed on a list before the coup; large-scale detention and torture, transforming Santiago's main football stadium into a prison; clandestine camps of torture and murder of political prisoners; and Operation Condor, an articulation between the dictatorships of the Southern Cone that internationalized the repression, conceived by the country's secret police chief, Manuel Contreras – these are all aspects of the state terrorism that destroyed the political and economic references associated with national developmentalism that had been prevalent since the 1930s. In this process, the objective and subjective conditions were generated for a refounding of the country, characterized by neoliberal fundamentalism. The boldness of democratic socialism was punished with its opposite, described as 'shock capitalism' (Klein 2008).

However, Chilean neoliberalism must first be understood as a paradigm – a set of values or a 'vision of the world' – rather than as a specific recipe, since it has lived with quite different monetary and exchange-rate policies. In particular, the severe crisis that erupted in the country between 1981 and 1982 led to counter-cyclical initiatives against the hitherto prevalent policies focused on trade and financial liberalization.

The diagnosis underlying the Chilean neoliberal project was that the country is small (17 million people in 2017) but has an exceptionally high number of natural resources in proportion to its population. This gives rise to two conclusions: it is unfeasible to develop a domestic industry based on this small domestic market, but if the country exploits its advantages it can obtain, through exports, the foreign exchange needed to import what it needs. In a nutshell, why manufacture what you can import?

Chilean neoliberalism supposes a strong state, which applies a high (regressive) tax burden and cultivates instruments of political and economic intervention, albeit in a liberal direction, according to the perspective of comparative advantages. Since the dictatorship, export sectors other than mining have been boosted. Wine, salmon, fruit and timber are among the segments supported by an aggressive Chilean export promotion policy, conducted since 1974 by Pro-Chile, part of the Ministry of Foreign Affairs.

The material substrate of various primary export modalities was the capitalist development of the countryside, which was based on the reversal of the agrarian reform carried out in the country by previous governments. However, the Pinochet agrarian counter-reform did not aim to restore land to former owners, but to create the conditions for the flourishing of a new agri-business oriented to the external market. Since the dictatorship, rural areas began to produce less food and more foreign exchange.

The other side of this policy was an accelerated de-industrialization. Between 1974 and 1983, the production value of the Chilean industrial sector fell by 25 per cent, while more than 5,000 establishments were closed, implying the loss of almost 150,000 jobs. (Faletto 2007: 55). The military took over the leadership of state-owned enterprises, many of which were privatized. The dictatorship maintained the previous government's management over state-owned mines, grouped together in the Corporación Nacional del Cobre de Chile (Codelco), which to this day directs 10 per cent of its profits to the armed forces. However, the conditions for foreign ownership and management have been restored, and the state's participation in mining has declined.

The world of work, shattered by the combination of terrorism and de-industrialization, had its legal framework completely remodeled. In 1978, the dictatorship annulled the law prohibiting dismissal without just cause. Temporary work contracts and the flexibility of working hours were also authorized, according to the convenience of the employer. The following year, a Labor Plan was adopted, which re-founded trade union legislation and enshrined the deregulation of the labor market. Collective bargaining and strikes by public employees were prohibited, hiring of workers to replace strikers was legalized, union formation by category was restricted (only by company), individual negotiation was encouraged, the idea of labor law ended (now considered as simply conflicts between individuals), among other devices in force until the present day. In short, a 'neoliberal model without democratic obstacles' has been established, laying the ground for a political culture in which 'talking about a strike is like talking about sex in a nunnery' (conversation with Kremerman 2017).[2]

It was in this same context that the dictatorship submitted a plebiscite to the constitution it drafted, also in force today. Designed under the sinister leadership of Jaime Guzmán, the constitution provided the legal framework for a deep commodification of social rights, which was implemented and improved in the following years, even after the dictatorship.

Despite propaganda to the contrary, the economic liberalization imposed by the dictatorship led the country to the brink of collapse. In 1982, Chile was one of the Latin American countries most affected by the debt crisis, facing a drop of 14.1 per cent in GDP in a context of bankruptcies, undercapitalized companies and high unemployment. The impact of the crisis explained the risks inherent in radical neoliberalism hitherto practised, provoking a revision towards a pragmatic course. For example, banks were nationalized (or saved), in a maneuver parallel to the privatization of the pension system. In spite of the growing challenges it faced, the dictatorship succeeded in regaining high levels of growth starting in 1984, which gave it economic backing for another season in power.

At this juncture, part of the left resumed armed struggle, at the same time that popular demonstrations against the regime provoked violent reactions. Between 1983 and 1986 there were various national protest days convened by trade unionists, in which dozens of deaths were recorded. In 1986, a botched attack against Pinochet, perpetrated by the Frente Patriotico Manuel Rodríguez (FPMR) group, served as a pretext to increase the brutality of the repression. The limits of armed action made the opposition change course and begin to concentrate their efforts in following years to overthrow the dictatorship through the institutional path (Muñoz 2008).

It was with the intention of avoiding popular protest that negotiations between the dictatorship and Christian Democracy, along with sectors of the Socialist Party, were unleashed – in the future they would be united in the Coalition of Parties for Democracy (Concertación).[3] The US, European Social Democracy and the Catholic Church were active in the process, in a context in

---

2   Labor and social security reforms were proposed to the Military Junta by José Piñera, brother of the current president Sebastián Piñera. Chilean wealth is concentrated in seven families, among them the Piñera.
3   The PS was divided since 1979 in two positions, led respectively by Clodomiro Almeyda, who defended a policy of left-wing unity (PS-PC), and Carlos Altamirano, who favored a democrat social identity and the rapprochement with DC.

which the legitimacy of the dictatorship declined with the waning of the Cold War. The process culminated in a plebiscite in 1988, in which the population was polled on the possibility of Pinochet's remaining in power until 1997. In a contested decision, the opposition opted for a campaign based on electoral marketing, projecting a Chile in which 'joy was coming' (*la alegría ya viene*) rather than a critique of the dictatorship's legacy. The main argument of this winning strategy is that a traumatized population did not want to put their finger on open wounds. On the other hand, the conditions of the campaign and victory itself limited the scope of the transition that had begun.

Pinochet was understandably surprised by defeat, and only accepted it under pressure from his peers (Muñoz 2008). Even the US was in favor of 'no'. However, during the year-and-a-half he had left in the La Moneda the dictator refined the structures of a transition controlled by the interests that sustained him. A key aspect of the negotiations was the derogation of the most aberrant aspects of the constitution, such as the banning of parties that spoke about class struggle or the presidential ability to dissolve the Chamber of Deputies, in exchange for quorums of up to two-thirds to reform the constitution itself (conversation with Grez 2017). However, in practice, supermajority quorums were made unfeasible by the infamous binomial system,[4] which consolidated the duopoly between the Concertación and the right in Chilean politics after the dictatorship, while limiting the participation of minority forces.

The result of this architecture is that although the coalition structured around the alliance DC and PS (Concertación, and later Nueva Mayoría, after the adhesion of the PC in 2013) won all subsequent presidential elections except for 2010, the constitution is the same until the present day. There were more than 200 minor reforms, but none that directly opposed Pinochet supporters, altering its essence. Since then, Concertación rhetoric has been that the right has blocked the reforms. However, during those years there were times when the Concertación had a majority to change it and did not, which supports the analysis of Sergio Grez, for whom this architecture was accepted by these parties precisely because it provides a pretext not to advance the reforms, thus disguising their accommodation to power (conversation with Grez 2017).

---

4   Electoral system providing for the election of two candidates in each electoral region. The vote is computed in lists, with the most voted in each list being elected, unless one of them obtains twice or more votes than the second placed candidate. In practice, Concertación and the right were often the two most voted in every region, but rarely doubled the rival's vote. On the other hand, candidates with many votes, but who are in lists that finish in third place or below, are not elected. The result is the sharing of legislative power between the two coalitions.

And what is the essence of this constitution? The crystallization of the dictatorship's legacy meant the institutionalization of a conservative neoliberalism. The notion of social rights is subsumed into the guarantee of economic freedom, which implies modifying the meaning of the intervention of the state. Understood as a 'subsidiary state' (Ruiz and Boccardo 2015), its role is to assume social roles only when private initiative is not interested. On the one hand, it ensures the unrestricted functioning of private initiative, seen as a support of individual freedom; on the other, it provides health, social security and education services to the poorest, often through targeted policies. The idea behind the privatization of social policies was not to disregard the individual, but to let him decide.

In line with this perspective, the right to education is subordinated to freedom of education. The constitutional text understands that parents have the 'duty to educate their children', and for this they have 'the right to choose the establishment of education for their children'. Similarly, freedom of education means the 'right to open, organize and maintain educational establishments'. In terms of health, 'each person will have the right to choose the health system in which he wants to be received, whether state or private', However, this choice is conditioned by the ability to pay, therefore the right becomes a commodity and citizenship is exercised as consumption. In practice, the transformation of social rights into niches of businesses protected and subsidized by the state became a fundamental pillar of Chilean capitalism.

In relation to work, the constitution provides that 'every person has the right to free employment and free choice of work with a fair retribution'. However, in the light of the Labor Code of 1979, which squeezed the organization of workers and made contracts more flexible, 'free choice' and 'just retribution' became precepts exercised unilaterally by the employer. Therefore, the Chilean constitution establishes equality between unequals. The real power of the worker, which depends on collective organization and the defense of rights, is depleted. Transformed into an individual whose supreme right is the freedom to consume, the worker is pushed to individualize his alternatives of life as well, having notable effects on Chilean sociability, culture and politics.

The Chilean Constitution also maintained the autonomy of the Central Bank; the existence of the Constitutional Court, which has the power to annul laws passed in Parliament or require a supermajority quorum for unanticipated issues; preserved the antipopular labor code; made state enterprises unfeasible by requiring supermajorities. Furthermore, it has removed national sovereignty over mining, forestry and also water resources, which in Chile were privatized; and criminalized abortion, which used to be legal for therapeutic purposes. Finally, the Constitution reinforced political rigidity with figures such as designated senators with lifelong mandates, while at the same time not envisaging a means for popular initiative or plebiscite, solidifying the irreformable character of Chilean neoliberalism (Ramirez 2017: 107).

The limits of the 'protected democracy' designed by Guzmán are evidenced by the privileges of the armed forces, perpetuated to this day. There was no intervention in the education policies modulated by reactionary doctrines; ties with the School of the Americas remained;[5] icons of the dictatorship are glorified – the library of the Military Academy is called Augusto Pinochet Ugarte, while a statue of Admiral José Toribio Merino was inaugurated in Valparaiso under the presidency of Lagos, when Michelle Bachelet was Minister of Defense;[6] there is no internal meritocracy; career privileges were maintained (the military was preserved from having its pensions privatized); and it continued to receive 10 per cent of Codelco's exports. According to the law, the text of which was kept secret until 2016, this amount should be completed by the Union if it is less than 180 million dollars. Emblematic of the military and civil collusion left by the dictatorship, Pinochet remained as head of the armed forces until 1998, when he was named senator for life: 'In the dawn of the tutored democracy, the dictator could walk in broad daylight, before all Chile, knowing himself to be untouchable, and the rest, knowing themselves to be in constant threat' (Alvarado and Roca 2017: 26).

4 Political Economy of the Concertación

4.1 *Concertación in Power*

The elections that followed the victory of the 'no' were won by the Christian Democrat Patricio Aylwin in 1989. A sequence of Concertación governments was inaugurated which, after the victory of Ricardo Lagos in 2000, alternated socialists in the presidency of the Republic.

At first, concessions to the dictatorship's legacy were justified in favor of political stability, sweetened as 'capacity for dialogue' and 'building consensus'. In fact, the military threat was not fantasy. Pinochet's coreligionists threatened

---

5 The School of the Americas was founded in 1946 under the US Defense Department and since the 1960s had as its priority counter-insurgency and anti-communist training. Most cadres of Latin American dictatorships were trained in this institution, which in 2001 was renamed Western Hemisphere Institute for Security Cooperation.
6 Chief architect of the 1973 coup, Toribio Merino defined the communists in the following words in 1986: 'There are two types of human beings: the ones I call human and the other humanoids. The humanoids belong to the Communist Party'. In 1993, he referred to the Bolivians: 'They are metamorphosed Andean camels who have learned to speak, but not to think'.

to leave the barracks at various times and thus stifled the corruption scandal, known as 'Pinochecks', involving the general's son in 1993. In time, however, there was a notable accommodation to inherited structures. The result was that the elected governments ended up legitimizing an order of spurious origin modeled under state terrorism and consolidated through armed blackmail. In particular, the capitulation of socialists, who had once elected Allende as president, narrowed the horizon of left-wing politics. This situation was exacerbated by the fact that the management of neoliberalism was not static, and implied new mechanisms of dispossession, commodification and financialization of rights, corroborating to make of Chile an advanced experiment of 'real neoliberalism'.

At the ideological level, the Concertación endorsed the discourse of international resonance that dissociated state terrorism from Chilean neoliberalism, as opposed to analyses that explain the nexus between them (Klein 2008). According to this ideology, the dictatorship exaggerated the repression, but got the economy right. Concertación then emerged as the ideal alternative, while maintaining the economic determinations of the model but without the terror. Implemented by socialists, who had once upset the world order with a proposal of 'socialism with red wine and empanadas', this arrangement deserved to be applauded, so much so that it was awarded a place in the Organization for Economic Cooperation and Development (OECD). Not even Josef Stalin could pull out a more eloquent retraction.

A number of factors colluded to that dénouement, between the trauma of repression, Eurocommunism and the seduction of power, as well as discussions about the UP experience, summarized in the debate between failure or defeat, which presumes an appreciation of the historical viability of this path.[7] Clearly, the coalition with the DC that flowed into the Concertación reflected that the UP should have been more flexible in relation to other political forces in the past.

Besides these political considerations, there was also a genuine adherence to the Chilean path to neoliberalism, interpreted as a successful modality of insertion in the globalized economy. According to this perspective, it was up to Concertación to cultivate a 'neoliberalism with a human face' which, in its most delirious ideological expressions, was considered as 'part of the (pre) history of Chilean socialism' (Atria 2013: 16).

This conviction was visible from the first moments of the Concertación. The Christian democratic leader under the dictatorship, Andrés Zaldívar, stated

---

7 'Failure' implies the strategic unfeasibility of the attempted path, while 'defeat' supposes tactical miscues.

that Pinochet's 'positive legacy' was 'economic transformation', while an aide to the Aylwin administration's finance minister said that 'the image of economic success of the military government' was 'strongly assumed by business groups', which became a determining factor for the strategic definitions of the new government (Fazio and Parada 2010: 7–8).

Between conviction and accommodation, the Aylwin government set a standard that was followed by later governments: nothing done by the dictatorship was deconstructed, and what was built was based on its foundation. The spirit of the future was summed up in the opening message of the National Congress in April 1990, when the president stated, in relation to the crimes of the dictatorship, that truth and justice would be done 'as far as possible'.

In this context, the privatizations carried out after the 1988 plebiscite were not reviewed, contrary to public promises. On the contrary, they were resumed at the end of his government. During this mandate, foreign investment reached unprecedented levels, surpassing, between 1990 and 1993, the total investment attracted throughout the Pinochet dictatorship. This data indicates that, as in South African apartheid, the dictatorship had become economically dysfunctional because of the political isolation to which it condemned the country. Driven by international capital, private mining exports outpaced those of the state sector for the first time in 1994 (Fazio and Parada 2010: 17).

Concertación transformed political necessity into economic virtue. The accommodation has been transformed into stability, making Chile a valued investment platform in the region. In the words of a former minister, the country would play the role of 'aircraft carriers', because it has 'political stability, natural resources and a highly specialized labor' (Fazio and Parada 2010: 27). This image has always been reinforced by careful marketing of economic success, for domestic and international consumption.

High levels of foreign investment stimulated economic growth while at the same time accelerating the de-industrialization of the country, which has become a service economy. In the midst of this trend, multiple credit and debt options were generated for families. As Tomás Moulian pointed out, the massification of credit was the other side of the flexible labor market. In objective terms, the increase in demand in the 1990s was not driven by wages, but by consumer credit, whose growth was always faster than that of the economy itself. On the subjective level, the massification of the 'citizen credit card' made the abandonment inherent to a commodified existence more tolerable through 'consumption as passion' (Moulian 1997).

However, the sociologist recalls that credit has two faces, as access to pleasure and as a device of domination: 'Credit allows a consummation of the desire to consume on the basis of a posteriori discipline. It is the gateway to the paradise of consumption through the purgatory of indebtedness' (Moulián 1997: 89). Credit and social discipline, consumption and political conformity go hand in hand in the contemporary Chile, where the collective is deprecated by an absolute individual reason. In Moulián's synthesis: 'The wage-worker, not mediated by the union, as the ideal of labor relations and the individual consumer as the ideal of consumer relations' (Moulián 1997: 100)

Viewed from the angle of necessary alienation, the Concertación's political role seems congruent. According to the analysis of a student leader: 'The Concertación project paved a path of distance between society and politics based on stability, in the tension dictatorship-democracy, which not only demobilized, but enabled a political culture disconnected from society' (Rojas 2017: 130).

The research of the anthropologist Julia Paley illuminates the demobilizing force of this project. When studying a health movement on the outskirts of Santiago in 1985, she noticed the strength of the community ties that sustained this popular demand, ignored at that moment by the authorities of the dictatorship. Years later, with the country already under democracy, she observed in the same place a commitment of the state to 'technicalize' social issues and to discredit popular protagonism, whose community base had weakened significantly. In this context, the government received the leadership but claimed to have no resources. And when the movements decided to take to the streets, they were labeled as traitors by officials (Paley 2001).

In spite of differences between governments, the fundamental determinations of Concertación's political economy remained intact when, in 2000, the socialist Ricardo Lagos succeeded the Christian Democrat Eduardo Frei Ruiz-Tagle, son of the former president. In fact, this administration deepened some important aspects of the prevaling historical trend.

The expectation that a socialist president would approach MERCOSUR, or governments identified with the left elected during the mandate of Lagos (2000–2006), was frustrated. The opposite happened because it was under the leadership of Lagos that Chile signed bilateral free trade agreements with the US and with the EU. This course of action was continued in 2006 by his successor, Michelle Bachelet, also a socialist. Currently, Chile is one of the countries with the largest number of free trade agreements in the world – more than 60 (conversation with Silva Flores 2017). Underlying this lack of interest in regional integration is the notion that Chile is in another stage of its economic evolution and, therefore, would have different objectives from the other countries of the region (conversation with Lara).

Lagos also promoted a constitutional reform, which removed aspects of what would be called 'authoritarian rubble' in Brazil, such as the figure of the senator for life. Other elements, such as the binomial system, in force until 2015, were not touched. Throughout this process, the president was widely criticized for endorsing the constitution inherited from the dictatorship, an act interpreted as legitimizing it.

Other controversial attitudes of the socialist president included his personal decision to keep the Torture Report secret for 50 years, the use of an antiterrorist law (another legacy of the dictatorship) to confront Mapuche protests and the intense commitment of his government to prevent Pinochet from being tried in Europe, where he had been detained since 1998, under the controversial argument that he should be tried by the Chilean justice system (Muñoz 2008). On the social front, the Lagos government accelerated the financialization of higher education by creating state-guaranteed credit (CAE), which will be analyzed below. The subsequent statement by President Sebastián Piñera (2010–2014, re-elected in 2017) that 'education is a consumer good' owes much of its materiality to the socialist mandate, which was remarkably popular among entrepreneurs.

His successor Michelle Bachelet sanctioned a fiscal responsibility law in the first months of her term, indicating that she did not intend to make any change from the previous government. In fact, when the businessman Sebastián Piñera broke the hegemony of Concertación in the following elections, senators and deputies of this group came together to 'ensure that [Piñera] does not distance itself from the path of fiscal responsibility'. When they felt that this happened in 2012, a public letter circulated 'making a call to the government of Sebastián Piñera to maintain fiscal responsibility as a patrimony of Chile that we must safeguard'.[8]

Despite the nuances that can be pointed out, the political economy of the Concertación governments did not change substantially under the presidency of Piñera, when the 'right', in the socialist saying, assumed the presidency. The main references of this regime are institutionalized neoliberalism, the constitution of the dictatorship, the commodification of social rights, the Labor Code, the service economy, the subsidiary state, the financialization of society, the citizen credit card, indebtedness, the sophistication of patterns of consumption, inequality, free trade agreements, betting on the comparative advantages in primary exports, repression of dissent and the Mapuche, and political duopoly. With the exception of this last element, which is in crisis at the present time, and of the repression of the native peoples, a legacy of the past, all originated in the dictatorship. In Chile, the connection between

---

8 The document is available at: <http://www.elmostrador.cl/media/2012/11/Preocupaci%C3% B3n-de-la-Oposici%C3%B3n-por-la-Responsbilidad-fiscal.pdf>.

dictatorship and neoliberalism is a direct one, while continuities between dictatorship and democracy have been mediated by Concertación.

4.2 Macroeconomics

It is possible to argue that Chile's political economy has been successful. Macroeconomic data often corroborates this reading. Between the end of the dictatorship in 1990 and 2007, Chile grew by an average of 5.5 per cent, resulting in a 96 per cent increase in per capita income (Sunkel and Infante 2009: 136). In the following years there was a slowdown, but the country nevertheless grew by an average of 3.2 per cent between 1998 and 2009. Between 1990 and 2009, public debt at 45 per cent of GDP declined to 7 per cent. The per capita GDP of the country surpassed Argentina and is only lower than Uruguay, while the United Nations Development Program (UNDP) attributes to Chile the highest Human Development Index (IDH) in South America (PNUD 2015).

A critical view points to a little diversified or sophisticated production base, subject to financial and productive cycles whose dynamics can not be controlled. The country remains dependent on primary exports, particularly copper. The weight of exports of this ore in the GDP doubled in the first decade of the twenty-first century, when mining accounted for between 50 per cent and 60 per cent of the total exported. It is a percentage lower than the UP years, when it reached 80 per cent but, on the other hand, the mining sector is now dominated by international capital. It is estimated that between 1974 and 2004 there were foreign investments of 19 billion dollars in mining, 87.5 per cent of them under Concertación governments. In 2006 alone, mining companies' profits reached 20 billion dollars (Galarce Villavicencio 2012: 193). For comparison purposes, exports of copper and by-products amounted to 70 per cent of Venezuelan oil revenues at the end of that decade, but Chile's population is lower: 17 million against 29 million in the Caribbean country (Galarce Villavicencio 2012). In parallel, pressure for the intensification of exploitation has provoked social-environmental conflicts, some of them led by the Mapuche.

Other Chilean exports include timber, fruits (grapes, apples, pears, dried fruits), wines and fish. Thus, although statistics indicate that the country exports 4,800 items to 90 countries, exports are poorly diversified and of items that incorporate low added value. China consumes about 28 per cent of the country's exports and the US, half (conversation with Silva Flores 2017).

The country suffered less than other primary exporters in the region from the effects of the 2008 crisis. The price of copper plummeted in that year, but rose again from 2009 onwards. In general, the price of this commodity is less volatile than that of others, such as oil. The civil construction boom, fueled by the 2010 earthquake and low oil prices, helped to mitigate the impact of the international crisis (conversation with Lara 2017).

However, in more recent years critical signs have reappeared. The economy has been stagnant since 2014, in a country where the financial system moves a volume three-and-a-half to four times greater than productive capital. There is a drop in productive investment, as well as an increase in corporate and individual indebtedness. There is evidence of deterioration in foreign trade: in 2016, exports contracted by 4.8 per cent and imports by 5.9 per cent. Copper faces Peruvian competition and rising costs of deep exploration over 1,000 meters underground (conversation with Lara 2017). In addition, the ecosystem that underpins primary competitiveness has deteriorated in recent years. In particular, the salmon industry was greatly affected by problems of this nature (Bengoa 2009).

Yet the axis around which the massive mobilizations in recent Chile gravitate is not economic. The social relations on which this macroeconomy is based have been questioned: it is a reaction to real neoliberalism. It is possible that this cleavage between economic dynamics and the social process expresses a deeper cleavage, described by Enzo Faletto as a 'dual segmentation of the economy and society' (Faletto 2007: 57). From this perspective, malaise comes from the realization that 'the economic model was enormously efficient in producing an increase of capital and investment in Chile but did not build society' (Mayol 2012: 172).

In order to understand the nature of the social problems of contemporary Chile, we will now examine the situation of education, particularly higher education, labor relations and the issue of social security. The commodification of life has reached other social dimensions, such as health, in which even the public sector involves the payment of fees for use; affordable housing, which the dictatorship turned into a business for contractors mediated by popular credit, inspiration for the Brazilian program Minha Casa Minha Vida; and culture, which has no ministry and works through projects and ubiquitous competition. However, the themes selected cover the life span of a Chilean worker, between education, work and retirement, allowing a transversal reading that will inform an appreciation of current dilemmas, beyond macroeconomics.

4.3   *Education*

In contemporary Chile public education is at risk of extinction, for even state education works under the logic of private business. The pattern of social reproduction in which the family produces, the state educates, and capital contracts no longer operates in Chile, where the student is educated and disciplined under the logic of capital.

In basic education, the voucher policy implemented by the dictatorship in the 1980s prevails and is said to have been taken from a chapter in Milton Friedman's *Capitalism and Freedom* (conversation with Orellana 2017). In this system, school management was municipalized, and public and private schools receive a financial subsidy per student from the state. The idea is that competition for funding between schools will reward the most competent, attract more students and, as a consequence, receive more money. The proposal is consistent with the spirit of the Chilean constitution, transforming education from a civil right into an individual responsibility.

In practice, the system generated distortions that were aggravated after 1993, when the Concertación government released a new form of financing to supplement meager state funds – the co-payment. The premise that schools which received complementary contributions should stop receiving state subsidies was modified, at the benefit of the private sector. From then on, more than 800 municipal schools were closed, while the number of private ones doubled, currently covering about 68 per cent of demand (Salazar 2014).

The state grant system that paid per student had two main consequences. On the one hand, it condemned the schools to an uncertain existence, since the directorates administered fixed costs with variable resources. The main challenge of school management became survival. To adapt to this dynamic, teachers' working conditions become more precarious. On the other hand, there has been a profound segregation of the Chilean school system. Free schools are frequented by the poorest, while subsidized private ones discriminate by location and price. It is a business with massive low-cost operators, but also high-cost exclusive operators: about 7 per cent of enrollments are in private colleges that do not receive state subsidies and are the most expensive (conversation with Orellana 2017).[9]

While medium-sized companies predominate in basic education, charging modest tuitions and receiving state subsidies, higher education is a business dominated by four business groups that cover more than half the demand. The turning point for private university expansion was the creation of the CAE (state-guaranteed credit) in the Lagos government. This policy succeeded in its stated purpose, which was to expand university coverage, with the number of enrolments in higher education almost doubling between 2005 and 2016 (663,679 to 1,247,135 students). However, 70 per cent of this increase was concentrated in 20 institutions linked to four major groups: Laureate International,

---

9   The last Bachelet government enacted a law in November 2017 that creates a new system of public education, which will gradually take public schools from municipal administration to a new institution of public education with the aim of increasing access to free education.

Santo Tomas, Universidad Tecnológica de Chile (Inacap) and Pontificia Universidad Católica. These institutions concentrate 67.1 per cent of the students that access the CAE and 67.7 per cent of the resources received by the entire Chilean higher education system in this way (Kremerman and Páez 2016). In this same period, enrollment in state-owned establishments only increased by 20,634 students and their total participation in the system dropped to 15.4 per cent. Receiving minimal budget allocation, forced to collect tuition, consulting and courses, the Chilean public university has become an appendage of the higher education system.

From an economic point of view, the CAE proved to be a big deal. The original argument for its implementation was that the state had budget constraints and needed the help of banks to finance the popularization of higher education. However, the banks did not agree to the proposal until the state pledged to subsidize them, buying 25 per cent of the contracted loans each year with a 6 per cent surcharge. In fact, since then the state has bought 48 per cent of the credits with a surcharge of 28 per cent (Kremerman and Páez 2016). In this operation, the student continues with the debt, but the bank receives its payment, and the university guarantees its business.

In a short time, the paradox of the program was evident. By 2009 the state had spent more on debts related to higher education than would be required to grant full scholarships to students receiving credit: 'The design had gone from inefficient to absurd' (Mayol 2012: 129). If at the beginning, in 2006, the CAE accounted for 2.4 per cent of the higher education budget, ten years later it reached 36.5 per cent.

Among OECD countries, Chilean students spend more on education in proportion to the state's investment: about 80 per cent of the expenditure falls on families, whereas the average in the OECD countries is 30 per cent (Brunner 2008). The country has the most expensive university education in the world, according to the ranking of this same organization. As a consequence, in March 2010 there were around 270,000 indebted youths, a number that in 2016 surpassed 730,000, while default within the system reached 38.7 per cent (Kremerman and Páez 2016).

From a qualitative point of view, the system is weak: there is no incentive to quality, no one fails and no knowledge is produced. The main mechanism of qualitative supervision (so-called 'accreditation') is also subordinated to the mercantile imperative, since it has become an essential requirement for accessing state-guaranteed financing. Promiscuous relationships prevail between companies and the technocracy that should oversee them, both in this and other businesses in the country (González and Guzmán 2012).

In spite of the extravagance of the system, it is possible to see that it was sustained because it produced an illusion of social integration. Many children of parents without a college education believed that they rose in life. But when they entered the labor market, they were confronted with a reality that hardly solved the debts and dreams they planted in college.

4.4 Labor Relations, Poverty and Debt

Those who work with macroeconomic data to highlight Chilean performance rarely analyze numbers associated with the living conditions of those who produce wealth. We present below some data related to working conditions, the situation of poverty and the indebtedness of Chilean workers.

In November 2016, the poverty line for an average household of four people in Chile was estimated at 410,000 Chilean pesos. However, half of the workers earned less than 350,000 pesos net, which means that they could not take their family out of poverty. Seven out of ten workers earn less than 500,000 pesos, and only 14.7 per cent receive more than 800,000 pesos net. Among women, 84.5 per cent of those with paid work earn less than 650,000 pesos net (Durán and Kremerman 2017a).

With the minimum wage set at 270,000 pesos in 2017, the Chilean usually has two jobs or an alternative source of income; 79.6 per cent of full-time employees have an income of less than 500,000 pesos, an eloquent indication of the precariousness of wage labor. By comparison, Croatia, which had a GDP per capita lower than Chile in 2013, had an average salary almost 45 per cent higher, while the average salary in Poland adjusted by purchasing power parity was 47.3 per cent higher even with a GDP per capita similar to Chile (Durán and Kremerman 2015).

The growth of salaried work in recent times is marked by less stability and high turnover: three out of four workers are subjected to flexible relationships (outsourcing, partial contract or contract work) and six out of ten jobs created in the last five years are outsourced. Public service work is also precarious, where many have temporary contracts and must issue a receipt in order to receive their pay, as if they were a small enterprise. In an estimated workforce of 8 million people, there are 1 million outsourced workers, 1 million employees without a work contract, 700,000 underemployed and 620,000 unemployed (conversation with Kremerman 2017).

At the end of 2016, 53.3 per cent of the employees were covered by the Labor Code, and 5.9 per cent by the Public Sector Administrative Statute. This means that 40.6 per cent of employed persons are not associated with any labor legislation and therefore have no possibility of legal protections or exercising collective labor rights, such as unionizing or striking (Brega et al. 2017).

The rate of unionization before the dictatorship reached 34 per cent, but currently is around 11 per cent. In general, the trade union movement has lost its ability to influence politics. In addition to the structural reasons pointed out, the lack of independence of the Central Unitaria de Trabajadores (CUT) in relation to Concertación and the accusations of fraud, together with the refusal to incorporate informal workers for fear of altering internal power relations, contributed to their discrediting (Aravena 2016).

The weakening of workers' organizations, labor precariousness and poverty coexist in Chile with increasing inequality, despite statistical efforts to disguise it: 'We hide inequality with measures that are not sensitive to it' (Mayol 2012: 82). The difference in autonomous incomes (salary plus other income) between the richest 5 per cent and the poorest 5 per cent of the population increased from 129 to 285 times between 1990 and 2013. The per capita autonomous income for the richest 0.01 per cent population is 459,446,908 pesos per month, while 50 per cent of Chileans receive, on average, 138,000 pesos. The richest thousandth of Chilean society (17,800 people) earns more than its poorest half (Fundación Sol 2014).

One of the ways to alleviate poverty in Chile is via conditional cash transfer programs. The state provides various forms of targeted assistance, in the form of family allowances (similar to Brazil's Bolsa Família), subsidies for school retention, and pensions for the poorest, as well as subsidies for water consumption. The calculation of poverty carried out in the country includes these cash transfers and the imputed rent,[10] which conceals the low level of wages. According to Sol Foundation calculations, when these two elements are disregarded, poverty in Chile reaches 26.9 per cent, not 11.7 per cent (Durán and Kremerman 2017b). In the case of people over 60 years of age, many of whom receive the basic solidarity pension and do not pay rent, this figure is five times larger. It should be added that research shows a high mobility between the situations of poverty and misery, indicating the precariousness of living conditions (Ruiz and Boccardo 2015: 70).

This precariousness is exacerbated by family indebtedness. It is estimated that 80 per cent of adults are in debt. Even more worrisome, data released in March 2017 indicates that more than 4.3 million Chileans have defaulted. This means that more than half the workers, or one in three over the age of 18, have a debt that they can not pay. Among the defaulters, 76.1 per cent have a monthly income of less than 500,000 pesos, while 21.2 per cent have an income of less than 225,000 pesos. Data reveals that 41 per cent of debts are due to retail purchases, an indication of cultural pressure for consumption (XVI Debt Settlement Debt First Quarter 2017). In 2014, 38 per cent of an average Chilean

---

10   Rent that would be paid by those who live on their own or ceded property is considered as income.

household's budget was allocated to paying monthly financial charges (Kremerman and Páez 2016).

Unfortunately, the drama associated with job insecurity is not alleviated by Chile's retirement system.

4.5   Pension Fund Administrators

The Chilean social security system was privatized in the early 1980s. Contributions remained compulsory, creating a kind of non-state tax of 10 per cent on wages, while employers were exempted from contributing. This compulsory savings began to be managed as a financial investment by Pension Fund Administrators (AFP). For pensioners, this means that retirement has turned into a financial product, in which they are forced to invest. For capital, these compulsory savings became a source of investment for the large economic groups to capitalize on, boosting the country's capital market. According to a representative of the No More AFP movement, this was the main objective of the reform, implemented in the context of the crisis that led to the dictatorship's intervention in Chilean banks (conversation with Guzmán 2017).

From this point of view, the change was a success. According to the second report of the Superintendence of Pensions, these administrators managed, in 2016, 112,673,743 trillion pesos (about 172 billion dollars), which is equivalent to 70 per cent of the Chilean GDP, a figure that would be higher were it not for the crisis (Superintendence of Pensions 2016). This is far in excess of the country's main fortunes, which also benefit from AFP investments: Luksic ($10.1 billion), Paulmann ($3.7 billion), Piñera ($2.5 billion) and Matte ($2.3 billion). For example, the first of these groups received investments of $ 3.4 billion in 2016. The political strength of the funds corresponds to their economic power. Since the dictatorship, the revolving doors between the government and the AFP have been notorious. At least twelve Pinochet ministers became directors of these funds, a practice that did not change under the Concertación (Matamala 2017).

AFPs have become the dynamic engine of the Chilean capital market since its creation, investing in financial and productive assets in the country and abroad. Originally there were 21 funds, but by 2017 the market concentrated in six carriers. In addition to the compulsory contribution, employees pay a monthly fee of around 1.9 per cent, which may vary according to the risk profile among five available modalities. In short, the Chilean worker is required by law to hand over part of her salary to six companies to speculate in the financial market. In Chile, the worker supports the capital market.

If the model is successful for the capital market, the same cannot be said from the point of view of taxpayer retirement. Subordinated to a financial dynamic that it does not control, the worker is sure of how much he pays, but not how much he will receive.

In practice, pensions are poor, relative to earned income. In 2016 the national average for a pension was 207,409 pesos per month, less than the minimum wage of 270,000 pesos. The state supplements pensions below 150,000 pesos, contributing 80,000 pesos monthly. The precariousness and instability of work generate long periods without contribution, which affect pensions. Women are the most disadvantaged because, apart from maternity leave, they are by culture more concerned with the care of children and the elderly. In Chile today, women accumulate less, live longer and retire earlier, receiving between 30 per cent and 40 per cent less than men in the same condition (conversation with Guzmán 2017).

There are no signs that the situation will improve. In 2013, a Central Bank adviser acknowledged that almost 60 per cent of Chileans will retire in the future with pensions of 150,000 pesos. In this context, there are pressures to raise the percentage of the contribution to 15 per cent and re-establish an employer contribution. Corporate profits rose 9.6 per cent between 2015 and 2016, though the average returns for pensions during the period was 3.34 per cent (Vasconcelos 2017).

If budget pressure were a central argument for privatizing the Chilean social security system, it must be noted that this option was costly for the state, and still is. The state continues to cover those still in the old system; pays solidarity pensions for the poorest 60 per cent; funds the provisional solidarity contribution that complements pensions below the minimum wage; and pays the recognition bonus offered as an incentive to those who changed to the new system.[11] Finally, it supports the retirement of those who have not been affected by the reform, such as *carabineros* and armed forces. Doing the numbers, the state has the social burden of the system, paying 70 per cent of the pension expenses, while the AFP keeps the revenue (conversation with Guzmán 2017).

The perverse effects of the AFP system are evident as more Chileans retire according to its rules. Guzmán describes the situation of twin teachers, where the one who retired in the old system receives eight times more than the sister who joined the AFP. One consequence of this reality is that people cannot stop working when they retire.

In summary, in Chile today, education brings debt, debt disciplines work, and work does not resolve past debt, nor future retirement. The Chilean lives under real neoliberalism as an eternal present.

---

11   There were state incentives ('recognition bonus') and private pressures (threat of dismissal), constraining adherence to the new model.

5 Crisis

The situation of education, working conditions, levels of poverty and indebtedness, besides the drama of retirement, are among the elements in the daily life of Chileans that corrode the image of a successful country. A critical turning point was the massive student mobilizations of 2011. Since then, the perception has spread that the society founded by the Chilean dictatorship and honed by Concertación is in crisis.

The main expression of this crisis is not economic: in 2011, the Chilean economy grew by 6 per cent and there was job creation. It is plausible that the maturation of innovations associated with this societal pattern – such as university credit, instability and labor precariousness, poor retirement conditions, the permanent fear of an expensive disease that will ruin the family, among others – has created a growing malaise. There is a gap between the Chile that is sold and the Chile that is lived, while 'the individualist foundation that linked economic growth with high expectations seems to have been fractured' (Mayol 2012: 181). In this context, collective struggles have resurfaced on the political horizon as a desirable and necessary alternative.

Initially, students from public and private universities took to the streets for issues related mainly to passes for school transport, but also to funding and scholarships. Then, the manifestations of 2011 became an uprising against the current educational model and, therefore, against the inheritance of the dictatorship and the subsidiary state (Amtmann 2017: 41). High school students, pioneers in shaking up the country in the 'penguin revolt' of 2006, added to these protests. A wave of school occupations was unleashed that would inspire Brazilian high school students in following years. The scope of their demands expanded rapidly, as well as the social adhesion to the movement, which was supported by indebted parents. What began as a student movement soon led to a social movement.

The movement had an ambiguous outcome from the point of view of its immediate objectives. The Piñera government did not approve any substancial gratuity, but the idea was incorporated into the program of Michelle Bachelet, elected in 2013. Predictably, the socialist government did not have the determination, nor did it accumulate the strength to carry out this reform as demanded – that is, as a universal right.

On the other hand, the massive mobilizations that lasted for almost a year had two important political effects: they broke with the culture of fear that had prevailed since the coup and they put neoliberalism under debate. It does not seem unconnected that the protagonists have been young people who were born after the dictatorship, within real neoliberalism.

In its most immediate political expression, the student revolt opened holes in the duopoly. Four young people from the student movement were elected deputies, none of them a candidate for the Concertación or for the right. In recent years, several organizations that emerged from or were strengthened by the mobilizations have converged into a *Frente Amplio* (Ample Front), which disputed the presidential elections of 2017 with its own candidate. The deep disrepute of conventional politics is reinforced by frustrations stemming from another socialist government by Michelle Bachelet and by successive corruption scandals reaching even the president's son, that discredit all professional politics, as well as increasing protests against various dimensions of real neoliberalism.

Beyond this crisis of representation, there is a progressive crisis of legitimacy. For many, the question is not whether the model works or not, but to the benefit of whom it works. The model's operating conditions are increasingly being questioned and considered illegitimate. In other words, the ability to build active consensus around real neoliberalism is declining.

On the other hand, there is a growing willingness to organize: it is estimated that the No More AFP movement took about 2 million people to the streets in their 2016 manifestations. The perception that depoliticization allows the model to function, that this depoliticization was the product of repression and it is this trauma that the current Chile rests upon, has motivated many Chileans to face the past and the present, recovering in the process the expectation of a different future.

6   Final Thoughts

Chile is one of the South American countries in which an important labor movement was constituted in the late nineteenth century as well as having a significant communist tradition since the beginning of the twentieth. With the founding of the Socialist Party in the 1930s, the political left was enriched, substantially influencing the country's politics. This protagonism fueled the illusion of Chilean singularity in the Latin American context, which would be associated with the stability of institutions and the strength of democracy. The participation of leftist forces in Popular Front governments in those years; the regularity of electoral succession in contrast with the political instability that typified neighboring countries – together with the discrete political profile of military in the period were among the elements upon which this perception was based.

At first, the election of the socialist Salvador Allende to the presidency seemed to confirm this idea. In Chile and abroad, the possibility of a 'Chilean way' to socialism that would modify the structures of underdevelopment without the use of weapons, aroused enthusiasm and sympathy. However, the sharpening of social contradictions led the Popular Unity experience to a tragic outcome.

Although a US-backed military coup was not exceptional in Latin America during the Cold War, nor in the Third World, the societal project unleashed by the dictatorship was. State terrorism cleared the ground for the pioneering implementation of neoliberal policies in all spheres of existence. In several cases, these formulations had an experimental character. If in the early 1970s the originality of the Chilean road to socialism captivated international attention, the dictatorship aroused interest as a kind of advanced laboratory of neoliberal policies.

In the early 1980s, the dictatorship faced a serious economic crisis that forced it to revise its radical liberalization, without losing its reference to the neoliberal paradigm. Other policies were created or improved, particularly the private pension plan that capitalized the capital market. Despite the resurgence of popular protest, the combination of repression and economic growth in the following years permitted the continuation of the regime, eventually defeated in a plebiscite at the end of the Cold War. Nevertheless, the conciliatory strategy of those who would form the Concertación implied accepting the constitution of the dictatorship complicated by the binomial system, a Trojan horse that tied the transition to the past.

Over time, impotence has become accommodation, concessions became self-interest, and ideology, an article of faith. Concertación's political economy perfected and deepened the neoliberal utopia modeled by the dictatorship, even when the socialists reached the presidency. This utopia has an economic and a societal dimension.

On the one hand, it is an open economy that believes in the comparative advantages of a specialized international role based on primary exports. By abdicating control over the national economic space, the country bets that it will remain a privileged destination for international business. This attractiveness refers to its liberality (in relation to capital flows, business and labor regulation) and modernity – a sophistication based on the concentration of income. But its main foundation is stability, secured by a socialist party that could not be more neoliberal. As long as the distinction between 'socialists' and 'right' prevails in the Chilean vocabulary – as if socialists were not part of the right – business will sleep peacefully.

At the corporate level, this utopia implies social relations mediated by the market and regulated by the law of supply and demand. The citizen exercises control over the quality and price of social services (education, health, social security) through the choices he makes as a consumer: the best providers with competitive prices impose themselves, while the less efficient ones break down. Consumer-mediated citizenship demanded financialization in a society where credit became a condition of citizenship: Moulian's 'citizen credit card'.

However, as often happens in capitalism, Chilean real neoliberalism did not foster competition, but monopoly. Social rights converted into business became privileged accumulation niches for economic groups whose profitability is guaranteed by the state, as analysis of student credit and AFP explicitly show. Those who are most marginalized because the country is unequal are supported by state subsidies. The transmutation of social rights into commodities is secured by the state at its two poles: to ensure the profitability of business and to mitigate the country's degradation.

It is possible to argue that this model has been successful. There is data indicating that since the 1980s Chile has had the best macroeconomic performance in the region, where it has been the most stable economy, in addition to achieving an important, though questionable, poverty reduction. On the other hand, inequality has grown, and daily life has become more expensive, precarious, selfish and insecure. The commodification of social relations reached the paroxysm, reflected in all spheres of existence: the anguish to stock up on food or fuel the car after the earthquake of 2010; the Communist Party that rents its rooms for militant activities; the passer-by who demands to pay for the cigarette he asked for; the beggar who dies without an identity card, but with loyalty cards from Falabella stores.

There is a diffuse but profound malaise in contemporary Chile, which is embodied in protests against education and social security, among others. Conventional political parties face an acute lack of prestige, aggravated by corruption scandals. In this scenario, the gaps opened since the protests of 2011 have widened the political landscape. For politics to go beyond neoliberalism will require instruments and practices different from the duopoly. The Frente Amplio appears as an alternative to the 'two rights' (conversation with Mundaca 2017), although embryonic and heterogeneous. Mobilization for a Constituent Assembly is another sign in this direction (Forum by the Constituent Assembly and Grez 2016).

However, given the depth and interconnection of the structures of Chilean neoliberalism, it will take more than an 'instant of legality' to disarm it.[12] As

---

12   Expression used by historian Sergio Grez when remembering that Chile never had a democratically produced Constitution in its history.

one teacher put it, reforming education in Chile today is like doing agrarian reform in the 1970s. The various dimensions of real neoliberalism are tied as a whole and will hardly be disarmed one by one. Looking at the situation in its totality, the conflict that arises is at the same time elementary and radical: it is the struggle to regain sovereignty over the processes of society and everyday life itself, expropriated from the worker in deeper and more absolute dimensions than the extraction of surplus value from work (Ruiz 2017: 137). In Chile, the confrontation between commodity and humanity, which is another way of naming the capital and labor contradiction, is exposed.

From this perspective, the radicalism of real neoliberalism poses both challenges and a unique political potential. Challenges because politicization is more difficult in a society in which the commodification of social rights has become naturalized. Moreover, Chile does not currently have the working world as the organizing ground for social struggles; instead, the victims of neoliberalism – indebted students and workers – are at the forefront against an order supported by the state. From this perspective, the Chilean experience finds few references or parallels. There is awareness that this is an experience of advanced and peripheral neoliberalism, which defies comparisons (conversation with Romero 2017).

This uniqueness is part of the challenge, but also its potential. It is easy to see that social struggles in the country need to be reinvented. This represents a challenge, because the starting point was lowered by decades of repression that attempted to dumb-down Chilean society. On the other hand, greater creative freedom is being tried out. Similarly, built-up apathy confronts the perception that it will not be possible to change parts of the problem without confronting the whole – which leads to radicalization, as daily life seems increasingly distressful.

Caught between the trauma of the past and the anguish of the present, the uncertainty of the future again hovers over the avenues, where one day, it is expected, free men will walk to build a better society.

CHAPTER 9

Perversion and Trauma: Impasses of Contemporary Peruvian Politics

> Water yes, gold no!
> *Ollanta Humala during election campaign, 2011.*

> ...I believe, as Head of State, that we can have both things, water and gold, not water or gold; water or gold is an extremist, antihistorical and antinational position.
> *Ollanta Humala in the presidency, 2012.*

1   Introduction

In the 1980s, the Peruvian left was considered to be one of the most powerful on the continent, and its future seemed promising. However, since then the right has regained the political initiative, a situation that still subsists. Three elements are fundamental to an understanding of this: the trajectory of the left; the ambiguities of the Alan García government from 1985 to 1990 which in turn are related to the history of the American Popular Revolutionary Alliance (APRA); and the specificity of Senderoism.

Although I am unable to explore the idea further in this chapter, I believe that the last two phenomena allow an analogy with the psychoanalytic notion of perversion.[1] The relationship of Alanism to the APRA[2] and the relationship

---

1 In general terms, psychoanalysis identifies three ways out of the Oedipus complex, conforming three patterns of the place of the subject in culture. The neurotic is subordinated to the rules of the culture to which it belongs, accepting them in conflict. It is the condition of 'normality'. The psychotic avoids social interdiction, forging a world of its own rules. The perverse instrumentalizes the prevalent rules according to their own interests. Senderoism, Alanism and Fujimorism are perversions in the sense that they take as reference a socially established norm in order to instrumentalize it in the opposite direction, configuring a deviation that results in a self-referenced normativity instrumentalized according to particular interests far from its original purpose.
2 Although the term 'Alanismo' is not common to designate the first APRA government, referring regularly to the segment of the party led by Alan García, presidential candidate in 2016, I use the term in the sense suggested by Aníbal Quijano, referring to the process of political degeneration of APRA synthesized by the trajectory of its main leader after Haya de la Torre.

of the Sendero Luminoso (Shining Path) to the guerrilla tradition are of this nature, as also is Fujimori's relationship to democracy, in a country where the Velasco military regime from 1968 to 1975 was not associated with repression. Taking a step further into psychoanalytic analogy, the conjunction between economic disorganization and Senderoist violence that marked the end of the García administration generated both the objective and subjective conditions for a radical political response at a time when the left was in disarray. To paraphrase Trotsky, Fujimorism, a traumatic response to a traumatic situation, established the foundations of present-day Peru.[3] In contrast to other countries in the region, the neoliberal clash in Peru was associated with a regime that pacified and, in the eyes of some, saved the country – which poses additional difficulties in confronting it. I shall analyze the historical roots of this singularity as part of the effort to understand trauma, and as a premise for overcoming it.

2   New Left and United Left

The roots of the so-called 'new Peruvian left' go back to the period between 1959 and 1965, when two short guerrilla experiences originated in two parties then identified with the left, the Popular American Revolutionary Alliance (APRA) and the Peruvian Communist Party (PCP). Shortly afterwards, the Revolutionary Vanguard came into being, an organization joined by former militants of Popular Action,[4] Trotskyists and independent Marxists. In the following decade, the guerrilla appeal gave way to connections with a growing peasant movement, consolidating what Carlos Malpica termed a 'national, *mariateguista* and *chola*' left.[5] A new socialist tradition within the Marxist left, not identified with the APRA or the PCP, was founded.

The other side of this left-wing radicalization in the 1960s was the accommodation to the establishment of the main opposition party, APRA. Founded in 1924 in Mexico City by the student leader Víctor Raúl Haya de la Torre, the APRA quickly left its original continental aspirations to become the largest

---

3   'Trauma is an event which, by its violence and suddenness, provokes an influx of excitement sufficient to call into question the usually effective defense mechanisms, often producing a state of sideration and leading, in a more or less long term, to a disorganization of the psychic economy' (Mijolla 2005: 1858).
4   President Fernando Belaúnde Terry, deposed by Velasco Alvarado in 1968, belonged to this party.
5   José Carlos Mariátegui (1894–1930) was the founder of the Peruvian Socialist Party and a key reference in Peruvian and Latin American Marxism.

Peruvian political organization of the twentieth century. The all-embracing character of the APRA organization has turned it into a kind of religious fraternity around which national politics revolved in the last century. Deployed mainly in areas of greater penetration of capitalist relations (such as the north coast of the country), the party's capacity for integration challenged the fragmented and impotent Peruvian bourgeoisie. However, the party's efforts to run the country faced systematic military hostility, going back to its insurrectional past. Politically, APRA evolved from a subversive organization with revolutionary rhetoric into a conventional party, deserving the sympathy of the US in the radicalized context of the 1960s.

Paradoxically, APRA's original nationalist program was implemented by military personnel who, while repressing the guerrillas in the 1960s, were touched by the gap that divided the country, relegating the indigenous majority to misery. They decided to act. The coup that brought General Velasco Alvarado to power in October 1968 should be understood in the light of a historical impasse between the weakness of the Peruvian bourgeoisie and the limited ability of APRA to channel popular energies towards change, in a moment of radicalization at the national level (occupations of land, guerrillas and urban movements) and international level (between the Cuban Revolution and May 1968). Under the Tupamara slogan 'Peasants: the boss will no longer eat from your poverty',[6] the Revolutionary Government of the Armed Forces (GRFA) set out to 'unlock' the country's economy, implementing a series of measures inspired by the Economic Commission for Latin America (ECLA) and guided by a political landscape that was neither communist nor capitalist (Quijano 1971; Cotler 1978). In order to prevent revolution, the GRFA formed a unique military regime, the antithesis of the state terrorism of other contemporary dictatorships. After initial success, the Velasquist government succumbed amid contradictory relations with social movements, which it intended to control, as well as the economic difficulties and health problems of its leader, who left the presidency in 1975.

The new left that did not identify itself either with the APRA or with the PCP was constructed politically and ideologically in opposition to the government of Velasco Alvarado. This implies another paradox, since the transformations driven by this regime had created the objective conditions for the advancement of the left on different fronts: in the countryside, where agrarian reform liberated peasants who had been subjected to servile relations; among the Indians, whose Quechua language was recognized by the state (they had been

---

6 Tupac Amaru led a major colonial rebellion in 1780 and since then has been identified with the spectre of indigenous revolt, like Tupac Katari in Bolivia.

prohibited even from walking on the pavements of many cities);[7] among the workers in general, since more unions were recognized during the seven years under Velasco than in the entire previous republican period; among public servants, a sector that expanded concomitantly with the state, and came to manage 50 per cent of the country's GDP; in the peripheries, where modalities of urban organization such as the Urban Self-Directing Cooperatives of Villa El Salvador were stimulated (albeit under a tutelary approach). In sum, in spite of the short time that the Velasquez reforms had to take effect and the democratic limits of a government that sought to monopolize power 'it can be said that in large part, the constitution, expansion and importance of the New Left can be explained by Velasquism, which creates processes and strengthens actors that would give solidity to the Peruvian left' (Gonsales 2011: 27).

The fact that it remained autonomous in relation to Velasco qualified this left to resist, with relative success, the anti-popular offensive of the GRFA, led by Morales Bermúdez, in the 'second phase' from 1975 to 1980. The vigor of the general strike of July 1977 persuaded the regime to negotiate a departure, mediated by conventional parties, to stem the rise of the masses, instead of implementing a repressive dictatorship inspired by the neighbors of the Southern Cone. It is at this time that the military and APRA reconciled in a conservative consensus, convening a constituent assembly the following year, presided over by this party (Diez Canseco 2011: 120).

Initially, the left was divided about conduct in the transition. After all, it disputed the constituent election in which – combined with different parties – it snatched a third of the votes. Only two associations did not join the legal process: PCP Patria Roja (PR), which participated in the next elections, and PCP Sendero Luminoso (SL), which declared war on the state shortly thereafter. Ambiguities permeated the process and some constituents such as Hugo Blanco, probably the Trotskyist who has received the most votes on the continent, did not sign the final document. On the whole, however, the prevailing view was that it was a priority to ensure that the military fell from power, which was only possible through a negotiated transition.

The constituent assembly was succeeded in 1980 by a presidential election that sharpened the dilemma of how a revolutionary left, for whom electoral participation predominantly meant giving in politically, would relate to the

---

7   On the other hand, the GRFA banned the use of the word 'Indian', a pejorative and invariably adjectival term in Peruvian society, such as 'dizzy Indian' or 'ignorant Indian'. The reduction of the indigenous to the condition of peasant in agrarian reform is relevant for understanding the discreet place of the Living Well ideology in the contemporary politics of the country, in contrast to Bolivia and Ecuador.

state. There was a deep-seated conviction that systemic forces would never allow a leftist government. In general terms, with the exception of Sendero, the fundamental question that arose within the left was not about electoral participation but the role it should play in a path to social transformation.

There was an attempt to bring together the most radical factions of the left around the Revolutionary Alliance of the Left (ARI) for the presidential elections of 1980, but this alliance only lasted for three months and was broken by minor differences between political leaders, generating for some a frustration hitherto unsurpassed. Appearing disunited in this election, the seven left-leaning candidates received about 13.6 per cent of the vote, less than half of what they had collected two years earlier. In a bitter irony, Francisco Belaúnde Terry, the president Velasco Alvarado had deposed in 1968, was elected in 1980.

The failure of the ARI did not mean the impossibility of a leftist alliance but, rather, that it was born out of a defeat, which had decisive implications. When the United Left (IU) was formed a few months later, the political leadership of this new front would belong to the more moderate sector of the leftist bodies that had supported Velasco. This tendency was personified in the figure of Alfonso Barrantes, whose main political advantage (apart from the charisma that propelled him to be elected mayor of Lima) was to not identify himself with any of the rival groups. IU adopted an electoral profile, and organic ties with the popular movement were little used. This detachment from grassroot politics resulted in interpersonal quarrels in place of joint projects as the driving force of the organization.

According to the self-critical testimony of another protagonist, Peru's left faced 'a new scenario with old tools' (Diez Canseco 2011: 176). Despite limitations on their political reach, popular forces resisted the anti-populist lashing of the Belaunde Terry government fairly effectively in a context of economic crisis, postponing the neoliberal onslaught for the next decade. On the electoral front, IU consolidated itself into the second political force in the country: in 1983, Alfonso Barrantes won the elections in Lima, becoming, as was said, the first socialist mayor of the Americas. The 1985 national elections were won by the APRA candidate Alan García, the youngest president in the country's history, who announced himself as a kind of reincarnation of the late Haya de la Torre. The same Barrantes was in second place in this election and, in a controversial decision, dropped out in the second round.

At that moment, the Peruvian left was reputed to be one of the most powerful on the continent and seemed to be ascending. A party affiliated with the Socialist International presided over the country and its main opposition was a coalition of parties to its left, while guerrilla movements were active in the countryside and in some cities. In fact, IU and its leader Alfonso Barrantes were seen as – and saw themselves as – favorites to succeed García in 1990. Nevertheless, the front broke down and the left arrived at these elections divided between two candidates who, together, gained 13 per cent of the votes, about 5 per cent of which was for Barrantes. The winner, with a meteoric rise at the end of the campaign, was a hitherto unknown underdog who won the second round – Alberto Fujimori.

What had happened? The issue has been discussed by the Peruvian left ever since. Examining the political situation in the country in 2015, Quijano attributed it to the convergence of three phenomena, which he refered to as 'Fujimontesinism' (which 'completes the degradation of the country, the putrefaction of its institutional apparatus'), in a process accelerated by 'Alanism' ('a son of APRA who has nothing to do with APRA') and 'Senderoism', interpreted as an 'ultra counter-revolutionary' (conversation with Quijano 2015). From a historical point of view it can be seen that Alanism and Senderoism brought the Peruvian left to face a number of impasses that allowed the right to resume the political initiative, generating the context in which the Fujimori dictatorship unfolded from 1990 to 2000.

3   Alanism and United Left

Politically, the collapse of the IU is associated with the ambivalence of its relationship with the country's main political force, APRA, and President Alan García. Specifically, the group around Barrantes believed in an unofficially agreed-upon presidential alternation, hinted at by García himself, whose government started pregnant with ambiguities and ended amid chaos.

García assumed a country that experienced an 'overflow of poor people', according to the formulation of Jose Matos Mar (1987). The growing migration to the cities as a result of economic decline aggravated the mismatch between rising popular demands and the limited possibilities of integration provided by the state and the market. In political terms, García tried to undermine the left and neutralize the right, while at the same time dealing with coup threats from the military and guerrillas in the countryside. On the economic front, the APRA leader assumed a country in a depression since 1983, within the framework of a debt crisis that plagued the region. Unlike his predecessor, he proposed a heterodox policy that was insufficient to prevent huge current transactions deficits. The problem was worsened by the international isolation of the government, which was unable to find support for the proposal to restrict the payment of debt to 10 per cent of export revenues, leading to ruptures with the International Monetary Fund (IMF) and International Bank for

Reconstruction and Development (IBRD) – even though in practice this goal has not been carried out.

On the whole, balance of payments problems accentuated by capital flight worsened the currency crisis and pushed inflation, which soon grew to hyperinflation. Michel Chossudovsky (1999: 129) criticizes APRA economic policy with these words:

> The economic model was defined in low level technical terms underpinned by a populist rhetoric: APRA had neither the social base nor the political will, let alone organized popular support, to implement important and sustainable social and economic reforms in areas such as tax reform, regionalization, reactivation of agriculture, and support for small-scale production units in the informal economy. Behind its populist discourse, the APRA government was not inclined to take any actions that directly opposed the interests of economic elites.

Amid the ambivalences of the process, the sealing of the government's fate was the sudden nationalization of the banking sector in July 1987. Announced in absentia of the group known as the '12 Apostles', which brought together the most powerful businessmen in the country and served as government interlocutor with this sector, the main effect of this measure was the 'instantaneous resurrection of the right', led by the writer Mario Vargas Llosa (Rudolph 1992: 132).

The initiative was fought by the financial sector, triggering a dispute that prompted the government to abandon the project. As a result, the trust between business and García was broken, accentuating the government's economic difficulties. According to the World Bank, GDP decreased by 8.8 per cent in 1988 and by 14 per cent in 1989; between December 1987 and October 1988 real wages in the private sector plummeted 52 per cent on average while in the public sector the fall was estimated at 62 per cent; the purchasing power of the minimum wage fell by 49 per cent between July 1985 and July 1990; inflation reached 1,700 per cent in 1988, 2,800 per cent in 1989 and 7,600 per cent in 1990. In this scenario, García lost control of the political agenda and in 1988 implemented the first attempt at an anti-inflationary shock – without success (Cano 2000: 132).

IU was one of the few social segments that publicly endorsed the nationalization of the banks, even calling for popular mobilization in Lima. Although the proposal was consistent with the left's historical agenda, its execution by a politically opportunistic government that plunged itself into contradictions and corruption undermined the political prestige of the IU. In the final analysis, this position refers to the ambivalence of the left in its relationship with APRA, a party that for long had not been progressive, but that deployed nationalist motives at a time when Peruvian politics were tilted to the left. However, the expectations of presidential alternation were frustrated because García disregarded protocol and intervened openly in the campaign for mayor of Lima in favor of the APRA candidate, who defeated Barrantes by a narrow margin. Despite the defeat in the capital, the number of votes obtained by the IU at the national level grew in 1986, confirming its position of strength.

However, when the presidential elections approached in 1990 the country was experiencing a very different moment, in which the economic problems were compounded by the increase in Sendero Luminoso's urban military action, which from 1989 onwards was believed to be closer to the 'strategic balance' that Mao spoke of (Degregori 2013: 223). It is in this context that the 'First National Congress of the United Left' was held, which was also its last, because its unity was undone during the Congress.

According to numerous testimonies, the cause of the split was the stand taken by Barrantes and his group, that it would be necessary to let go the most combative sectors of IU to attract the moderate voter and win the elections (Ames 2011; Guerra García 2011, Pease 2011; Zapata 2011). It was also thought that the army would hardly tolerate a more radical government at a time of great uneasiness over the Senderoist insurgency. As we saw, the result of the split was that Barrantes gained even fewer votes (5 per cent) than Henry Pease's IU bid (8 per cent), and they totaled 13 per cent between them. But to understand this defeat of the Peruvian left, beyond the addictions of 'the microparties with corporate logic that camouflaged themselves with an ideologically radical discourse' (Adrianzen 2011: 58) it is necessary to examine the phenomenon of the Shining Path.

4   Sendero Luminoso

Contrary to what the Mexican ideologist Jorge Castañeda (1994) suggests in '*La Utopia Desarmada*', Sendero Luminoso has no affinity with what is described as a 'second wave' of guerrilla movements on the continent, including the Central American movements and the Colombian M-19. Understanding the uniqueness of this insurgency is a complex task to which a number of notable intellectuals, mainly Peruvians, have dedicated themselves (Degregori 2013; Renique 2015). As did Benedict Anderson (1983) when he suggested that the nature of nationalism is closer to kinship or religious structures than to ideological phenomena such as liberalism or socialism, I understand that the

Senderoist insurgency is related to social problems in a country in transit from national-developmentalism to neoliberalism, which in Latin America has also increased the likelihood of phenomena such as neo-Pentecostalism and criminal gangs.

Evidently, it is necessary to embed this general framework in the particularities of Peru by articulating the uneven development pattern of the country and its regions; the ambivalent legacy of Velasquism; the authoritarian cultural patterns in the relations between the *misti* (non-Indians) and the indigenous peasants; and entrenched prejudices about Andean culture and racism. A critical examination is required of a certain Marxist tradition, perverted by Sendero as a megalomaniacal mode of reasoning, supported by anti-democratic and fanatical practices that have resulted in violent and anti-popular politics. With the impossibility of giving a proper account of this 'opaque and elusive object of study' (Degregri 2013: 23), I will outline some fundamental aspects of the phenomenon, because it is necessary for an understanding of Peru today.

Sendero Luminoso was born as a Maoist-oriented split in the heart of the PCP in the 1960s, and flourished in the mountainous region of Ayacucho, one of the poorest in the country, with a notable indigenous presence. Its main hub was the University of Sán Cristóbal de Huamanga, the re-opening of which in 1959, in the city of Ayacucho, had the effect of a social earthquake, multiplying by ten the number of university students in a few years in the most backward region of the country (Degregori 2013). Originally, the political organizing of university students was a reaction to the Belaúnde government's intention to cut the institution's funding, as it was accused of supporting the guerrillas. Yet the path of the Senderoists (led by the professor of Philosophy, Abimael Guzman) during the 1970s included numerous political defeats, in both university politics and in the peasantry. It did, however, solidify the unity of a group that was intensely proselytizing among secondary school and university students in the region, as well as teachers and employees (Degregori 2010).

Contrary to the mass movement that arose in the late 1970s, Sendero did not support the 1977 general strike and did not endorse participation in the constituent process. In 1980, while the Peruvian left debated tactics and strategy forming the IU, Sendero decreed the beginning of an extended popular war, made public with the burning of electoral material in the Chuschi *'pueblo'*.

Following this symbolic act, Sendero carried out armed activity in the countryside that, despite its brutality, won sympathy among the rural population at first. They murdered hated figures such as farmers and businessmen; they distributed livestock and land; mobilized against state cooperatives, which were repudiated by the peasantry; punished cattle theft as well as various moral infractions including alcoholism and adultery. In regions where the little the state does often has a repressive character, the Senderoist presence could at first be considered a guardian of order. But the Senderoist intervention was hardly different from that of a good boss who removes the old '*misti*' not to suppress it but to take its place. For, contrary to encouraging peasant autonomy, its practice replicated the 'most authoritarian, closed, excluding, and pre-modern aspects of Peruvian political culture' (Degregori 2013: 192). The Senderoist culture intended to be more just, but not more democratic.

Considering that Sendero had a 'de-peasanted' and 'de-indianized' rural population as a social base, it can be said that it was a departure from the *mariateguista* tradition in the political arena, because it never bet on peasant protagonism. In fact, it had difficulties penetrating into the regions where peasant organization existed. It was also distant on the socio-economic level, because it aimed to eradicate from the countryside everything that was not Senderoist or peasant (what was described as 'clearing the field'), with no intention of establishing links with local political or economic traditions. Finally, it differed ideologically, because it dissociated the agrarian question from the indigenous question, eliminating the specificity of the Peruvian formation emphasized by Mariátegui.

Consequently, Senderoist policies quickly antagonized peasants. The dissonance was evidenced in the 1982–1983 harvest, when the movement prohibited the access of producers to the markets because it intended to establish autarkic productive circuits. This was the context in which the first acts of peasant resistance to the presence of the Senderoist were registered.

But in this same period the first civil government for 12 years overcame its hesitation about military intervention, and the army went up the mountains. A statement by the minister of war, Luis Cisneros Vizquerra, summarizes the reasons the military had resisted intervening and, at the same time, announced the form of this action. In order to take control of Ayacucho 'they would have to start killing Sendero members as well as non-members, because that is the only way they could ensure success. Kill sixty people and at best there are three Senderoists there...' (Cisneros Vizquerra 1983: 50).

The repression unleashed by the army fueled an escalation of violence that bloodied Ayacucho and spread the conflict to other regions. Several analysts point out that the conduct of the armed forces was counter-productive, as it forced the population to choose the lesser evil, and often this seemed to be Sendero (Burt 2011; Degregori 2013). Composed mostly of recruits from the coast, few of whom spoke Quechua, the army was perceived by many as an invader. At the height of this policy in 1984, more than 4,000 murders and forced disappearances were registered (Comisión 2008).

From the point of view of the insurgency, the government response fit Guzman's politics like a glove. 'President Gonzalo', as he referred to himself, preached that the Senderoist action would make state violence more explicit, compelling the peasantry to stand against the state and ultimately to take the cities. This reading reached extreme tones in the following years, with actions of unsuspected destructiveness. Thus, when Alan García assumed the presidency in 1985 and announced a new strategy focused on social development to combat the insurgency, Guzman replied that it would be necessary to 'take away his progressive mask'. The simultaneous uprising of incarcerated Senderoista on the days in which APRA hosted a socialist congress in Lima, an episode that ended in the execution of three hundred prisoners, was conceived with this objective. According to this rationality the uprising was successful, as there was a repressive escalation of the state, attested by the number of politically motivated murders that rose from 5.4 per day in 1987 to 8.8 in 1988 and 9.4 in 1989 (Burt 2013: 126). Meanwhile, Guzman proclaimed that 'blood does not stop the revolution, but waters it', and estimated that the revolution could cost a million lives.

The Senderoist leader faced militants of the left through the same lens: class traitors who smoothed the sharpness of social contradictions, delaying the revolution. Consequently, the movement persecuted and murdered hundreds of leftist social and political leaders. More shockingly, Senderoist rationality determined that killing was often not enough, but had to be done in an exemplary way: the popular Afro-Peruvian leader Maria Elena Moyano was dynamited in the presence of her children.

If, in retrospect, the antipopular character of the Senderoist insurgency, which could qualify as terrorist by the contemporary left, is evident, this reading was not clear in the 1980s. After all, as Degregori analyzes, Sendero emerged as a triple surprise – for the state and intelligence services; for political parties and social organizations; and for the academic community. Among the factors that hindered an accurate reading of the nature of the insurgency, three stand out: Marxist rhetoric in a country with a rich socialist tradition and in the middle of a radical series of events; the isolation of Ayacucho from the coast; and Andean prejudices,[8] confusing Sendero with a millenarian or indigenist movement. The scenario became even more complex with the armed actions of the

---

8 The US anthropologist Orin Starn works with the notion of 'Andeism' as analogous with the term 'orientalism' of Edward Said (STARN 1991)

Túpac Amaru Revolutionary Movement (MRTA) initiated in 1982, a conventional urban guerrilla organization whose activity grew during the Alan García government.

Although Senderoist destructiveness was evident for those who had direct contact with what happened in Ayacucho, many did not have that contact. For them, it was only when activity intensified in Lima that it became clear that Sendero was a national challenge. This occurred in the late 1980s, when Guzman estimated that the confrontation was approaching a 'strategic balance' and intensified efforts to penetrate the periphery of Lima with the intention of establishing a kind of insurgent belt around the city. Contrary to appearances, this decision corresponded to a moment of weakening in the rural positions of the organization, threatened by the growing peasant resistance, mainly in the form of peasant rounds (*rondas campesinas*). In this period the state changed its strategy and, without ceasing to practise the 'dirty war', invested in intelligence work and relations with peasant organizations, which became committees of peasant self-defense. Unlike their Colombian counterparts, these committees did not turn into delinquent paramilitary squads, but played a decisive role in the Senderoist defeat.

The decision to move forward on Lima emerges more as an 'escape forward' rather than an unfolding of organic growth. But at the time there was a genuine fear of insurgent power, as the repercussion of Shining Path action in the capital was amplified – and the firepower of the organization seemed to grow: the number of attacks between 1988 and 1989 nearly tripled those of 1981 and 1982. More frightening from the point of view of the state, 47 per cent of the attempts and attacks perpetrated by the organization between April 1989 and December 1992 (907 actions) were held in the capital. In the early 1990s, Lima appeared to be a besieged city (Rénique 2015: 154). At that moment, 32 per cent of Peruvian territory and 49 per cent of the population were under military command.

It was in this context that IU was disbanded, and the elections were held in which Fujimori won. Although testimony indicates that the condemnation of Sendero was unanimous in the IU, there is also widespread recognition that this insurgency has irreparably damaged the ongoing political effort because it has hampered internal consensus in addition to killing leaders and militants. And in the long run it has stigmatized the left to a point from which they have not yet recovered, as former senator Rolando Ames acknowledges: 'Sendero pushed public opinion against the discourse and image of any left, all left or center left. They also spoke of Mariátegui, of Marxism, Leninism, Maoism, etcetera – and they carried out terrorism!' (Ames 2011: 210).

5 Fujimori

The connections that Naomi Klein (2008) establishes between 'shock doctrine' and neoliberalism, using Chile under Pinochet as a paradigmatic case, find resonance in Peru led by Alberto Fujimori. In the Peruvian case, the disorder generated by the degeneration of the APRA government and accentuated by the devastation of the Senderoists created an atmosphere conducive to the combination of dictatorship and neoliberalism that marked the regime. If the conjunction of Alanism and Sendero challenged the rise of the Peruvian left, the Fujimori dictatorship flourished in this context, using economic unrest, widespread violence and the weakness of the left to his advantage. The prevailing conservatism in Peru is still related to the feeling that, despite the means employed, the 'Chino' put order in the house.

In order to assess the meaning of this regime, it is necessary to remember that Fujimori was elected in opposition to the candidacy of the writer and Nobel laureate Vargas Llosa, who assumed neoliberal adjustments as his platform. A political neophyte who projected himself in the final month of the campaign cultivating an image of honesty, technology and work, three characteristics associated with the Japanese immigrant, Fujimori's slogan was 'Vote No to Shock!'. Taking advantage of the deep distrust of politicians and the demoralization of the left to fuel an anti-party discourse, the candidate of 'Cambio 90' had the support of the APRA apparatus, once Vargas Llosa became García's arch-nemesis, besides benefiting from the rejection of the creole arrogance of his rival, who did not even live in the country.

Once elected, Fujimori formed an alliance with the military through the sinister figure of Vladimir Montesinos, who became the strong man of the regime: 'Montesinos was Mr Fix-it, not only for Fujimori, but also for the US government' (McClintock and Vallas 2003: 55). There are indications that the military was plotting to seize power and implement a decades-long national reordering project that would have been adjusted in the wake of the new president's unexpected complicity (converstation with Javier Torres 2015). This approach required the approval of the military high command; therefore, the government deposed enemies and promoted officers close to Montesinos. Broadly speaking, the division of labor established dictatorial powers for the president, while the armed forces had carte blanche to deal with the insurgency – and both immersed themselves in corruption.

Once in command, Fujimori issued a state of emergency throughout the country. A few days later, he promulgated the set of measures known as 'fujishock', when in flagrant contradiction to his electoral discourse he implemented a radical neoliberal program. Eliminating price controls in the private sector and raising energy and other public services prices, the shock caused an immediate price increase of between 300 per cent and 1,000 per cent, increasing the number of poor by 70 per cent in one day. The ultimate goal was, in the end, to regain the confidence of financial markets and multilateral institutions, reinserting Peru into international financial circuits.

This objective was achieved through different measures. The first was the stabilization program adopted in August 1990, aimed at controlling inflation and regularizing the payment of debt services. Subsequently, from February of the following year, pro-market institutional reforms were implemented, including the deregulation of the financial and labor markets, as well as privatizations. The commitment to discipline national policy in accordance with neoliberal guidelines has led to Peru's return to international financial circuits. It is relevant to note that Fujimori's rise coincided with the collapse of the Soviet Union and the end of the Cold War, accentuating the neoliberal pressure.

The conditions of this reinsertion would be consolidated by the so-called 'autocoup', when Fujimori closed the Congress and intervened in judicial power in April 1992, decreeing in Argentine fashion a 'government of emergency and national reconstruction'. Perverting democracy, the president used the increasing disbelief in institutional politics, sharpened by the failure of the Popular Action (Belaúnde) and APRA (García) governments, in addition to the IU's collapse, to claim popular support for the measure. At the same time, this regime, in which the executive branch centralized up to 75 per cent of the national budget, implemented an extensive clientelist network lubricated by a poverty alleviation program supported by IMF, the World Bank and Fondo de Coperación para el Desarrollo (FONCODES). This combination of dictatorial practices, popular support, and neoliberal policies led analysts to propose that it was a 'neopopulist' government, an imprecise category that blurred the repressive nature of the regime and was effectively deconstructed by Vilas (Weyland 1996; Vilas 2004).

Despite some effort to keep up appearances, the political mainstay of the regime was not elections, which were always fraudulent, but the army. On the day of the auto-coup tanks circulated through cities, press outlets were occupied and opposition leaders were arrested. The press was subjected to a combination of cooption and coercion, which ensured its alignment with the regime. But what gave social cohesion to Fujimorism was the stabilization of the economy, despite its high social cost and, especially, the end of the armed conflict.

A careful analysis of the facts shows that the defeat of Sendero Luminoso must be attributed to processes unleashed outside of this government. The decision to move from a reactive policy to a planned policy, to invest in intelligence work and policies of collaboration with the peasantry instead of extermination, all preceded the elections, as did the Senderistas setbacks in rural areas, which precipitated the assault to Lima. In the city, the escalation of attacks sharpened the rejection, including by many among the left, of the organization. Sendero's strategy at this time was to deepen the chaos, hoping to provoke a US intervention that would create a scenario analogous to interwar China, where nationalism and communism would converge on resistance to the invader. Guzmán stated that the murder of Maria Elena Moyano in February 1991 was inscribed in this perspective, which at the time was not sheer madness: at the beginning of 1992 the under secretary of state for inter-American affairs, Bernard W. Aronson, warned the leaders of the Congress of that country that it was necessary to prepare to prevent Sendero from coming to power, unleashing the 'third genocide' of the twentieth century (Burt 2013: 176).

But a few months later Abimael Guzmán was arrested at his hiding place in Lima and the Senderoist organization was quickly dismantled, facilitated by its high degree of centralization. This process was accelerated by the capitulation of the leader himself who, in contradiction with previous rhetoric, sought a peace agreement with Fujimori, announcing entry into a new stage of the political process. The MRTA, an organization of comparatively reduced social impact, was literally liquidated in an armed action overseen by the CIA in 1996, when a kidnapping at the Japanese ambassador's house was thwarted, and the guerrillas executed despite surrendering.

The careful work done by the Truth and Reconciliation Commission, formed shortly after Fujimori's fall, concluded that 69,280 people had died or disappeared as a result of the conflict, of which more than half were Sendero's victims. This is an extraordinary proportion when we remember that nowhere on the continent has insurgency caused more than 5 per cent of deaths whereas state terrorism and paramilitarism account for over 90 per cent. It is estimated that three-quarters of the victims were peasants from the poorest regions of the country who spoke Quechua, 40 per cent of them residing in Ayacucho. Among the victims 1,503 political authorities (mayors, governors, judges and local leaders) perished; 2,267 peasant leaders and 1,674 'members of the forces of order' (Comisión 2008).

These figures give an indication of the climate of insecurity, and often of terror, that hovered over the country during the period. This environment was exploited in several ways by the Fujimori regime. On the one hand, it attributed to itself the merits of having broken up the insurgency and pacified the country, which gave it a high level of approval, in a context in which many violations of democracy were taken as a sort of collateral damage. On the other hand, the regime manipulated widespread fear in society with the aim of self-legitimization, justifying the continued legal, political and military mechanisms characteristic of a state of exception, even with the decline of the conflict. In addition to legal persecution facilitated by draconian anti-terrorist legislation, the presidency authorized the murder and disappearance of teachers, students, peasants and worker leaders on the pretext of combating subversion. Frequently, the killings were attributed to Sendero, as in the assassination of trade unionist Pedro Huilca, a persistent critic of the regime's policies. In rural areas, maintaining the state of emergency meant that the armed forces exercised maximum authority in many parts of the territory.

On the economic front, the effects of the combination of stabilization and structural reform within the framework of neoliberalism are well known. Inflation was controlled through mechanisms that led to currency appreciation combined with increased imports, which had destructive effects on domestic industry, aggravating the deficits in current transactions covered by privatizations and IMF loans. Thus, external debt doubled during the Fujimori government, reaching 53 per cent of GDP (much higher than Chile, Mexico or Brazil), while annual payments quadrupled (McClintock and Vallas 2003). The growth of 59 per cent in exports between 1989 and 1998 did not accompany the explosion of imports, which increased by 264 per cent, making the balance of trade negative throughout the decade (Cano 2000: 486). Capital market reform, tax reform, labor market reform and generalized privatizations complemented the opening.

In short, what was left of the *velasquistas* structures was dismantled in the city as in the countryside, where a 'reform of agrarian reform' was implemented. Informal work and the criminal economy exploded: over the 1990s, the number of workers with temporary employment contracts doubled, while under-employment reached three-quarters of the economically active population by the end of the decade. The ideology that transforms the precariousness of labor relations, from a social problem to an entrepreneurial opportunity, has prospered in this situation (De Soto 1992).

Although the limits of this economic policy were already evident in the late 1990s, the fall of the regime was precipitated by political motives. The traumatic solution to a traumatized society, the 'Fujimontesinismo' that Quijano speaks of, collapsed from the inside, but was also pushed from the outside. The scandals detonated by the '*Vladivídeos*', recorded by Montesinos to discipline his followers and documenting the regime's endemic corruption, surfaced at a time of rising street protests intensified after fraudulent elections in 2000. In reality, the very participation of Fujimori in the election was farcical, since the constitution he himself promulgated prohibited a third mandate. The US also considered withdrawing its support to the regime, a decision hastened when an operation involving Montesinos with drug trafficking and the Revolutionary Armed Forces of Colombia (FARC) came to light.

Faced with the corrosion of the apparatus of power that he raised, protests in the streets and the US withdrawal, Fujimori sent his resignation by fax from Japan in 2001. The fact that the dictator fell from power instead of descending was significant, as it created the climate for the investigations of internal Peruvian conflict under the coordination of the CVR that, despite limits and difficulties, illuminated the recent history of the country, besides subsidizing the judgment of numerous criminals, among them Fujimori himself.

6 Fujimorista Legacy

In the election that followed Fujimori's resignation, Alejandro Toledo, who led the protests against fraud and electoral abuses committed by the regime in its last moments, was elected president. In the subsequent election, Alan García triumphed narrowly over Ollanta Humalla, a military man who at that time was associated with the left and Hugo Chávez.

In his second term, from 2006 to 2010, García abandoned leftist whims and carried out a frankly neoliberal government. Although he criticized the mining model on which Peru's growth was based, virtually exempting companies from tax or environmental obligations, his government maintained the normative framework inherited from Fujimori. On the trade front, the Free Trade Agreement (FTA) with the US signed during the Toledo administration came into force on 1 February 2009, without any opposition from the government.

In the following elections in 2011, Ollanta Humalla, who in the 2006 campaign took a stand against the FTA, a fact that contributed to his being associated with Hugo Chávez, made a commitment to distance himself from the Venezuelan by signaling an identification with Brazilian PTism, which supported and advised his winning campaign.

Beyond the nuances among the leaders, some paradoxes draw attention to Peruvian politics during the period. First, since the end of the military regime in the 1970s no ruler has elected his successor: the opposition candidate has always won. However, the new president often openly contradicts his platform, configuring a succession of electoral frauds, a flagrant expression of the hypocrisy that characterizes contemporary democracy (Panitch and Leys 2005). Evidently, this phenomenon further corrodes partisan legitimacy, fueling a depoliticization that favors conservatism. Fujimori, who was the most radical expression of the electoral lie, consciously managed this depoliticization. The lies of president Ollanta Humala are also notorious, such as the promise to privilege water over gold exploration ('water yes, gold no!'), but which collapsed in the face of conflicts over the Conga mining project.

Beyond politics as a lie, the recurrence of victories of an opposition that soon rejects its electoral discourse, suggests constraints to modification of the socio-economic structures bequeathed by Fujimori. In spite of his being discredited and imprisoned,[9] and the decline of the prestige of the military institution – a direct partner of the violence and corruption that devastated the regime – the foundations of the capitalist reproduction pattern that he established remain unquestioned.

Broadly speaking, an open economy was affirmed which anchors its international position in the export of minerals backed by international investments attracted by low fiscal, labor and environmental requirements. The legal framework of this model had its milestone with the Framework Law for the Growth of Private Investment of November 1991, and was consolidated in the constitution promulgated in 1993, which guaranteed privileged terms, as well as legal stability, to international investments. The new text, which is still valid, also eliminated the inalienable character of the lands of peasant and native communities, as well as determining that natural resources would cease to be the exclusive patrimony of the nation (Bebbington et al. 2014: 35).

Since then, Peruvian economic growth is an outcome of the extraordinary expansion of multinational mining. Growth peaks were reached in the 1990s, with 10.9 per cent (1993), 15.2 per cent (1994), 10.8 per cent (1997), 16 per cent (1999) (Alayza and Gudynas 2012: 65). Overall, investment increased in the post-Fujimori years in the context of international commodity price increases: Foreign Direct Investment (FDI) rose from 4.5 per cent of GDP between 1990 and 2000 to 25 per cent in 2007. In 2009 Peru was the largest recipient of mining investments on the continent, and the third largest in the world after Canada and Australia. For comparative purposes, in 2011 Brazilian expenditure on geological research was equal to 60 per cent of Peruvian investment, although its territory is seven times more extensive.

A territorial expression of this expansion, in the early 1990s mining concessions occupied 2.3 million hectares – currently they are close to 25 million. Mining activity ceased to focus on the Andean mountains, expanding into the valleys, the coast and even the Amazon. There are departments where mining concessions approach or exceed half of the territory, such as Arequipa, Ancash, Lima, La Libertad, Moquegua, Huancavelica and Tacna (Mansur 2014: 75). By

---

9 Fujimori was pardoned by president Pedro Pablo Kuczynski in December 2017. Although humanitarian reasons were alleged, the move was part of PKK's attempt to circumvent an impeachment process. Although successful at that time, PKK was impeached in March 2018.

2015, Peru was the largest Latin American producer and among the world's largest producers of silver (first), gold (sixth), zinc (second), tin (third), lead (fourth) and copper (second). It also accounted for 40 per cent of the world's gold reserves in 2008.

After 20 years of expansion, the country's dependence on this sector of the economy has intensified. Around 22 per cent of internal revenue between 2007 and 2010 was derived from mining, and about 6 per cent of GDP and 60 per cent of exports are currently derived from these activities. However, the regulatory framework of the sector has frustrated any substantive increase in the collection of internal taxes, for example, the so-called 'surplus' exemptions. Some say the paradox of unpopular rulers in the context of economic growth in Peru shows the limited possibilities of the state to convert this wealth into social programs, in contrast to other countries in the region (Barros and Hitner 2010).

This limitation is aggravated by the fact that contemporary mining is an activity that requires high capital investments but employs relatively little labor power. Thus, the other side of the policy of commercial deregulation and attraction of foreign investment that favored mining to the detriment of sectors associated with national production was the growth of unemployment and the informal economy, enhancing the 'criminal economy' which revolves around piracy, smuggling and drug trafficking. Peru today is one of the main exporters of cocaine on the continent. At the same time, there is an increase in security problems related to common delinquency, in the context of the degradation of the country's social fabric. At the sociological level, Francisco Durand observes that the mixture between informality and delinquency is so rooted in contemporary Peruvian sociability that it ends up 'forming an integral part of the country's institutional matrix' (Durand 2007: 69).

Yet another aspect of mining growth is the increase in socio-environmental conflict in the country. In contrast to the impotence of institutional policy, there are numerous cases in which popular resistance has interrupted projects linked to the 'extractivist economy', such as the mining projects in Tambogrande and Conga, or the Inambari hydroelectric plant. Among the socio-environmental conflicts registered, 64 per cent are related to mining and some involve a high degree of violence: between 2006 and 2011, 195 deaths were recorded in social conflicts, in addition to 2,312 wounded in clashes between civilians and police officers – the continent's highest number in the period. The most lethal episode was the so-called Bagua massacre in 2009, when 34 people were killed, including 24 policemen and 10 indigenous people resisting one of the largest gold projects in the world today (Guevara Aranda 2013).

Despite bold popular resistance to projects of diverse socio-environmental impact, from displacement and water depletion to various levels of environmental contamination, there has been no change in the means or ends of state policy since Fujimori. In the same year as the Bagua massacre, the minister of economy and finance announced that there would be fines and lawsuits against civil servants who extend the 100-day deadline for the preparation of environmental impact studies, a requirement prior to the approval of mining projects (Mansur 2014: 74). In this scenario, there is the perception among those who resist that mining expansion involves a continuous effort but of intermittent intensity, which means that discontinued projects will return in the future, with refined strategies for convincing communities or imposing on their interests (conversations with Gamboa 2015; Choquehuanca 2015).

In this perspective, while the Humalla government announced a list of new mining projects worth more than US$41 billion, data of the Defensoría del Pueblo registered 210 social conflicts in January 2015, of which 140 were of a social-environmental nature. Until mid-2015, there had been 65 fatalities in social conflicts during this government, which took office in 2011. To cite an episode, in mid-2018, Arequipa, a principal city of the country, was occupied by the army, owing to the conflicts arising from the Tia María mine project.

Complementary to this 'accumulation by spoliation' is the state policy of presenting Peru as a brand, the so-called 'Peru brand', which explores some niches of sophisticated consumption, notably gastronomy, exporting speciality foods such as asparagus, paprika, artichoke, avocado and quinoa. This promotion of the country for external consumption, mobilizing motives between the cult and the exotic, is symmetrical to Peruvian international engagement, in which the market defines not only its position in the international division of labor, but also the national identity itself. In the description of a university professor, television advertising of the 'Peru brand' is intended to teach Peruvians themselves who they are, preparing them for tourists (conversation with Pease 2015). It is marketing making up for the insufficiencies of history, by resolving, through a simulacrum, the national identity that the Creole aristocracy, Mariátegui and Velasco, among others, were unable to affirm.

Typically, the contradictions between extractivism and 'Marca Perú' are exposed in the threat to the hydrobiological resources of the country. The increase in global animal protein consumption since the late 1980s, pushed by China, has raised prices for anchovy, of which Peru is one of the largest global exporters. In a process analogous to the expansion of soybeans on the continent, anchovy serves as a raw material for fishmeal and fish oil, which in turn feeds captive-bred fish in other countries. However, the growth of anchovy industrial fishing on the Peruvian coast threatens the subsistence of other fish, notably those appreciated as 'ceviche', the main dish of Peruvian gastronomy promoted worldwide (Sueiro 2012).

7 Final Thoughts

Social mobilization fermented in the heart of *velasquismo* was insufficient to transcend it, but it prepared the popular resistance for the neoliberal onslaught in the 1980s, when the Peruvian left was in the vanguard of the continent. However, two perverse processes put their organized political expression, the Izquierda Unida, in the face of impasses that precipitated its sudden decline amid the ambiguities of the APRA, which eventually reached the government with Alan García. The progressive symbolism and rhetoric of Garcia's mandate disguised the opportunism and venality that drove it, resulting in ambivalences that led the country to socio-economic chaos, preparing the ground for the shock policies that followed. The song of the APRA mermaid has enchanted part of the left, delighted by the possibility of an electoral alternation that only sharpened its internal contradictions, while the support for an inconsequental nationalization of the banks showed up the difficulties of affirming an autonomous social leadership, at a moment in which the right recovered the political initiative.

This scenario became even more nebulous with the expansion of an original political phenomenon that perverted the rhetoric and political culture of the left, making a terrorist organization appear as a Marxist guerrilla. After sowing civil war in impoverished corners of the country, Sendero Luminoso intensified its urban activity towards the end of the decade, announcing a raid to surround the capital carried out through the murder of numerous leftist civilian leaders and attacks that frightened the country. Faced with the challenges posed by this remarkably complex conjuncture, IU did not differentiate itself clearly from Alanism and Sendero, but succumbed to internal differences, exposing a political culture trapped by dogmatism and personalism.

Fujimori was elected president in this critical context, with a platform that seemed to capture, at the same time, the popular rejection of Creole politics personified by Vargas Llosa and a distrust of the ambiguities of the left that oscillated between a radical past like Sendero and a future in the presidency like APRA. Making the armed forces his party, Fujimori relied on the generalized discrediting of politics and the pacification of the country to solidify a dictatorial regime, whose relative successes affirmed the framework in which Peruvian society currently operates: neoliberalism, mineral extractivism, free-trade, labor informality, criminal economy, drug trafficking. Party alternation since Fujimori's fall in 2000 hardly disguises the conservatism of national politics, whose lack of belief in institutions is exacerbated by the naturalness with which candidates elected by the opposition renege on their campaign promises.

This acute narrowing of the political landscape is evidenced by the candidacies in the middle of 2015 likely to succeed Humalla in elections scheduled for the following year. In a context where the then president showed low approval ratings, three candidates were competitive: Alan García, icon of conventional politics and corruption; Keiko Fujimori, daughter of the former dictator imprisoned and who promised to grant him amnesty; and Pedro Pablo Kuczynski, former minister of economy in the Toledo government (2001–2006), a prominent neoliberal figure, the US's leading lobbyist, a man who lived at the Sheraton while his family lived in the US and encouraged Peruvians to learn English to eventually leave the country.[10]

On the left there were two poles that have been difficult to unify. Congressman Sergio Tejada presented himself as a candidate of the Popular National Bloc, claiming a center-left position in the institutional tradition of IU (to which the former mayor of Lima, Susana Villarán, is affiliated), linked to the coalition known as Únete. On the other hand, there were efforts to combine resistance to territorially-dispersed extractivism into a national political alternative. This movement has as its main figure the former priest Marco Arana, founder of the Movimiento Tierra y Libertad, one of the organizations that make up the Frente Amplio. Arana was defeated in internal elections by the young Cusco representative, Verónika Mendoza, who became the coalition's presidential candidate. At the political level, the main cleavage between the two poles is the stance in relation to mining, where Frente Amplio criticises extractivism as a whole, while Únete favors the negotiation of better terms for the state, in the fashion of its Andean neighbors. But it is not a linear cleavage: the regional governor and leader against mining projects in Cajamarca, Gregorio Santos, flirted with the second organization, although his political mobility has been blocked since he was jailed on corruption charges in 2014 – which did not prevent him from being re-elected later the same year, even though he could not take office.[11]

---

10   PKK beat Keiko in the second round with a narrow margin of 0.24 per cent of votes.
11   Veronika Mendoza placed third in the first round, having received 18.8 per cent of the votes, shortly behind PKK, who had 20.99 per cent. Tejada resigned his candidacy to support Frente Amplio, while Gregorio Santos had 4 per cent of the votes, which was more than the difference between Mendoza and PKK.

The conditions for spreading an alternative discourse to extractivism have advanced. For example, in 2012 the National March for Water and the protest that followed gathered around 20,000 people in Lima against the Conga mining project. The main slogan was in defense of water and not the demands for more income that characterize similar protests. However, there are several historical and political factors that differentiate the Peruvian context from Bolivia and Ecuador, where indigenous protagonism in recent struggles brought the theme of 'Living Well' to the national agenda. These singularities involve objective aspects such as the character of the Velascist agrarian reform, which prioritized Yugoslavian-inspired cooperativism to the detriment of indigenous forms of production, but also subjective ones, such as the subsumption of indigenous identity to a peasant identity.

On another level, the violent upheavals that have succeeded the GRFA, itself the protagonist during a period of rapid change, seem to have fostered accommodation to a system that seems stable, after all. The drama of contemporary Peruvian politics is that the recovery of peace and stability is associated with a combination of state repression and neoliberal fundamentalism. This perception is key to understanding the prestige of Keiko Fujimori, despite the international demoralization of her father. Resistance to change is exacerbated by the superficial prosperity backed by mineral exports, the criminal economy, and more recently, the self-emulation evoked by the 'Peru Brand'.

The paradoxes of contemporary Peruvian politics – where governments elected as opposition practise continuity; where no president has elected his successor despite economic growth; where extractive fishing threatens the flagship of the 'Peru brand'; and where popular protest has stopped extractive projects but without proposing a national alternative – express, in a particularly adverse context, the impasses of politics in Latin America today. Neoliberalism has no legitimacy to reproduce itself, but perpetuates itself based on a political system impermeable to popular yearnings, that naturalizes lies, corruption and exploitation, which is only viable because of the corrosion of the social fabric, the forms of organized resistance and the utopian horizon that their own implementation implied, a process that was particularly traumatic in Peru.

CHAPTER 10

War and Peace in Colombia in Historical Perspective

> Colombia was, and continues to be, evidence that gradual reform in the framework of liberal democracy is not the only and even the most plausible alternative to social revolutions, including those that fail or are aborted. I discovered a country in which failure to make a social revolution made violence the constant, universal and ubiquitous core of public life.
>
> Eric Hobsbawm, *Interesting Times: A Life in the Twentieth Century*

> [Juan Manuel] Santos opens the way to 'castrochavismo' when he makes a pact with the FARC.
>
> Álvaro Uribe, 2014

1 Introduction

Colombian politics at the beginning of the twenty-first century was associated with the very opposite of the progressive wave. In a country with a long history of armed conflict, the signing of Plan Colombia with the United States in 2001 toppled with the election of Álvaro Uribe in 2002, intensified the repression of the guerrillas and the criminalization of all dissent. In more than a reactionary indulgence in counter-terrorist rhetoric since the attack on the Twin Towers in New York, Uribe incarnated a project of power identified with so-called 'parapolitics', which brutalized and poisoned the country's political culture.

It is necessary to analyze the meaning and resonance of the phenomenon of Uribismo to understand the obstacles to a negotiated end of the armed conflict and the defeat of the plebiscite for peace in 2016 which concluded the negotiations between the government of Juan Manuel Santos and the Revolutionary Armed Forces of Colombia-People's Army (FARC-EP) started in 2012 in Havana. Uribismo takes root in the singular violence that characterized the pattern of class struggle in contemporary Colombia, reconstituted in this chapter with the purpose of situating the inherent dilemmas of the peace process in a historical perspective. My hypothesis is that Colombia exposes, in an extreme manner, the impediments to change within the system in Latin America, explaining the anti-national, anti-democratic and anti-popular character of the dominant classes on the continent. The dilemma of the Colombian guerrilla as part of the left lay in the choice between two disjunctive paths: prolonging armed struggle and subjecting all opposition to state criminalization, or dropping weapons altogether and exposing itself to the possibility of massacre as in the past. In this reality, the disjunctive choice between reform or revolution is an empty one: before the permanent counter-revolution, reform *is* revolution.

2   Background

Cautious statistics indicate that, between 1958 and 2012, 220,000 people of which 81 per cent were civilians, were murdered for political reasons in Colombia (National Center for Historical Memory 2013: 10). However, it was the period just before this, beginning with the assassination of the popular liberal leader Jorge Eliécer Gaitán in 1948, that became known in literature as *La Violencia* (the violence): it is estimated that there was a similar number of political victims in those years.

Many of the dead were public figures, like the three presidential candidates assassinated during the 1990 election campaign, or the soccer player Andrés Escobar, who scored an own goal, which eliminated the Colombian team from the 1994 World Cup. Others were militants: according to the testimony of leaders of the Union Sindical Obrera (USO), of every hundred trade unionists murdered in the world in recent years, 51 were Colombians, accounting for 2,652 murdered workers (conversation with Gomez 2014). Many of these deaths were perpetrated by hired killers (*sicarios*) who leave no trace and were carried out in the outlying areas of urban centers or in the countryside.

In addition to the selective murders, there are numerous massacres. Between 1985 and 2012, there were almost 2,000 bloodbaths, victimizing 11,751 people. Some deaths have caused national repercussions, as when nine investigators of paramilitary action in the Magdalena Medio region were murdered in 1989 (conversation with Páez 2014), but most of these crimes receive less attention than massacres elsewhere in the world. In this same period, 25,007 forced disappearances were registered. There are 2,700 cases of 'false positives', youths dressed in guerrilla uniforms who were murdered by the army in order for their executioners to receive a reward (set in 2005 at around 1,900 dollars) (conversation with Fundación Lazos de Dignidad 2014).

The murder and disappearance of civilians have been used to intimidate the populace, forcing them to swear allegiance to a group claiming the domination of a territory. Paramilitaries are responsible in most of the cases: 'Their distinctive mark has been to kill in a massive or selective manner, disappearing with their victims, stripping them of their lands, carrying out crimes with violence and exercising sexual violence' (Centro Nacional de Memoria Histórica 2013: 25).

However, it is wrong to interpret paramilitaries as a 'third actor' in a conflict between the army and the guerrillas, as the relationship of the paramilitaries to the public forces is notorious, both in origin and in their mode of operation as well as their alleged disarmament. At present, the links between the state, paramilitaries and drug trafficking have shaped the phenomenon known as parapolitics. Moderate estimates indicate that one-third of the country's parliamentarians, including the senator and president from 2002 to 2010, Álvaro Uribe, have direct links to illegal activities (conversation with Avella 2014). In addition to lethal violence, other forms of violence such as forced removal, personal violence, anti-personnel mines and kidnapping are widespread.

As a result of the violence in the countryside, Colombia produced 5 million internally displaced persons and about 9 million refugees – only the Democratic Republic of the Congo went through a comparable drama at the time. Between 1998 and 2008, approximately 760,000 families were removed, leaving behind some 5.5 million hectares of land. It is estimated that 45 per cent of Colombian national territory is covered by landmines. Over the past three decades, 10,000 people (2,000 of whom have died) were hit by landmine explosions. Violence has transformed the roles culturally attributed to men, since forced removal often distanced them from their work and community. Many have lost their status as providers, being forced to accept jobs that they consider degrading – or even begging (Red Derecho e Desplazamiento 2010; Centro Nacional de Memoria Histórica 2013).

On the other hand, the focus of guerrilla violence in its more than 50 years of existence has been the fight against state forces, damage to property and kidnapping for political and economic purposes. There are 27,023 documented cases of kidnapping, of which 16,000 occurred between 1996 and 2002. Among those perpetrated by the guerrillas, 318 mayors, 332 councilors, 52 deputies, 54 congressmen and 790 soldiers and police were taken (Centro Nacional de Memoria Histórica 2013). One of the most extreme episodes was the capture of the Palace of Justice by the 19 April Movement (M-19) in 1985, an operation that ended with the invasion of the army and the death of the guerrillas and their hostages, the Supreme Court magistrates. From a liberal point of view, it is affirmed that a democratic regime prevailed in the twentieth century, with the exception of the period from 1953 to 1957 in which General Gustavo Rojas Pinilla was in power. From a legal point of view, however, the country was in a quasi-continuous state of siege between the 1940s and the 1991 Constitution, a condition resumed by Álvaro Uribe four days after his inauguration in 2002. At that moment, which was packed with the rhetoric of 'war on terror', the guerrillas' political status was denied, and the criminalization of social protest sharpened.

Currently, there are numerous cases of the persecution of popular leaders, trade unionists, students and university professors. Professor Miguel Ángel Beltrán, for example, was illegally deported from Mexico in 2009 and spent two years imprisoned, charged with the 'crime of rebellion' due to an article in which he defended the right to rebellion. Fired by the National University of Colombia, he had his political rights limited for 13 years (conversation with Ángel Beltrán 2014). By the middle of 2015 he was again incarcerated.[1] The former senator Piedad Córdoba, Senator Iván Cepeda and Bogota Mayor Gustavo Petro are among the public figures who, in 2015, were prosecuted by the Attorney General's Office, led by Alejandro Ordoñéz, a Catholic fundamentalist who acts as an inquisitor of the left, recycling processes based on evidence known to be illegal, such as the alleged files found on computers in the bombing that killed FARC commander Raúl Reyes in Ecuadorian territory in 2008, an illegal action in itself (conversation with Córdoba 2014). In the countryside, the situation is even more dramatic, and many leaders are forced to move or live in hiding, as in the time of the Southern Cone military dictatorships. By 2015, it was estimated that there were more than 9,000 political prisoners in Colombia, fewer than half of them linked to the guerrillas (Encuentro Nacional por la Libertad de lxs Prisionerxs Politicxs 2011).

3   Roots of Violence

The roots of violence that shape Colombian class struggle is a controversial subject with an extensive bibliography (Bergquist et al. 1992). Some authors place its origins in the nineteenth century or even during colonization (Sánchez 1992). In fact, between 1830 and 1903 there were 29 changes of the constitutional order; three military coups in the country; two wars with Ecuador; fourteen local civil wars; and nine national civil wars, including the split that gave rise to Panama. However, this political instability also happens in other regions of the continent and is linked to the difficulty of consolidating a

---

[1] In September 2016, Beltrán was acquitted by the Supreme Court of Justice and released. In May 2018, the State Council suspended the interdiction imposed by the Attorney General's office to hold public office.

national state in societies of colonial formation, in which civil war becomes an instrument of political alternation (Halperin Donghi 1989).

As in Mexico, marked by the peasant political protagonism since the colonial period (Katz 1990), the key to Colombian singularity is the pattern of popular organization and resistance. As Forrest Hylton pointed out in the context of what Hobsbawm named as *The Age of Capital (1848–1875)*, 'radical-popular mobilization has placed Colombia at the most advanced end of Atlantic republican democracies' (Hylton 2006: 15). The reaction to this radical popular mobilization, expressed, for example, in the spread of Democratic Societies in the context of the 'liberal revolution' of 1849–53,[2] resulted in conservative dominance for half a century, from 1880 to 1930, with a centralist orientation and a strong Catholic presence (Tirado Mejía 1985). Although Colombia evolved differently from many Latin American countries, where liberal politics prevailed during this period, its trajectory is not unique if one remembers, for example, that it is contemporaneous with the conservative Old Republic in Brazil.

On the economic front, the rates of capital accumulation in Colombia were lower than those of Peru, Chile or Bolivia during the nineteenth century. It is estimated that by the end of the 1870s, while Brazil was exporting to the value of approximately 90 million dollars Colombian exports were valued at 11 million dollars. At the beginning of the twentieth century the country had 8 per cent of the value of foreign investment per capita in relation to the rest of the continent, a proportion higher only than that of Haiti (Checchia 2007: 107). These numbers made Colombia the Latin American country with the lowest degree of integration into the world economy, prior to the coffee expansion, which began in the 1910s (Ocampo 1984). The obstacles to market integration were linked to the challenges of national integration, boosted by a rugged geography, which led to the view that the country was still, in the twentieth century, an archipelago of disjointed regions, as portrayed in the literature of Gabriel García Márquez (Kalmanovitz 2003).

From the 1910s onwards there was a notable expansion of coffee production, making Colombia the second largest exporter (after Brazil) of that crop in the interwar period. Coffee revenues were the basis of capital accumulation in the country until the 1980s, corresponding to a relative diversification of production anchored in the domestic market. In the geopolitical sphere, Colombia is also a country of the Caribbean, a region considered by the US since the nineteenth century as an internal sea. Its presence was decisive in transforming

---

2   One of the earliest forms of political organization in independent Colombia, that organized professionals in trade associations, having an important role in the political and social life of the time.

a bloody civil war (known as the War of A Thousand Days, from 1899 to 1902) between Colombian liberals and conservatives into the territorial division that gave rise to Panama. A few months after the end of the confrontation, the new republic signed a treaty that ratified US rights over the area of the future canal, a document drafted in English and signed in the United States, as was the case with Plan Colombia a hundred years later (Jaramillo Levi 1976).

As in other Central American countries, about three-quarters of Colombian foreign trade in the early twentieth century involved the United States, and United Fruits Company banana plantations duplicated the traits of an enclave (García 1984: 181). A strike of banana workers in 1928, which ended in massacres (portrayed in the García Marquez novel *One hundred years of solitude*), was a founding episode of workers' struggles in the country and propelled the lawyer Jorge Eliécer Gaitán into national politics. Originally of liberal persuasion, Gaitan embodied the yearnings and ambiguities inherent in the pressures for social change within the framework of Colombian liberalism in the 1940s. In the interwar period, pressures for democratizing the access to land intensified, prompting the enactment of Law 200 of 1936, which established the effective occupation of land as a condition for its possession. The period of liberal political domination, between 1930 and 1948, came together with a combination of urban social protest and an incipient import substitution industrialization.

However, the self-titled Revolution in March, begun by President Alfonso López Pumarejo in 1934, increased expectations of change without generating the means to consummate it. In his second term, between 1942 and 1945, a law known as '*La revancha*' removed the possibilities for agrarian reform contained in Law 200. In the context of an upswing of social movement in the countryside and cities, Gaitán tried a rupture with the bipartisanship prevalent in the country since independence, pointing to a popular reformist political movement. In the words of Antonio García, Gaitán projected himself as a '*caudillo* of a radicalized mass movement' (García 1984: 192). This possibility of people's participation in politics, simultaneously triggered a reaction of Falangist inspiration, supported by Catholic values, and a repressive culture, led by Laureano Gómez. The political tumult that followed López Pumarejo's resignation in 1945 and the election of a conservative, at a time when the liberals were divided by the ascent of Gaitán, reached its climax when he was assassinated on 9 April 1948, while the conference that gave rise to the Organization of American States (OEA) was being held in Bogotá.

Several Latin American countries experienced a sharpening of social contradictions after the Second World War; and the ideological polarization within the Cold War framework endorsed repressive outcomes (Bethell and Roxborough 1992). In the Colombian case, the popular insurrection triggered by the assassination of the favorite in upcoming presidential elections gave rise to the persecution and murder of leaders and workers associated with liberalism, in both the cities and in the countryside. It can be said that the conservative reaction began a process of 'replacement of the liberal republic model – economic interventionism and political liberalism – by political absolutism and economic liberalism' (García 1984: 198).

The election of Laureano Gómez as president in 1950, notorious for his fascist inclinations, in a poll in which he ran unchallenged, expanded the violence against liberals, fueled by a spurious identification of them with Gaitanism and communism – which often legitimized the expropriation of their property. As in the Thousand Days' War at the beginning of the century, when 100,000 Colombians (4 per cent of the population) died in clashes between liberals and conservatives, the deaths unleashed by the *Bogotazo* brought to a peak what became known as *La Violencia,* which lasted from 1946 to 1957. From this moment on, open violence typified the pattern of class struggle in the country.

It is possible to paint different phases in this process in broad strokes. In the first phase, which coincides with political polarization under the rise of Gaitanism and the conservative reaction, violence is predominantly urban. From the *Bogotazo* onwards, as tensions spread to the countryside, conventional patterns of popular insubordination prevailed, guided by traditional political allegiances framed by bipartisanship. As a rule, peasants fought within the system through their local political bosses (Bejarano 1985).

However, as a result of repression, the weakening of the sectors associated with Gaitán favored an understanding among the dominant classes between conservatives and liberals, which united against workers. Abandoned many times to its own fate, popular insubordination often took an autonomous path, strengthened by communist cadres who were persecuted in the cities and then joined the rural struggle. A qualitative change in the conflict is observable, summed up in the following terms:

> When the peasant had to begin to fight equally against the police as an armed branch of official repression and against the liberal landlord, the nature of the struggle changed. It was no longer a civil war, it was class struggle.
> SANCHEZ 1976: 26

Proposals for programmatic unification in the countryside, showing an increase in the autonomy of popular organizations, corresponded to a compromise solution between the factions of the ruling classes around the dictatorship commanded by General Rojas Pinilla (1953–1957). The government announced peace in the countryside, while persecuting the better-organized peasant groups. That promises of reconciliation were not fulfilled is illustrated by the assassination of the leader Guadalupe Salcedo, who had demobilized about 10,000 men under his command, still within the framework of the liberal guerrilla. *Pajaros* and *Chulavitas*, precursors of the paramilitaries, proliferated since the government of Laureano Gómez at the same time as the Colombian army was modernized with US assistance. Colombia was the only country in the region to send troops to the Korean War (1950–1953).

Faced with indications that the general intended to maintain himself in power by organizing workers in corporatist ways, the two ruling-class parties agreed to a division of powers, the *Frente Nacional*, analogous to the contemporary *Pacto de Punto Fijo* in Venezuela. This agreement provided for management of the state apparatus, including presidential alternation, shared between liberals and conservatives. It also determined the centralization of power in the executive, through a legal regime of exception that normalized situations such as state of siege, economic emergency and extraordinary powers to the president, while alternative social forces were proscribed. Formally in force until 1974, the political milestones established by the agreement proved to be long-lived, so that the first president-elect who was not affiliated with any of these parties was Álvaro Uribe, a liberal dissident, in 2002. The only occasion on which the bipartisanship was threatened was in 1970, when there were strong indications that electoral fraud prevented the victory of General Rojas Pinilla.

Students and other social movements participated in the mobilizations that overthrew the dictatorship in 1957, creating expectations of the solution to social conflicts through legal means. However, resistance to agrarian reform, combined with constraints against opposition within the system, resulted in an upswing of guerrilla struggle. The government advanced proposals for mercantile land reform within the framework of the US Alliance for Progress, conceived to prevent communism (Reyes Posada 2004). The political result in Colombia, as in other countries on the continent, was to exacerbate tensions in the countryside.

Simultaneously, the doctrine of 'national security' grounded counter-insurgency policies that included the grooming of rural communities and the formation of paramilitary groups. In this context, the bombing of territories managed by peasants converted sedentary self-defense militias into mobile forces. This is the main origin of the Colombian guerrillas whose activities stretched into the twenty-first century – the FARC and the National Liberation Army (ELN).

4 Insurgency and Counter-insurgency in the 1980s

Insurgent pressure in Colombia intensified in the early 1980s, boosted by the triumph of the Sandinista Revolution in 1979 and the offensive of guerrilla movements in El Salvador and Guatemala. Between 1984 and 1994, the Colombian guerrillas reached their apogee, when their numbers went from approximately 5,000 to 10,000 militants to more than 40,000. Paradoxically, this was a time when many guerrillas demobilized in Latin America, in a situation unfavorable to social change, aggravated regionally by the Sandinista defeat in 1990 and the collapse of the Soviet Union. Peru and Colombia are the only two countries on the subcontinent where armed confrontation continued through the 1990s, corresponding to repressive states comparable to the Southern Cone dictatorships that militarized social conflict, in the context of the expansion of what has been described as the 'criminal economy' (Durand 2007). They were also the two countries in which the degeneration of conventional parties that typified regional politics under neoliberalism did not translate into the electoral advance of progressivism.

The rise of insurgent pressure corresponded to a socio-economic inflection, in that a system of accumulation based on the internal market grounded on a national development landscape, gave way to a project based on commercial and financial liberalization, pointing to the de-nationalization of the economy from the second half of the 1980s. The adoption of measures identified with neoliberalism had negative socio-economic effects on the Colombian social fabric, the most visible of which was the expansion of drug trafficking.

Initially, the focus was the production of marijuana. In 1978, Colombia provided between 60 per cent and 65 per cent of the product consumed in the United States, growing between 20,000 and 25,000 hectares (Tokatlian 2004: 75). Despite extensive crop-spraying and increased production in the United States, ten years later the country was again the main supplier in this market.

The business with the greatest impact on Colombian society and its economy was cocaine. Unlike other Andean countries, Colombia is not a traditional producer of coca leaf tied to aboriginal cultures. Its original entry to the international division of drug trafficking was as a refiner and distributor of cocaine, a role it played in the 1980s, when powerful cartels were formed. In this decade, cocaine revenues exceeded that of coffee. Economists indicated that the weight of drug trafficking in the Colombian economy was one of the decisive elements for the country not to suffer the effects of the debt crisis in the period, a unique situation in the region (López Restrepo 2004: 27).

The country's relations with the US have since been shaped by policies targeting drug trafficking. Crop spraying, extraditions and the militarization of the drug issue are the pillars of a policy that has often been instrumental in criminalizing social movements and the insurgency – the guerrillas. The tone of this association was given by Ambassador Lewis Tambs, who coined the term 'narcoguerrilla' in 1984. Thus, the 1997 extradition agreement between Colombia and the US, which represented a flagrant violation of national sovereignty, has since been manipulated for political purposes. In addition to providing for the extradition of guerrillas such as Simón Trinidad, the agreement has sent criminals linked to drug trafficking and paramilitarism – and who would have compromising information involving members of the Colombian ruling classes and powerful politicians – to the United States.

The links between the state, paramilitarism and drug trafficking became closer during the 1980s. Drug trafficking infiltrated politics, institutions and high society in Colombia. Pablo Escobar, for example, became a Liberal Party congressman in 1982. Figures opposing the penetration of drug trafficking in this party, such as the minister of justice, Rodrigo Lara Bonilla, and the presidential candidate of the so-called new liberalism, Luis Carlos Galán, were murdered.

From an economic point of view, drug trafficking was among the sectors that actively supported neoliberal policies, as the links between financial liberalization, the criminal economy and money laundering are well known (Strange 1998). On the other hand, they perpetrated, for selfish reasons, a violent campaign in opposition to the policies of extradition to the US: better a grave in Colombia than a prison in the US, as Escobar said.

The growth of the insurgency pari passu with the expansion of narco-trafficking led to repressive responses from the state, supported by the US and resulting in the militarization of Colombian society. The links between the state, paramilitarism and drug trafficking intensified and proliferated. In 1981, important traffickers organized the Death to Kidnappers (MAS), a squad dedicated to the assassination of left-wing militants. The counter-insurgency techniques promoted by the US in Central America spread throughout the country. Farouk Yanine Díaz, a disciple of the notorious School of the Americas, implemented strategies based on coercing the population to cooperate with counter-insurgency in the Magdalena Medio, a pole of dynamic social protest in the country. Accused of complicity in numerous massacres perpetrated by paramilitaries, such as the nine paramilitary investigators in La Rochela in 1989, Diaz became commander of the national military forces the following year. Israeli advisers also acted in the country – for, example the mercenary Yari Klein, who trained several paramilitary groups. Later condemned by Colombian justice, Klein stated that he had been in the country at the invitation of the national police. In turn, leading paramilitary leader Carlos Castaño wrote in his autobiography that he had trained in Israel in 1983, and had copied the concept of Israeli paramilitary force. He said that he applied the lessons learned in Lebanon, the West Bank and the Gaza Strip to the Magdalena Medio region (Cepeda and Uribe 2014; Centro Nacional de Memoria Histórica 2014; Hylton 2006).

Cultivated by the state with US support, and financed by ranchers, multinationals, and drug traffickers, the political power of paramilitarism evolved throughout the 1980s and 1990s in line with the social sectors that supported it, becoming an obstacle to peace in the country (Lozano 2006). In 1982, the Betancur government established a Peace Commission that opened dialogues with the main insurgent forces, which led to the La Uribe accords signed with the FARC in 1984, foreseeing a bilateral ceasefire and the search for a political solution to the conflict. In this context of negotiation, which stipulated the constitution of an opposition movement incorporating the insurgency into political legality, the Unión Patriótica (UP) emerged in 1985 – a leftist front inspired by the experience of Popular Unity in Chile. From the beginning, the organization was harassed by the right wing and by the paramilitaries, leading to the rupture of the peace process.

Nevertheless, in the elections carried out the following year the UP became the third largest national political force, obtaining a significant vote for president and electing diverse parliamentarians and councilmen. In the years that followed, the sustained growth of the group unleashed an extraordinarily repressive wave. Between 1988 and 1995 there were 6,177 political murders in the country; 10,556 assassinations, presumably motivated politically; 9,140 deaths in combat between the army and guerrillas; and 1,451 forced disappearances (Giraldo 1996). For comparative purposes, the estimate of political murders in 17 years of dictatorship in Chile is around 3,000, a higher number than under Brazil's dictatorship (Giraldo 1996).

The dead include nearly all politicians elected by the UP: senators, deputies, mayors and councilors, as well as two presidential candidates, Jaime Pardo Leal and Bernardo Jaramillo. In the presidential campaign of 1990, two other candidates with progressive leanings were also assassinated: Luis Carlos Galán, leader of the new liberalism, and Carlos Pizarro, by the M-19, the guerrilla that had surrendered arms a month-and-a-half previously, as part of the constituent process. The extermination of members of the UP is one of the rare Colombian denunciations received by the Inter-American Commission on Human Rights (CIDH), which generally ignores petitions from the country's human rights organizations (conversation with Gallardo 2014).

5 Neoliberalism and Parapolitics

Although it is possible to trace the antecedents of neoliberal politics in Colombia to the 1970s, there is consensus that the government of President César Gaviria between 1990 and 1994 was a turning point (Estrada Álvarez 2004). At first, the constituent assembly gathered in 1991 intended to respond to the crisis in the political regime, negotiating the demobilization of some insurgent organizations, such as M-19 and the People's Liberation Army. Paradoxically, the new constitutional text affirmed economic and social rights, while at the same time laying the groundwork for the deregulation of the economy and the so-called fiscal discipline, consolidating a process that began before the assembly itself and which extends to the present. It was at this moment, for example, that the autonomy of the Central Bank became constitutional.

According to Jairo Estrada Álvarez, from then on 'the construction of a neoliberal order became state policy' (Estrada Álvarez 2009: 234). Consolidated amid the bloodbath unleashed by the rise of the UP, the affirmation of neoliberalism in Colombia has characteristics of the 'shock capitalism' that marked its pioneering deployment in Chile under Pinochet and in Peru under Fujimori. Similarly to what happened in Brazil, social rights enshrined in the Constitution were sidelined as part of the ongoing deterioration of the social action of the state in the framework of fiscal adjustment policies.

Neoliberalism redefined the role of the state in Colombia, as it became a key promoter of new markets and businesses for the private sector and multinationals. The decline of national markets as a reference for accumulation corresponded to the consolidation of a legal system that made national law innocuous, consecrated by the signing of a Free Trade Agreement (FTA) with the US. Although presented as a negotiation between states, this treaty deprived the Colombian state of its legal-economic prerogatives by subordinating it to a supranational norm subservient to transnational corporations:

> FTAs are the expression of a project of building a private capitalist order that regulates relations between private capitalist enterprises, especially multinational corporations, but which is coated with the state form of regulation and endowed with protection mechanisms that the state can provide.
>
> ESTRADA ÁLVAREZ 2009: 257

These 'protection mechanisms' involve the functions of surveillance and control, exercised within the prerogatives of the administration of justice and the monopoly of legitimate violence by the state. The process of militarization of the state and social relations in Colombia became more acute, since the UP genocide led to the rise of the armed insurgency. The degradation of politics in this context was exposed by proof that Gaviria's successor, the liberal Ernesto Samper, received support from drug traffickers in his election campaign. At this point, there was some staging in which, behind the presumed indignation of the US, and its suspension of the visa of a cowed president, the Americanization of the fight against drugs in the country had been completed (Tokatlian 2004: 103).

The corrosion of the social fabric engendered by the combination of neoliberalism and the criminal economy, with a militarist tinge, has affected all spheres of social relations. The workers' movement, hampered by the precariousness of labor relations and the growth of the informal economy in a country where trade unionism has become a high-risk activity, has not carried out a protest of national impact since the 1977 civic strike. In urban peripheries, the lack of a life perspective based on a regular job turns organized crime into an attractive career.

In rural areas, the deleterious effects of trade liberalization led many peasants to opt for illicit crops, making the country an important cultivator. In the words of a rural leader, 'It is not the will of the peasantry to sow coca, poppy or marijuana. The situation of marginality obliges [it to do so]' (conversation with Peasant Association of the Cimitarra River Valley 2014). As a result, the area of coca production tripled in the second half of the 1980s, while poppy production, which did not exist until then, reached 61 tons in 1999. At this time, illicit crops covered about 100,000 hectares, of which more than half were dedicated to coca. It is estimated that in the late 1990s, Colombia supplied 40 per cent of US marijuana imports and 90 per cent of cocaine. On the other side of the coin, the percentage of Gross Domestic Product (GDP) from agricultural production declined from 43 per cent in 1980 to 13 per cent in 1998, while food imports tripled in this decade (Hylton 2006; Tokatlian 2004; López Restrepo 2004).

In this context, the insurgent movements, notably the FARC, also became involved in the criminal economy. From the point of view of the peasantry, the guerrillas offered protection and stability to rural workers who would otherwise be expelled from their lands due to economic liberalization policies and the spiral of violence: 'prohibiting [cultivating coca] would imply isolating it [the guerrillas] from their bases' (Gros 2004: 114). On the other hand, although the guerrillas appropriated a fraction of the revenue from drug trafficking through taxes on planting and the commercialization of crops (a business in which about 7 per cent of the money remained in Colombia), this relationship weakened the legitimacy of the FARC. It was a dilemma, as the involvement with drug trafficking allowed the guerrillas to become stronger in the context of the continued degradation of the Colombian social fabric, which social struggles were powerless to reverse. The country's second guerrilla group, the ELN, refused to participate in drug trafficking, and has increased its reliance on other sources of income such as kidnappings, levies collected from multinationals that exploit the country's natural resources, and other forms of local taxation.

In 1992, the short-lived attempts at peace talks in Caracas and Tlaxcala (Mexico) were stopped by the government, which declared 'total war' against the insurgency. The spreading of military strategies involving peasant cooperation has resulted in an increase in civilian casualties. Although carried out by the paramilitaries and the state, which in many circumstances acted in the same way, the sharpening of repression also increased the brutality of the insurgency. This process, amplified extensively by the media, has alienated part of the civil support enjoyed by the guerrillas, in an international context frankly hostile to armed struggle.

However, more impressive than the growth of the guerrillas in the 1990s was the consolidation of paramilitarism – that is, armed groups operating on the margins of legality, often with state support. As governor of Antioquia since 1995, Álvaro Uribe played a decisive role in promoting and legalizing counter-insurgency militias which, in addition to terrorizing the civilian population in the face of guerrilla warfare, were invariably linked to criminal activities, further blurring the line that separates organized crime from politics (Cepeda and Uribe 2014). Uribe stimulated the creation of state Rural Surveillance Cooperatives (Convivir), modeled after the Peruvian peasant patrols and Guatemalan Civil Self-Defense Patrols of the 1980s, attempts to arm the peasantry as an ally of the state. Military strategies involving the coercion of peasants, begun by General Yanine Díaz in the Magdalena Medio in previous years, were perfected.

When in 1999 the Convivir was judged illegal by the country's Supreme Court, because of the numerous massacres of civilians attributed to it, many of its members simply went to the United Self-Defense Forces of Colombia (AUC). Considered to be the deadliest paramilitary organization in the country, the AUC also flourished in the shadow of Uribe, particularly in Cordoba and Uraba. In this banana region, homicide rates reached 700 in every 100,000, almost a hundred times more than in the US in the same period (eight in every 100,000). One year after the end of his tenure as governor, the rate declined to 300 per 100,000 (Hylton 2006: 94).

This violence was not only directed at political ends, but also fostered land concentration for the benefit of the governor and his allies (Cepeda and Uribe 2014). The brutal methods of territorial conquest based on massacres and terrorism that characterized the AUC (with Uribe's complicity) spread to other regions of the country. Following a geography coinciding with coca plantations, the organization commanded by the Castaño brothers became a leading drug trafficker in the country.

If the trajectory of the Uribe family has indelible marks of its relationship with *narcotrafico* – symbolized by the fact that he was taken to meet his father, killed by the FARC in 1983, in a helicopter belonging to Pablo Escobar – the project defended by the ex-president is of another nature: it involves the political organization of a diversified and powerful sector of Colombian society, which makes violence a means of life and thrives on war:

> Based on a discourse of self-defense with which they sought to legitimize themselves, the paramilitaries and their managers involved the poorest people in the war offering the possibility of social ascension during difficult times, creating a regime of terror and complicity that, far from limiting itself to the struggle against the counter-insurgency allowed them to conquer land, prefectures, governments,vacancies in Congress, to control and silence criticism, influence and participate in economic activity and to seek, as proposed by those who signed the celebrated Pact of Ralito, 'the re-foundation of the homeland'.
>
> CEPEDA and URIBE 2014: 76

When the conservative Andrés Pastrana won the presidential elections in 1998, proposing peace negotiations, a demilitarized zone in Colombian territory the size of Switzerland, known as *el Caguan*, was created – and conversation began again. In addition to the historical obstacles to a democratic solution to the conflict, there was an explicit commitment by the AUC, as part of a sector of society that opposed any peace attempt, to sabotage the talks. At the same time, transnationals which paid fees to the guerrillas channeled much more substantive resources to US lobbies in favor of a military solution to the conflict. The ambivalence of the government in this process, in which the talks did not imply a military truce, was shown in the adoption of Plan Colombia at a time when dialogue was still in progress. It was a sign that parapolitics was ready to culminate its assault on the state.

6   The War Party in Power

Plan Colombia should be interpreted in light of the constraints faced by the Colombian ruling class to end the armed conflict while neoliberalism simultaneously aggravated the social causes of the insurgency and weakened the means of the Colombian state to confront it. Viewed from this angle, the deepening of the US involvement reveals the nexus between the anti-democratic and anti-national dimensions of the country's bourgeoisie, as blocking the social change advocated by the insurgency led the ruling classes to blatantly compromise Colombia's national sovereignty.

Originally conceived in the US and drafted in English, the plan completed US intervention in Colombian politics under the pretext of combating drug trafficking by consolidating ties that would make the country a long-term ally in the region – an alliance which was strengthened by the signature of the FTA in 2006. The extradition of Colombians and the use of the country's military bases, coupled with US money, weapons, and advice for repression, came hand-in-hand with supranational business regulations and the devastation of natural resources under the label of free trade, to constitute a counter-revolutionary enclave in South American territory that is often compared to Israel.

The numbers are eloquent. US military aid to Colombia rose from US$317 million in 1999 to nearly US$1 billion in 2000, accounting for 80 per cent of total military and police assistance for all of Latin America. Globally, Colombia received the third largest military allocation from the US, after Israel and Egypt. Army personnel jumped from 80,000 soldiers in 1990 to 278,000 in 2002 and 386,000 in 2006, recently reaching some 500,000 soldiers, a mark that surpasses the army of Brazil, a country with a population five times greater. Revenues allocated to the armed forces rose from 2.2 per cent of GDP in 1990 to 5.3 per cent of GDP in 2005. If US contributions associated with Plan Colombia are included in the calculation, this rises to 6.1 per cent of GDP in 2005 (Caycedo 2009: 218–20; Silva 2013).

As might be expected, military action was concentrated in areas under guerrilla influence, leaving untouched the regions dominated by drug trafficking and paramilitarism. Since 2004, the so-called Plan Patriota has been implemented in the wake of Plan Colombia, and has contributed to the regionalization of the conflict, the culmination of which was the bombing of FARC bases in Ecuadorian territory in 2008. The paramilitaries also overflowed national boundaries, aggravating the problem of crime in Venezuela. According to Hylton, more than a hundred Colombians were jailed in that country for conspiring to assassinate Hugo Chávez in coordination with paramilitaries and the Administrative Department of Security (DAS), the intelligence service that answers to the president (Hylton 2006: 116). On the ideological level, the Uribe government of 2002 to 2010 denied the political status of the insurgency, a premise on which previous peace talks were anchored, and surfed on the rhetoric of the fight against terrorism, globalized after 9/11. By categorizing the guerrillas as terrorist organizations, the government denied the political roots of the conflict, laying the foundations for the broad criminalization of social protest.

This movement was neither initiated nor terminated in Uribe's government. In 1997, a Constitutional Court ruling modified the relationship between rebellion and common crimes, implying that if a guerrilla killed a soldier he was to stand trial for murder. This scenario made other legal tools such as pardon and amnesty even more remote. However, under Uribe the persecution of the opposition intensified, often with the accusation of 'crime of rebellion' in processes that forged spurious associations between his opponents and the insurgency. By 2015 there were more than 9,000 political prisoners estimated in the country, with widespread persecution of members of trade unions, universities and the countryside (Encuentro Nacional por la Libertad de lxs Prisionerxs Politicxs 2011; conversations with Asociación Campesina del Valle of the Rio Cimitarra 2014, Gallardo 2014; Rivera 2014).

Colombia is a country where not only the rich but also activists circulate in armored cars provided by a state incapable of guaranteeing the physical safety of an opposition that it criminalizes. This is not a matter of ceremony: Aída Avella, the leftist alliance candidate for vice president in the 2014 elections, had survived a mortar bomb thrown at her car in downtown Bogota in 1996. It is not uncommon for militants to wear bulletproof vests or to take precautions characteristic in a dictatorship, such as avoiding set routes to prevent identification of their daily locations.

The harassment of militancy is only one of the faces of an overall militarization of society, continued by Uribe's successor. Between 2000 and 2011 the country's penal code was amended 36 times, creating 47 new offenses and at the same time increasing the penalties for 80 crimes. In the same period, the prison population doubled, and in the next two years it increased by 20 per cent to 120,000 inmates in a prison system whose capacity also doubled, but which was still less than 78,000. Underpinned by legislation that does not discriminate political from other crimes, life in prison is hellish in all its dimensions, from obstacles to visits, to convictions that arbitrarily prolong their stay in prison. Held together with common prisoners, they are often tortured and stigmatized in jail (National Encounter for Freedom of Political Prisoners 2011).

In contrast, the Uribe government moved mountains to accommodate the paramilitaries in legality, in an international context in which organizations like the AUCs were considered to be terrorist. Under Uribe, the search for peace with the insurgency turned into peace with the paramilitaries. This commitment culminated in the Justice and Peace Law of 2005, a kind of pardon for paramilitaries hitherto regarded as political criminals (Lozano 2006: 99). Some became legal, while others demobilized the old organizations and constituted so-called criminal bands (*bacrim*), which are still active. More serious cases carried sentences of up to eight years, and people in several regions of the country are now apprehensive about the imminent release of these criminals.

From the socio-economic point of view, peasant expulsion under the aegis of combating narco-terrorism reached unprecedent levels, making Colombia one of the largest producers of refugees on the planet. The economic rationality of these forced removals – that were accompanied by the expansion of African palm plantations (raw material for biofuels) illicit crops, mining and oil extraction – was defined by several authors as 'accumulation by disposession', following David Harvey (Harvey 2006; Bautista 2013; Estrada Álvarez 2009). In other cases, the plundered land has become a source of wealth, exacerbating land concentration. According to a report by the United Nations Development Program (UNDP) in 2011, 39 million hectares of land were destined for livestock, and only 4 million for agriculture – in a country that is not a major meat producer – suggesting sparse and unproductive occupation of land and corroborating one of the world's worst concentration rates of land tenure (Programa Naciones Unidas para el Desarrollo 2011). Colombia was self-sufficient in food in 1988; 25 years later it imported 11 million tons of food. War is felt less in cities, although the militarization of life, normal for ordinary citizens, is evident to the eyes of a tourist. Violence permeates all spheres of existence, including cultural production: sensitive films about the conflict coexist with serials and feature films that replicate the police dynamics of US productions, often creating folklore around some of the most nefarious figures associated with drug trafficking, such as Pablo Escobar and the Castaño brothers.

Bogota has become a service center where real estate and financial speculation flourish. As in other countries of the region, speculation has dominated production, accentuating the vulnerability of the economy to the movements of international capital, while the world of work is degraded. The growth of the informal economy is the other side of this process. Thus, paramilitary territorial control in rural areas corresponds to paramilitary control of urban peripheries, and the command of the informal economy. With the election of Uribe, the composite group of interests that thrive under the violence arrived at the Palace of Nariño. The political association set up by the president, ironically called Centro Democratico (Democratic Center), had all of its congressmen condemned or investigated for ties with paramilitarism (Cepeda and Uribe 2014). Gone were the days when former president Samper was harassed internally and externally for receiving campaign money from drug traffickers.

The political project led by Uribe concealed class violence behind an ideology of national interest, expressed in the notion of 'democratic security' proclaimed by his government. In addition to poisoning the political environment by criminalizing social protest – supported by the rhetoric of terrorism and replicated by the mainstream media – the intention was to consolidate both the subjective and objective bases of a project of power. In other words, the Uribe bloc set out to contest hegemony over Colombian society.

The material foundations of this policy are diverse. Beyond the direct beneficiaries of the political economy of violence – such as drug traffickers, the high military command, agri-business and landowners – an economy has been created which is dependent on militarism and which transcends even the criminal economy. The degradation of the formal economy has transformed the army into a valuable professional opportunity, the military into a lifestyle and the soldier into a good starting point. With an estimated 500,000 soldiers and the creation of approximately two additional jobs for each soldier in support activities, a total of about 1.5 million Colombians were involved, meaning that about 3 per cent of the population was subsisting directly from the war (conversation with Estrada Álvarez 2014).

The government also invested in a social program in the style of the Brazilian *Bolsa Família*, Families in Action, which aimed to reach 2.5 million families – an estimated 40 million people. In terms of propaganda, there was massive investment in advertising campaigns aimed at building a consensus around the elimination of insurgency as the road to peace (conversation with Rocancio 2014).

Uribe's high levels of popularity over the course of his term explain a poisoning of politics and culture in a militarized society that favors repressive outlets, as if violence could be resolved with more violence. This trend in Colombian society should be understood in light of a combination of factors, among which the following stand out: the political and social effects of the extermination of a generation of militants linked to the UP; the blockage of emerging political alternatives within the system; the de-structuring of the world of work in the context of neoliberalism; the further criminalization of social protest; apathy as a consequence of the narrowness of the political landscape, expressed in high levels of electoral abstention; indifference as a psychic defense against endemic violence in which the citizen perceives himself as impotent; a discourse that spreads hatred while concealing the social roots of the perpetuation of violence, in a global context resonant with this rhetoric. Uribe's sustained popularity allowed for the constitutional reform that permitted his re-election, as well as allowing him to elect his successor in 2010.

7 Dilemmas of the Peace Process

A politician from a traditional lineage in the country's ruling classes, Juan Manuel Santos was elected in 2010 with talk of continuity with the Uribe government, of which he had been defense minister. In fact, no substantive changes were observed in economic policy or social programs, and the criminalization of popular movements continued.

Nonetheless, Santos's choice of reopening dialogue as a way to peace in Colombia, establishing a negotiation process with the FARC in Havana in 2012, caused a distancing from Uribe. Expressive of the suffocating conservatism that prevailed, the cleavage between the two politicians of liberal origin polarized the electoral dispute of 2014. The central issue in this contest was security policy. Uribe's candidate, Oscar Iván Zuluaga, defended the break in the dialogues of peace, in contrast with Santos. Zuluaga gained more votes in the first round, and then the polarization sharpened.

In the second round, there was relative agreement in the popular camp to support Santos as a vote for peace. Peasant movements, in full confrontation with the government after a successful national stoppage in 2013, discreetly lifted the pressure. The more than 15 per cent of the votes obtained by the left-wing candidate in the first round were claimed by the peace process. In this context, Santos was re-elected.

From a class point of view, there was no substantive difference between the projects disputing the second round. Santos represented the segments of the Colombian ruling classes, whose business is favored by a peaceful environment, while Uribe was sustained by those who prosper best during war. However, this difference translates into very different political landscapes. And with Santos's victory, negotiations continued in Havana.

The premise for the dialogue on the side of the FARC, considerably weakened after the Uribe war, was that the takeover of the state was no longer a goal of the insurgency. From the government's point of view, the premise was that the end of the war would be less costly and more effective through conversation, since the resilience of the insurgency had been attested to. However, there was no ceasefire, suggesting that, as in previous negotiations, the government was simultaneously carrying out dialogue and war, especially to weaken the guerrilla position as the talks unfolded in Havana.

Among popular organizations there was an expectation that a political solution to the confrontation would open chinks in the autocratic structure of the Colombian state, which would be widened by the rise of a mass movement (Chagas and Pismel 2014). The left's support of the process was almost unanimous: the prevailing understanding being that the burden of perpetuating the insurgency – used to legitimize the persecution of all opposition in the country – was not compensated by the guerrillas' capacity to keep in check the monopoly of violence by the state, particularly as the armed struggle was isolated internationally. Specifically, it was intended for the dialogues in Havana to culminate in the convening of a Constituent Assembly, broadening the base of support for the agreements. This was because the five themes of the talks (integral agrarian development, political participation, end of conflict, solution to the problem of illicit drugs, victims of violence) concerned the whole of Colombian society and presupposed its radical democratization (Voz 2013).

Underlying the peace process was an impasse: the government believed that it would lead the guerrillas to disarmament through minimum concessions, which could be reversed without bloodshed in the near future, as had happened in Central America. Its adherence to the process had a perverse feature in that it sought to turn around the explicit meaning of peace (to pacify the country through change) and aimed to freeze change in order to achieve peace. On the other hand, the popular field, which includes the guerrillas, understood that it would be possible to take advantage of the dialogues to build a social movement around peace, politicizing its content from the agenda advanced in the dialogues. The common ground between both was the intention to dispute Uribist hegemony.

However, the guarantor of the negotiations was a government that sailed in dangerous waters, limited on the one hand by a state colonized by parapolitics, and on the other by the constraints to social democratization. Santos showed little autonomy or willingness to confront parapolitics, nor did he point to social changes. His strategy was to consolidate a political field opposed to Uribe, in order to assert himself as the hegemon of the bourgeois order.

In short, the government and social movements were provisionally unified against the war party. Santos, however, intended to assert himself as an alternative within the system, while the popular field aimed at changing the social structures that underpin a system which found political expression in Uribism, but also in Santos. In a word, the first proposed an alternative to Uribe's political project, while the second projected an entirely different society. Ultimately, the government and social movements intended to use the process of dialogue for contradictory purposes: one to freeze change and the other to unleash it.

However, it was an unequal negotiation, in which the government had the power to set the pace and timing of the process, and thus subordinate it to its political agenda. It was from this perspective that, on 2 October 2016, the signing of the agreements negotiated in Havana was submitted to a popular plebiscite. Far from any democratic concern, the plebiscite was conceived by the government as an occasion to reaffirm its position of strength to the detriment of Uribism, which had been losing ground at all levels since the previous elections. With more space in the media, and with a great advantage in the polls, the government took for granted a victory in the plebiscite. The Uribe-led 'no' campaign also predicted its defeat and, for this reason, opposed the referendum.

The shot, however, backfired. In a tight election, marked by the high rate of abstention that characterized the country's elections (62.67 per cent), the 'no' won by a small margin: 50.21 per cent of the votes against 49.79 per cent 'yes' vote. The electoral map expressed social fractures that refer to the very origin of the insurgency – a majority 'yes' vote in territories affected directly by the conflict but defeat in areas with lower incidences of violence. In the end, contrary to strengthening the president, the plebiscite indicated a fall in his popularity: for many, a no vote was more a rejection of Santos than of peace. Consequently, instead of preparing the government for the following presidential elections, the plebiscite signaled its political unraveling.[3]

In addition to Santos's calculations, the result made explicit, once again, the poisoning of Colombian politics, exploited by parapolitics and the Uribe bloc. In a dishonest campaign aimed at arousing indignation instead of clarifying (as its coordinator acknowledged), it was widely reported that the agreements represented 'castrochavismo' (a blend of Cuba's Castro and Venezuela's Chávez), bankruptcy of the family and the economy, opening the door for the FARC to preside over the country. It was announced that the guerrillas would not surrender their weapons; that each insurgent would receive a scholarship of around 700 dollars from the government (which would mean reducing the pensions of other workers); that the FARC would have 26 seats in Congress (not 10) – and more. The key message was that the government was in the process of turning the country over to terrorists. On the other hand, the 'yes' campaign had difficulties in countering those messages. Although the mainstream media was mostly sympathetic to peace, this same press had criminalized armed struggle for decades. It was not trivial to defend the political integration of those who had always been portrayed as an internal enemy.

The setback of the plebiscite did not abort the peace process, since the consultation was political rather than normative in nature: it decided whether the president of the Republic would sign this specific agreement but did not cover its content. In the following weeks, parties signed a new agreement, modifying minor aspects of the original text. In 2016, Santos submitted it for the approval of Congress, where he enjoyed a majority, without risking a new plebiscite. On the other side, the war party questioned the process in its entirety, sowing

---

3 In presidential elections the following year, the two candidates close to Santos, Germán Vargas Lleras and Humberto de la Calle, totaled about 9 per cent of the votes in the first round, ranking fourth and fifth.

instability and discord in order to present itself in the next elections as the alternative party of order.[4]

In short, the defeat of the plebiscite did not make the peace agreement unfeasible, but it did reveal its contradictions, as well as the ways in which the Colombian counter-revolution in the twenty-first century has re-established itself, blocking change as a path to peace.

---

4   The elections held in 2018 were won by Uribe's candidate, Iván Duque, who defeated Gustavo Petro, identified with the center-left, in the second round. The FARC participated as a political party, the Fuerza Alternativa Revolucionaria del Común, which, following the agreements signed in Havana, will hold a quota of ten of the 280 seats in Congress.

CHAPTER 11

Where is the Cuban Revolution Going? Dilemmas of Primitive Socialism

> This country can self-destruct itself; this Revolution can destroy itself, who cannot destroy it are they; we can destroy it and it would be our fault.
>
> *Fidel Castro, 2005*

> In the United States we have a clear monument of what Cubans can build: it's called Miami.
>
> *Barack Obama in Havana, March 2016*

1   Introduction

Cuba is not in South America and was governed by the left long before the progressive wave began. However, since the 1959 revolution the island has become a reference and foothold for anti-capitalist politics in the region. Reciprocally, Cuban politics was conditioned by the regional environment, a perception crystallized since the nineteenth century in the ideal of *Nuestra America* forged by José Martí. During the Cold War, the triumph of the revolution ignited hopes of change, which in turn strengthened the resolve of counterrevolutionary reaction as expressed in numerous dictatorships in Latin America. On the other hand, Cuba's regional isolation was decisive in its decision to approach the Soviet Union, a move that influenced the revolution for both good and evil. Boycotted, defamed and isolated, Cuba resisted the end of real socialism as a reference to another possible world under increasingly adverse circumstances.

In this inhospitable setting that put socialism on the defensive, the election of progressive governments in South America was a breath of fresh air. As always, the island supported friendly governments and actively sought out mutual support. It did business with Brazil and with Venezuela it established a relationship of trust that resulted in diverse, formal and informal exchanges, reciprocated with economic and political support as materialized in the Bolivarian Alternative for the Americas (ALBA). In other words, relations with Cuba influenced the South American progressive wave, while the scope and limits of this process determined the margin of maneuver for the Cuban revolution. What happened and is happening in Cuba is a thermometer of the possibilities of structural change in the region.

2 Revolution against Underdevelopment

The Cuban Revolution that triumphed in 1959 was a reaction to underdevelopment. From this perspective, it established egalitarianism and national sovereignty as central values. However, the realization of these values through the first measures of the revolutionary government provoked the intolerant reaction of the ruling classes and imperialism, making explicit the link between external dependence and social asymmetry in peripheral capitalism. Almost immediately the Cubans faced a dilemma between radicalizing or reversing the changes the revolution had initiated. It is this dynamic that led a national democratic and popular project to the socialist path. In the words of Florestan Fernandes: 'The "revolution within the system" was a real moment of the Cuban revolution. It lasted little time and was quickly extinguished because only the wretched of the Earth mobilized to fight for it. The "revolution against the system" has, alternatively, become a permanent reality and in increasing acceleration' (Fernandes 2007: 35).

Initial government measures included: suppressing lotteries and gambling; declaring the country's beaches to be for public use; reducing drug prices and telephone charges; establishing a minimum wage for sugarcane cutters; creating the Ministry of Recovery of Misappropriated Goods to take back assets appropriated by the dictatorship; carrying out the trial of accomplices of the dictatorship through popular tribunals; and, constituting the Committees for the Defense of the Revolution (CDRs). This set of measures did not have a socialist orientation. Urban reform, which reduced rents by 50 per cent and converted rent payments into real estate amortization, was conceived against rentism. Property was limited to just one residence and former landlords who had no other income received a state pension.

Even the land reform initially enacted, which sealed the United States' hostility to the revolution, can be described as moderate. It sought to combat rentism in the countryside by distributing idle land holdings to landless workers but allowed large estates with a yield 50 per cent higher than the national average on any crop. On the whole, the proposal did not deviate from the ECLA objectives of diversifying production, industrializing agriculture and integrating the population through work. At the same time, agrarian reform extended private land ownership to 200,000 families (Vasconcelos 2016).

Initially, the United States sought to cripple the Cuban revolution through economic means by reducing sugar purchases. Fidel Castro summed up the revolution's response by stating that as the US cuts Cuba's quota pound for pound, Cuba will take US sugar mills one by one. At the same time, the Cubans began a rapprochement with the Soviets, which until then had had nothing to do with the revolution. When US refineries refused to process Soviet oil, a situation that if continued would have paralyzed the island's economy, the revolutionaries decided to nationalize them. The government of Dwight D. Eisenhower suspended the purchase of Cuban sugar and in his last days as president, broke US diplomatic relations with the country (Faya and Rodríguez 1996).

At the same time, preparations were accelerated for a military invasion of the island by mercenaries trained and funded by the CIA, which subsequently took place in the early months of John F. Kennedy's administration in 1961. In a visible nod to the Soviet Union, Castro declared the socialist character of the revolution on the eve of the invasion. Even at this delicate moment, when the survival of the revolutionary process was threatened by US-sponsored violence, Fidel spoke of a revolution of the humble. In a speech that defied Marxist orthodoxy Castro stated: 'Workers and peasants, this is the socialist and democratic revolution of the humble, with the humble and for the humble (Applause). And for this Revolution of the humble by the humble and for the humble, we are ready to give life' (Castro 1961a). As Fernando Martínez Heredia has argued, the revolution was an assault against oligarchies, but also against revolutionary dogmas (conversation with Martínez Heredia 2016).

The failure of the Bay of Pigs invasion (known in Cuba as *Playa Girón*), which was defeated in less than three days, only intensified imperial hostility to the revolution. From that point on US policy was marked by: economic sanctions, military threats, covert operations, assassination attempts, political and diplomatic isolation, media campaigning, dissident financing and other aggressions (conversation with Acosta González 2016). Symptomatically, the invasion occurred in the middle of an extraordinary national literacy campaign that mobilized the country's secondary and university youth and eventually eradicated illiteracy. The booklet used in the campaign introduced students to vowels through the acronym OEA (Organization of American States); an outfit from which Cuba had ironically, recently been expelled.

Throughout the 1960s, the Cuban state became an active participant in and supporter of, the movement of non-aligned countries. Faced with the servility of Latin American states, that systematically endorsed the US condemnation of the revolution in international forums, Cuba welcomed and encouraged revolutionary organizations and those committed to the sovereignty of peoples in the region. A few months before Che Guevara was assassinated in Bolivia in

1967, the conference that gave rise to the Latin American Organization of Solidarity (OLAS) was held.

Cuba's gravitation towards the Soviet sphere, which was consummated in the 1970s, must be understood within the country's double limitation: the regional isolation of the revolution in a context in which military dictatorships prevented any trajectory analogous to that of Cuba on the subcontinent; and the significant obstacles to confronting the economic dimensions of underdevelopment and industrialize the country.

In the early years of the revolution, there were intense debates about the economic development strategy to be adopted. Among other issues discussed were: the role of sugar in the economy; the possibilities of industrialization; the scope of economic planning; the role of the market; and, material stimuli versus moral motivations (Guevara et al. 2006). However, at the end of the 1960s it was agreed that Cuba's specialized insertion in the Soviet economic sphere as a supplier of sugar was the most desirable route to follow. The worsening of the blockade imposed by the United States and the obstacles to overcoming the colonial legacy in a small economy lacking diversity, converged with geopolitical and security considerations to seal the decision. The Cuban representative at the Council for Mutual Economic Assistance (Comecon), into which the island was integrated in 1972, summed up the situation: 'This dependence is the only condition in which we can maintain our independence' (Rodríguez in Vasconcelos 2016: 332).

The relationship with the Soviets left contradictory marks on the Cuban Revolution, which Limia Díaz synthesizes in two ways: on the one hand, the undeniable reality that the Soviets helped and defended the island, a fact recognized by Cubans in general; on the other hand, a dogmatism and bureaucracy that left a legacy harmful to Cuban politics and culture. In this regard though, it is necessary to clarify that the relationship between Cuba and the Soviets cannot be compared to that between the Soviets and east European countries, because the island was never subordinated to the Soviet Union. For example, there was no Soviet participation in discussions of the Cuban Communist Party (conversation with Limia Díaz 2016 and Padron 2016).

The Soviets imported sugar at fixed prices, which were often above international market prices. Simultaneously they provided cheap loans and technical assistance in a variety of fields, from defense to sports. These measures provided precious stability for the island, which had unprecedented conditions to organize and plan development. At the same time, Martínez Heredia notes that the Soviets never paid more than a third of what it would have cost them to produce sugar beet. Further, they never agreed for example, to sell a steel factory to Cuba. In short, the relationship with the Soviets did not establish the bases for greater economic autonomy nor for industrialization but was fundamental to universalize the social achievements for which the island is known worldwide (conversation with Martínez Heredia 2016).

As a result, Cuba entered the 1980s with the best indices in health, education, employment, culture and sports in Latin America, if not all of the Third World. These were achieved in an economy with characteristics typical of underdevelopment, such as external dependence, modest industrialization, low productive diversification and low wages, although structural unemployment and overexploitation of labor were alien to the island.

However, the potential for social achievements was limited by the incorporation of traits associated with the Soviet regime, which restricted the possibilities of political contestation and artistic creation. This is not a criticism from the liberal framework that simply highlights the lack of freedom and democracy associated with political prisoners and the multiparty system.[1] The policy of early years of the revolution in this field was outlined by Fidel in 1961, in his address known as 'A Word to the Intellectuals': 'Inside the revolution, everything; against the revolution, nothing' (Castro 1961b).[2] However, by the 1970s there was a notable overlapping of political and cultural practices, which were often subject to dogmatism and bureaucracy under the guise of revolutionary criteria. In the final analysis, they emanated from a conservative version of revolution itself, which restrained its necessary renewal.

By the 1980s the Cuban revolutionary leadership understood that the imperative of survival was exacting an excessive price on revolutionary freedom. Or perhaps it realized, with the rise of Mikhail Gorbachev in 1985, that survival would require counter-measures. In 1986, a rectification was initiated against Cuban 'followism' of the Soviet Union, which expanded the role of the market and material incentives; at the same time, the reformist route diffused in Eastern Europe was rejected. (Gott 2004: 309).

In fact, when the Soviet Union broke up, Russian President Boris Yeltsin implemented a policy that reduced Cuba's trade with Russia by 94 per cent; until then, 85 per cent of Cuba's international trade had been reliant on Comecon. In addition, the Russians inscribed the Cuban debt within the Paris Club (an international forum representing international creditors created in the 1950s) as if it were in US dollars, with all the associated interest and monetary conditionalities (Rodríguez 2011).[3]

---

[1] On the Cuban political system, consult: August, 2014; Rafuls Pineda, 2014; and, Guanche, 2012.
[2] On the context and significance of this phrase, consult: Martínez Heredia, 2010, pp. 42–52.
[3] In 2003, during the Vladimir Putin presidency, 90 per cent of the debt was canceled with the remaining 10 per cent having to be paid, with favorable terms, over 10 years.

The end of the Soviet Union and Comecon was devastating for the Cuban economy. Between 1989 and 1993, the Gross Domestic Product (GDP) fell by almost 35 per cent; the capacity to import fell by 70 per cent; the country ran out of credit; as a result of oil shortages, power cuts were such that Cubans joked about having '*alumbrones*' (light-ins) rather than '*apagones*' (blackouts); bicycles occupied cities where there were few cars or buses; oxen pulled plows instead of tractors; malnutrition, eradicated in previous years, returned (though not overall hunger); and, spare parts, fertilizers and consumer goods were lacking. By 1993, Cuba was importing only 17 per cent of the same goods it had imported in 1989.

And yet, even while the 'socialisms' of the Soviet Union and Eastern Europe were coming to an end and Latin American neighbors were plunging into neo-liberalism, the Cuban Revolution survived: 'Few societies have been able to cope with such an economic catastrophe and come out unscathed', wrote the historian Richard Gott, who is not an advocate of the regime (Gott 2004: 323).

Efforts to overcome adversities of this magnitude were compared by Fidel to a war situation: hence the reference to a 'special period in times of peace'. To get through this period, the leadership radicalized the distributive criterion that always prevailed in the revolution, establishing priorities that everyone understood: milk is for children; dollars are for medicines and not for guns; and, everyone has only a little bread. Cubans understood the situation and relied on strategies to deal with them, backed by a leadership that had, over thirty years, proven that they were not corrupt, economically or ideologically. They also understood that the alternatives practiced in Eastern Europe or Latin America would jeopardize the very social gains and sovereignty associated with the revolution that every Cuban treasures.

However, it is wrong to say that Cuban society left the special period unscathed, as Gott has suggested. The precept of fundamental equality that had characterized it was split in two senses. First, the economic crisis compromised the State's capacity to respond to the basic needs of the population, which was expressed in a growing disparity between wages and workers purchasing power.

This situation generated multiple distortions. The main one was a booming US dollar black market, where scarce products circulated. Gradually, a new reality arose in which every Cuban needed to access dollars to supplement their income. As the State opted for the reactivation of tourism as the main source of foreign exchange, access to dollars was provided through three basic channels: tourism; remittances from relatives abroad; and, involvement in the black market itself.

Second, this economic duality promoted a growing inequality between those who had and those who did not have access to foreign currency. In this context, many teachers went to work in tourism while medical enrollments exploded in the hope of serving on a foreign mission. Cuba must be the only country in the world where the hosts are at an educational and cultural level superior to the tourists that visit them. And, it is certainly the only one where the medical services it provides around the world are its principal source of external income.

The alternatives pursued by the Cuban leadership to respond to these challenges implied a controlled opening to private initiative and foreign investment, as well as the attempt to discipline internal disparities that could not be avoided. An economy that for decades was among the least commodified in the world took a number of counter-measures. The state monopoly on foreign trade was abolished. A new law, which required a change in the 1976 Constitution,[4] allowed consortiums between the state and international investors in any area except health, education and defense, while limiting international participation to a maximum of 49 per cent. The number of joint ventures jumped from 2 in 1990 to 112 in 1993. So-called 'self-employment' ('*cuentapropismo*') has been legalized, allowing a diversity of small private businesses, with the most successful being linked to tourism such as restaurants, cafes and room rentals. The tax system, in which previously Cuban workers did not pay taxes, was reorganized. In rural areas, many state farms were transformed into Basic Units of Cooperative Production (UBPC), aiming to increase food production. Agricultural products markets were created, as were markets for industrial and artisanal products. The state reformed the banking system, legalized the ownership of dollars and opened currency exchanges and stores selling foreign exchange products, with the aim of disciplining the mercantile circuit in hard currency (Gott 2004; López Segrera 2010; Tablada 2001).

In the following years, monetary duality was institutionalized through the creation of the convertible Cuban peso (CUC) in place of the US dollar.[5] The gap between current transactions in the national currency of Cuban pesos (CUP) in which state salaried employees are paid, and those in convertible pesos, which assume access to foreign exchange, continues to defy social equality.

The difficulties faced by the island were intensified by American policies. Whoever had imagined that the United States would soften anti-Cuban policy

---

4 The Constitution prohibited non-state forms of ownership of the means of production as well as businesses with foreign capital.
5 In 2016, the CUC was quoted at 24 Cuban pesos (CUP).

with the end of the Cold War underestimated the nature of imperialism. Initially, the United States stiffened the economic blockade by means of the Torricelli Act in 1992, figuring that the sharpening of the crisis would lead to the overthrow of the Castro 'regime'. At the same time, terrorist organizations based in Miami carried out attacks on tourist targets on the island, which were aimed at sabotaging the revitalization of the sector.[6] When the island's economic recovery was evident in 1996, the Bill Clinton administration passed the Helms-Burton Act[7] days after the shooting down of two planes, illegally being flown over the island by anti-Castro organizations. In addition to insisting on the demand for 'democracy' as part of its terms to recognize the Cuban government (opposition parties with access to the media, free, fair and internationally supervised elections, advances in a market economy, specific clauses vetoing Fidel or Raul in government, etc.), the Helms-Burton Act stipulated that any individual or company negotiating with Cuban properties that belonged to an American citizen (or a Cuban with US citizenship) and which had previously been nationalized, would be sued in US courts. While the main purpose of the law was to scare off any foreign investment on the island, this particular clause has been interpreted as a violation of international law, including by the European Union, and as such, its implementation has been suspended by the president every six months through a legal subterfuge (Gott 2004: 342).

On the whole, the measures implemented during the special period, which were discussed between January and March 1994 by 3 million members of the Workers Central Union of Cuba (CTC) as well as debated in assemblies in more than 80 thousand places of work and in a special session of the National Assembly, had the desired economic effect (Gott 2004: 329). In that same year the economy came out of recession and from 1996 onwards it resumed growth, led by the tourism sector which expanded on average by 18 per cent a year during the special period. Between 1995 and 2005, the country grew at an average rate of 4.5 per cent. In 2006, when the GDP had returned to the level of 1989, the Ministry of Economy declared that Cuba had overcome the 'special period' (López Segrera 2010: 31).

Despite overcoming a crisis of colossal proportions in a peripheral and isolated nation while preserving the fundamental milestones of the revolution,

---

6 The Cuban government's intelligence efforts to prevent these actions, which resulted in the arrest of ten Cubans accused of espionage in the United States, is vividly narrated by Fernando Morais (Morais 2011).

7 The Helms-Burton Act prevents the President of the United States from changing the rules of the embargo or eliminating it, something that can only be done by Congress. The legislation also obliges the president to vote against Cuba's entry into multilateral organizations, depriving the island of important sources of credit.

the perception that revolutionary values were threatened provoked reactions. In 2000 the government announced a 'Battle of Ideas', a set of social initiatives aimed at mitigating potential inequalities but centered around a discourse revealing that the impact of the end of the socialist bloc went beyond its economic effects, affecting subjectivity as well. At the end of 2005 when Fidel Castro was about to leave the government, he gave a speech to the youth in which he stressed the risk that the revolution could destroy itself, but not because of the actions of external adversaries: 'This country can self-destruct itself; this Revolution can destroy itself, who cannot destroy it are they; we, yes, we can destroy it and it would be our fault' (Castro 2005b).[8]

When he assumed the presidency of the Council of State in February 2008, Raul Castro faced these same dilemmas.

3 Reform or Update?

Echoing the state's version, the president of the Federation of University Students (FEU) affirmed that 'Cuba is not making reforms but updating its economic model' (conversation with Martínez 2016). And yet, many understand that 'although we may not like the word, we are facing a reform' (Cobo et al. 2013: 70). What this speaks to is the core of current dilemmas, which is linked to the limitations in universalizing social rights in an underdeveloped economy, aggravated by modernizing pressures towards a consumption pattern associated with a digital society. In other words, they refer to the contradictory possibilities of realizing a 'primitive socialism' in a hostile international environment (Martínez Heredia, 2003).

At the root of the ongoing changes are the economic problems that erupted in the special period, accentuated by neoliberal domination and the crisis of world capitalism. Favorable relations with Venezuela allowed some relief to the island, which exported social and medical services on a large scale and received oil on favorable terms, but these have declined with the falling price of commodities.

Between 2008 and 2010, GDP growth slowed to an average of 2.5 per cent, while the fiscal deficit worsened. The Cuban state's inability to sustain workers past standards of living is revealed by analysis of the basic expenditures of families that depend on wages or retirement funds. In 2011, spending on food consumed between 59–74 per cent of the Cuban family income, since the basic basket to which every worker is entitled (*libreta de abastecimiento*) only

---

8 A book organized by Guanche compiles debates motivated by this speech (Guanche, 2007).

satisfied the minimum caloric consumption of children up to seven years old. In that same year, it was estimated that the deficit of income to meet the basic needs of reproduction of life ranged from 185 CUP (a family with two workers and one retiree) to 747 CUP (a family with one worker) (García, Álvarez and Anaya Cruz 2014). These numbers reveal that every Cuban family whose main income comes from the state is forced to seek complementary sources of income.

José Luis Rodríguez, an economist who piloted the island's economy through the special period, summed up the current challenges: reducing the balance of payments deficit; increasing labor productivity; and, expanding and improving infrastructure (conversation with Rodríguez 2016). In principle, these goals involve cutting state spending, breaking with the egalitarianism of remuneration and attracting foreign financing and investment. They point, therefore, to measures that are contrary to the values of equality and sovereignty and closer to the neoliberal spectrum.

However, the affinity with neoliberalism is at most formal, since in Cuba social expenditures as a proportion of the GDP have never been reduced, state ownership and employment remain dominant and the relationship with international capital is disciplined. Moreover, contrary to the opacity that characterizes global fiscal adjustment policy, decisions of this nature are subject to wide popular consultation (Martínez 2001). This was the case in respect of the 'Guidelines for Economic and Social Policy' (*Lineamientos de la política económica y social*) that has guided Cuban policies since 2011 and which was debated in more than 163000 meetings involving 8 million participants at the base. It was only after this participatory process that the policy was finalized during the 4th Congress of the Communist Party of Cuba, resulting in the modification of 197 of the original 291 guidelines and the addition of 20 new guidelines (4th Congress of the Communist Party of Cuba 2011).

Broadly speaking, the need to increase the dynamism and efficiency of the Cuban economy is being carried out by expanding the role of the market and private initiative, as opposed to the State economy. The State is expected to regulate the market, disciplining private enterprise and foreign investment in order to preserve the social gains of the revolution and national sovereignty.

In line with this reading, the Guidelines approved in 2011 begin by reaffirming the commitment to economic planning that must 'take into account the market' (Communist Party of Cuba 2011). Within this framework, the decentralization of the economy and support for small-scale private initiative and foreign investment were boosted. The Guidelines are based on a perspective that it is necessary to reduce state employment and improve the efficiency of public companies. As a result, a process of reorganization of the State and its companies has been undertaken, providing for the relocation of 1.2 million workers where some are relocated within the public sector, others migrate to self-employment and many retire along the way. The longer-term intention is to transfer at least 20 per cent of the workforce over to the non-state sector, while at the other end of the process, 178 activities were approved for self-employment possibilities (Díaz Vázquez 2011: 130), noting that it is common for state employees and retirees to also be involved in self-employment activities (conversation with Piñeiro Harnecker 2016).

There are sectors of Cuban society that are betting on the strengthening of a genuine cooperativism as an alternative to self-employment, linked to self-management and with high autonomy in relation to the state. Piñeiro Harnecker noted that the Guidelines encouraged, for the first time, the formation of cooperatives outside the agricultural sector. However in practice, opening a cooperative is more bureaucratic and time-consuming than a regular business since it requires approval from the State Council. Between 2013 and 2014, 498 cooperatives were formalized but by the end of 2016 the creation of new units was paralyzed (conversation with Piñeiro Harnecker 2016).

On the other hand, guideline 17 provides that state-owned or insolvent cooperatives may be closed or privatized, while guideline 219 provides for the sale or leasing of industrial equipment from the state to individuals (Communist Party of Cuba 2011). While there are provisions that are contrary to the concentration of ownership of the means of production (guideline 3), this does not prevent maneuvers to circumvent them, such as self-employed entrepreneurs with businesses in the name of family members.

The communist principle, 'of each according to his ability; to each one, according to their needs' made way in the guidelines for a salary remuneration linked to productivity.[9] In this perspective, guideline 171 breaks with the simultaneous increase of wages at all levels, prioritizing the activities 'that bring benefits of particular economic and social impact' (Communist Party of Cuba 2011). Thus, while scientists in the biotechnology industry received wage increases and dockworkers continue to receive bonuses in strong currency when they unload ships quickly, teachers' salaries remained unchanged. Little surprise then that in 2016 there were no candidates enrolled for the teaching profession (conversation with Fernández 2016).

---

9 Guideline 170 states the following: 'Ensure that wages guarantee that each receives according to their work, that it generates products and services with quality and increases production and productivity, and that wage income allows for meeting the basic needs of workers and their families' (Communist Party of Cuba 2011).

At the social level the Guidelines foresee the gradual abolition of the *libreta* and other universal subsidies, proposing that this kind of assistance be focused on those most in need.[10] It is in this sense that one can understand statements criticizing egalitarianism in Cuba: 'Accustomed after so many years of egalitarian policies, so pernicious to the economic and political system, and to the psychology and ideology of people, it will also be very complex to convince them that egalitarianism is not synonymous with equality or social justice and that it is necessary to end this phenomenon' (Duharte et al. 2011: 75). Social security is also being modified, demanding greater contributions from workers in the state and non-state sector (Communist Party of Cuba 2011: Lineamientos 165).

The buying and selling of homes and automobiles is allowed (Lineamientos 297 and 286) while the opening of credit lines for the acquisition of durable consumer goods and construction materials is also permissible (conversation with Hernández Pedraza 2016). In a country where previously only foreign companies and the private sector paid taxes, new taxes are expected in line with the expansion of self-employment and market transactions.

In the countryside, emphasis has been on continuing the conversion of idle state land to better use, a process triggered by decree-law 259 in 2008 (Lineamientos 187, 189 and 198). In 2006, about 60 per cent of national lands were identified as unproductive; by 2016 40 per cent had been distributed. Juan Valdés Paz suggests that a fourth agrarian reform is underway in the country. Unlike the special period, when the formation of cooperatives was stimulated from state-owned properties, there is an attempt to 'repeasantize' Cuban fields to encourage peasant production (conversation with Valdés Paz 2016). The main objective is to increase food production to reduce imports.

However, in an urbanized country where the majority of Cubans in rural areas work for a public service, few want to return to the hard work of the countryside. A similar dilemma faces the construction sector that is expanding but faces a shortage of labor. The revolution faced an analogous situation in its early years, when the need to export ran counter to Cubans' rejection of sugarcane plantations which were associated with overexploitation of labor. At present, the state is trying to incentivize with high rates of profit, in addition to the possibility of building homes and other benefits. It is assumed that the

---

10   Guideline 173 states: 'Eliminate undue gratuities and excessive subsidies, under the principle of compensating those in need and not subsidizing products, in general'. And guideline 174 states: 'Implement the orderly and gradual elimination of the *libreta de abastecimiento*, as a form of regulated, egalitarian distribution and at subsidized prices' (Communist Party of Cuba 2011).

announced constitutional reform will replace the practice of usufruct of the land with ownership. (conversation with Valdés Paz 2016).

Finally, Guidelines related to foreign capital simultaneously reaffirm the need to attract and discipline investments (Lineamientos 96–107). This is a delicate equation in that international capital demands business-friendly rules. In this light, the main incentive for such investment in Cuba is a highly qualified and cheap labor force. Although at this juncture there are certainly Cubans who prefer to receive hard currency from a capitalist rather than orders from a bureaucrat – the 'happy exploited' as they say – the prevailing intention is to reconcile foreign investment with national development.

However, Cubans refer with striking parsimony to the Chinese regime, an important political and economic partner for whom critics are difficult to find. On the contrary, there are frequent appreciative readings. For example, in a 50-year review of the Cuban Revolution, Carlos Alzugaray Treto enumerates aspects of 'the reform process in China that apply to Cuba': the emphasis on results, citing Deng Xiaoping's famous phrase, 'it does not matter if the cat is white or black, what matters is that it catches rats'; the 'recognition and use of monetary-market relations through the formula of a "socialist market economy"'; and, the creation of a large middle class (Alzugaray Treto 2009: 43). Fidel Castro, speaking to Chinese authorities in 2004, said that, 'China has become objectively the most promising hope and best example for all Third World countries' (Castro 2004).

More broadly, there is an ongoing kind of arm-wrestling match between the Cuban government and foreign capital, where the former gropes at what would be minimum concessions needed to attract desired levels of investment. In 2014 a new foreign investment law was promulgated, allowing the operation of 'totally foreign' companies. Among other incentives to international capital is the exemption from taxes: on profit during the first eight years of investment; on reinvested earnings; on the personal income of foreign partners; on the salaries of the labor force (in addition to the social security contribution of 14 per cent); and, the exemption from customs duty during the investment period, among other provisions. In the same year, a 'Foreign Investment Opportunities Portfolio' was circulated for the first time, presenting 246 projects in search of investors on the island, many of them in the Special Development Zone (ZED) around the port of Mariel. By 2016, fifteen new agreements were registered in ZED Mariel and 54 elsewhere, moving a total of US$ 1.3 million, a figure still below government expectations (López and Herrera Carlés 2015; Concepción et al. 2016).

The dilemma is illustrated by an anecdote circulating in the country: the Cuban government offers a portfolio of possible investments to a foreign capitalist in Mariel and explains each of the possibilities; his interlocutor listens, closes the folder and says: 'What I want to know is how much Mariel is worth' (conversation with Valdés Paz 2016).

On the whole the Guidelines express the reading as summarized by economist Gladys Hernández; namely, that Cuba needs to promote a mixed economy since the state cannot guarantee full employment and society does not accept high levels of unemployment. The preservation of universal public services would provide an important 'social mattress' to soften the shock of growing inequality (conversation with Hernández Pedraza 2016). Valdés Paz echoes the opinion of many when he says that Cuba remains a planned economy, where the state controls strategic economic (finance, industry, hotels) and social (health, education, science) sectors. In the antithesis of the free market, he affirms that 'in Cuba, nobody is alone, nor is there anything loose' (conversation with Valdés Paz 2016).

Differing with those who understand that socialist experiences 'underestimated market laws' (Alzugaray Treto 2009: 46), former Minister Rodríguez is among those who admit an essential contradiction between socialism and the market. But in the face of the ineluctability of change, he refers to an effort to implement the measures slowly, in order to release social tensions without losing control over the timing of the process. In the words of Raúl Castro: 'No rush but no pause' (Raúl Castro 2011). Rodríguez summed up his understanding by saying that Cuba is a planned economy that contemplates the market, while China and Vietnam are market economies with socialist modulation, since they have redistributive aspirations. And finally, he reaffirms the prevailing political will to not allow a capitalist restoration to take place on the island (conversation with Rodríguez 2016).

4   Current Dilemmas

In recent years, Cuba has been going through its biggest public debate in 60 years of the revolution. Those who envision a totalitarian ideology in a static country in the midst of a silenced and apathetic society do not understand what is happening on the island. Rafael Hernández, an intellectual director of the magazine *Temas* and one of the most vital spaces in the country for debates called *Ultimo Jueves*, enumerated the main points under discussion (conversation with Hernández 2016):

1) The problem of inequality, which has quadrupled in 25 years, parallel to the theme of growth: is inequality a cost to pay for growth?
2) Super centralization versus control: how to decentralize without losing control, or how to generate new forms of control? In this regard, the Cuban debate is not governed by the ideology of a minimal state, since

the perception that the State plays a fundamental role prevails and its extinction is impracticable under imperialism. The original problem posed by the revolution – 'how the hell am I going to make a strong state, but one that does not eat me?' – has now been updated (conversation with Martínez Heredia 2016).

3) The space of the non-state sector, both private and cooperative, informed by different views on how to animate and democratize the economy.

4) To modify what Raúl Castro describes as an 'old mentality' associated with political and cultural vices inherited from Soviet influence, such as dogmatism and bureaucracy. In this discussion there is a paradox, since those responsible for reform could well lose power.

5) The role of law and in particular, the mismatch between the current changes and the law, which is slow to change. Hernández has mentioned the need to reform municipal laws, electoral law, the law of associations, the law of worship, and labor legislation among others. For example, there is a new general labor code, but it does not include the self-employed sector since all of those in the sector are recognized as self-employed, even though they often operate like small companies. Indeed, many of those who work for small and medium-sized entrepreneurs do not have regulated working hours, a minimum wage, vacation, or maternal leave, among other guarantees (conversation with Hernández 2016).

There are two central issues that cut cross these debates and are connected: economic reform and the democratization of politics. There is consensus among Cubans about the need for both, but there are different ways of interpreting them.

Camila Piñeiro Harnecker describes three currents in the economic debate: (1) the statist vision which defends minimal changes and is usually associated with the state bureaucracy; (2) an economistic view which favors private ownership and initiative, often emulating the Chinese example; (3) those who defend a democratization of productive relations linked to collective and non-individual interests, mainly in the form of cooperativism (conversation with Piñeiro Harnecker 2016). In addition to these, there is a minority sympathetic to liberalization *tout court*, just as there are voices at the opposite pole that view the ongoing process as a renunciation of the ideals of the revolution (Hernández 2016; Katz 2014). Overall, what prevails is the engagement with and defense of, discrepant but equally convinced paths of realizing revolutionary ideals in present conditions.

This common denominator has not always resulted in a convergence of ideas or greater clarity in the debate. Often, socialist values are imbued with a vocabulary typical of capitalist rationality. The term 'human capital', commonly used in present-day Cuba, is representative of this phenomenon (Salazar Fernández 2012). Fidel Castro referred to the term in the following words: 'Human capital implies not only knowledge, but also – and essentially – conscience, ethics, solidarity, truly human feelings, a spirit of sacrifice, heroism and the ability to do very much with very little' (Fidel Castro 2005a). Another example is propagating the image of Cuba as a 'country brand' in the international tourism market (Ricardo Luis 2014).

Recent debates on the updating of socialism reveal widely varying goals. There are those who defend the importance of 'forming a competitive business culture, in which the entrepreneur perceives himself as a creator of wealth, committed to the customers to whom he destines his production, his services and acquire a true meaning of his social responsibility' (Cobo et al. 2013:71). On the other hand, some criticize the 2011 guidelines saying that, 'what is being proposed is a greater autonomy for business, read management; the document does not mention the participation of workers or the population'; in a nutshell, 'we need the power of the people and not only the property of all the people' (Alonso et al. 2013: 72)

While some suggest that 'development lies in entrepreneurial development' (Nova et al. 2013:75) others ask, 'if not now, when will we be ready for self-management?', while defending the strengthening of a 'culture of equals' (conversation with Piñeiro Harnecker 2016).

The complex relation between means and ends in a society that proposes to overcome capitalism has, in the relations of production, a central theme. And also, in this field, socialist values risk taking on a mercantile rationality. In an analysis of the labor relations within the Guideline updates, José Luis Martin Romero considers that Cuba, by 'not abandoning vertical, salarial and centralizing management schemes, renounced the comparative advantage (of socialism) of having the involvement and commitment of workers' (Martin Romero 2015). Would it not be a paradox to overcome alienated labor, which socialism aims to do, in order to obtain 'comparative advantage' in the contemporary capitalist world?

At the heart of this debate are two divergent paths: the use of capitalist means which are intended to be subordinated to socialist ends, versus the orientation of the winds of change towards a democratization of all dimensions, including relations of production. This dilemma involves considering the feasibility of change in the hierarchical relations of production, which further implies questioning the extent to which the Cuban Revolution has constructed subjects of an emancipated society. When Pineiro Harnecker asks, 'if not now, when will we be ready for self-management?', we must remember that in the early years of the revolution Cubans certainly were not ready: at the time, the absolute majority of the rural workers chose to serve a state farm rather than constitute a cooperative. Since the legacy of slavery and sugar monoculture does not favor self-management, a culture shift in this direction would need to be forged.

It is at this point that the economic and political challenges of the revolution meet. For despite the high level of education and the remarkable political culture of the ordinary citizen, which impresses any visitor to the island, there is a general evaluation that there are limits to the formation of an emancipated subject.

Educator Ariel Dacal recalls that Cuban education has reached levels of excellence routinely attested to by the United Nations Educational, Scientific and Cultural Organization (UNESCO), but always in the mold of what Paulo Freire called 'banking education'. In his view, while Cuba is a highly informed society it has limited capabilities to produce politics from this information (conversation with Dacal 2016).

This is a problem for those who consider it imperative to counter the growing mercantile pressure with critical engagement in defense of revolutionary values. This concern about depoliticisation is surprising for foreigners who are accustomed to levels of alienation not seen in Cuba, where citizens are generally much more politicized. In particular, the situation of youth is discussed, linked as it is to a critical appraisal of the educational system and political participation.

In a debate over these issues, one participant has observed that, 'our education is planned, organized and projected in a depoliticized way, because when it is politicized it is done as ritual, dogma or memorization of circumstances' (Fernández Estrada et al. 2013: 75). Bringing this critical perspective to politics, journalist Luis Sexto has said: 'If we keep insisting that slogans and phraseology is the best way to unite, to do politics, we will continue to be mistaken [...]' (Sexto et al. 2013:76). In a similar approach, Julio Cesar Guanche, one of the foremost critics on the left has related depoliticisation to the decreasing legitimacy of the government: 'In Cuba, depoliticisation expresses the crisis of official politics; that is, the disconnection, the untying, the breaking with official policy that is under way. When one becomes depoliticized it is because one has been dispossessed of politics' (Guanche et al. 2013: 78). Another participant in the debate offers a distinctly different view: 'Our society is completely politicized. The fact of thinking differently ... I do not call it depoliticisation but being politicized in a different direction' (Garces 2013: 78).

The issue of politicization is linked to political participation and the question of values. From this angle, Hernández asks: 'Can there be a change of mentality and values without changing the modes of participation, the access to power, the established hierarchies?' (Hernández et al. 2013b: 78). In fact, there are pressures from diverse origins within the revolutionary field, for changes in this direction.

These issues are particularly sensitive when it comes to the youth, whose revolutionary commitment is a source of skepticism abroad. Although an individualist ideology prospers, synthesized in the motto, 'there is only one life' – and this life is yours – there are also those who call for greater participation in the debate about the country's directions by becoming engaged (conversation with Limia Díaz 2016).

In a corresponding debate about the relationship between youth and the revolution, one participant stated: 'We Cubans are not tested in participation and the exercise of power. Nor do we have clarity of what we want and the ways of achieving it' (Rojas et al. 2008: 159). Another young woman participant summarized the rejection of guided 'participation': 'We young people do not want you to let us play like Revolution: we want to make the revolution' (Ortega González et al. 2008).

Beyond the role of youth, political scientist Julio Fernández Estrada has observed that in Cuba people have become accustomed to popular participation supported by the state. Obviously, this stems from the unique origins of the Cuban state as well as its renewed legitimacy as a defender of revolutionary values and as the embodiment of unity against the aggressiveness of the United States, which was never rhetorical. In this context, his observation that the people have little practice of political struggle and need to gain experience is remarkable, as it implies a modified relationship with the state (conversation with Fernández Estrada 2016). This raises a pertinent question: Will the renewal of Cuban politics correspond to a sharpening of the contradictions that typify a class society?

A loosening of the grip of the state is foreseen by many, in which dogmatism and control associated with Soviet influence are put in check, opening up fresh possibilities of doing politics and culture in Cuba. However, this will occur within a context of the commodification of life which militates against sovereignty, equality and internationalism as collective values. Luis Morlote recalls that as far as culture is concerned there has never been a blockade, and the American way of life circulates in television, radio, movies and tourists (conversation with Morlote 2016). The delicate paradox of democratic radicalization in revolutionary unity, between the crossfire of imperialism and bureaucracy, was summed up by a young man: 'The call to discipline within the revolutionary ranks must be compensated by an indiscipline urged by the need for change' (Pérez et al. 2008: 155).

In Cuba, the commodification of social relations and the penetration of foreign capital affect social dynamics and create divisions. While, as Piñeiro Harnecker says, there must be self-employed people who 'want to contribute to the country', as in all probability they will look to guarantee their profits first, which involves the exploitation of labor even if at this moment that labor can be 'happily exploited'. In broad terms, Cubans want a fair project but as the paths are not clear, they 'resolve their own first' (conversation with Dacal 2016). As such the tensions between the expectation of a progressive update and, the corrosion of collective values, demarcates the debates and disputes about changes on the island.

It is likely that the open contradictions of the Cuban transition – the 'loose threads' in the words of Valdés Paz – will continue to surface and ultimately lead to constitutional reform announced by the government in 2018. In the draft approved unanimously by parliament in July 2018 the word 'communism' was removed from the text, although it emphasizes that socialism continues to be state policy. Even so, there is no clarity about how the reform process will take place or about its content and scope. Regardless, its urgency is certain since many of the ongoing 'updates' are, in practice, unconstitutional. Some ponder that it might be necessary, after all, to produce a new Constitution (conversation with Fernández Estrada 2016).

The new stage for this ongoing reform process was sealed with the retirement of Raúl Castro, whose post as president of the Council of State was occupied by then-first Vice President Miguel Díaz-Canel who was born after the revolutionary triumph.[11]

5 Final Thoughts

The current dilemmas have plunged the island into an intense 'process of introspection' (García et al. 2013: 80), which provokes reflections on the totality of the revolutionary process. Of particular note, is the coincidence between the claim of the absolute need for an alliance with the Soviet Union in the past and the almost unanimous recognition of the need to broaden the role of the market today, while advocating a regulatory role for the state.

I have no pretensions to argue against the past policy of approaching the Soviet Union or to question current guidelines. In both cases, I am convinced that these are policies undertaken by a leadership committed to the Cuban people and with incomparable experience, which endows them with political and moral arguments of unquestionable solidity. However, at a time when the

---

11 Even so, Raul continues influencing the country's politics, since he remains president of the Communist Party of Cuba and maximum commander of the Armed Forces.

failure of the progressive wave forces the rethinking of the means and ends of social change in Latin America in the 21st Century, with a view to putting revolution back on the agenda, I consider some reflections relevant.

1. The relationship with the Soviet Union had two important and related consequences. At the economic level, Cuba's specialized productive insertion within the framework of a comparatively favorable relationship, which was treated as a permanent reality, overlooked the structural dimensions of the colonial legacy. Its main expression was the incompatibility between a relatively narrow production base and the universalization of a pattern of consumption associated with industrial societies.

Despite significant growth during the period, the exchange with the Soviets frustrated any expectation of accumulation in an industrial direction, as that did not coincide with the partner's intentions. Cuba did not overcome its historic condition of primary exporting and dependence as a country, and the inherent weaknesses of an underdeveloped economy resurfaced when the Soviet Union collapsed. It is undeniable that the American blockade has aggravated the burden of poverty but it is not its cause nor will its suspension one day be its solution.

Any revolution on the periphery of capitalism that confronts the developmental illusion and assumes the material limits that underdevelopment imposes, at least in a context of isolation, must compensate its economic weakness with political strength. In fact, it is what a dependent bourgeoisie does, albeit with a contrary purpose, to perpetuate underdevelopment (Fernandes 1975).

The legitimacy of every revolution stems from its ability to defend the interests of the people. Initially in the Cuban process, these interests were identified with the assertion of the nation; but overcoming neocolonialism unleashed a dynamic that pushed the process toward communism, which assumes substantive equality. By breaking with the parameters of bourgeois society the revolution committed to radicalize in this direction. The equal distribution of wealth is a fundamental dimension of this political landscape, but it is not the only one: the end of hierarchies at work, political participation and equality of gender and color are also part of it.

Substantive equality is necessarily a collective ideal, a premise for the realization of individuality. This is freedom in the communist view. In opposition to communism, capitalist ideology assumes that the human being operates individually. Presided over by competition and not by cooperation, liberal achievement is associated with merit, which in turn refers to the capacity for accumulation. In an ideology that naturalizes the market, individual achievement is mediated by consumption, an illusion that can only thrive amidst frustrated human beings.

Communism offers a radically opposite path because the human is realized through what one does, and what is done conditions who one is. Thus the individual is free only when what they are doing is free from coercion. This does not mean the abolition of labor in the sense of one's material production of existence, but the overcoming of work deprived of meaning for whoever does it. As work as well as politics takes place in the social sphere and not in the private sphere, it can be said that the communist being realizes him or herself in the social sphere.

The heavy hand of Soviet influence inhibited revolutionary achievement in this direction. Bureaucracy in the economy militated against free labor, dogmatism in politics against popular power, and cultural realism against creative originality. Even if one admits rapprochement with the Soviets as necessary, the justification of assuming these traits in order to maintain unity is debatable. Given the minimal Soviet interference in the internal affairs of the island, it is more likely to represent a genuine belief in the merits of the Soviet pattern. It is also worth noting that this was a selective incorporation: Cuba's revolutionary process has been peaceful and has never been riven by the convulsions and purges that marked both the first workers and peasants' state in history and its Chinese rival.

In sum, the convergence between bureaucracy, dogmatism and socialist realism prevented political renewal in generational terms, but mainly affected the very possibilities of revolution within the revolution or, to use a heretical term, of permanent revolution: it inhibited the 'indiscipline urged by the need for change'.

2. By gravitating to the Soviet camp and adopting practices associated with it, the Cuban Revolution deepened its focus on a path associated with the development of productive forces. As an analogy, it bet on winning in the Olympics and succeeded: during consecutive editions, Cuba won more medals than the rest of Latin America altogether. Alongside this though, it reinforced the logic of competitive high performance sports, aligned with national criteria, despite preserving the amateur character of sports practice (a policy that is presently under review).

Soviet 'followism' involved the option for a certain civilizing pattern, linked to the notion of development. This option had as a consequence, whether necessary or not, policies antithetical to economic self-management, critical formation and creative freedom. On the whole, it was a combination of conservative factors that limited the realization of the humanistic ideal of revolution: the 'natural man' of Martí, or the 'new man' of Che Guevara.

It is possible that the material advances of the 1970s widened the space for future maneuvering. Rodríguez believes that the revolution would not have withstood the impact of the special period without the prosperity of previous years. But this is problematic reasoning, as is every counterfactual in history: it is possible to argue that without the insertion into the Soviet orbit, the impact of its collapse would be different or in fact, that there would not even have been a special period. It is impossible to speculate widely on what Cuba would have been without its attachment to the Soviet orbit, a relationship which was only consummated a decade after the revolutionary triumph.

What is certain is that this path also conditioned future political options. If a revolution of values had been carried out, the scope of future alternatives, including economic ones, would have been enlarged. However, such possibilities were limited by the truncation of democratic and cultural radicalization. It is likely that the very field of theoretical and political alternatives considered by the revolutionary leadership – the 'maximum possible consciousness' in György Lucáks's expression – has narrowed over time. There are objective and subjective links between the need for rapprochement with the Soviets in the past and the need for mercantile openness in the present.

Finally, the reasoning for the necessary rapprochement with the Soviets implies recognizing the impossibility of socialism in the periphery without international protection. In this perspective, the limits of the Cuban Revolution are inscribed in the contradictions of the Soviet experience. While this approach is justified at the level of the material realization of communism, which supposes the world revolution, from the political point of view the Cuban trajectory itself defies this reading, a quarter of a century after the Soviet collapse.

The alternative to economic constraints is to radicalize a revolution's political sustenance, which points to an alternative civilizing pattern not only to capitalism but also to communism. This is because primitive socialism, as Third World socialism is bound to be, confronts inequality in conditions where equality in abundance is impossible. This disjuncture is evident in the present in Cuba: in the face of barriers to material sustenance, global political isolation, the overwhelming entertainment industry, consumer seduction, and the modernities of the digital world, primitive socialism must be based on radically different values, beyond equality and sovereignty. Its safeguard would be popular unity around a project of nation based on substantive equality, allowing the fruition of a set of values that are an alternative to the seduction of consumption: equality, participation and freedom. To reject this historical possibility is tantamount to resigning oneself to a modality of 'dependent socialism', and underestimating the humanist radicalness implicit in Marxism, in which human realization far transcends economic motives.

3. The Cuban process had limits to overcoming the alienation of work and politics, and consequently to generating an emancipatory culture. In this respect, it must be noted that everything depends on the ruler with which you measure: Cuba is a more democratic, self-conscious and cultured society than any bourgeois state.

It is also much more humane: Cubans have little experience of many core aspects of bourgeois life and society: police violence; fights between sports team fans; telemarketing calls; talking to electronic recordings; memorizing passwords; revolving doors; turnstiles; advertising in the streets, in television, in newspapers and in magazines; electoral marketing; parliament as a business; the notary office; organized crime; private security; massacres; overcrowded prisons; education, health, welfare and culture as businesses; expensive cinema, ballet, books, medicines and public transportation; university entrance exams; fast-food; evictions; children who work; children out of school; working mothers with nowhere to leave their child; illiteracy; reality TV shows; radar speed traps; traffic; shopping centers; lotteries; Bingo; the prosperity gospel (although neo-Pentecostalism is growing); pornography; hunger; unemployment; abandoned children; and, helplessness in old age. In short, a Cuban has little familiarity with abandonment.

It is clear that there are many problems and difficulties: insufficient and crowded buses, low wages, jobs far below the capacity of many Cubans, lines, little product variety, occasional shortages of goods, power outages, crumbling houses, excessive bureaucratization, arbitrary or uncommitted employees, a boring press and a precarious internet; no doubt, this is a list that could be lengthened by any Cuban.

Some of these problems are the same as those to be found in other parts of the world, while others are different but not necessarily worse. Cubans complain about state bureaucracy but they have no idea what it is to be served by an electronic voice, download a form on the internet, pay a fee and go back another day and not be served. In Cuba, people still talk to people.

Racism and machismo persist, but many Afro-Cubans are doctors, leaders and teachers, while women are the majority in universities and in sectors such as public health, science and culture. The inefficiency of the State is often recalled, but it is a state that feeds, clothes, educates, cares, defends and gives culture to all its population. Inefficiency depends on your point of view.

Measured by the ruler of contemporary capitalism, Cuba is a kind of ecological reserve of human values that the world tries to denaturalize. As a

Brazilian colleague who was unsure if he would receive medical attention on the island was told: 'For us, you are not a foreigner, you are a human being'. 'Cuban doctors are the best in the world, because they are the most affectionate', a father said.

But the challenge of sustaining 'primitive socialism' in a very primitive and non-socialist 21st century requires a democratic radicalization of both the economy and politics. This must be rooted in an increase in the critical awareness and creativity of its population, seeds that were not sowed when Cuba was within the Soviet orbit. When the revolutionary leadership began self-criticism in the mid-1980s, it was feared that the challenges posed by the special period amid the impending collapse of Soviet/Eastern European socialism would make democratic radicalization a risky enterprise. In that context, national cohesion survived as a value because the people understood what was happening and incorporated adversity as their own.

The current situation is more ambiguous because change also blows on mercantile winds. An expression of this ambivalence in relation to the state is that Cubans want to change, but also to preserve social conquests; to bet on the market but on a regulated one; to attract international capital but simultaneously defend sovereignty.

There is a component of conformism, but there is also critical awareness in this ambivalence. The Cuban who emigrates rarely carries the illusion of the American dream but does cherish the social security he/she leaves behind. People rarely leave the country for ideological motivation but rather because they think they deserve more. As one sage Cuban said, the young man migrates as if leaving home because he cannot stand his parents anymore and wants to go his own way, not because he has stopped loving them.

Finally, ambiguity exists because life is not only difficult but sometimes seems meaningless. If consumption fills the existential voids in capitalism, the socialist antidote is to provide ways of existential realization, depriving consumerism of meaning.

In Cuba, much progress was made in this direction: a culture was forged in which pride was not attached to one's material goods, but rather to the solidarity Cubans gave to Angola. It is a revolution in which respect for wealth, private property and imperialism have been lost. Perhaps they are not the revolutionaries 'moved by a deep feeling of love' as idealized by Che, but they most definitely have healthy teeth: at least they already have the teeth of the new man, as Martínez Heredia put it.

Nowadays, money has regained its power, and is gradually regaining its legitimacy. Some families now spend what they do not have on a party for their fifteen-year-old, or on an ostentatious wedding. One observes behaviors aimed at the other's gaze, characteristic of a narcissistic society. These are conservative positions, in discord with the revolutionary ethic in which Cuban emancipation was forged, but not necessarily counterrevolutionary. More serious is the perception that, little by little, the components of capitalism are becoming naturalized, such as accepting as normal that one buys something that the other cannot. Or, as the notion of 'human capital' refers, to note the advance of neoliberal rationality understood not as an economic prescription but as a structural logic that colonizes other spheres of existence. In this context, Martínez Heredia has argued that in Cuba the revolutionaries are not losing the battle, but neither are they winning it (conversation with Martínez Heredia 2016).

4. In Cuba today, the state has lost the monopoly on questions and answers about the future of the country. The social order, in which the state is responsible for addressing the problems of its citizens as part of a trajectory that points to communism, is in crisis. The changes initiated in the special period no longer seem provisional or reversible and the communist utopia has cooled down. There is now a moment of transition, in which the previous paradigm loses weight in reality but an alternative with comparable mobilizing capacity has not yet been consolidated (conversation with Dacal 2016). As one young man said, 'we are not clear about what we want and the ways we can achieve it'.

The meaning of change on the island is in dispute and this means the country can be envisaged in numerous ways. Barack Obama shared his vision with Cubans while visiting the country: 'In the United States we have a clear monument of what Cubans can build: it's called Miami' (Obama 2016).

Domestically, there is a high level of consensus around a national project that preserves the universality of social achievements and sovereignty. The spontaneous reactions to Fidel's death testify to this: those who spoke of youth being indifferent to the death of the commander expressed a desire and a lie. *En masse,* Cubans honored the leader of the process that created their nation, despite their differences. In doing so, they were recognizing those who defended the people in the past, but also paying tribute to the present and sending a message to the future. And politically, the manifestations had an important demonstrative effect on the United States and the world (conversation with Garces 2016).

As the president of FEU said, the problem is not those who are against the revolution but the direction the revolution will take. In this respect the key question is: to what extent will it be possible to preserve the value of equality in the face of the changes taking place, and how is this to be done? The future that Cubans are looking to is no longer the utopia of a society with no state, no classes nor private property. Rather, it is a combination of free and quality universal rights with mercantile relations disciplined by a sovereign state.

Given this scenario, two dilemmas are posed for the revolution that, 'assault the oligarchy but also revolutionary dogmas': To what extent will the mercantilization of social relations be compatible with the preservation of revolutionary ideals, albeit in their minimalist version? Will the State be able to discipline capital in defense of a nation on the global periphery in the middle of the 21st century?

As historian Eusebio Leal says, in the 'moral regeneration oeuvre of the Cuban Revolution' the optimism of the will faces the pessimism of the intellect.

Conclusion

The concluding remarks that follow are organized in three sections. Initially, I reconstitute the general determinations of the movement of history in which the progressive wave was inscribed. Although the quantity and diversity of countries limits the possibility of detailed comparisons, I emphasize the common traits and the most relevant particularities in an exercise of historical comparison.

I then analyze convergences and divergences between the different governments related to regional integration. My hypothesis that the progressive wave attests to the narrow space for change within the system, unfolds in the realization that a regional integration that does not confront dependency structures is doomed to reproduce it. Taken together, there is a correlation between national progressive processes and the effort at regional integration, where political change within economic continuity has constrained it to the surface of politics.

Finally, I articulate nine propositions related to the political motivation behind the analysis of the progressive wave. My intention here is to contribute to thinking about the politics required to build the needed change.

1   The Movement of History

> The Democratic and Cultural Revolution is made with votes, not with bullets; with militant political consciousness and without ambitions or greed.
> *Evo Morales in a statement on Twitter, December 16, 2016*

> By confusing democracy with revolution, its champions sponsor the immobility of order and the permanent counterrevolution.
> *Florestan Fernandes*

Contrasting the trajectory of South American countries reveals similarities and differences, as is the case with any historical comparison. The fundamental similarity is in the general sense of movement that stems from a common colonial past, perpetuated in the combination of dependence and inequality. In the economic sphere, it is possible to representationally synthesize this movement through the sequence of import substitution industrialization, internationalization of domestic markets, debt crisis, inflation, neoliberalism, the commodity super cycle and, recession. In the political sphere, the representational sequencing involves national-developmentalism, revolution versus counterrevolution, transition, weakening of conventional political parties, progressive wave and finally, conservative ascent.

There is no precise link between economic and political terms, nor do they follow an exact chronological sequence in the different situations. Just as some countries did not advance in the industrial direction, subsisting as enclave economies, there were those who did not elect presidents identified with the progressive field in the early 21st century. In spite of these peculiarities, the succession of these moments provides a general sense of the history in the last hundred years in the region. Its relative simultaneity in the different countries concretizes the meaning of imperialism – and of dependence – in the subcontinent. Conversely, the finding that the Cuban trajectory differs substantially from this itinerary illustrates what it means to break with these moorings.

The specificities are given for each socioeconomic formation, articulated more or less cohesively around national states from the 19th century. To the structural particularities of each country, such as underdevelopment with an abundance of foreign exchange in Venezuela, the variegated society in Bolivia, or violence in Colombia, are added the multiple vicissitudes inherent in historical processes. For example, although Fidel Castro argued that where one finds dozens of revolutionaries assembled as in the Granma, there will always be a Che, a Raul, a Cienfuegos and a Fidel, the role of the individual in history is unique.

In a wider historical frame, the movements that converged in the progressive wave should be referenced to the triumph of the counterrevolution in the period of the Cold War, a period that froze historical change in many national situations in the wake of the Cuban Revolution. This process was more visible in the Southern Cone dictatorships, but change was also blocked in regimes where politics was restricted to the closed circuit of oligarchic pacts, as in Venezuela and Colombia.

The freezing of change meant not only the defeat of revolution but also of reform. The intensification of multinational penetration bypassed pressures for social reform and regional integration, which were understood as means to overcome the exhaustion of substitute industrialization. Politically and ideologically the dissociation between development and national integration was sealed, breaking with the reference to post-war Economic Commission for

Latin America (ECLA) thinking, which mutually associated industrialization and nation.

The region's growing external indebtedness in the 1970s was one of the dimensions of deepening dependency, laying the foundations for the end of national developmentalism and the dominance of financial capital. When the debt crisis broke out during the following decade, countries faced a combination of economic stagnation and inflation. Economic problems contributed to destabilizing existing dictatorships, but in all cases the transition was a controlled process, although less so in the Argentine situation and more so in the Chilean case.

As a result, governments that identified with the previously allowed opposition to the dismantled regimes prevailed, in situations in which there was no correlation of forces or political interest in confronting the legacies of dictatorships. In other words, previous defeats modulated the harsh conditions with which so-called democratic governments then faced the crisis. The universal result of this impotence – which was also shared by those countries that did not emerge from dictatorships – has been the progressive subordination of national policies to international financial institutions, notably the International Monetary Fund (IMF). As globalization accelerated, neoliberal adjustment programs put the last nails into the coffin of national developmentalism.

The rhythm and intensity of the incorporation of the countries of the region into the neoliberal fold varied in inverse proportion to the social devastation produced by the previous regimes. That is, the more devastated the social movements, as in the cases of Argentina and Peru, the more radical the implementation of neoliberalism. At the political level, this agenda was implemented in some cases by people previously identified with nationalism, such as the Peronists in Argentina, Victor Paz Estenssoro in Bolivia and Carlos Andrés Pérez in Venezuela. In Chile, where the relationship between dictatorship and neoliberalism dispensed with mediations, the socialists managed the system. At the same time, the self-declared social democrats in Brazil proved the impossibility of a center-left in Latin America, gravitating towards the liberal right.

On the whole the implementation of the neoliberal agenda eroded old political forces and opened space for new ones. The corrosion of traditional instruments of class politics such as trade unions and workers' parties weakened the material base of projects for change associated with the working class. This worldwide phenomenon was catalyzed by the demise of the Soviet Union, which provided an ulterior neoliberal offensive synthesized in the notion of the end of history. Cuba has defied this verdict and survived as an aberration but has been on the defensive ever since.

On the other hand, new political actors emerged, organized mainly as social movements. Beyond the landless in Brazil, the piqueteros in Argentina and the Zapatistas in Mexico, the most striking political results were achieved by peasant movements linked to indigenous identity in Bolivia and Ecuador, where several presidents were overthrown at the beginning of the 21st century.

The conjunction between the weakening of conventional politics and the rise of social protest opened space for electoral novelty. In some cases, organizations traditionally associated with the left triumphed, such as the Brazilian Workers Party (PT) or the Uruguayan Frente Amplio. In other cases individual figures identified with change emerged, such as Hugo Chávez in Venezuela, Evo Morales in Bolivia, Rafael Correa in Ecuador and Fernando Lugo in Paraguay. In Argentina, Néstor and Cristina Kirchner embraced the slightest possible change, to appease a radicalized context. In Chile, socialists took the lead in *Concertación* but frustrated any expectation of change. Only Peru and Colombia explicitly turned to the right, generating regimes with dictatorial characteristics that combined neoliberalism, 'carnal relations' with the United States, assistencialism and repression. In turn, these were the only countries where armed struggle survived in the 1990s; in the Peruvian case as a perversion of Cold War guerrillaism, which in the eyes of part of the population legitimized state terrorism.

In the vanguard of the progressive wave was Venezuela. Determined to regain state control over oil revenues, the Chávez-led movement faced the intolerance of the ruling classes who did everything to topple him in his early years. Victorious on the streets and through the ballot box, the singularity of the Bolivarian process in relation to its contemporaries, all of whom retreated, was its gradual radicalization. This course was given added impetus by the swearing in of Luiz Inacio Lula da Silva in Brazil and Néstor Kirchner in Argentina in 2003, followed by electoral victories of the left in Uruguay, Bolivia, Ecuador and Paraguay. As such, when the Union of South American Nations (UNASUR) was created in 2008, Álvaro Uribe's Colombia felt forced to join in order to not isolate itself in the region.

However, despite the revolutionary rhetoric it adopted the Bolivarian process never transcended bourgeois institutionality. On the contrary, it constantly resorted to polls to legitimize itself, a course followed by the Citizens' Revolution in Ecuador and the process of change in Bolivia where revolutionary rhetoric was more discreet. This resulted in the dominance of processes framed by parliamentary dynamics, an indication of the vulnerability of the alleged revolutionary design. Symptomatically, in 2016 popular sectors in Chile and Colombia evoked a constituent assembly as an instrument to thaw out politics in countries where the left had been silenced for decades. In these countries, as in Peru, progressive fronts grew as a second or third electoral force, with a discourse and practice that resurfaced the progressive illusion.[1]

On the tactical level, in electing parliament as the forum for resolving social tensions progressive governments opted for class reconciliation, even where there was the notable potential for popular radicalization. Often, the parliamentary route served as a means of taking the people off the streets and returning politics to institutions, a route that restored order in Argentina, Bolivia, and Ecuador. At the opposite pole the electoral game was effective in changing presidents in Peru and Colombia, countries in which the left was practically proscribed, as was the case in Chile, where it was frozen by socialism.

Invariably progressive parliamentary politics articulated strategies to neutralize the disruptive potential of social movements, ranging from cooptation to open confrontation, while dealing with conservatives implied concessions. In each case there were popular sectors who were motivated by a mixture of conviction and benefits that joined the government, while those who preserved their autonomy were accused of doing the right a favor. On the whole, so-called progressive governments became managers of the system and were all the more effective because they neutralized their country's main dissenters.

The centrality of parliament also implied strategies oriented to electoral prestige, an approach that dominated the political landscape. Progressives advocated change but by conventional means. In addition to pursuing conservative alliances and militating against popular autonomy they adopted all sorts of practices identified with bourgeois alienation, such as marketing, demagogy, clientelism, and personalism, as well as relying on liberal economic ideologies such as the myth of growth and the illusion of consumption. On the whole, command of the state ceased to be a means for change but rather became an end in itself.

In the Venezuelan case, it is possible to argue that there were efforts to build a correlation of forces favorable to radicalization. However, the design to promote change from the state ran into the very real contradictions inherent in the plan to strengthen popular power through an institutional framework. This dilemma reached its extreme in the Cuban Revolution, where the demands of a state defending the island from imperialism, conflicted with the need to radicalize popular power as the democratic basis of the revolution. However,

---

1 The election of López Obrador in Mexico in 2018 took place in a similar manner: i.e., political alternation within the system. In the Mexican case, the fundamentals of the subordinate relationship with the United States, which the dominant classes sealed in the 1980s, will not be questioned.

unlike Venezuela, Bolivia, or Ecuador, the Cuban process was based on a popular revolution and not on a constitution rewritten under a newly elected president. Significantly, the revolution only adopted a constitution seventeen years after its triumph, equivalent to the length of the Bolivarian process when it lost elections in 2015.

Finally, class reconciliation meant that progressive governments discarded structural transformations. In other words, they bet on change without facing the root of problems. This approach implied economic continuity, which deprived the traditional right of its role. Often, the right became a recalcitrant opposition gathering those displaced from power. However, there was little resonance amongst the right given that its relevance came from the power of money, which financed parties of the left and right within the system and was left undisturbed during the progressive wave. In countries where the left was stigmatized in the midst of civil wars or kidnapped by socialist transformism as in the Chilean case, there was even less need for negotiation and capital slept more tranquilly.

The choice of modifying without confronting structural questions limited the landscape of change to the distributive policies of state revenue, related mainly to the proceeds from the export of primary goods. Therefore, the other side of the diffusion of cash transfer programs encouraged by the World Bank, such as the *Bolsa Família* in Brazil, was infrastructure works that promoted the circulation of commodities. While both policies were adopted by all governments in South America, in some cases efforts were made to increase state income as in Venezuela and Bolivia, or to expand program coverage as in Brazil. As such, the reduction of poverty rates was generalized in the region while inequality remained untouched. Cumulatively, the process was lubricated by the extraordinary revenues enjoyed during the commodity super-cycle, which benefited everyone and facilitated the reconciliation of divergent interests in the case of progressive administrations. On the other hand, characteristics of the colonial legacy such as economic dependence, overexploitation of labor and environmental devastation were deepened.

On the whole, the prevailing trend was the reproduction of societies incapable of controlling their own fate and advancing towards degradation in all spheres of existence, a characteristic of contemporary capitalism. If the speed towards barbarism was slower under progressive administrations, the direction of societal movement remained unchanged. In implementing policies that weakened the very social movements that elected them, these governments helped to create the conditions for the anti-popular reaction underway, as evident in the cases of Paraguay and Brazil.

In short: the politics associated with the progressive wave proved successful in winning elections but insufficient to change the respective countries. The bet on class reconciliation implied different strategies of demobilization and instrumentalization of social movements, at the same time that businesses prospered and were strengthened. In a wider historical perspective, the progressive interlude can be seen as conducive to the reproduction of order because it contained the possibilities for change in situations where the insurgency against neoliberalism, latent in Brazil, Paraguay and Uruguay and open in Argentina, Ecuador and Bolivia, threatened the system itself. In this perspective, the decline of the progressive wave is related with the loss of this political functionality – i.e., the containment of change – in a context in which the waning of the commodities super-cycle aggravated the capitalist crisis on the subcontinent and catalyzed more aggressive and unpopular policies.

The contemporary impasses in Venezuela illuminate the paradoxes involved, as it is where progressivism advanced the furthest and defiance of the system was rehearsed. Unable to root change in society but solidifying the support of the poor it represented, the Bolivarian process became entrenched in the state, where it resisted giving up power. In 2017, its strength was also its weakness: state power still allowed it to avoid an electoral exit as in Argentina, or a coup as in Brazil. The paradox is that in order to sustain itself in power the Bolivarian process transmuted into a conservative political factor, sustained by the military. In Bolivia and Ecuador, there was a comparable political degeneration, although in these countries the progressive governments were not identified with social change for long. On the other hand, the speed and intensity of the Venezuelan crisis defies parallels. In short, where progressivism turned out to be stronger, the more conservative it became and where it has set deeper roots, the crisis has been more acute. In this light the Maduro government emerges as an unfolding of Chavism itself and not as an inflection, just as the Temer government is the metastasis of the PT. Viewed between its political vanguard (Venezuela) and its economic engine (Brazil), the progressive wave revealed itself to be another face of barbarism, not its opposite. By 2017, it survived only as an empty shell, or an ideology.

2   Regional Integration

> Let's explore South America, which is both so close and far away at the same time.
>
> *Luiz Inácio Lula da Silva, 2003*

CONCLUSION

> In foreign policy, what we might informally call a progressive and revolutionary international at the continental level will be constituted.
> *Álvaro García Linera, 2016*

If it can be said that Venezuela was at the forefront of the progressive wave, the region's dynamic engine was the Brazilian process, taking place as it did in a country that commands about half of South America's territory and economy.

The driving force of integration was the internationalization of oligopolized sectors of Brazilian capital, leveraged by public money from the National Bank for Economic and Social Development (BNDES). The competitiveness of these 'national champions' was linked to the overexploitation of work and natural resources, as well as venal relations with the state. Within this framework, regional integration could only be an extension of domestic support to primary exports and civil construction, materialized in the export corridors designed by the Initiative for the Integration of Regional Infrastructure in South America (IIRSA). The articulation of regional organizations, notably UNASUR, served as a foundation for Brazilian political leadership and raised the country's status on the world stage.

Conceived within the parameters of orthodoxy at both domestic and international levels, Brazilian foreign policy condemned to isolation the most daring ambitions of Venezuela under the aegis of the so-called Bolivarian Alternative for the Americas (ALBA). While it is true that the Bolivarian process favored friendly governments, it is also true that the Brazilian option restricted its anti-hegemonic partnerships to the limited possibilities of Cuba. To put it directly, PT empathy helped the Bolivarians survive, provided they accept the proposed order.

At the other pole, Colombia, Chile and Peru constituted an explicit support axis for the US agenda in the region. Beyond Plan Colombia, a radical expression of this complicity, convergence among countries was expressed in the Pacific Alliance, which Mexico also joined. Constituted as a counterpoint to the regionalist aspirations of the progressive bloc in 2011, the alliance was articulated around multilateral trade liberalization, bringing together countries in the region that had free trade agreements with the United States.

However, this divergent international alignment did not prevent all of them from joining together in UNASUR. The fact that South American countries unanimously adhered to this initiative and its backbone, the IIRSA, shows the limits of progressivism in the region. The export of raw materials was a common denominator among those who joined the Alliance of the Pacific and those who aligned themselves with ALBA. Even governments that described themselves as revolutionaries were unable to advance an alternative to the extractivist export model.

Bolivarian Venezuela tried to tackle the issue but with less than satisfactory results. On the other hand, governments that had never consistently questioned this pattern prevailed despite rhetoric to the contrary, as is the case in the Constitutions of Ecuador and Bolivia as well as in the neo-development discourse in Brazil and Argentina. Seen through the lenses of the 'commodity consensus' the contrasts between South American governments have become ever more diluted (Svampa 2017).

Viewed from the perspective of economic continuity and social conservatism, the progressive wave emerges as a kind of recycling in which political novelty was instrumental in reproducing the old pattern of domination, described by Florestan Fernandes as the 'Bourgeois Autocratic State'. This was the case with the PT governments in Brazil, whose regional project can be synthesized in two vectors: economic dependence framed by extractivism, albeit while producing relative benefits for Brazilian corporations that are often weak links in business chains that they do not command; and relative political autonomy, limited by the interests of the United States in the region.

In summary, there is a relationship between the scope and the limit of the processes identified with the progressive field at the national level and with the dynamics of regional integration. More specifically, there was political change within the framework of economic continuity. At the regional level UNASUR emerged as a positive political novelty, even if associated with IIRSA whose logistical framework deepened dependency structures. This paradox of economic continuity and political newness replicating prevailing national dynamics explains the convergence of the South American countries in these regional initiatives, whose innovative potential was, as a consequence, limited. On the other hand, the ambiguity between political progressivism and economic conservatism generated contradictory situations as in the case of Paraguay, where the Brazilian state's support for economic sectors that opposed political change ended up reversing it.

If the progressive wave offers practical proof of the constraints on reformism as a route to national change, the impasses of regional integration reveal another side of the same coin. The pretension of creating openings in South American space for the reconciling of sovereignty and imperialism, replicated on an international level the magic that Lulism and related governments intended to carry out at the domestic level; i.e., reconciling capital and labor, the bourgeoisie and the nation. However, the vulnerability of change anchored in economic continuity was made explicit when the fall in the price of commodities fueled various crisis situations in the region. The corrosion of the bases associated with the Lula social pact, the electoral defeat of Kirchnerism and, the crisis faced by Bolivarianism all affected the process of regional integration whose fragility was evident in 2016.[2]

Thus, if reform is not an open path to social change in the region reconciliation with imperialism is not a path to sovereignty either. In the second independence of Latin America sovereignty is inseparable from equality, just as regional integration is inseparable from the revolution.

3 Nine Propositions

> A thousand times worse than defeat is to deviate for a long time from the fight, there where it became inevitable.
> *Rosa Luxemburg*

> Only by imagining other worlds will this one be changed.
> *Alberto Acosta*

As the purpose of an analysis of the progressive wave from a perspective committed to change is to contribute to its happening, I now develop propositions on the articulation between sovereignty, equality and continental integration, understood as references of a project for change yet to be built. This approach emphasizes continental unity since each national situation has its peculiarities, but also because the expression 'progressive wave' presupposes some level of interrelation between the recent processes which nurtured different views on regional integration. As they unfold the nine propositions shed light on the timidity of what has been recently envisaged, while they aim ultimately to broaden the landscape for imagining and devising present politics.[3]

3.1 *Integration Is a Dimension of the Latin American Revolution*
In the 21st century, Latin American unity proves to be a necessary but insufficient condition to safeguard the region from the disintegrative tendencies that typify contemporary capitalism. Viewed from this perspective, integration must articulate national processes of change that incorporate continental

---

2 In April 2018, Argentina, Brazil, Chile, Colombia, Peru and Paraguay announced that they would leave UNASUR, deepening a crisis in the institution that had had no General Secretary since February 2017.
3 These notes incorporate reflections on revolutionary processes outside the continent, notably the Russian Revolution. After all, the Latin American revolution must be neither more nor less than a chapter of the necessary world revolution.

unity as a historical necessity. In other words, regional integration reemerges as a dimension of a movement that we can describe as a Latin American revolution, aimed at taking control of one's destiny and subordinating the economy to the needs and aspirations of the population as a whole. For as José Carlos Mariátegui reminded us almost one hundred years ago, it is impossible to articulate incompletely formed nations:

> But what separates and isolates Latin American countries is not this diversity of political agendas. It is the impossibility that among incompletely formed nations, among nations barely sketched in the majority, that they successfully conspire and articulate an international system or conglomerate. In history, the commune precedes the nation. The nation precedes any society of nations.
> MARIÁTEGUI 1990: 14

In contemporary Latin America, nation, continental unity and socialism are indissociable in resistance to barbarism.

3.2 History Requires its Own Solutions to its Own Problems

Any integration oriented to overcoming the ties between dependence and inequality must assume as a premise the singularity of the socioeconomic formation of the region. Its main feature in Latin America is the permanence of a colonial legacy, which is expressed in the outward orientation of its economic base, despite the advances of industrialization and the deepening of the internal market in several countries.

These realities have two political consequences. First, an original historical formation requires unique integration proposals. Transplanted schemes of European experiments have proven to be inadequate for continental reality. Integrationist projects that deny Latin American specificity risk re-living debates like those that informed the democratic field in the 20th Century, such as Walt Whitman Rostow's takeoff myth[4] or the controversy surrounding the existence of Latin American feudalism (Rostow 1974; Assadourian and Cardoso et al. 1973).

Toward the end of the 19th century, José Martí pointed out similar difficulties when analyzing the obstacles faced by independence leader Simón Bolívar:

---

[4] Conceived in the 1960s by American economist Rostow, this refers to one of the phases of economic development through which countries would have to pass to achieve development.

> By chance, in his dream of glory for America and for himself, he did not see that the unity of spirit, indispensable for the salvation and happiness of our American peoples, harmed, more than helped, with their union in theoretical and artificial forms which were not in accord with the secure of reality [...].
>
> MARTÍ 2000: 282

3.3 Latin American Integration Will Be against the Economy

The second consequence of the external orientation of the economy is the precariousness of the material bases for an integrationist project. It starts from a productive structure firmly situated, since the colonial period, in the framework of a subordinated insertion as a primary exporter to the international market. Correspondingly, transportation, communication and energy infrastructures are designed to connect export-producing centers to their outlets on the coast.

Intra-regional exchange levels are historically low as redundancy between national productive bases prevails rather than complementarity, imposing competition between countries rather than cooperation. Undoubtedly this is a result of the historic obstacles that have faced countries in the region in their efforts to control their own destiny. Such obstacles are expressed on the one hand in the perpetuation of dependency bonds characteristic of a center-periphery relationship and, on the other in the impotence to assert relations of regional collaboration. These were aggravated by their cultural expressions, since ideological influences and political and academic ties prevail with the countries of the center to the detriment of mutual knowledge and intra-continental intellectual cooperation.

What this indicates is that Latin American integration is not inscribed in the economic evolution of the region in the way that the development of productive forces would generate the objective conditions for socialism. This is because development has reaffirmed the articulation between dependence and the over-exploitation of labor. And with this, the general determinations that impede integration in the economic, political and cultural spheres are reproduced.

In this perspective, starting from an adverse economic trajectory, regional integration will be a political design emanating from the historical movement of these societies. This is the antithesis of barbarism, which is reserved for the condition of dependence. Although Jorge Abelardo Ramos's analysis of the 'Latin American nation' published in 1968 evokes a problematic 'essential unity' of the continent, his conclusion indicates this path:

> It is clear from what has been said that the unity of Latin America is not today posited as a demand for the development of productive forces in search for a great internal market of the twenty republics, but precisely for the opposite reason. In order to launch ourselves resolutely on the path of civilization, of science and culture, and precisely to develop the economic potential of our peoples, whether by capitalist means, through State capitalism, through a Creole socialism or by a combination of all the options mentioned, Latin America needs to unite in order not to degrade. It is not the progress of capitalism, as happened in Europe or the United States that demands the unity of our states today, but rather the deep crisis and the exhaustion of the semi colonial condition that we suffer.
>
> ABELARDO RAMOS 2012: 551

The Latin American revolution will be against the economy, or more precisely, it will mobilize politics against the outward orientation of the economy. Ultimately, it will be necessary to confront the myth of economic development, a peripheral expression of the ideology of progress.

3.4   Development Must Be Equal and Combined – with the People and the Planet

The Russian Revolution and all the revolutions that followed it were referenced to the Marxist paradigm of the development of productive forces. The fundamental premise of that paradigm is the need to accelerate the industrialization and mechanization of rural production as conditions for the realization of communism in the periphery, so that the socialization of production does not become the socialization of poverty. At the political level, communism can be understood as the historical solution to the contradiction between the social character of production and the private appropriation of wealth in capitalism. As such, communism would put the productive potential, the fruits of capitalist progress, at the service of the working majority.

The idea behind the Marxist paradigm is unassailable: communism strives for equality in abundance. However, difficulties emerge in history when the imperative of the development of productive forces collides with the political demands of change. Perhaps the best-known example is the forced collectivization of peasant production in the Soviet Union where plans for the mechanization of rural production, seen as necessary to provide cheap food and labor for industrialization, collided with the way of life of peasants. As a result, the collectivization was advanced through a bloodbath.

The outcome of this process was paradoxical, since the accelerated industrialization turned the Soviet Union into an economic power but sacrificed popular support for the revolution. So these are not easy questions, but dilemmas: problems for which foreseen solutions are difficult. If the Soviet Union had not become an industrial power, it would probably have been annihilated by Nazism. On the other hand, the path chosen for development alienated the peasant majority, putting in question the very raison d'etre of the revolution. The Cuban process has also experienced and continues to experience its own dilemmas. For example, in the 1970s a paradoxical position prevailed that saw Soviet dependence as necessary to preserve the island's independence in the Cold War.

In the 21st century there are at least three reasons to revisit this paradigm. First, as has already been mentioned, is that the imperative of progress trampled popular aspirations, alienating revolutionary reason. Second, is the tension between centralization – associated with national defense and the development of productive forces – and popular democratization. Finally, there is a question of order: i.e., the world can end if anti-capitalist forces do not subvert the ideology of progress. Indeed, ecological imperatives force us to review the approach to nature as a productive force, just as the emancipation of labor is impossible while treating people as human resources.

The equation between the needs of economic development and the ecological imperative is not a simple matter nor is it consensual among the Latin American left. In practice, it often results in a dilemma between the practical reasoning of the state and ideology, illustrated tersely in Ecuadorian president Correa's recurrent statement that Ecuadorians cannot be beggars seated on a sack of gold.

Conversely, the principle of *Living Well* illuminates the impasses of a devised regional integration. First, it reveals a popular rejection of extractivism, in line with the yearning for economic diversification but also points to the rejection of the pattern of development anchored in economic growth. This second critical dimension implies a broader rejection of what can be synthesized in Karl Marx's phraseology, as the 'society of commodities'. In short, *Living Well* claims the Aboriginal legacy as a source of inspiration for an alternative civilizing project, consistent with the regional reality, in which the determinations of economic development are subordinated to the needs and aspirations of society as a whole, including ecological concerns. From this angle, South American integration based on the IIRSA is identified with the perpetuation of the colonial legacy.

Privileging social determinations does not imply disregarding the economic dimension of regional integration, but rather points to the imperative of politics driving the economy, not the other way around. An emancipatory integration must transcend free trade agreements or infrastructure interconnections, aiming to constitute as Celso Furtado observed 30 years ago, an authentic regional economic system:

> It is now more or less evident that, far from being a simple matter of trade liberalization, the real problem is to promote the creation of a *regional economic system*, which will not be a small task, given the previous orientation of development, the risks of aggravating geographical concentrations both in economic activities and in the appropriation of the fruits of development, the considerable autonomy with which powerful international consortia operate in the region, that control not only traditional export activities but also a large part of the modern manufacturing sector, the divergences between national policies in the control and orientation of economic processes and other factors of no less importance.
> FURTADO 1986: 267–268

In short, regional integration must be associated with sovereignty, which requires a policy that reverses the meaning of the economy and in which overcoming the colonial legacy necessarily leads to an alternative civilizational pattern.

3.5 *Progress Is Walking with your Own Legs, with your Head Where your Feet Step*

The development of productive forces and the modernization of consumption patterns are two aspects of the paradigm of progress that the left must overcome.

In addition to equality in abundance, the emphasis on productive forces rested on a second premise: that socialism would be more productive than capitalism. At the end of World War II, the impressive Soviet victory encouraged estimates of how many years it would take to overtake Western powers. Such prognostications were further fuelled by the Soviets' fairly quick success in developing a nuclear bomb and sending a dog into space.

In hindsight, many on the left think these were illusions: socialism proved to be inefficient from the point of view of production and would have lost the struggle with capitalism in the field of economics (Blackburn 2005). I do not want to discuss which system is and/or could be most productive, although I am convinced that communism, which we have not yet experienced, will be more productive. The point to emphasize is that the superiority of socialism need not be located in the realm of productivity but in meeting the wants and needs of people.

To put the issue in Weberian terms, the debate on economic efficiency framed in terms of productivity dissociates the means from ends. It has become commonplace to argue that the Cuban state is inefficient. Yet, when a state shelters, nurtures, educates, cares for and defends its entire population in the midst of underdevelopment, under what criteria would it be considered inefficient? By accepting the terms of a debate framed by economic efficiency, then reduced to productivity, the left has historically incorporated capitalist references to gauge socialist success.

This issue is crucial in respect of the development of an anti-capitalist imagination in Latin America, where it is impossible and undesirable to generalize the consumption patterns of central countries. Latin American integration must build another civilizational landscape, grounded in the fundamental values of economic self-determination, political sovereignty, social integration and cultural self-reference.

Such reasoning is not unprecedented in the history of the subcontinent's critical thinking. Analogous problematizations were proffered by at least two intellectuals who dealt with the problem of continental integration in different historical moments and national realities. At the end of the 19th century, José Martí suggested a rejection of the 'class hatred' that typified Western societies, pointing to a civilizing path for Cuba angled around the notions of 'natural man' and 'world balance'. Almost a century later, Celso Furtado problematized the reproduction of consumption patterns of the capitalist center in peripheral societies, where the narrow productive base required a concentration of income as a condition for capitalist realization. From this perspective, the Brazilian economist formulated an acute criticism of the 'cultural mimicry' of the dominant classes in Latin America, indicating the impossibility of reconciling patterns of imported consumption and integration of the population through labor. In the 21st century, the ideology of *Living Well* has in its own way, taken on a similar problem, pointing to the need for an alternative civilizing landscape.

These reflections indicate that it is necessary to subordinate economic development to the interests of the population as a whole, which, in the light of contemporary ecological problems, implies questioning the civilizational paradigm anchored in the notion of progress. Following in the footsteps of Martí and Furtado, this does not mean the rejection of the advances of industrial civilization, but rather the subordination of means to ends. For Latin America, the paradigm of progress has proven to be both unfeasible and undesirable, noting that even its successful version produced societies marked by individualism, alienation and competition, instead of life, freedom, and the pursuit of happiness, as promised by Declaration of Independence of the United States. Where it was implemented advanced capitalism resulted in societies driven by accumulation based on the exploitation of workers and the environment, both at home and abroad. We must remember that in this reality, as Walter Benjamin said, every document of culture is also a document of barbarism.

If we adopt a different perspective then Latin American integration as well as socialism can be seen as a utopia of abundance that points to the future, but a future that does not stop in Miami. In other words, it is necessary to adapt the pattern of consumption to the material bases of peripheral societies. This necessarily involves a cultural decolonization and a productive reorientation that breaks with concentration and privilege in favor of social integration. Of course, the abundance that is sought is not based on consumerism shaped by the advertising industry. Cultural emancipation also implies freedom from the modulation of human needs to the imperatives of capital; in short, to control the pace, time and orientation of social innovation. People must walk with their own legs, with steps that are their size and in the direction of common interest.

3.6   Values not only Opposed to, but Different from, those of Capitalism

The understanding that neoliberal hegemony articulates coercion and consensus means assuming culture as a contested field, in which the main anticapitalist weapon is radically different values.

Socialism will eventually be a social system of greater productive efficiency, but it needs to be immediately superior on political, social and cultural levels. It must be politically more democratic because the antithesis of bourgeois liberalism is not workers in parliament but workers parliaments, as were the original soviets. It must be socially more humane because it addresses the basic needs of the population, as opposed to the destitution that marks contemporary societies. It must be culturally different because it is governed by values antithetical to capitalism, such as solidarity, altruism and contentment. The superiority will also be economic, but the immediate criterion should not be productivity but the practice of democratic production relations, favoring the reappropriation of labor by the worker.

In Latin America, this changeover of values must be associated with a profound cultural decolonization: it must be made clear that equality imposes other cultural references and other patterns of consumption. This proposition indicates the need for a continuous and long-term effort to dismantle what Antonio Gramsci called 'common sense', constructing a counter-hegemonic view of the continent's civilizing horizon. This effort has three main dimensions.

First, and as has been previously mentioned, it is necessary to make explicit the incompatibility of integration of the population as a whole, with and through labor and consumption patterns copied from the central countries. Contrary to the myth of economic growth, the democratization of consumption requires an adaptation of the productive structure to meet the needs of the population as a whole, in a movement that contradicts dependent modernization. It is further necessary to clarify the links between the modernization of patterns of consumption and income concentration, to reveal the antithetical relationship with control over economic space and social equality (Furtado 1974). In short, it is necessary to point out that in the current historical moment, one must choose between modernization and concentration, or sovereignty and democratization.

A second dimension is the importance of cultural decolonization. Easier said than done, this proposition has multiple implications ranging from consumption patterns to social theory, through to racism and cultural references. Far from being a phenomenon restricted to the dominant classes, the admiration of the cultural expressions of central capitalism and the United States in particular is something that permeates all social classes and also different political orientations, albeit in varying degrees of intensity.

The other side of this phenomenon is a feeling of inferiority in relation to what is native. For this reason, the starting point for facing cultural colonialism is the valorization of what is one's own in all its dimensions, which also involves an explicit recognition of continental specificities. It is not only a humanistic question, demanding the civilizational status of different cultures, but it is a central political issue for a future of self-determination because the values by which the success of a Latin American enterprise is evaluated must be different, referring to autonomy and democratization, ecological balance and the realization of human potential.

The third dimension points to an awareness of the historical determinations that influence the destiny of Latin American countries. Despite the economic, historical and cultural obstacles to continental integration, the movement towards the internationalization of production and the financialization of capital, which correspond to the formation of regional blocs, makes it even more improbable to overcome common dilemmas on a national scale. Continental unity reemerges in the 21st century as a historical necessity.

It will be necessary to overcome an instrumentalist vision of integration between neighboring countries. An integration of emancipatory meaning cannot be guided by the logic of economic competition and political domination but must be guided by the search for the common good, the privileging of economic cooperation and political solidarity as well as respect for people's right to self-determination. A diplomacy of generosity must be assumed and practiced with pride in the region, especially by Brazil, in order to cultivate a 'marriage' to be sealed not only for money but also for love.

3.7 Equality in the Workplace against Capital

The premise that overcoming underdevelopment in Latin America requires overcoming capitalism and has as its landscape substantive equality, necessarily leads to a critical reflection on the Soviet process, which haunted the right with the specter of revolution and cast a shadow over revolutionary politics in the last century.

In his analysis of the Soviet Union, the Hungarian intellectual István Mészáros saw a post-capitalist society that did not go beyond capital. In his view, capital is constituted by the triad of private property, wage labor and state. Breaking only with the first element of this triad, the Soviet Union shook a fundamental element of capitalism – private ownership of the means of production – but the metabolic system of capital remained intact. Hence, the Soviet Union is described as a post-capitalist society that has not overcome the tyranny of capital (Mészáros 1996).

This analysis suggests that the revolutions against capital in the 21st century will be more and not less radical than the Soviet experience. In addition to overcoming the private ownership of the means of production – the contradiction between the social character of production and the private character of appropriation – the other two legs of capital must also be confronted.

Therefore, it will be necessary to break with hierarchy in labor relations. Historical experience shows that abolishing private ownership of the means of production is a necessary but insufficient condition for overcoming the alienation of labor. Realizing the latter will require producers to appropriate the production process: i.e., socialism understood as the self-management of associated producers.

This is also not a simple or immediate task because, among other things, one dimension of capitalist alienation is to make workers stop believing or being interested in the appropriation of work, as well as in politics. Earlier, a concrete example from the Cuban Revolution was provided, when the absolute majority of rural workers opted to work for the state instead of joining a cooperative. In the penultimate country to abolish slavery in the Americas, the peasants seemed content to have a decent boss and did not want to command themselves.

So the revolutionary hypothesis faces another dilemma: how do institutions and human beings forged under capitalism build a non-capitalist society?

3.8 A Strong State that does not Eat Me

The notion of socialism as the transition from capitalism to communism comes from the understanding that it is necessary to construct the objective and subjective conditions for a society without private property, without social classes and without a state. The underlying diagnosis is that institutions, social relations and individuals molded under capitalism cannot simply plunge into communism without mediations, and thus risk a social disorganization that would ultimately lead to capitalist restoration.

In 'The State and Revolution', the book that Lenin had hurriedly finished because he considered it 'more useful and pleasant to experience revolution rather than write about it'; the state was consecrated as the main instrument of this transition. Consistent with communist ideology, it was assumed that the state is an institution of class domination, but that in this historical situation it would serve the interests of the majority through the revolutionary form of 'the dictatorship of the proletariat'. Faced with the impossibility of liquidating this pillar of capital, the revolution sought to reverse it (Lenin 1986).

Since then, the main path to build an anti-capitalist society where the revolution triumphed has been the workers and peasants state. In practice however, the conception of the state as an instrument of the transition to communism, which would be a stateless society, encountered a difficult paradox: how to affirm the post-revolutionary state as an instrument of transition and, at the same time make it expendable? In short, how to strengthen and weaken the state at the same time?

Besides this propositional argument, the state dilemma has a second dimension of a defensive character. The centralization of power has been shown to be necessary to face the very counterrevolution triggered by any revolution. Historical experience, from the French Revolution to the Cuban Revolution and including frustrated processes like the Mexican Revolution or the Spanish Civil War, reveals this impasse: the centralization of power as necessary and effective to defeating the counterrevolution but militating against the original democratizing potential of these processes.

In the Soviet case the centralization required by the civil war was partially undone in the economic sphere with the adoption of the New Economic Policy (NEP). However, there was no analogous shift at the political level, which contributed to the later consolidation of Stalinism. In the Cuban case, where a remarkable commitment by the state to equality and sovereignty persisted, Martínez Heredia synthesized the dilemma posed by the demand for centralization of power in the following terms: 'How to make a strong state that does not eat me?'

In Latin America, where capitalist domination has been described by Florestan Fernandes as 'total imperialism', the defense of revolution will always be pressing (Fernandes 1975). Despite the abuses and distortions that can be pointed out there is undeniable wisdom in the Cuban process that has lasted for decades, during a time when Bolivian nationalists, Chilean socialists and the Sandinistas among others, succumbed. The need to defend revolution is frequently ignored by formulations that refer to Zapatismo, that point to changing the world without taking power or that have *Living Well* as a reference. While these elaborations provide a pertinent and necessary critique of the anti-popular character of state politics on the subcontinent, including under progressive governments, one must respond in theory and in practice to the concrete challenges posed by imperialism.

Just as small-scale industrial production is unlikely to meet the material needs of contemporary societies, so too is decentralized policy unlikely to effectively defend a country from imperialism. This double realization of the constraints to generalizing abundance in peripheral societies – though emancipated from the patterns of capitalist publicity – coupled with the demand to defend the revolution within the framework of imperialism, is what renews the currency of communism as a world utopia.

In other words, as long as economic integration is subordinated to mercantile rationality and imperialist domination is a reality, the national state will be a necessary instrument to economically and militarily defend societies that defy the system. In the 21st century, equality in abundance and a stateless society remain in force as paradigms of communism, as does the idea of world revolution.

3.9   *There Is no Alternative to Popular Power*

The democratization of relations of production as well as the democratization of politics were contained in past revolutions due to the imperatives of production and defense. Faced with men and women forged by the societies they wanted to overcome, revolutionary leaders understandably distrusted popular protagonism, centralizing the direction of economics and politics.

However, the hierarchization of labor and the strengthening of the state blocked efforts to overcome capital; capitalist restoration relied on these two legs of the tripod. Based on historical experience the solution to the centralization versus democratization dilemma seems to be clear: the infallibility of the central committee must give way to the spontaneity of popular power (Luxembourg 2017). The dictatorship of the proletariat will give way to a transition conceived of as a pedagogy of praxis.[5]

---

5   The notion of praxis understands history as an unlimited process of double transformation of human's relations with the environment, which forges its own nature. According to this

If the origin of communism in the 19th century was linked to science and its first historical essays in the 20th Century were ossified as dogmas, 21st century praxis will need to believe in spontaneity as the way to the self-determination of workers. Less science and more spontaneity understood not as voluntarism or improvisation but as creative expressions of human beings. The creativity intrinsic to the dawn of revolution, the moment when workers 'storm heaven', reveals that with a new historical situation an original historical response emerges. This was seen in the Paris Commune in 1871.

The Bolshevik strategy in 1917 had as its background the massacre with which the brief experience of the Commune ended. In the Russian revolution, which influenced all subsequent revolutions, the demand for the centralization of power to defeat the counterrevolution was succeeded by the fear of counterrevolution from within and without, which was addressed with further state centralization as a means to control the process.

The fact that the Bolsheviks seized and sustained power, opening the possibility of building for the first time in history a society in which class exploitation was abolished, is an extraordinary political feat. Yet, the survival imperative stifled the original creativity of the process. Quickly, defending the revolution was confused with defense of the state, and *raison d'État* supplanted world revolution. In the Soviet Union as in other revolutions that followed, the state distanced itself from the ideology that legitimated it at its origin, often acting in a counterrevolutionary sense. Just as was the case with economic development, the command of the state became an end in itself. On the whole, economic power and political power were alienated from their original purpose: popular power.

Popular power is the only way to confront the economic and cultural power of capital in the 21st century. The solutions to the dilemmas of efficiency versus democratization of production, of defense versus democratization of politics, will be found not only in historical experience itself but in experiences that rely on the initiative of the working class. This is also the way to assert a radically different culture, laying the foundations for the popular support necessary for any egalitarian revolution. Workers will defend a society that is theirs, however imperfect it may be.

It is possible that this path of popular power will have more curves than straight lines. Regardless, the most important thing is to break with the metabolic system of capital and not to walk in circles, even if it's a decades-long

---

perspective, there would not be an immanent human essence, but it is its practical and historical nature as a social being that defines it. It is this awareness of production and self-production as constitutive characteristics of human nature that is at the root of the unity between theory and practice and which underlies the problem of the formation of class consciousness and the overcoming of capitalism from the point of view of historical materialism. On this, see Sánchez Vázquez 2007.

circle. In this perspective, the means prove to be as, if not more, important than the ends. The Leninist bet on the workers and peasants state in the 20th century will have to coexist in the 21st century with the hypothesis of the self-determination of the masses of Rosa Luxemburg. One hundred years after October 1917, the observation that it is preferable to make mistakes with the people than to get it right without them seems to be inescapable.

After all, a less efficient but happier society seems desirable. We may not plant the red flag on the moon or win the Olympics but who knows, perhaps we will cultivate the wisdom of Uruguayan children, who play soccer on the streets and sing: 'We win, we lose, equally we have fun' (Galeano 1995).

Bibliography

Argentina

Altamira, Jorge. Entrevista em: Fioretti, Martín; Shinzato, Federico. Las izquierdas en la política argentina. Buenos Aires: Divino Tesoro, 2009.

Aspiazu, Daniel; Basualdo, Eduardo. El proceso de privatización en Argentina. Bernal: Universidad Nacional de Quilmes, 2002.

Ayerbe, Luis Fernando. Estados Unidos e América Latina. São Paulo: Unesp, 2002.

Basualdo, Eduardo. 'Evolución de la economía argentina en el marco de las transformaciones de la economía internacional de las últimas décadas'. In: Basualdo, Eduardo; Arceo, Enrique (comp.). Los condicionantes de la crisis en América Latina. Buenos Aires: CLACSO, 2009, pp. 321–382.

Basualdo, Eduardo. Sistema político y modelo de acumulación em la Argentina. Bernal: Universidad Nacional de Quilmes, 2001.

Bobbio, Norberto; Matteucci, Nicola; Pasquino, Gianfranco. Dicionário de política. Brasília: UNB, 1983.

Cano, Wilson. Soberania e política econômica na América Latina. São Paulo: UNESP, 1999.

Catela, Ludmila da Silva. Situação-limite e memória. A reconstrução do mundo dos familiares de desaparecidos na Argentina. São Paulo: Hucitec, ANPOCS, 2001.

CELS: 2017. Disponível em: <http://www.cels.org.at/blogs/estatisticas/>. Acesso em outubro de 2017.

Cortés Conde, Roberto. The growth of the Argentine economy c.1870–1914. In: Bethell, Leslie (Org.). The Cambridge History of Latin America. Cambridge: Cambridge University Press, 1986.

El Descamisado. Apuntes políticos 2001–2014. Buenos Aires: 2015.

Fioretti, Martín; Shinzato, Federico. Las izquierdas en la política argentina. Buenos Aires: Divino Tesoro, 2009.

Frondisi, Silvio. La realidad argentina. Ensayo de interpretación sociologica. Buenos Aires: Praxis, 1955.

Furtado, Celso. Formação econômica da América Latina. 2. ed. Rio de Janeiro: Lia, 1970.

Gaggero, Alejandro; Schorr, Martín; Wainer, Andres. Restricción eterna: el poder económico durante el kirchnerismo. Buenos Aires: Futuro Anterior ediciones, 2014.

Gallo, Ezequiel. La Pampa Gringa. Buenos Aires: Edhasa, 2004.

Germani, Gino. Política y sociedad en una época de transición. De la sociedad tradicional a la sociedad de masas. Buenos Aires: Paidos, 1965.

GRR. Grupo de Reflexión Rural en diálogo con Ignacio Lewkowicz. Estado en construcción. Buenos Aires: Tierra Verde, 2003.

Kaplan, Marcos. '50 años de historia argentina (1925–1975): el laberinto de la frustración'. Em: González Casanova, Pablo. América Latina: historia de medio siglo. México: Siglo XXI, 1984 (1977).

Katz, Claudio. 'Contrasentidos del neodesarrollismo'. Em: Estrada Álvarez, Jairo. América Latina en medio de la crisis mundial. Trayectorias nacionales y tendencias regionales. Buenos Aires: CLACSO, 2014.

Katz, Claudio. 'Anatomía del kirchnerismo'. Em: Rebelión. 17/1/2013.

Katz, Claudio. Entrevista em: Fioretti, Martín; Shinzato, Federico. Las izquierdas en la política argentina. Buenos Aires: Divino Tesoro, 2009.

Kirchner, Néstor. Palavras do presidente Néstor Kirchner na assinatura da ata de apresentação do programa de assistência creditícia em operações de curto prazo. 29/3/2003. Disponível em: <http://www.casarosada.gob.ar/informacion/archivo/24456-blank-90565382>. Acesso em 28/8/2017.

Kosacoff, Bernardo. Marchas y contramarchas de la indústria argentina (1958–2008). Santiago: Cepal, 2010.

Lynch, John. The River Plate Republics. In: Bethell, Leslie (Org.). Spanish America after Independence. Cambridge: Cambridge University Press, 1987.

Murmis, M.; Portantiero, J.C. Estudos sobre as origens do peronismo. São Paulo: Brasiliense, 1973.

Novaro, Marcos; Palermo, Vicente. A ditadura militar argentina (1976–1983). São Paulo: EDUSP, 2007.

O'Donnell, Guillermo. El Estado Burocrático Autoritario. Buenos Aires: Editorial de Belgrano, 1982.

Repetto, Nicolás. Mi paso por la política. Buenos Aires: Santiago Rueda Editor.

Rock, David. El Radicalismo Argentino, 1890–1930. Buenos Aires: Amorrortu editores, 2001.

Romero, José Luis. Breve historia de la Argentina. Buenos Aires: Tierra Firme, 2001 (1965).

Sartelli, Eduardo. La plaza es nuestra. Buenos Aires: Ediciones RyR, 2007.

Schincariol, Vitor. 'A recuperação da economia argentina nos anos 2000'. Em: Revista Galega de Economia, 2013.

Schorr, Martin; Aspiazu, Daniel. 'Industria y economía (1976–2007)'. Em: El descamisado. Apuntes políticos 2001–2014. Buenos Aires: 2015.

Svampa, Maristella. Del cambio de época al fin de ciclo. Gobiernos progresistas, extractivismo y movimientos sociales en América Latina. Buenos Aires: Edhasa, 2017.

Varesi, Gastón Ángel. 'Crisis mundial, modelo de acumulación y lucha de clases en la Argentina actual'. In: Estrada Álvarez, Jairo (coord.). La crisis capitalista mundial y América Latina. Lecturas de economía política. Buenos Aires: CLACSO, 2012, pp. 145–159.

Conversations between 10/7 to 14/7, 2017 in Buenos Aires and Surroundings

CTA. Leaders of Central de Trabajadores de Argentina – Autonoma.
CTEP – Activists from Confederación de Trabajadores de la Economia Popular.
Gallo Mendoza, Guillermo. Rural issues specialist.
Gambina, Julio. Economist.
Gringo. CTEP leader.
Hourcade, Sol. Human Rights Lawyer. Centro de Estudios Legales y Sociales.
Isacovich, Paula. Professor at Universidad Nacional de Jose Carlos Paz (UNIPAZ).
Marcos, Daniel. Movimento Emancipador Peronista.
MOI. Leaders from Movimiento de Ocupantes e Inquilinos.
MTL governista. Leader of Merendero la Colmena.
MTL. Leader of Movimiento Territorial Liberácion.
Palmisano, Tomás. Grupo de Reflexão Rural do Instituto de Investigaciones Gino Germani.
PCCE. Centro Cultura Roque Centurión.
Petz, Inez. Grupo de Reflexão Rural do Instituto de Investigaciones Gino Germani.
Tufró, Manuel. Centro de Estudios Legales y Sociales.

Bolivia

Agee, Philip. O diário da CIA. São Paulo: Círculo do livro, 1976.
Albo, Xavier. 'Algunos de nuestros desafíos ambientales'. Pagina Siete, La Paz, abril de 2015, p. 20.
Almaraz, Alejandro. 'La frustración agraria'. Pagina Siete, La Paz, abril de 2015, p. 23.
Archondo, Rafael. 'El periodismo en la era Evo Morales'. Pagina Siete, La Paz, abril de 2015, p. 34.
Arguedas, Alcides. Pueblo enfermo. La Paz: Ercilla, 1937 (1910).
Arze Vargas, Carlos; Espada, Juan Luis; Guzmán, Juan Carlos; Poveda, Pablo. Gasolinazo: subvención popular al Estado y a las petroleras. La Paz: Cedla, 2011.
Arze Vargas, Carlos; Gómez, Javier. 'Las contradictorias nociones del Vivir Bien y las estrategias para alcanzarlo'. Em: Lander, Edgardo; Arze, Carlos; Gómez, Javier; Ospina, Pablo; Álvarez, Víctor. Promesas en su laberinto. Cambios y continuidades en los gobienros progresistas de América Latina. La Paz: IEE, CEDLA, CIM, 2013.
Barrientos, Rene. Teoria y programa de la Revolución Boliviana. La Paz, 1966.
Boff, Leonardo. 'Os equívocos do PT e o sonho de Lula'. Fevereiro de 2016. Disponível em: https://leonardoboff.wordpress.com/2016/02/06/os-equivocos-do-pt-e-o-sonho-de-lula/. Acesso em 12/2/2016.

Borón, Atilio. 'El no nace en Washington'. La Jornada, 11 de fevereiro de 2016. Disponível em <http://www.jornada.unam.mx/2016/02/11/opinion/031a1mun#texto>. Acesso em 13 de fevereiro de 2016.

Colque, Gonzalo. Expansión de la frontera agrícola. Luchas por el control y apropiación de la tierra en el oriente boliviano. La Paz: Fundación Tierra, 2014.

Condori, Ivan. 'La Cumbre Agropecuaria definirá lineamientos para la Agenda 2025'. La razón, La Paz, 5/4/2015. Disponível em: <http://www.la-razon.com/economia/Cumbre-Agropecuaria-definira-lineamientos-Agenda_0_2246775352.html>. Acesso em 8/2/2016.

Costa Neto, Canrobert. Políticas agrárias na Bolívia (1952–1979). Reforma ou revolução? São Paulo: Expressão Popular, 2005.

Crabtree, John. Patterns of protest. Politics and social movements in Bolivia. London: Latin American Bureau, 2005.

Dangl, Benjamin. El precio del fuego. Las luchas por los recursos naturales y los movimientos sociales en Bolivia. La Paz: Plural, 2009.

Dinges, John. Os anos do condor. São Pualo: Cia das Letras, 2004.

FIDES. 'García Linera asegura que Fundación Tierra y CEDIB mienten en favor de los extranjeros'. 8/8/2015. Disponível em: <http://www.noticiasfides.com/g/politica/garcia-linera-asegura-que-la-fundacion-tierra-y-el-cedib-mienten-en-favor-de-los-extranjeros-37114/> Acesso em 8/10/2015.

FIDES. 'Morales exige enjuiciar a financiadores de VIII Marcha Indígena'. 10/12/2013 Disponível em: <http://www.noticiasfides.com/g/politica/tipnis-morales-exige-enjuiciar-a-financiadores-de-viii-marcha-indigena-19376/> Acesso em 8/10/2015.

Fundación Tierra. Marcha indígena por el TIPNIS. La lucha en defensa de los territorios. La Paz, Fundación Tierra, 2012.

Gandarillas, Marco; Rodríguez Cáceres, Gustavo. Mitos de la inversión extranjera. El caso de los hidrocarburos en Bolívia. Cochabamba: CEDIB, sem data.

García Linera, Álvaro. Geopolítica de la Amazonía. Poder hacendal-patrimonial y acumulación capitalista. La Paz: Vicepresidencia, 2013c.

García Linera, Álvaro. 'El Capitalismo Andino Amazonico'. Le monde diplomatique, Santiago, janeiro de 2006a. Disponível em: http://www.lemondediplomatique.cl/El-capitalismo-andino-amazonico.html. Acesso em 6/2/2016.

García Linera, Álvaro. 'El evismo: lo nacional popular en acción'. Observatorio Social de America Latina, año VI, no. 19. CLACSO, Consejo Latinoamericano de Ciencias Sociales, Buenos Aires, Argentina: Argentina. julio. 2006b.

García Linera, Álvaro. El 'oenegismo', enfermedad infantil del derechismo. La Paz: Vicepresidencia, 2013a.

García Linera, Álvaro. Las empresas del Estado. Patrimonio colectivo del pueblo boliviano. La Paz: Vicepresidencia, 2013b.

García Linera, Álvaro. Las tensiones creativas de la revolución. La Paz: Vicepresidencia, 2014 (2011).

García Linera, Álvaro. Socialismo Comunitario. Un horizonte de época. La Paz: Vicepresidencia, 2015.

Gott, Richard. Guerrilla movements in Latin America. New York: Doubleday, 1971.

Guevara, Jean Paul. 'Política exterior del Estado Plurinacional'. Pagina Siete, La Paz, abril de 2015, p. 8.

Halperin Donghi, Tulio. Hispanoamerica despues de la Independencia. Consecuencias sociales y economicas de la emancipación. Buenos Aires: Paidos, 1972.

Hylton, Forrest; Thomson, Sinclair. Revolutionary horizons. Past and present in Bolivian politics. London: Verso, 2007.

Kennedy, John. Public Papers of the Presidents of the United States. Washington, 1961.

Klein, Herbert. Bolivia: the evolution of a multi-ethnic society. New York: Oxford University Press, 1982.

Loayza Bueno, Rafael. Eje del MAS. Ideología, representación social y mediación en Evo Morales Ayma. La Paz: Konrad Adenauer, 2011.

Mesa, José de; Gisbert, Teresa; Mesa Gisbert, Carlos D. Historia de Bolivia. 3a ed. La Paz: Gisbert, 1999.

Miranda, Boris. 'Bolivia: el millonario caso de corrupción que involucra a exministros, parlamentarios y dirigentes del partido de Evo Morales'. BBC, dez 2015. Disponível em <http://www.bbc.com/mundo/noticias/2015/12/151205_millonario_escandalo_corrupcion_partido_evo_morales_bm>. Acesso em 6/2/2016.

Molina, Fernado. 'Donde el "proceso de cambio" choca con el subdesarollo'. Pagina Siete, La Paz, abril de 2015, p. 27.

Ormachea, Enrique S.; Ramirez, Nilton. Políticas agrarias del Gobierno del MAS o la agenda del 'poder empresarial-hacendal'. La Paz: Cedla, 2013.

Rada Vélez, Alfredo. 'En defensa de los movimientos sociales'. Pagina Siete, La Paz, abril de 2015, p. 4.

Requena, Cecília. 'El Vivir Bien y sus malestares'. Pagina Siete, La Paz, abril de 2015, p. 21.

Reynaga, Fausto. La revolución india. El Alto: Fundación Amautica Fausto Reynaga, 2001 (1971).

Rivera Cusicanqui, Silvia. Oprimidos pero no vencidos: luchas del campesinado aymara y quechwa de Bolivia, 1900–1980. La Paz: Hisbol-CSUTCB, 1984.

Rivera Cusicanqui, Silvia. 'Luchas campesinas en Bolivia'. Em: Gonzalez Casanova, Pablo. Historia política de los campesinos Latinoamericanos. México: Siglo XXI, 1985.

Rivera Cusicanqui, Silvia. Mito y desarrollo en Bolivia. El giro colonial del gobierno del MAS. La Paz: Plural, 2013.

Schavelzon, Salvador. Plurinacionalidad y Vivir Bien/ Buen Vivir. Dos conceptos leídos desde Bolivia y Ecuador post-constituyentes. Quito: Abya Yala/CLACSO, 2015.
Silva, Fabrício Pereira da. 'Equilíbrios precários: a trajetória do movimento ao socialismo e seus dilemas'. Domingues, José Maurício et al. A Bolívia no espelho do futuro. Belo Horizonte: UFMG, 2009.
Soruco, Ximena (cord.). Los barones del Oriente. El poder en Santa Cruz ayer y hoy. Santa Cruz, Fundación Tierra, 2008.
Stefanoni, Pablo; Alto, Hervé do. Evo Morales: de la coca al palacio. Una oportunidad para la izquierda indígena. Bolivia: Malatesta, 2014.
Stern, Steve J. (compilador). Resistencia, rebelión y conciencia campesina en los Andes (siglos XVIII al XX). Lima: Instituto de Estudios Peruanos, 1990.
Tamayo, Franz. Obra escogida. Caracas: Ayacucho, 1986 (1910).
Tapia, Luis. 'Sociedad abigarrada. Repensando la democracia multicultural en Bolivia'. Entrevista em: RELACSO, México, 2011. Disponível em: <http://relacso.flacso.edu.mx/repensando-la-democracia-multicultural-en-bolivia>. Acesso em 10/2/2016.
Urioste, Miguel. 'La marginalización de la agricultura campesina e indígena'. Pagina Siete, La Paz, abril de 2015, p. 22.
Urquidi, Vivian. Movimento cocaleiro na Bolívia. São Paulo: Hucitec, 2007.
Webber, Jeffery. 'From Left-Indigenous Insurrection to Reconstituted Neoliberalism in Bolivia: Political Economy, Indigenous Liberation, and Class Struggle, 2000–2011'. In: Webber, Jeffery; Carr, Barry. The new Latin American left. Cracks in the Empire. Lanham: Rowman & Littlefield Publishers, Inc., 2013, pp. 149–190.
Zavaleta Mercado, René. Lo nacional-popular en Bolivia. La Paz: Plural, 2008 (1986).
Zavaleta Mercado, René. 'Consideraciones generales sobre la historia de Bolivia'. Em: Gonzalez Casanova, Pablo. América Latina: historia de medio siglo. México: FCE, 1984 (1977).
Zavaleta Mercado, René. Clases sociales y conocimiento. La Paz: Amigos del libro, 1988.
Zavaleta Mercado, René. El poder dual en América Latina. México: Siglo XXI, 1973.

Conversations in Santa Cruz, Cochabamba and La Paz between 5/7/2015 and 15/7/ 2015

Almaraz, Alejandro. Former vice-minister of land under Evo Morales (2006–2010).
Ávila, Hernán. Director of Centro de Estudios Jurídicos e Investigación Social (CEJIS).
Campero, Ariana. Physician and Minister of Health.
Campos, Isau; Tosito, Franklin; Romero Zolando. Leaders of Central Obrera Departamental.
Chávez, Adolfo. Leader of Confederación de Pueblos Indígenas de Bolivia (CIDOB).
Escobar, Sílvia. Economist and researcher from Centro de Estudios para el Desarrollo Laboral y Agrario (CEDLA).

Gandarillas, Marco Antonio. Director of Centro de Documentación e Información Bolívia (CEDIB).
Méndez, Fernando. Coordinator of Casa del ALBA – Alianza Bolivariana para los Pueblos de Nuestra América Latina, Cochabamba.
Paz, Sarela. Researcher.
Peredo, Osvaldo 'Chato'. Former guerrilla leader and Santa Cruz MAS city councellor.
Perez Peña, Miguel Angel. Petrobras Bolívia S.A.
Ribera Arismendi. Marco Antonio. Director of Liga de defesa del meio ambiente (LIDEMA).
Sallari, Andrés; Vázquez, Mariano. Journalists of Abya Yala state TV channel.
Saravia, Ramiro. Red Tinku.
Saucedo, Erwin. Former state Deputy, Health minister and professor.
Vadillo, Alcides. Lawyer and director of Fundación Tierra. Served on Ministry of Land Reform.
Villanueva, Amaru. Director of Centro de Investigaciones Sociales de la Vicepresidencia (CIS).
Villegas, Pablo. CEDIB researcher.

Equador

Acción Ecológica, Comisión Ecumênica de Derechos Humanos; Fundación Regional de Asesoría en Derechos Humanos. Criminalización a Defensores de Derechos Humanos y de la Naturaleza en Ecuador. In: Chérrez, Cecilia; Padilla, César; Otten Sander; Yumbla, María Rosa (orgs.). Cuando tiemblan los derechos: extractivismo y criminalización en América Latina. Quito: Observatorio de Conflictos Mineros de América Latina/ Acción Ecológica/ Broederlijk Denle, 2011.
Acosta, Alberto. Breve história econômica do Equador. Brasília: Funag, 2006.
Acosta, Alberto. La Maldición de la abundancia. Quito: Abya Yala, 2009a.
Acosta, Alberto (coord.). Análisis de coyuntura política, económica y social del Ecuador: Una lectura de los principales componentes económicos, políticos y sociales de Ecuador durante el año 2009. Quito: FLACSO/ Friedrich Ebert Stiftung/ ILDIS, 2009b. Disponível em: <http://www.fes-ecuador.org/fileadmin/user_upload/pdf/393%20ANACOY2010_0509.pdf>. Acesso em 26/08/2010.
Acosta, Alberto. La firma del fideicomiso para la Iniciativa Yasuní-ITT. 3 ago. 2010. Disponível em: <http://www.vientosur.info/documentos/Alberto%20Acosta.pdf> Acesso em 26/08/2010.
Acosta, Alberto; Guijarro, John Cajas. Ocaso y muerte de una revolución que al parecer nunca naci. Rebelión, Quito, 2016. Disponível em: <http://www.rebelion.org/docs/216525.pdf>. Acesso em 20/11/2017.

Acosta, Alberto; Olivares, Susana López; Villamar, David. El aporte de las remesas a la economía ecuatoriana. La Insignia, Equador, set. 2006.

Ávila Santamaría, Ramiro. De la utopía de Montecristi a la distopía de la revolución ciudadana. In: Machado, Decio et al. El correísmo al desnudo. Quito: Montecristi Vive, 2013.

Báez, René et al. Ecuador, pasado y presente. Quito: Libresa, 1995.

Batista, Genaro. Represión a los shuar. Revista Memoria, 2011. Disponível em: <http://www.revistamemoria.com/noticia.php?id=79>. Acesso em 9/3/2011.

Breda, Tadeu. O Equador é verde: Rafael Correa e os paradigmas do desenvolvimento. São Paulo: Elefante, 2011. Disponível em: <http://www.editoraelefante.com.br/wp-content/uploads/2015/09/o_equador_e_verde_TB2.pdf>.

Carpio Benalcázar, Patrício. 'El buen vivir más allá del desarrollo: la nueva perspectiva constitucional'. Alai, 11/6/2008. Disponível em: <https://www.alainet.org/es/active/24609> Acesso em 10/2/2018.

Correa, Rafael. Ecuador: de Banana Republic a la no republica. Bogotá: Random House Mondadori, 2009.

Correa, Rafael. El desafío de Rafael Correa [15 jan. 2012]. Guaiaquil, El Telégrafo. Entrevista concedida a El Telégrafo. Disponível em: <http://www.eltelegrafo.com.ec/noticias/especial-desafio-rafael-correa/1/el-desafio-de-rafael-correa>. Acesso em 20/11/2017.

Cueva, Agustín. Ecuador: 1925–1975. In: Casanova, Pablo González. América Latina: Historia de medio siglo. 4. ed. México: Siglo XXI, 1984.

Cuvi, Juan (org.). La restauración conservadora del correísmo. Quito: Montecristi Vive, 2014.

Dávalos, Pablo. Reflexiones sobre el sumak kawsay (el buen vivir) y las teorías del desarrollo, América Latina en Movimiento. 5 ago. 2008. Disponível em: <http://alainet.org/active/25617&lang=es>. Acesso em 26/8/2010.

Dávalos, Pablo. Alianza País o la reinvención del poder. Siete ensayos sobre el posneoliberalismo em el Ecuador. 1. ed., Bogotá: Ediciones desde abajo, 2014.

Eguez, Alejandro. Las remesas de emigrantes en Ecuador tras la dolarización. Observatorio de la Economía Latinoamericana, 2001. Disponível em: <http://www.eumed.net/cursecon/ecolat/ec/Eguez-remesas-A.htm>. Acesso em 9/3/2011.

El Universo. Presidente Rafael Correa reta a grupos opositores a reunir firmas para consulta sobre Yasuní. Quito, 17/8/2013. Disponível em: <https://www.eluniverso.com/noticias/2013/08/17/nota/1302246/presidente-rafael correa-reta-grupos-oposi tores-reunir-firmas>. Acesso em 20/11/2017.

Houtart, François. El desafío de la agricultura campesina para el Ecuador. In: Cuvi, Juan (org.). La restauraciónconservadora del correísmo. Quito: Montecristi Vive, 2014.

Hurtado, Osvaldo. El poder politico en el Ecuador. Quito: Letraviva, 1988.

Maiguashca, Juan; Maiguashca, Liisa North. Orígenes y significado del Velasquismo: lucha de clases y participación política en el Ecuador, 1920–1972. In: Quintero, Rafael (org.). La questión regional y el poder. Quito: Corporación Editora Nacional, 1991.

Machado, Decio et al. El correísmo al desnudo. Quito: Montecristi Vive, 2013.

Muñoz Jaramillo, Francisco (org.). Balance crítico del gobierno de Rafael Correa. Quito: Universidad Central de Ecuador, 2014.

Observatorio Social de América Latina. Cronología del conflicto social. Equador. CLACSO, out 2008.

Ospina Peralta, Pablo. Estamos haciendo mejor las cosas con el mismo modelo antes que cambiarlo. In: Ospina Peralta, Pablo et al. Promesas en su laberinto. Cambios y continuidades en los gobiernos progresistas de América Latina. La Paz: IEE/ CEDLA/ CIM, 2013a.

Ospina Peralta, Pablo. La revolución ciudadana en Ecuador: conflicto social, régimen disciplinario y proyecto de Estado. In: Quintero, Rafael (org.). La cuestión regional y el poder. Quito: Corporación Editora Nacional, 1991.

Ramírez Gallegos, Franklin (coord.). Democracia, participación y conflictos. Ecuador 2009–2012. Quito: FES/ ILDIS/ FLACSO, 2013.

Brazil

Arantes, Pedro. 'Da (anti) reforma urbana brasileira a um novo ciclo de lutas nas cidades'. Em: Sampaio Jr., Plínio. Jornadas de junho: a revolta popular em debate. São Paulo: ICP, 2014.

Badaró, Marcelo. Junho e nós: das jornadas de 2013 ao quadro atual, Blog Junho, disponível em: http://blogjunho.com.br/junho-e-nos-das-jornadas-de-2013-ao-quadro-atual/. Acessado em 2/7/2015.

Bonomo, M., Brito, R., & Martins, B. (2014). Macroeconomic and financial consequences of the after crisis government-driven credit expansion in Brazil. Working paper 378. Rio de Janeiro: Banco Central do Brasil.

Braga, Ruy. Precariado e sindicalismo no Brasil contemporâneo: Um olhar a partir da indústria do call center. Revista Crítica de Ciências Sociais, Coimbra , n. 103, pp. 25–52, maio 2014a. Disponível em <http://www.scielo.mec.pt/scielo.php?script=sci_arttext&pid=S2182-74352014000100003&lng=pt&nrm=iso>. Acesso em 15/7/2016. http://dx.doi.org/10.4000/rccs.5532.

Braga, Ruy. 'As jornadas de junho no Brasil: crônica de um mês inesquecível'. Em: Sampaio Jr., Plínio. Jornadas de junho: a revolta popular em debate. São Paulo: ICP, 2014b.

Braga, Ruy. 'Contornos do pós-lulismo'. Entrevista à revista Cult, 206. São Paulo, nov. 2015.

Carneiro, Ricardo de Medeiros (2008). Impasses do desenvolvimento brasileiro: a questão produtiva. Textos para discussão n° 153 IE/Unicamp, 2008.

Cervo, Amado Luiz. 'Política exterior e relações internacionais do Brasil: enfoque paradigmático'. Rev. bras. polít. int., Brasília, v. 46, n. 2, Dec. 2003.

Coutinho, Carlos Nelson. A democracia como valor universal e outros ensaios. São Paulo: Salamandra, 1984.

Dardot, Pierre; Laval, Christophe. La nouvelle raison du monde. Essai sur la societé neoliberal. Paris: La Découverte, 2010.

DIEESE. 'Salário mínimo nominal e necessário'. Disponível em: <http://www.dieese .org.br/analisecestabasica/salarioMinimo.html.>. Acesso em 10/5/2016.

Esposito, Maurício. 'Desindustrialização do Brasil: uma análise a partir da perspectiva da formação nacional'. Revista da Sociedade Brasileira de Economia Política, n. 46, 2017.

Fatorelli, Maria Lucia; Avila, Rodrigo. 'Gastos com a dívida pública em 2014 superam 45% do orçamento federal executado'. 5/2/2015. Disponível em: <http://www.audi toriacidada.org.br/blog/2015/02/24/gastos-com-a-divida-publica-em-2014-super aram-45-do-orcamento-federal-executado/>. Acesso em 5/5/2016.

Fiori, José Luís. 'A miséria do "novo desenvolvimentismo"'. Carta Maior, 2011. Disponível em: <http://www.cartamaior.com.br/templates/colunaMostrar.cfm?coluna_ id=5334>. Acesso em 28/07/2016.

Garcia, A.E.S. A internacionalização de empresas brasileiras durante o governo Lula: uma análise crítica da relação entre capital e Estado no Brasil contemporâneo (Unpublished doctoral dissertation). Pontifícia Universidade Católica, Rio de Janeiro, 2012.

Hilsenbeck, Alex. O MST no fio da navalha: dilemas, desafios e potencialidades da luta de classes. Tese de Doutorado. Campinas: Universidade Estadual de Campinas. Instituto de Filosofia e Ciências Humanas, 2013.

Krein, José Dari; Manzano, Marcelo; Santos, Anselmo Luis dos. 'A recente política de valorização do salário mínimo no Brasil'. Texto no prelo, nov. 2015.

Loureiro, Isabel; Singer, André. As contradições do lulismo: a que ponto chegamos? São Paulo, Boitempo, 2016.

Machado, Fernando D'Angelo & Sampaio Jr., Plínio Soares de Arruda. 'Capital internacional e vulnerabilidade externa'. Os bancos e a sociedade brasileira. Jornal dos economistas, n. 275, Rio de Janeiro, jun. 2012.

Mercadante, Aloísio. As bases do novo desenvolvimentismo: análise do governo Lula. Tese (Doutorado) – Instituto de Economia da Universidade Estadual de Campinas – IE Unicamp, Campinas, 2010.

Newsweek. 'Brazil's Lula: the most popular politician on Earth'. 21/09/2009. Available at: <http://www.newsweek.com/brazils-lula-most-popular-politician-earth-79355>. Retrieved in 5/7/2018.

Oliveira, Ariovaldo Umbelino de. 'A questão agrária no Brasil: não reforma e contrarreforma agrária no governo Lula'. In: Sader (Org.). 10 anos de governos pós-neoliberais no Brasil: Lula e Dilma. Boitempo, FLACSO Brasil: São Paulo, 2013, pp. 287–328.

Oliveira, Francisco de. Crítica à razão dualista: O ornitorrinco. São Paulo: Boitempo, 2003.

Paulani, Leda. Brasil Delivery. São Paulo: Boitempo, 2008.

Pochmann, Marcio. Nova classe média? O trabalho na base da pirâmide social brasileira. São Paulo: Boitempo, 2012.

Rodrigues, E. 'Brasil faz obras nos vizinhos temendo a China'. Folha de São Paulo, 27/09/2009. Available at <http://www1.folha.uol.com.br/fsp/dinheiro/fi2709200910.htm> Retrieved in 5/7/2018.

Sampaio Jr., Plínio de Arruda. 'Desenvolvimentismo e neodesenvolvimentismo: tragédia e farsa'. Serv. Soc. Soc., São Paulo, n. 112, Dec. 2012. Available from <http://www.scielo.br/scielo.php?script=sci_arttext&pid=S0101-66282012000400004&lng=en&nrm=iso>. access on 28 Oct. 2014. http://dx.doi.org/10.1590/S0101-66282012000400004.

Sicsú, J.; Paula, L.F.; Michel, R. Novo desenvolvimentismo: um projeto nacional de crescimento com equidade social. São Paulo: Manole, 2005.

Singer, André. Os sentidos do lulismo. São Paulo: Cia. das Letras, 2012.

Souza, Josias de. 'Ibope: 75% dos brasileiros apoiam os protestos', UOL Notícias, 22 jun. 2013, disponível em <http://josiasdesouza.blogosfera.uol.com.br/2013/06/22/ibope-75-dos-brasileiros-apoiam-os-protestos/>, acesso em 12 nov. 2013.

Tautz, C., Siston, F., Pinto, J.R.L., & Badin, L. 'O BNDES e a reorganização do capitalismo brasileiro: um debate necessário'. In: Os anos Lula: contribuições para um balanço crítico, 2003–2010 (pp. 249–286). Rio de Janeiro: Garamond, 2010.

UNIDO. Industrial and Development Report. Viena: Unido, 2011.

Zagni, Rodrigo Medina. 'Carta aos calouros ou bem-vindo à pátria educadora'. Boletim Adunifesp. São Paulo: maio, 2016. Em: <http://www.adunifesp.org.br/artigo/carta-aos-calouros-ou-bem-vindos-patria-educadora-por-rodrigo-medina-zagni>. Acesso em 2/7/2016.

Paraguay and Brasiguayos

ABC Color Digital. 'Paraguay denuncia otra triple Alianza'. Assunção, 26/6/2012. Disponível em: http://www.abc.com.py/nacionales/denuncian-otra-triple-alianza-contra-paraguay-419073.html. Acesso em 18/8/2012.

ABC Color Digital. 'Brasiguayos' pedirán a Itamaraty que respalde a Franco. Assunção, 24/6/2012. http://www.abc.com.py/edicion-impresa/politica/brasiguayos-pediran-que-itamaraty--respalde-a-franco-418087.html. Acesso em 15/8/2012.

ABC Color Digital. 'Ejecutan brasileño y queman tres topadoras en estancia en Ajote'y'. Assunção, 30/6/2012. Disponível em: <http://www.abc.com.py/edicion-impresa/judiciales-y-policiales/ejecutan-a---brasileno-y-queman-tres-topadoras-en--estancia-de-azotey-420573.html.>. Acesso em 14/8/2012.

Albuquerque, J.L.C. Fronteiras em movimento e identidades nacionais. A imigração brasileira no Paraguai. Fortaleza, 2005. Tese (Doutorado) – Programa de Pós-Graduação em Sociologia, Universidade Federal do Ceará.

Albuquerque, J.L.C. A dinâmica das fronteiras: deslocamento e circulação dos 'brasiguaios' entre os limites nacionais. Horiz. antropol. [online]. 2009, vol. 15, n.31 [cited 2012-02-23], pp. 137–166.

Alderete, Luciano & Navarro Ibarra, Liliana (2009). Paraguay en la encrucijada: movimiento campesino y governabilidad durante el periodo 1989–2008. Disponível em: http://paraguay.sociales.uba.ar/files/2011/08/P_navarro_alderete_2009.pdf. Acesso em: 18/5/2012.

Alves, J.L. Brasiguaios: destino incerto. São Paulo: Global, 1990.

Arditti, Benjamín; Rodríguez, José Carlos. La sociedad a pesar del Estado. Movimientos sociales y recuperación democrática en el Paraguay. Asunción: CDE, 1987.

BASE IS. Los impactos socioambientales de la soya en Paraguay. Asunción: BASE IS, 2010.

BASE IS. Brasiguayos, Itaipu y Mercosur. Memorias del IV seminario binacional sobre brasiguayos. Documento de Trabajo 68. Disponível em: <http://www.portalguarani.com/detalles_museos_otras_obras.php?id=87&id_obras=1981&id_otras=295> Acesso em 18/5/2012.

Batista, L.C. Brasiguaios na fronteira: caminhos e lutas pela liberdade. São Paulo, 1990. Dissertação (Mestrado) – Faculdade de Filosofia, Letras e Ciências Humanas, Universidade de São Paulo.

Benitez Leite, Stela; Macchi, Maria Luisa; Acosta, Marta. Malformaciones congenitas asociadas a agrotoxicos. Assunção: BASE IS, 2011; Palau, Tomas et al. Los refugiados del modelo agroexportador. Impacto del monocultivo de soya en las comunidades campesinas paraguayas. Asunción: BASE IS, 2007.

Ceceña, Ana Ester; Aguilar, Paula; Motto, Paulo. IIRSA: territorialidad de la dominación. Buenos Aires: Observatorio Latinoamericano de Geopolitica, 2007.

Chiavenatto, Júlio José. O genocídio americano: a guerra do Paraguai. São Paulo: Brasiliense, 1988.

Comisión de Justicia y Verdad. Informe Final de la Comisión de Verdad y Justicia. Tomo IV: Tierras Mal Habidas. Asunción: Comisión de Justicia y Verdad, 2008. Disponível em: <http://www.meves.org.py>. Acesso em 20/3/2012.

Cortêz, C. Brasiguaios: os refugiados desconhecidos. Brasil Agora, 1994.
Couto e Silva, Golbery do. Geopolítica do Brasil. Rio de Janeiro, 2ª edição, Livraria José Olympio Editora, 1967.
Doratiotto, Francisco Doratiotto. Maldita Guerra- nova história da Guerra do Paraguai. São Paulo: Cia. das Letras, 2002.
Dros, Jan Marteen. Managing the boom: two scenarios of soy production expansion in South America. AID Environment. Amsterdam, June 2004.
Ferrari, Carlos Alberto. Dinâmica Territorial na(s) fronteira(s): um estudo sobre a expansão do agronegócio e a exploração dos brasiguaios no norte do departamento de Alto Paraná – Paraguai. Dissertação de Mestrado. Universidade Federal da Grande Dourados (UFGD), 2009.
Figueredo, Oscar Augustín Torres; Lovois, Andrade Miguel (2006). A modernização da agricultura e os brasiguaios no Paraguai. Disponível em: <http://www.sober.org.br/palestra/5/970.pdf> Acesso em 15/2/2012.
Fiorentin, Marcia Izabel. A experiência da imigração de agricultores brasileiros no Paraguai (1970–2010). Dissertação de Mestrado apresentada ao Programa de Pós-Graduação em História da Universidade Federal do Paraná, 2010.
Fogel, Ramón. La región de la triple frontera: territorios de integración y desintegración. Sociologias no. 20 Porto Alegre July/Dec.2008.
Fogel, Ramón; Riquelme, Marcial. Enclave sojero: merma de soberania y pobreza. Asunción: Ceri, 2005.
Fogel, Ramón. Tierra y democracia: la lucha de los campesinos paraguayos. Nueva Sociedad. Julio-Agosto 1988, n. 96, pp. 163–173.
Fogel, Ramón. Movimientos campesinos y su orientación democrática en el Paraguay. Compilador/es: Hubert C. de Grammont (En publicación): 'La construcción de la democracia en el campo latinoamericano'. Buenos Aires: CLACSO, 2006.
Fogel, Ramón. Entrevista concedida a Fatima Rodriguez para o periódio E'A, em 25/07/2011. Disponível em: <http://ea.com.py/ramon-foguel-este-es-el-unico-pais-donde-los-inmigrantes-son-los-que-discriminan-a-los-locales/> Acesso em 10/4/2012.
Garzón, Luiz Fernando Nóvoa. IIRSA: neoliberalismo físico ou versão territorial do livre-comércio. Em: Korol, Claudia; Palau, Marielle. Restistencias populares y recolonización del continente. Talleres de la triple frontera. Asunción: BASE IS, 2009, pp. 64–68.
Garzón, Luiz Fernando Nóvoa. IIRSA: o futuro do continente como mercadoria. Em: Korol, Claudia; Palau, Marielle. Restistencias populares y recolonización del continente. Talleres de la triple frontera. Asunción: BASE IS, 2009, pp. 69–74.
Gimenez, Heloisa Marques. O desenvolvimento da cadeia produtiva da soja na Bolívia e a presença brasileira: uma história incomum. São Paulo, 2010. Dissertação de mestrado apresentada no PROLAM-USP.

Glauser, Marcos. Extranjerización del territorio paraguayo. Asunción: BASE IS, 2009.
González, David. 'Paraguay por primera vez superará 3 millones de hectáreas en soja'. Assunção: 5 dias, 30/8/2011. Disponível em: http://www.5dias.com.py/5310-paraguay-por-primera-vez-superar-3-millones-de-hectreas-en-soja. Acesso em: 15/8/2012.
Grain, ¡Se adueñan de la tierra! El proceso de acaparamiento agrario por seguridad alimentaria y de negocios en 2008, Documentos de análisis, octubre 2008.
Informe IWGIA. El caso Ayoreo. Paraguai, sem data.
ISA (Instituto Sócioambiental) ONG paraguaia denuncia desmatamento promovido por empresas brasileiras na região do Chaco. Notícias socioambientais, 13/10/2008. Em: <http://www.socioambiental.org/nsa/detalhe?id=2773>. Acesso em 16/2/2012.
Klipphan, Andres; Enz, Daniel. Tierras S/A. Cronicas de un pais rematado. Buenos Aires: Alfaguara, 2006.
Korol, Claudia; Palau, Marielle. Restistencias populares y recolonización del continente. Talleres de la triple frontera. Asunción: BASE IS, 2009.
Laino, D. Paraguai: fronteiras e penetração brasileira. São Paulo: Global, 1979.
Maestri, Mário. A Guerra Contra o Paraguai: História e Historiografia: Da instauração à restauração historiográfica [1871–2002]. Estudios Historicos – CDHRP- Agosto 2009 – N° 2 – ISSN: 1688–5317.
Marques, Maria Eduarda Castro Magalhães. A Guerra do Paraguai – 130 anos depois. Rio de Janeiro: Relume- Dumará, 1995.
Mello, Leonel Itaussu Almeida. Brasil e Argentina em perspectiva. Rev. hist., São Paulo, n. 147, dez. 2002. Disponível em https://doi.org/10.11606/issn.2316-9141.v0i147p211-224.
Mendez, Idilio. (2011) Monsanto golpea en Paraguay: Los muertos de Curuguaty y el juicio político a Lugo. Disponível em: http://www.atilioboron.com.ar/2012/06/porque-derrocaron-lugo.html. Acesso em 5/8/2012.
Menezes, Alfredo da Mota. A herança de Stroessner: Brasil – Paraguai, 1955–1980. São Paulo: Papirus, 1987.
Moraes, Ceres. Interesse e colaboração do Brasil e dos Estados Unidos com a ditadura de Stroessner (1954–63). Diálogos, v. 11, n. 1 e 2, pp. 55–80, 2001.
Mota, Alfredo Menezes. A herança de Stroessner. Brasil- Paraguai (1955–1980). Campinas: Papirus, 1987.
Nickson, Andrew R. 'Brazilian colonization of the Eastern Border Region of Paraguay', Journal of Latin American Studies n. 13 (maio de 1981), Republicado como: Colonización brasileña de la región oriental del Paraguay. Em: Fogel, Ramón; Riquelme, Marcial. Enclave soyero merma de soberanía y pobreza. Assunción, CERIS, 2005, pp. 219–239.
Palau, Tomas. Es logico que una sociedad agredida se defienda. Asunção: BASE IS, 2012.

Palau, Tomas. Brasiguaios. In: Migrações Internacionais – Contribuições para políticas. Brasília: CNPD, 2001.

Palau, Tomas. Tomas. El movimiento campesino en el Paraguay: conflictos planteamientos y desafíos. Em: OSAL (Observatório Social de América Latina). Año 6, n.16 (jun 2005). Buenos Aires: CLACSO, 2005.

Palau, Tomas. et al. Los refugiados del modelo agroexportador. Impacto del monocultivo de soya en las comunidades campesinas paraguayas. Asunción: BASE IS, 2007.

Pastore, Carlos. La Lucha por la tierra en el Paraguay. Montevideo: Editorial Antequera, 1972.

Pébayle, Raymond. Les Brésilguayens, migrants brésiliens au Paraguay. In: Revue européenne de migrations internationales. Vol. 10 N°2. pp. 73–86

Pomer, Leon. A guerra do Paraguai: a grande tragédia rioplatense. São Paulo: Global, 1981.

Programa Democratización y Construcción de la Paz. Monitoreo de la Política de Reforma Agraria del Gobierno Lugo. Síntesis a Diciembre 2011. Asunción, febrero de 2012.

Riquelme, Quintin. Los sin tierra en Paraguay. Conflictos agrarios y movimiento campesino. Buenos Aires: CLACSO, Septiembre. 2003.

Riquelme, Quintín; Rojas, Luis & Palau, Tomas. Acciones del Gobierno Lugo para la Reforma Agraria entre agosto de 2008 y junio de 2010. Informe final de consultoría. Assunção, dez. 2010.

Rivarola, Domingo (editor) Los movimientos sociales en el Paraguay. Asunción: CPES, 1986. Outras obras referentes incluem: Keikel, Maria Victoria; Palau, Tomas. Los Campesinos, el Estado y las Empresas en la frontera agrícola. Assunção: BASE ISEC, PISPAL, 1987.

Rivarola, Milda. Vagos, pobres y soldados – La domesticación estatal del trabajo en el Paraguay del siglo XIX. Asunción: Servilibro: 2010.

Rojas, Luis. Actores del agronegocio en Paraguay. Asunción: BASE IS/ Diakonia, 2009.

Rulli, Javiera. Republicas unidas de la soya. Cordoba: GRR, 2007. Disponível em: <http://lasojamata.iskra.net/es/republicasunidas> Acesso em 10/4/2012.

Salim, Celso. Migración brasiguayos y MERCOSUR. Fuerza de trabajo rural en el centro-oeste brasilero. En publicacion: Migración brasiguayos y MERCOSUR. Fuerza de trabajo rural en el centro-oeste brasilero. Asuncion: BASE IS, 1994.

Santa Bárbara, M. Des-caminhos brasileiros em terras paraguaias. Rio de Janeiro, 2005a. Dissertação (Mestrado) – Departamento de Geografia, Universidade Federal Fluminense.

Santa Bárbara, M. Brasiguaios: território e logos de identidades. In: Neto, H.P.; Ferreira, A.P (Org.) Cruzando fronteiras disciplinares – Um panorama dos estudos migratórios. Rio de Janeiro: Revan, 2005b.

Santos, Fabio Luis Barbosa dos. 'A destituição de Lugo e os limites da democracia na América Latina'. Brazilian Journal of Latin American Studies. São Paulo: PROLAM, 2013.

Santos, M.E.P. O cenário multilíngüe/multidialetal de fronteira e o processo identitário de alunos brasiguaios no contexto escolar. Campinas, 2004. Tese (Doutorado) – Instituto de Estudos da Linguagem, Universidade Estadual de Campinas. Silva, Maria Aparecida de Moraes; Melo, Beatriz Medeiros de. Soja: a expansão dos negócios. Le monde diplomatique, 5/2/2009. Disponível em: <http://www.diplomatique.org.br/artigo.php?id=311&PHPSESSID=7344ed5e82e51d5534f731688bd39468> Acesso em 12/2/2012.

Souchaud, S. La formation d'un espace brésiguayen dans l'Est du Paraguay. Migrations pionnières brésiliennes et organisations socio-spatiales dans l'Oriente du Paraguay. Potiers, 2001. Thèse (Doctorat en Géographie) – Université de Poitiers.

Souchaud, S. Pionniers brésiliens au Paraguay. Paris: Kaethala, 2002.

Souchaud, S.; Carmo, Roberto Luiz do; Fusco, Wilson. Mobilidade populacional e migração no Mercosul: a fronteira do Brasil com Bolívia e Paraguai. Teoria & Pesquisa, VOL XVI, n.1, jan-jun 2007.

Souchaud, S. Nouveaux espace en Amerique du Sud: la frontière Paraguayo-Brésilienne. Mrappemonde, 2001, pp. 19–23.

Souchaud, S. A visão do Paraguai no Brasil. Contexto int. vol. 33 no. 1 Rio de Janeiro Jan./June 2011.

Sprandel, M.A. Brasiguaios: conflito e identidade em fronteiras internacionais. Rio de Janeiro, 1992. Dissertação (Mestrado) – PPGAS, Museu Nacional.

Sprandel, M.A. Brasileiros na fronteira com o Paraguai. Estud. av., São Paulo, v. 20, n. 57, Aug. 2006.

Tana, Kyle. South America's soy bean wars. 31/5/2010. Disponível em: <http://www.thecuttingedgenews.com/index.php?article=12194&pageid=89&pagename=Features> Acesso em 18/5/2012.

Tiburcio, James. Brazilians in Paraguay: A Growing Internal Problem or a Regional Issue? Paper presented at the annual meeting of the ISA – ABRI Joint International Meeting, Pontifical Catholic University, Rio de Janeiro Campus (PUC-Rio), Rio de Janeiro, Brazil, Jul 22, 2009.

Urioste, Miguel. Concentración y estrangerización de la tierra en Bolívia. La Paz: Fundación Tierra, 2011.

Wagner, C. Brasiguaios: homens sem pátria. Petrópolis: Vozes, 1990.

Wagner, C. País-bandido: crime tipo exportação. Porto Alegre: RBN, 2003.

White, Richard Alan. La primera revolución radical de America (1811–1840). Asunción: La Republica, 1984.

Zaar, Miriam H. 2001. 'A Migração Rural No Oeste Paranaense / Brasil: A Trajetória Dos "Brasiguaios"', Scripta Nova. Vol. 88, No. 94, p. 2.

Interviews between 31/7 to 4/8, 2012, in Asunción

Aguayo, Luis. Leader of Mesa Nacional de las Organizaciones Campesinas (MNOC).

Alderete, Alberto. Former-Director of INDERT (Instituto Nacional de Desarrollo Rural y de la Tierra).

Bordenave, Juan Díaz. Consejo Nacional de Educación y Cultura.

Fogel, Ramón. Sociologist.

Flecha, Victor-Jacinto. Sociologist.

Lovera, Miguel. Former Director of SENAVE (Servicio Nacional de Calidad y Sanidad Vegetal y de Semillas).

Méndez, Idilio. Journalist and economist.

Riquelme, Quintín. Sociologist.

Rivarola, Milda. Historian and agronomic engineer.

Rojas Villagra, Luis. BASE IS coordinator.

Wehrle, Andrés. Former Vice-minister of Agriculture and Livestock.

Brazil and Regional Integration

Bonomo, M. Brito, R. and Martins, B. 'Macroeconomic and Financial consequences of the after crisis government-driven credit expansion in Brazil'. Working paper 378. Rio de Janeiro: Banco Central do Brasil, 2014.

Campos, Pedro Henrique. 'As origens da internacionalização das empresas de engenharia brasileiras'. Em: Fundação Rosa Luxemburgo. Empresas transnacionais brasileiras na América Latina: um debate necessário. São Paulo: Expressão Popular, 2009.

CEPAL – Comissão Econômica Para a América Latina e O Caribe. El regionalismo abierto en América Latina y el Caribe: la integración económica al servicio de la transformación productiva con equidad. In: CEPAL. Cincuenta años de pensamiento en la Cepal: textos seleccionados. 1994. v. 2.

Cerezal, Manuel; Simarro, Ricardo Molero; Soler, Alberto Montero. 2013. 'El Sucre: orígenes, funcionamiento y perspectivas de futuro para la integración latinoamericana'. Em: Martins, Carlos Eduardo. Los retos de la integración y América del Sur. Buenos Aires: CLACSO, 2013.

Cervo, Amado Luiz. 'Política exterior e relações internacionais do Brasil: enfoque paradigmático'. Rev. bras. polít. int., Brasília, v. 46, n. 2, Dec. 2003.

COSIPLAN. Cartera de Proyectos (2014). Montevideo: V Reunión ordinaria del COSIPLAN, 4/12/2014. Disponível em: <http://www.iirsa.org/admin_iirsa_web/Uploads/Documents/cn25_montevideo14_Cartera_COSIPLAN_2014.pdf>. Acesso em 1/9/2015.

Desidera Neto, Walter; Teixeira, Rodrigo. 'La recuperación del Desarrollismo en el Regionalismo Latinoamericano'. In: Desidera Neto, Walter; Teixeira, Rodrigo. Perspectivas para la integración de América Latina. Brasília: CAF; IPEA, 2012.

Estado de São Paulo. 'BNDES aposta R$ 7,5 bi no Friboi'. São Paulo, 15/02/2010.

Estado de São Paulo. 'BNDES empresta 3915 mais em 5 anos e supera em 3,3 vezes o Banco Mundial'. São Paulo, 10/3/2011. Available at: <http://economia.estadao.com.br/noticias/geral,bndes-empresta-391-mais-em-5-anos-e-supera-em-tres-vezes-o-banco-mundial-imp-,689817>. Retrieved on 21/5/2016.

Fiori, José Luís. A miséria do 'novo desenvolvimentismo'. 2011. Disponível em: <http://www.cartamaior.com.br/templates/colunaMostrar.cfm?coluna_id=5334>. Acesso em 28/10/2014.

Folha de São Paulo. 'Brasil faz obras nos vizinhos temendo a China'. São Paulo: Caderno Dinheiro, B6, 27/09/2009.

FUNAG. A América do Sul e a integração regional. FUNAG: Brasília, 2012.

Fundação Dom Cabral. Ranking FDC das Transnacionais Brasileiras. São Paulo, 2010.

Garzon, L.F.N. 'A esfinge, o BNDES e as "campeãs" que nos devoram'. Correio cidadania. 03 de Maio de 2013. Disponível em: <http://www.correiocidadania.com.br/index.php?option=com_content&view=article&id=8329%3Amanchete030513&catid=34%3Amanchete&amp.> Acesso em 8/8/2014.

Gonçalves, José Botafogo. In: Paz, Leonardo (org.). O CEBRI e as Relações Internacionais no Brasil. São Paulo: SENAC, 2013.

Luce, M.S. O subimperialismo brasileiro revisitado: a política de integração regional do governo Lula (2003–2007). Dissertação de Mestrado em Relações Internacionais, Porto Alegre: Universidade Federal do Rio Grande do Sul, 2007.

Lula da Silva, Luis Inácio. 2014. 'Oposição e governo iniciam diálogo na Venezuela com a mediação da Unasul'. Disponível em: <http://oglobo.globo.com/mundo/oposicao-governo-iniciam-dialogos-na-venezuela-com-mediacao-da-unasul-1-12127392>. Acesso em 22/7/2016.

Mercadante, Aloísio. As bases do novo desenvolvimentismo: análise do governo Lula. Tese (Doutorado). Instituto de Economia da Universidade Estadual de Campinas. IE Unicamp, Campinas, 2010.

Paulani, Leda. Brasil Delivery. São Paulo: Boitempo, 2008.

Pinto, Luiz; Reis, Marcos. (2016): 'Long term finance in Brazil: the role of the BNDES'. Chapter to the book: Grivoyannis, Elias. The New Brazilian Economy. New York: Palgrave Macmillan. Forthcoming.

Rice, Secretary Condoleezza. Remarks With Brazilian Foreign Minister Celso Amorim. Brasilia, Brazil, March 13, 2008. Disponível em: <http://2001-2009.state.gov/secretary/rm/2008/03/102228.htm>. Acesso em 10/5/2014.

Saggioro Garcia, Ana. A internacionalização de empresas brasileiras durante o governo Lula: uma análise crítica da relação entre capital e Estado no Brasil contemporâneo. Tese de Doutorado. Rio de Janeiro: PUC, 2012.

Sampaio Jr., Plinio de Arruda. 'Desenvolvimentismo e neodesenvolvimentismo: tragédia e farsa'. Serv. Soc. Soc., São Paulo, n. 112, Dec. 2012. Available from <http://www

.scielo.br/scielo.php?script=sci_arttext&pid=S0101-66282012000400004&lng=en&nrm=iso>. access on 28 Oct. 2014. http://dx.doi.org/10.1590/S0101-66282012000400004.

Sanahuja, José Antonio. 'Regionalismo post-liberal y multilateralismo en Sudamérica: El caso de UNASUR'. In: Serbin, Andrés; Martínez, Laneydi; Ramanzini Júnior, Haroldo; El regionalismo 'post–liberal' en América Latina y el Caribe: Nuevos actores, nuevos temas, nuevos desafíos. Anuario de la Integración Regional de América Latina y el Gran Caribe 2012. Buenos Aires: Coordinadora Regional de Investigaciones Económicas y Sociales, 2012.

Santos, Fabio Luis Barbosa dos. 'A problemática brasiguaia e os dilemas da projeção regional brasileira'. In. Desiderá Neto, Walter Antonio (org.). O Brasil e Novas Dimensões da Integração Regional. Brasília: IPEA, 2014.

Sherman, Wendy. Under Secretary for Political Affairs. Remarks to the Council of the Americas and the Center for Strategic and International Studies (CSIS). Carnegie Endowment for International Peace Washington, DC February 28, 2012 http://www.state.gov/p/us/rm/2012/184853.htm Acesso em 15/5/2014.

Sicsú, J.; Paula, L.F.; Michel, R. Novo desenvolvimentismo: um projeto nacional de crescimento com equidade social. São Paulo: Manole, 2005.

Silva, André Luiz Reis da. As transformações matriciais da política externa brasileira recente (2000–2010). Meridiano 47 (UnB), v. 120, pp. 1–10, 2010.

Tautz, Carlos; Siston, Felipe; Lopes Pinto, João Roberto; Badin, Luciana. 'O BNDES e a reorganização do capitalismo brasileiro: um debate necessário'. Em: Os anos Lula contribuições para um balanço crítico: 2003–2010. Rio de Janeiro, Garamond, 2010.

Thorstensen, Vera. 'Ficar atrelado ao Mercosul é afundar o Brasil', em Carta Capital, 19 mai. 2014. Disponível em <http://www.cartacapital.com.br/economia/ficar-atrelado-ao-mercosul-e-afundar-o-brasil-804.html>. Retrieved at 28/10/2014.

Vigevani, Tullo & Cepaluni, Gabriel. 'Política externa de Lula: a busca de autonomia pela diversificação', em Vigevani, Tullo & Cepaluni, Gabriel. A política externa brasileira: a busca de autonomia, de Sarney a Lula. São Paulo: Editora UNESP, 2011.

Vizentini, Paulo F. Relações internacionais do Brasil: de Vargas a Lula. São Paulo: Fundação Perseu Abramo, 2008.

Zavaleta Mercado, René. Clases sociales y conocimiento. La Paz: Amigos del libro, 1982.

Interviews and Conversations

Acosta, Alberto. Former leader of Constitutional Assembly in Ecuador and former minister at Rafael Correa´s government. Quito, September 2015.

Araujo, Joaquim. Brazilian Embassy at Peru. Lima, July 2015.

Barros, Pedro Silva. Director of Ecomomic Affairs at UNASUL. Quito, September 2015.

Cerezal, Manuel. Advisor to Central Bank of Venezuela, researcher at Universidade Bolivariana da Venezuela. Caracas, November 2015.

Constant, Hector. Diplomat and professor at Universidad Central de Venezuela. Caracas, November 2015.

Nascone, Mariano. Director of Social Affairs at UNASUL. Quito, September 2015.

Paes, Pedro. Economist, chief designer of a 'new financial architecture' for South America. Quito, September 2015.

Paloschi, Jonas. Brazilian Embassy at Peru. Lima, July 2016.

Parkinson de Castro, João Carlos. General Coordinator of Economic Affairs at South America (Brazilian Government). Montevideo, December 2015.

Ramírez, Kenneth. Director of Consejo Venezolano de Relaciones Internacionales. Caracas, November 2015.

Ramos, Felippe. Instituto de Pesquisa Econômica Aplicada (IPEA) mission in Venezuela. Caracas, November 2015.

Urbina, Elvis. Venezuela National Coordinator at COSIPLAN. Montevideo, December 2015.

Chile

Alvarado, Constanza; Roca, Persida. 'La plaga de Chile post tenebras lux'. Em: Zerán, Farid (ed.). Chile actual: crisis y debate desde las izquierdas. Santiago: Lom, 2017.

Amtmann, Carla. 'Mito, esperanza y vacío: la travesía de una crisis'. Em: Zerán, Farid (ed.). Chile actual: crisis y debate desde las izquierdas. Santiago: Lom, 2017.

Aravena, Antonio. 'Neoliberalismo, transición democrática y sindicalismo en Chile'. Em: Faure, Antoine; Gaudichaud, Franck et al. Chili actuel: gouverner et résister dans une société néolibérale. Paris: L´Harmattan, 2016.

Atria, Fernando. Veinte años después. Neoliberalismo con rostro humano. Santiago: Catalonia, 2013.

Bengoa, José. La comunidad fragmentada. Nación y desigualdad en Chile. Santiago: Catalonia, 2009.

Blakemore, Harold. British nitrates and Chilian Politics, 1886–1996. Londres, 1974.

Brega, Carla et al. Informe Mensual de Calidad del Empleo (IMCE). Análisis de los microdatos liberados el 30 de Enero de 2017 correspondiente al trimestre móvil Octubre-Diciembre 2016. Santiago: Fundación Sol, janeiro de 2017.

Brunner, José Joaquín. El sistema de educación superior en Chile: un enfoque de economía política comparada. Avaliação (Campinas), Sorocaba, v. 13, n. 2, pp. 451–486, June 2008 . Available from <http://www.scielo.br/scielo.php?script=sci_arttext&pid=S1414-40772008000200010&lng=en&nrm=iso>. access on 13 Sept. 2017. http://dx.doi.org/10.1590/S1414-40772008000200010.

Carlos, Newton; Freitas, Galeno de; Vettori, Marcia. Chile com Allende, para onde vai? Rio de Janeiro: Gernasa, 1970.

Casanova, Pablo. América Latina: historia de medio siglo. México: Siglo XXI, 1984.

Concertación. 'Responsabilidad fiscal. Un patrimonio de Chile que todos debemos resguardar'. Senadores y deputados de la oposição, 6/11/2012. Disponível em: <http://www.elmostrador.cl/media/2012/11/Preocupaci%C3%B3n-de-la-Oposici%C3%B3n-por-la-Responsabilidad-fiscal.pdf.> Acesso em 3/9/2017.

Constituição do Chile. 1980. Disponível em: <http://www.senado.cl/capitulo-iii-de-los-derechos-y-deberesconstitucionales/prontus_senado/2012-01-16/093413.html>. Acesso em 5/7/2017.

Deves Valdes, Eduardo. Los que van a morir te saludan. Historia de una masacre: Escuela Santa María de Iquique, 1907. Santiago: Lom, 2002.

Dinges, John. Os anos do Condor. Uma década de terrorismo internacional no Cone Sul. São Paulo: Companhia das Letras, 2005.

Durán Sanhueza, Gonzalo; Kremerman, Marco. Panorama de los Verdaderos Sueldos usando la Encuesta CASEN. Santiago: Fundación Sol, agosto de 2017a.

Durán Sanhueza, Gonzalo; Kremerman, Marco. Pobreza y la fragilidad del modelo chileno Nuevos indicadores para el debate de pobreza en Chile. Santiago: Fundación Sol, julho de 2017b.

Durán Sanhueza, Gonzalo; Kremerman, Marco. Los Verdaderos Sueldos en Chile. Panorama Actual del Valor del Trabajo usando la Encuesta NESI. Santiago: Fundación Sol, janeiro de 2015.

Elgueta, Belarmino; Chelén, Alejandro. 'Breve historia de medio siglo en Chile'. Em: GonzálezCasanova, Pablo (org.). América Latina: história de médio siglo: México: Siglo XXI, 1984.

Faletto, Enzo. 'De la teoría de la dependencia al proyecto neoliberal: el caso chileno'. Em: Faletto, Enzo. Dimensiones sociales, políticas y culturales del desarrollo. Santiago: FLACSO, 2007 (1999).

Fazio, Hugo; Pareda, Magaly. Veinte años de política económica de la Concertación. Santiago: Lom, 2010.

Foro por la Asamblea Constituyente; Grez, Sergio. Asamblea constituyente. La alternativa democratica para Chile. Santiago: Lom, 2016.

Fundación Sol. El Chile del 50%, del 1%, el 0,1% y del 0,01% (2014). Gráfico disponível em: <http://www.fundacionsol.cl/graficos/el-chile-del-50-del-1-del-01-y-del-001/>. Acesso em 3/9/2017.

Galarce Villavicencio, Graciela. 'La propaganda engañosa sobre Chile. Agotamiento relativo del capitalismo neoliberal'. In: Estrada Álvarez, Jairo (coord.). La crisis capitalista mundial y América Latina. Lecturas de economía política. Buenos Aires: CLACSO, 2012, ps. 189–198.

Garcés, Joan. Allende e as armas da política. São Paulo: Scritta, 1993.

Gil, Frederico G. The political system of Chile. Boston: Houghton Mifflin Company, 1966.

González, Maria Elena. 'El poder contra el poder. Nacionalismo, progreso y libertad en la presidencia de Balmaceda'. Em: González, Maria Elena; Muñoz, Hernán; Rodríguez, Luis Cipriano. Tres momentos del nacionalismo en Chile. Caracas: Tropykos, 1989.

González, Monica; Guzmán; Juan Andrés. 'Las pruebas confirman la venta de acreditaciones a universidades privadas'. Santiago, Ciper, 10/12/2012. Disponível em: <http://ciperchile.cl/2012/12/10/las-pruebas-que-confirman-la-venta-de-acreditaciones-a-universidades-privadas/>. Acesso em 23/11/2017.

Jobet, Julio Cesar. Ensayo critico del desarrollo economico-social de Chile. Santiago: Editorial Universitaria, 1955.

Klein, Naomi. A doutrina do choque: a ascensão do capitalismo de desastre. São Paulo: Nova Fronteira, 2008.

Kornbluh, Peter. Los EEUU y el derrocamiento de Allende. Una historia desclasificada. Santiago: Ediciones B, 2003.

Kremerman, Marco; Páez, Alexander. Endeudar para gobrernar y mercantilizar: el caso de CAE. Santiago: Fundación Sol, abril 2016. Disponível em: <http://www.fundacionsol.cl/estudios/endeudar-gobernar-mercantilizar-caso-del-cae/>. Acesso em 7/9/2017.

Matamala, Daniel. O poder impotente. São Paulo: Correio da Cidadania, 4/7/2017. Disponível em: <http://www.correiocidadania.com.br/internacional/30-america-latina/12679-afp-o-poder-impotente>. Acesso em 8/8/2017.

Mayol, Alberto. El derrumbe del modelo. La crisis de la economía de mercado en el Chile contemporáneo. Santiago: Lom, 2012.

Moulián, Tomas. Chile, anatomia de un mito. Santiago: Lom Editorial, 1997.

Muñoz, Heraldo. À sombra do ditador. Memórias políticas sob Pinochet. Rio de Janeiro: Zahar, 2008.

Necochea, Hernán Ramírez. Balmaceda y la contrarrevolución de 1891. Santiago: Editorial Universitaria, 1972.

Paley, Julia. Marketing democracy. Power and social movements in post-dictatorship Chile. Berkeley: University of California Press, 2001.

Peck, James. Ideal illusions: how the U.S. Government co-opted human rights. New York: Metropolitan books, 2011.

Pinto, Anibal. Chile: un caso de desarrollo frustrado. Santiago: Editorial Universidad de Santiago, 1996 (1959).

Pinto, Julio; Salazar, Gabriel. Historia contemporánea de Chile II. Actores, identidades y movimiento. Santiago: Lom, 1999.

PNUD. Projeto Latinoamerica. 2015. Disponível em: <http://www.projetolatinoamerica.com.br/idh-2015-america-latina/>. Acesso em 5/7/2017.

Ramírez, Felipe. 'Chile: el desafío de superar la crisis desde la izquierda'. Em: Zerán, Farid (ed.). Chile actual: crisis y debate desde las izquierdas. Santiago: Lom, 2017.

Rojas, Camila. 'Lo que nos tocó vivir, Lo que nos toca cambiar'. Em: Zerán, Farid (ed.). Chile actual: crisis y debate desde las izquierdas. Santiago: Lom, 2017.
Ruiz, Carlos; Boccardo, Giorgio. Los chilenos bajo el neoliberalismo. Santiago: Fundación Nodo XXI, 2015.
Sader, Emir. Cuba, Chile, Nicarágua. São Paulo: Atual Editora, 1992.
Salazar, Gabriel. Historia de la acumulación capitalista en Chile. Apuntes de clase. Santiago: Lom, 2003.
Salazar, Paulina. 'A 20 anõs de la explosión del financiamento compartido'. Santiago: La tercera, 8/6/2014. Disponível em: <http://www.latercera.com/noticia/a-20-anos-de-la-explosion-del-financiamiento-compartido/>. Acesso em 7/9/2017.
Silveira, Fábio Vidigal Xavier. O Kerensky chileno. São Paulo: Editora Vera Cruz, 1967.
Sunkel, Osvaldo; Infante, Ricardo. 'Chile: hacia un desarrollo inclusivo'. Santiago: Revista Cepal, n. 197, pp. 135–154, abril de 2009.
Superintendencia de Pensiones. Valor y rentabilidad de los fondos de pensiones. Santiago, junho 2016. Disponível em: <https://www.spensiones.cl/portal/informes/581/articles-10988_recurso_1.pdf>. Acesso em 8/9/2017.
Vasconcelos, Joana Salem. 'Aqui se fabricam pobres'. A previdência chilena como antimodelo. São Paulo: Correio da Cidadania, 18/4/2017. Disponível em: http://correiocidadania.com.br/internacional/30-america-latina/12492-aqui-se-fabricam-pobres-a-previdencia-chilena-como-antimodelo. Acesso em 8/9/2017.
Verdugo, Patricia. Los zarpazos del puma. Santiago: Cesoc, 1989.
Vitale, Luis. Interpretración marxista de la historia de Chile. De semicolonia inglesa a semicolonia norteamericana (1891–1870). Barcelona: Fontamara, 1980.
XVI Informe de Deuda Personal Universidad San Sebastián – Equifax. Primer trimestre 2017. Disponível em: http://www.uss.cl/economia-y-negocios/wp-content/uploads/sites/12/2017/05/XVI-Informe-de-Deuda-Morosa-1er-trimestre-2017-USS-Equifax.pdf. Acesso em 2/9/2017.
Zerán, Farid (ed.). Chile actual: crisis y debate desde las izquierdas. Santiago: Lom, 2017.

Conversations between 1/7 to 8/7 2017 in Santiago and Valparaíso

Aguilar Carvajal, Santiago. Former MIR activist; cultural activist.
Alvarez, Rolando. Historian.
Bolados, Paola. Geographer at Universidad de Valparaíso.
Boric, Gabriel. Federal Deputy representing Movimiento Autonomista.
Caputo, Orlando. Economist, director of Companhia Nacional del Cobre (CODELCO), during Allende's goverment.
Chonchol, Jacques. Minister of Agriculture during Allende's government.
Correa, Felipe. Economic Comission for Latin America (ECLA) Economist.
Garcés, Magdalena. Human rights lawyer.

Grez, Sergio. Historian and activist at Foro por la Asamblea Contituyente.
Guzmán, Jaime. Lawyer and activist at No + AFP movement.
Kremerman, Marco. Fundación Sol.
Lara, Cláudio. Economist.
Mansilla, Pablo. Geographer at Universidad de Valparaíso.
Mundaca, Rodrigo. Leader of Movimiento de Defensa por el Acceso al Agua, la Tierra y la protección del Medio ambiente (MODATIMA).
Olivares, Valentina. Nueva Democracia.
Ponce, Maria Ignacia. Universidad de Valparaíso.
Romero, Nicolás. Movimiento Autonomista.
Rubio, Pablo. Historian.
SAAVERA, Valentina Saavera. Izquierda Autonóma.
Silva Flores, Consuelo. Coordenator of CLACSO workgroup on regional integration.
Titelman, Noam. Revolución Democratica.
Ugarte, José Luis. Worker rights lawyer.
Orellana, Victor. Sociologist, Fundación Nodo XXI.

Colombia

Bautista, Sandra Carolina. 'La paz como construcción social'. In.: Estrada Álvarez, Jairo (coord.). Solución política y proceso de paz en Colombia. México: Ocean Sur, 2013.
Bejarano, Jesus Antonio. 'Campesinado, luchas agrarias e historia social en Colombia: notas para un balance historiográfico'. In.: González Casanova, Pablo (coord.). Historia Política de los campesinos Latinoamericanos. México: Siglo XXI, 1985.
Bergquist, Charles et al. (eds.) Violence in Colombia: the contemporary crisis in historical perspective. Willington: SR Books, 1991.
Bethell, Leslie; Roxborough, Ian (eds.). Latin America between the Second World War and the Cold War, 1944–1948. Cambridge: Cambridge University Press, 1992.
Caycedo, Jayme. 'Militarização e alternativa popular: outro olhar sobre as lutas sociais na Colômbia'. In: Ceceña, Ana Esther. O desafio das emancipações em um contexto militarizado. São Paulo: CLACSO/Expressão Popular, 2009.
Centro Nacional de Memoria Historica. Desaparición forzada, Tomo III: entre la incertidumbre y el dolor: impactos psicosociales de la desaparición forzada. Bogotá: Imprenta Nacional, 2014.
Centro Nacional de Memoria Historica. Basta Ya! Colombia: memorias de guerra y dignidade. Resúmen. Bogotá: Imprensa Nacional, 2013.
Cepeda, Iván; Uribe, Alirio. Por las sendas de El Ubérrimo. Bogotá: Ediciones B, 2014.
Chagas, Rodrigo Simões; Pismel, Matheus Lobo. Colômbia: movimentos pela paz. Florianópolis: Insular, 2014.

Checchia, Cristiane. Terra e capitalismo. A questão agrária na Colômbia. São Paulo: Alameda, 2007.
Durand, Francisco. El Perú fracturado. Formalidad, informalidade y economía delictiva. Lima: Fondo Editorial del Congreso, 2007.
Encuentro Nacional Por La Libertad De Los Prisioneros Políticos. Bogotá: Campaña Traspasa los Muros, 2011.
Estrada Álvarez, Jairo. Construcción del modelo neoliberal en Colombia (1970-2004). Bogotá: Aurora, 2004.
Estrada Álvarez, Jairo. 'As reformas estruturais e a construção da ordem neoliberal na Colômbia'. In.: Ceceña, Ana Esther. O desafio das emancipações em um contexto militarizado. São Paulo: CLACSO/Expressão Popular, 2009.
García, Antonio. 'Colombia: medio siglo de história contemporânea'. In.: González Casanova, Pablo. América Latina: historia de medio siglo. México: Siglo XXI, 1984.
Giraldo, Javier. Colombia: the genocidal democracy. Monroe: Common Courage Press, 1996.
Gros, Christian. 'Los campesinos frente a la guerrilla y a la droga: actores o víctimas?' In.: Gros, Christian; Ramirez Tobón, William; Reyes Posada, Alejandra. Guerra en Colombia: democracia y conflito agrário. Bogotá: IPRI/ FIC, 2004.
Halperin Donghi, Tulio. História da América Latina. Rio de Janeiro: Paz e Terra, 1989.
Harvey, David. 'O "novo imperialismo": acumulação por espoliação'. In.: Panitch, Leo; Leys, Colin. O novo desafio imperial. Socialist Register 2004. Buenos Aires: CLACSO, 2006.
Hylton, Forrest. Evil hour in Colombia. Londres: Verso, 2006.
Jaramillo-Levy, Enrique (comp.). Una explosión en América: el canal de Panamá. México: Siglo XXI, 1976.
Kalmonovitz, Salomón. Economía y nación. Uma breve historia colombiana. Bogotá: Norma, 2003.
Katz, Friederich. Revuela, rebelión y revolución: la lucha rural en México del siglo XVI al siglo XX. Era: México, 1990.
Klein, Naomi. Shock Capitalism. The rise of disaster capitalism. Nova Iorque: Picador, 2007.
López Restrepo Andrés. 'El cambio de modelo de desarrollo de la economía'. In.: Tokatlian et al. Colombia: economía y política internacional. Bogotá: Iepri/FICA, 2004.
Lozano, Carlos A. Guerra o paz en Colombia? Cincuenta años de un conflicto sin solución. Bogotá: Ocean Sur, 2006.
Ocampo, José Antonio. Colombia y la economía mundial. 1830-1910. Bogotá: Siglo XXI, 1984.
Programa Naciones Unidas Para El Desarrollo (PNUD). Colombia rural: razones para la esperanza. Bogotá: PNUD, 2011.

Red Derecho y Desplazamiento. Informe sobre política pública y desplazamiento forzado. Bogotá: ILSA/ ACNUR / NRC, 2010.

Reyes Posada, Alejandro. 'La violencia y el problema agrario'. In.: Gros, Christian; Ramirez Tobón, William; Reyes Posada, Alejandra. Guerra en Colombia: democracia y conflito agrário. Bogotá: IPRI/ FIC, 2004.

Sánchez, Gonzalo. 'The violence: an interpretative synthesis'. In: Bergquist et al. (eds.) Violence in Colombia: the contemporary crisis in historical perspective. Willington: SR Books, 1991.

Sánchez, Gonzalo. Los Bolcheviques del Líbano (Tolima). Bogotá: Mohan, 1976.

Santos, Fabio Luis Barbosa dos. 'Dilemas da Revolução Bolivariana'. Contra a corrente. Revista marxista de teoria, política e história contemporânea. Vol. 4, pp. 57–64, 2010.

Silva, Luiza Lopes da. A questão das drogas nas relações internacionais: uma perspectiva brasileira. Brasília: FUNAG, 2013.

Strange, Susan. Mad Money: when markets outgrow governments. Michigan: The University of Michigan Press, 1998.

Tirado Mejía, Álvaro. 'Colombia: medio siglo de bipartidismo'. In.: Arrubla, Mario et al. Colombia Hoy. Bogotá: Siglo XXI, 1985.

Tokatlian, Juan Gabriel. 'Política antidrogas de Estados Unidos y cultivos ilícitos en Colombia. La funesta rutinización de una estrategia desacertada'. In.: Tokatlian et al. Colombia: economía y política internacional. Bogotá: Iepri/FICA, 2004.

Voz. 100 propuestas para La Habana. Bogotá: Fundación Semanario Voz, 2013.

Conversations between 19/7 and 26/7 2014 in Bogotá and Barrancabermeja

ACVC (Asociación Campesina del Valle del Río Cimitarra)

Angel Beltrán, Miguel. Sociogist and professor at Universidad Nacional de Colombia (UNC).

Avella, Aída. Political leader, vice-president candidate in 2014.

Córdoba, Piedad. Former federal deputy and senator.

Estrada Álvarez, Jairo. Economist.

Fundación Lazos de Dignidad

Gallardo, Gustavo. Lawyer and Marcha Patriotica leader.

Gomez, David. Marcha Patriotica.

Paez, Annye. ACVC advisor.

Rivera, Jairo. Student leader.

Roncancio, Germán. Congreso de los Pueblos.

Cuba

Alonso, Aurelio et al. Debate: 'Actualizando el modelo: economía política y cultura'. La Habana: Temas. N. 73: 70–80, enero – marzo de 2013.

Alzugaray Treto, Carlos. 'Cuba cincuenta años después: continuidad y cambio político'. La Habana: Temas. N. 60: 37–47, octubre – diciembre de 2009.

Armas, Ramón de. La revolución pospuesta. La Habana: Centro de Estudios Martianos, 2002.

August, Arnold. Cuba y sus vecinos. Democracia en movimiento. La Habana: Ciencias Sociales, 2014.

Castro, Fidel. 'Al tribunal de urgencia'. 24/3/1952. Disponível em: <http://www.fidelcastro.cu/es/articulos/al-tribunal-de-urgencia>. Acesso em 19/1/2017.

Castro, Fidel. Discurso pronunciado por Fidel Castro Ruz, Presidente de la República de Cuba, en las honras fúnebres de las víctimas del bombardeo a distintos puntos de la república, efectuado en 23 y 12, frente al cementerio de Colón, el día 16 de abril de 1961(a). Disponível em: <http://www.cubadebate.cu/noticias/2015/04/16/una-revolucion-de-los-humildes-por-los-humildes-y-para-los-humildes/#.WIDeoVMrLIU>. Acesso em 10/1/2017.

Castro, Fidel. Discurso pronunciado como conclusão das reuniões com os intelectuais cubanos, efetuada na Biblioteca Nacional no 16, 23 e 30 de junho de 1961(b). Disponível em: <http://www.cuba.cu/gobierno/discursos/1961/esp/f300661e.html>. Acesso em 8/1/2017.

Castro, Fidel. Discurso pronunciado por el Comandante en Jefe Fidel Castro Ruz, Primer Secretario del Partido Comunista de Cuba y Presidente de los Consejos de Estado y de Ministros, en la ceremonia de condecoración con la Orden 'José Martí', a Hu Jintao, Secretario General del Partido Comunista de China y Presidente de la República Popular China, en el Palacio de la Revolución, el 23 de noviembre de 2004. Disponível em: <http://www.granma.cu/granmad/secciones/visitas/china/art04.html>. Acesso em 14/01/2017.

Castro, Fidel. Discurso pronunciado na orimeira graduação da Escola Latinoamericana de Medicina (ELAM) em 20 de agosto de 2005a. Disponível em: <http://www.cuba.cu/gobierno/discursos/2005/esp/f200805e.html>. Acesso em 18/01/2017.

Castro, Fidel. Discurso pronunciado por Fidel Castro Ruz, Presidente de la República de Cuba, en el acto por el aniversario 60 de su ingreso a la universidad, efectuado en el Aula Magna de la Universidad de La Habana, el 17 de noviembre de 2005b. Disponível em: <http://www.cuba.cu/gobierno/discursos/2005/esp/f171105e.html>. Acesso em 12/01/2017.

Castro, Raul. Discurso del General de Ejército Raúl Castro Ruz, Presidente de los Consejos de Estado y de Ministros, en el VIII Período Ordinario de Sesiones de la Asamblea Nacional del Poder Popular, el 23 de diciembre del 2011. Disponível em: <http://www.cubadebate.cu/opinion/2011/12/23/discurso-de-raul-castro-en-el-parlamento-de-cuba/#.WHio-VMrLIU>. Acesso em 8/01/2017.

Cobo; Narciso et al. Debate: 'Actualizando el modelo: economía política y cultura'. La Habana: Temas. N. 73: 70–80, enero – marzo de 2013.

Díaz Vázquez, Julio A. 'Un balance crítico sobre la economía cubana. Notas sobre dirección y gestión'. La Habana: Temas. N. 66: 123–133, abril – junio de 2011.

Diez Acosta, Tomás. Octubre de 1962: a un paso del holocausto. La Habana: Editorial Política, 2008.

Duharte, Emilio et al. Debate: 'Actualizando el modelo: economía política y cultura'. La Habana: Temas. N. 73: 70–80, enero – marzo de 2013.

Faya, Ana Julia; Rodríguez, Pedro Pablo. El despliegue de un conflicto. La política norteamericana hacia Cuba: 1959–1961. La Habana: Editorial de Ciencias Sociales, 1996.

Fernandes, Florestan. A revolução cubana – da guerrilha ao socialismo. São Paulo: Expressão Popular, 2007.

Fernandes, Florestan. Capitalismo dependente e classes sociais na América Latina. Rio de Janeiro: Zahar, 1975.

Fernández Estrada, Julio Antonio et al. Debate: 'Politización/ despolitización en la cultura contemporánea'. La Habana: Temas. N. 76: 72–82, octubre – diciembre de 2013.

Fernández Retamar, Roberto. Cuba Defendida. La Habana: Letras Cubanas, 1984.

Garcés, Carlos. Debate: 'Politización/ despolitización en la cultura contemporánea'. La Habana: Temas. N. 76: 72–82, octubre – diciembre de 2013.

García Álvarez, Anicia Esther; Anaya Cruz, Betsy. Gastos básicos de familias cubanas pensionadas y salario-dependientes. Havana: Revista Temas, n. 79: 89–94, julio–septiembre de 2014.

García, Tania et al. Debate: 'Actualizando el modelo: economía política y cultura'. La Habana: Temas. N. 73: 70–80, enero – marzo de 2013.

Gott, Richard. Cuba: uma nova história. Rio de Janeiro: Zahar Editores, 2004.

Guanche, Julio Cesar et al. Debate: 'Politización/ despolitización en la cultura contemporánea'. La Habana: Temas. N. 76: 72–82, octubre – diciembre de 2013.

Guanche, Julio Cesar. 'La participación ciudadana en el Estado cubano'. La Habana: Temas. N. 70: 69–79, abril-junio de 2012.

Guanche, Julio Cesar (org). En el borde de todo. El hoy y el mañana de la revolución en Cuba. Bogotá: Ocean Sur: 2007.

Guerra Villaboy, Sergio; González Arana, Roberto; Maldonado Gallardo, Alejo. Revoluciones Latinoamericanas del Siglo XX. México: Universidad Michoacana de San Nicolás de Hidalgo, 2006.

Guevara, Ernesto Che (et al.). El gran debate sobre la economía en Cuba (1963–64). Melbourne: Ocean Press, 2006.

Guevara, Ernesto Che. Revolução Cubana. São Paulo: Edições Populares, 1979.

Halperin Donghi, Tulio. Reforma y disolución de los impérios ibéricos. Madrid: Alianza, 1985.

Harnecker, Marta. Fidel. A estratégia política da vitória. São Paulo: Expressão Popular, 2000.

Hernández, Rafael et al. Debate: 'Valores em crise?'. La Habana: Temas. N. 75: 67–80, julio – septiembre de 2013.

Hernández, Rafael et al. Debate: 'Politización/ despolitización en la cultura contemporánea'. La Habana: Temas. N. 76: 72–82, octubre – diciembre de 2013.
IV Congreso del Partido Comunista de Cuba. Información sobre el resultado del Debate de los Lineamientos Maio de 2011. Disponível em: <http://www.cubadebate.cu/wp-content/uploads/2011/05/tabloide_debate_lineamientos.pdf>. Acesso em 23/2/2017.
Katz, Claudio. La epopeya cubana. Disponível em: <http://katz.lahaine.org/?p=243>. Acesso em 12/4/2016.
Le Riverend, Julio. Cuba: del semicolonialismo al socialismo (1933–1975). Em: González Casanova, Pablo. América Latina: historia de medio siglo. 2a ed. México: Siglo XXI, 1984.
Limia Díaz. Ernesto. Cuba: fim da história? Colômbia: Ocean Sur, 2017.
López R., Felipe; Herrera Carlés, Humberto. 'Inversión extranjera: clave para el futuro de Cuba'. Em: Forbes México, marzo 2015. Disponível em: <http://www.forbes.com.mx/inversion-extranjera-clave-para-el-futuro-de-cuba/#gs.V6HkLeE>. Acesso em 14/1/2017.
López Segrera, Francisco. La revolución cubana. Propuestas, escenarios y alternativas. España: El viejo topo, 2010.
Malmierca, Rodrigo. Entrevista: 'Necesitamos atraer el capital extranjero'. Em: Cuba Debate. Novembro de 2016. Disponível em: <http://www.cubadebate.cu/noticias/2016/11/01/rodrigo-malmierca-en-fihav-2016-necesitamos-atraer-el-capital-extranjero/#.WHecUVMrLIU>. Acesso em 12/1/2017.
Martin Romero, José Luis. 'Las relaciones de trabajo: una asignatura pendiente en la política de la Actualización'. Temas, n. 83: 66–74, julio-septiembre de 2015.
Martínez Heredia, Fernando. 'Un socialismo primitivo'. Em: Cuestiones de América. N. 13, Febrero – marzo de 2003. Disponível em: <http://www.cuestiones.ws/revista/n13/feb03-fsm-cuba-fmh.htm>. Acesso em 6/1/2017.
Martínez Heredia, Fernando. A viva voz. La Habana: Editorial de Ciencias Sociales, 2010.
Martínez, Osvaldo. 'Cuba en el contexto de la economía mundial'. Em: Tablada, Carlos. Cuba: transición... hacia donde? Madrid: Editorial Popular, 2001.
Morais, Fernando. Os últimos soldados da guerra fria. São Paulo: Cia. das Letras, 2011.
Moreno Fraginals, Manuel. El Ingenio. 2 ed. La Habana: Editorial de Ciencias Sociales, 1986.
Moreno Fraginals, Manuel. Cuba- Espanha- Cuba. Uma história comum. Bauru: Edusc, 2005.
Nova, Armando. Debate: 'Actualizando el modelo: economía política y cultura'. La Habana: Temas. N. 73: 70–80, enero – marzo de 2013.
Obama, Barack. 'Discurso del presidente Obama al pueblo cubano'. Havana, 22/3/2016. Disponível em: <https://obamawhitehouse.archives.gov/the-press-office/2016/03/22/discurso-del-presidente-obama-al-pueblo-cubano>. Acesso em 20/7/2017.

Ortega González, Diosnara et al. Debate: 'Que es para ti la Revolución: los jóvenes opinan'. La Habana: Temas. N. 56:152–160, julio – septiembre de 2008.

Partido Comunista de Cuba. Lineamientos de la política económica y social del Partido y la Revolución (Resolución del IV Congreso del PCC), junio de 2011. Disponível em: <www.congresopcc.cip.cu>. Acesso em 6/1/2017.

Pérez, Ernesto et al. Debate: 'Que es para ti la Revolución: los jóvenes opinan'. La Habana: Temas. N. 56:152–160, julio – septiembre de 2008.

Pérez Jr., Louis. 'Cuba, c. 1930–1959'. Em: Bethell, Leslie. Cuba: a short history. Cmbridge: Cambridge University Press, 1993.

Rafuls Pineda, Daniel. El sistema electoral cubano: de la representación formal a la participación real. La Habana: Temas. N. 78: 64–71, abril-junio de 2014.

Ramonet, Ignacio. Fidel Castro: biografia a duas vozes. São Paulo: Boitempo, 2006.

Ricardo Luis, Roger. 'Prensa e imagen Cuba ante el espejo de la realidad'. La Habana: Temas. N. 77: 49–55, enero – marzo de 2014.

Rodríguez, José Luis. 'Cuba, su economía y la Unión Soviética'. Havana: Revista Temas. N. 68: 114–121, outubro-dezembro de 2011.

Rojas, Fernando Luis et al. Debate: 'Que es para ti la Revolución: los jóvenes opinan'. La Habana: Temas. N. 56:152–160, julio – septiembre de 2008.

Sader, Emir. Cuba: um socialismo em construção. Petrópolis: Vozes, 2001.

SalazarFernández, Diana (cord). La red Capital Humano. La Habana: Editorial Academia, 2012.

Sexto, Luis et al. Debate: 'Politización/ despolitización en la cultura contemporánea'. La Habana: Temas. N. 76: 72–82, octubre – diciembre de 2013.

Taibo II, Paco. Ernesto Guevara, também conhecido como Che. São Paulo: Expressão Popular, 2008.

Vasconcelos, Joana Salém. História agrária da revolução cubana. São Paulo: Alameda, 2016.

Vitier, Cintio. Ese sol del mundo moral. La Habana: Unión, 2008 (1970).

Conversation in La Habana between 5/12/2016 and 14/12/2016

Acosta González, Yoan Karell. Centro de Estudios Hemisféricos y sobre Estados Unidos.

Dacal, Ariel. Education activist, Centro Martin Luther King.

Fernández Estrada, Julio Antonio. Lawyer, former professor at Facultad de Derecho de la Universidad de La Habana.

Garcés, Raul. Journalist, Revista Temas.

Hernández Pedraza, Gladys. Economist at Centro de Investigaciones de la Economía Mundial.

Hernández, Rafael. Director of Revista Temas.

Limia Díaz, Ernesto. Advisor at Ministry of Culture.

Martínez Heredia, Fernando. Centro de Estudios Juan Marinello.
Martínez, Jenifer. Head of Federación de los Estudiantes Universitários (FEU).
Morlote, Luis. Vice-president of Unión de los Escritores y Artistas de Cuba (UNEAC).
Padrón, Juan Nicolas. Writer.
Piñeiro Harnecker, Camila. Centro de Estudios de la Economía Cubana. Cooperativism activist.
Rodríguez, Jose Luis. Former Minister of Economy.
Valdés Paz, Juan. Agrarian issue specialist.

Peru

Adrianzén, Alberto (editor). Apogeo y crisis de la izquierda peruana. Hablan sus protagonistas. Lima: IDEA/UARM, 2011.
Adrianzén, Alberto. 'La izquierda derrotada'. Em: Adrianzén, Alberto. (editor). Apogeo y crisis de la izquierda peruana. Hablan sus protagonistas. Lima: IDEA/UARM, 2011.
Aguero, José Carlos. Rendidos: sobre el don de perdonar. Lima: IEP, 2015.
Alayza, Alejandra; Gudynas, Eduardo. Transiciones postextractivistas y alternativas al extractivismo en el Perú. 2a ed. Lima: CEPES, 2012.
Ames, Rolando. Entrevista em: Adrianzén, Alberto (editor). Apogeo y crisis de la izquierda peruana. Hablan sus protagonistas. Lima: IDEA/UARM, 2011.
Anderson, Benedict. Imagined communities. Londres: Verso, 1983.
Barros, Pedro; Hitner, Verena. 'A economia política do Peru: da ruptura interrompida aos dilemas contemporâneos'. Rio de Janeiro, Revista Oikos, vol. 9 n. 2, 2010, ps. 143–164.
Basadre, Jorge. La vida y la historia. Lima: Orbis Ventures, 2005.
Bebbington, Anthony; Chaparro, Anahí; Scurrah, Martin. 'El Estado compensador peruano y la persistencia del modelo neoextractivista: seis hipótesis sobre el (no) cambio institucional. Debate agrario. Análisis y alternativas'. N. 46. Lima, 2014, pp. 29–50.
Blanco, Hugo. Terra ou morte. São Paulo: Versus, 1979.
Bonilla, Heraclio. Guano y burguesia en el Peru. Quito: FLACSO, 1994.
Bonilla, Heraclio. La trayectoria del desencanto. El Perú en la segunda mitad del siglo XX. Lima: Fondo Editorial San Marcos, 2009.
Bonilla, Heraclio. 'Continuidad y cambio en la organización política del Estado en el Perú independiente'. Em: FloresGalindo, Alberto (comp.). Independencia y revolución (1780–1840) Vol. 2. Lima: Instituto Nacional de Cultura, 1987.
Bonilla, Heraclio. Un siglo a la deriva. Ensayos sobre el Perú, Bolívia y la guerra. Lima: IEP, 1980.

Burt, Jo-Marie. Violencia y autoritarismo en el Perú: bajo la sombra de Sendero y la dictadura de Fujimori. 2a ed. Lima: IEP, SER, EPAF, 2011.
Cano, Wilson. Soberania e política econômica na América Latina. São Paulo: UNESP, 2000.
Castañeda, Jorge. Utopia desarmada. São Paulo: Cia das Letras, 1994.
Chaterjee, Partha. 'Comunidade imaginada por quem?' Em: Balakrishnan, Gopal. Um mapa da questão nacional. Rio de Janeiro: Contraponto, 2000.
Chossudovsky, Michel. A globalização da pobreza. Impactos das reformas do FMI e do Banco Mundial. São Paulo: Moderna, 1999.
Cisneros Vizquerra, Luis. Entrevista a Raúl Gonzáles. 'Ayacucho: la espera del gaucho. Entrevista a Luis Cisneros Vizquerra'. Quehacer, 20, 1983. p. 50.
Comisión de la Verdad y Reconciliación. Informe final. Versión en cinco fascículos. Lima: IDDH-PUC, 2008.
Cotler, Julio. Clases, estado y nación en el Perú. Lima: IEP, 1978.
Cotler, Julio. 'Perú: Estado oligárquico y reformismo militar'. Em: González Casanova, Pablo. América Latina: historia de medio siglo. 4a ed. México: Siglo XXI, 1984.
De Echave, José. 'La mineria peruana y los escenarios de transición' Em: Alayza, Alejandra; Gudynas, Eduardo. Transiciones postextractivistas y alternativas al extractivismo en el Perú. 2a ed. Lima: CEPES, 2012.
De Soto, Hernando. El otro sendero. Lima: Sudamerica, 1992.
Degregori, Carlos Iván. Que difícil es ser Dios. Lima: IEP, 2013.
Degregori, Carlos Iván. El surgimiento de Sendero Luminoso. 3a ed. Lima: IEP, 2010.
Delgado Olivera, Carlos. Testimonio de lucha. Lima: Peisa, 1973.
Diez Canseco, Javier. 'Exorcizando Izquierda Unida'. Em: Adrianzén, Alberto (editor). Apogeo y crisis de la izquierda peruana. Hablan sus protagonistas. Lima: IDEA/UARM, 2011.
Durand, Francisco. El Perú fracturado. Formalidad, informalidad y economía delictiva. Lima: Fondo Editorial del Congreso del Perú, 2007.
Flores Galindo, Alberto. 'Buscando a un inca'. Em: Stern, Steve J. (compilador). Resistencia, rebelión y conciencia campesina en los Andes (siglos XVIII al XX). Lima: Instituto de Estudios Peruanos, 1990, ps. 187–202.
García-Naranjo, Aída. Entrevista em: Adrianzén, Alberto (editor). Apogeo y crisis de la izquierda peruana. Hablan sus protagonistas. Lima: IDEA/UARM, 2011.
Gavilán Sánchez, Lurgio. Memorias de un soldado desconocido. 3a reimpr. Lima: IEP, 2014.
Gonsales, Omar. 'La izquierda peruana: una estructura ausente'. Em: Adrianzén, Alberto (editor). Apogeo y crisis de la izquierda peruana. Hablan sus protagonistas. Lima: IDEA/UARM, 2011.
González Prada, Manuel. Paginas libres. Horas de lucha. 2a ed. Caracas: Ayacucho, 1985.

Gott, Richard. Guerrilla movements in Latin America. New York: Double Day, 1971.
Gudynas, Eduardo. 'Si eres tan progresista porque destruyes la naturaleza? Neoextractivismo, izquierda y alternativas'. Quito: Ecuador Debate, 2010, ps. 61–81.
Guerra García, Francisco. 'Notas preliminares sobre la experiencia de la Izquierda Unida'. Em: Adrianzén, Alberto (editor). Apogeo y crisis de la izquierda peruana. Hablan sus protagonistas. Lima: IDEA/UARM, 2011.
Guevara Aranda, Roberto. Bagua: de la resistencia a la utopía indígena. Lima, 2013.
Haya de la Torre, Victor Raul. El antiimperialismo y el APRA. Lima: Ed. Chan Chan, 1980 (1936).
Klein, Naomi. Shock doctrine: the rise of disaster capitalism. Canada: Knopf, 2007.
Letts, Ricardo. Entrevista em: Adrianzén, Alberto (editor). Apogeo y crisis de la izquierda peruana. Hablan sus protagonistas. Lima: IDEA/UARM, 2011.
Löwy, Michael (Org.). O marxismo na América Latina – uma antologia de 1909 aos dias atuais. São Paulo: Perseu Abramo, 2003.
Luna Vargas, Andrés. 'Perú: reformas agrárias en América Latina'. Em: Palau, Tomás; Ortega, Guillermo; Reformas agrarias en América Latina. Asunción: BASE IS, 2009.
Mallón, Florencia. Peasant and nation. The making of post-colonial Mexico and Peru. Berkeley: University of California Press, 1995.
Manky Bonilla, Walter Omar. 'Democracia, crecimiento economico y sindicalismo en el Perú del siglo XXI. Continuidades y rupturas'. Rio de Janeiro: Revista da ALAST, ano 19, N. 31, 2014, pp. 195–228.
Mansur, Maíra Sertã. 'Peru: agricultura x mineração'. Em: Malerba, Juliana (org.). Diferentes formas de dizer não. Experiências internacionais de resistência, restrição e proibição ao extrativismo mineral. Rio de Janeiro: FASE, 2014.
Matos Mar, Jose. Desborde popular y crisis del Estado. 5a ed. Lima: IEP, 1987.
Mariátegui, José Carlos. Siete ensayos de interpretación de la realidad peruana. 50a ed. Lima: Biblioteca Amauta, 1985 (1928).
McClintock, Cynthia; Vallas, Fabian. Cooperation at a cost: the United States and Peru. New York: Routledge, 2003.
Mijolla, Alain de (dir.). Dictionnair international de la psychanalyse, v. 2. Paris: Hachette, 2005.
O'Phelan Godoy, Scarlett. 'El mito de la independencia concedida: los programas políticos del siglo XVIII y del temprano XIX en el Perú y el Alto Perú (1730–1814)'. Em: Flores Galindo, Alberto (compilador). Independencia y revolución (1780–1840). Lima: Instituto Nacional de Cultura, 1987.
Panitch, Leo; Leys, Colin. Telling the truth. Socialist Register 2006. London: Merlin, 2005.
Pease, Henry. Entrevista. Em: Adrianzén, Alberto (editor). Apogeo y crisis de la izquierda peruana. Hablan sus protagonistas. Lima: IDEA/UARM, 2011.

Portocarrero, Gonzalo. La urgencia por decir 'nosotros'. Los intelectuales y la idea de nación en el Perú republicano. Lima: PUC, 2015.

Quijano, Anibal. Nacionalismo, neoimperialismo y militarismo en el Perú. Buenos Aires: Periferia, 1971.

Rénique, José Luis. Incendiar la pradera. Un ensayo sobre la revolución en el Perú. Lima: La siniestra, 2015.

Rudolph, James D. Peru: the evolution of a crisis. Westport: Praeger, 1992.

Silva, Rogério Forastieri. Colônia e nativismo. A história como 'biografia da nação'. São Paulo: Hucitec, 1997.

Starn, Orin. 'Missing the Revolution: anthropologists and the war in Peru'. Em: Cultural Anthropology, v. 6, n 1, 1991.

Stern, Steve J. (compilador). Resistencia, rebelión y conciencia campesina en los Andes (siglos XVIII al XX). Lima: Instituto de Estudios Peruanos, 1990.

Sueiro, Juan Carlos. 'Explotación de los recursos hidrobiológicos en el postextractivismo: el caso de la anchoveta'. Em: Alayza, Alejandra; Gudynas, Eduardo. Transiciones postextractivistas y alternativas al extractivismo en el Perú. 2a ed. Lima: CEPES, 2012.

Velasco Alvarado, Juan. Mensaje a la nación con motivo de la promulgación de la ley de la Reforma Agraria (1969). Disponível em: <https://www.marxists.org/espanol/tematica/agro/peru/velasco1969.htm> Acesso em 14/8/2015.

Vilas, Carlos. ¿Populismos reciclados o neoliberalismo a secas? El mito del 'neopopulismo' latinoamericano. Rev. Sociol. Polit., Curitiba, n. 22, June 2004. Available from <http://www.scielo.br/scielo.php?script=sci_arttext&pid=S0104-4478200400 0100011&lng=en&nrm=iso>. Retrieved on 18/10/2012. http://dx.doi.org/10.1590/S0104-44782004000100011.

Weyland, Kurt. 'Neo-Populism and Neo-Liberalism in Latin America: Unexpected Affinities', Studies in Comparative International Development, 32:3 (Fall 1996), pp. 3–31; reprinted in Pretextos (Lima) 10 (1997), pp. 7–43.

Zapata, Antonio. Entrevista em: Adrianzén, Alberto (editor). Apogeo y crisis de la izquierda peruana. Hablan sus protagonistas. Lima: IDEA/UARM, 2011.

Conversations in Lima and Puno between 18/7/2015 and 25/7/2015

Adrianzén, Alberto. Intellectual and politician.
Azcueta, Michel. Leader at Villa El Salvador.
Blanco, Hugo. Former guerilla leader and federal deputy.
Chao, Alan. Director of Odebrecht.
Choquehuanca, Zenon. Servicios Educativos Rurales (SER), Puno.
Cueto, Maria Rosa. PUC.
Durand, Anahi. Tierra y Libertad.

Espinosa, Oscar. Anthropologist (PUC).
Gamboa, Cesar. Derecho Ambiente y Recursos Naturales.
Lunas Vargas, Andrés. Former senator.
Paese, Maria Angélica. Psychologist at PUC.
Paloschi, Jonas. Brazilian Embassy.
Quijano, Aníbal. Sociologist.
Torres, Javier. La Mula & SER.

Venezuela

Álvarez, Victor. 'La transición al socialismo de la Revólucion Bolivariana: gobierno socialista o revolución socialista?' Em: Valero, Jorge (compilador). Democracias nuevas o restauradas: el caso de Venezuela. Caracas: El perro y la rana, 2012, pp. 189–207.

Azellini, Darío. 'Participación y poder popular – Consejos Comunales y Comunas'. Em: Valero, Jorge (compilador). Democracias nuevas o restauradas: el caso de Venezuela. Caracas: El perro y la rana, 2012, pp. 117–132.

Briceño Mendez, Manuel. Estado Comunal: la nueva geometría del poder. Caracas: Fondo Editorial de la Asamblea Nacional Willian Lara, 2014.

Cano, Wilson. Soberania e política econômica na América Latina. São Paulo: UNESP, 2000.

Carrera Damas, Germán. Una nación llamada Venezuela. 5ª ed. Caracas: Monte Avila, 1997.

Carrera Damas, Germán. El culto a Bolívar. 5ª ed Caracas: Aldafil, 2003.

Chávez, Hugo. El libro azul. Caracas: Ediciones Correo del Orinoco, 2013.

Coroníl, Fernando. El Estado Mágico. Naturaleza, dinero y modernidad en Venezuela. Caracas: Alfa, 2013.

Defensoría del Pueblo. Tortura, asesinato y desaparición forzada en el período 1958–1998. Caracas: Defensoría del Pueblo, 2013.

Díaz Rangel, Eleazar. 'El proceso venezolano: obstáculos para su desarrollo'. Em: Valero, Jorge (compilador). Democracias nuevas o restauradas: el caso de Venezuela. Caracas: El perro y la rana, 2012, os. 33–40.

Dietrich, Heinz. Hugo Chávez y el socialismo del siglo XXI. Buenos Aires: Nuestra América, 2005.

Fernandes, Florestan. Sociedade de classes e subdesenvolvimento. Rio de Janeiro: Zahar, 1968.

Fernandes, Florestan. Capitalismo dependente e classes sociais na América Latina. Rio de Janeiro: Zahar, 1975.

Furtado, Celso. Ensaios sobre a Venezuela. Subdesenvolvimento com abundância de divisas. Rio de Janeiro: Contraponto/ Centro Internacional Celso Furtado, 2008.

Gott, Richard. À sombra do libertador. São Paulo: Expressão Popular, 2004.

LaFeber, Walter. The new Empire: an interpretation of American expansion (1860–1898). Cornell: Cornell University Press, 1963.

López Maya, Margarita. Del viernes negro al referendo revocatorio. 2ª ed. Caracas: Aldafil, 2006.

López Maya, Margarita. Democracia participativa en Venezuela (1999–2010). Orígenes, leyes, percepciones y desafios. Caracas: Fundación Centro Gumilla/ Universidad Católica Andrés Bello, 2011.

Maduro, Nicolás. 'Encuentro del presidente Nicolás Maduro con el Consejo de Movimientos Sociales del Gran Polo Patriótico'. Caracas, 22/5/2013. Disponível em: http://www.revolucionomuerte.org/index.php/discursos/discursos-de-nicolas-maduro/891-lea-la-intervencion-integra-del-presidente-nicolas-maduro-en-el-encuentro-con-el-consejo-de-movimientos-sociales-del-gran-polo-patriotico. Acesso em 10/9/2014.

Maringoni, Gilberto. A Venezuela que se inventa. São Paulo: Perseu Abramo, 2004.

Maza Zavala, D.F. 'Historia de medio siglo en Venezuela: 1926–1975'. Em: González Casanova, Pablo (org.). América Latina: historia de medio siglo. 4ª ed. México: Siglo XXI, 1984.

Mommer, Bernard. 'Petroleo y socialismo'. Em: Corena Parra, Jaime; Mommer, Bernard; Trómpiz Valles, Humberto. Renta petroleira y Revolución Bolivariana. Caracas: El perro y la rana, 2013a.

Mommer, Bernard. 'Venezuela, país petrolero: hacia el primer centenário'. Em: Corena Parra, Jaime; Mommer, Bernard; Trómpiz Valles, Humberto. Renta petroleira y Revolución Bolivariana. Caracas: El perro y la rana, 2013b.

Monedero, Juan Carlos. 'Venezuela y la reinvención de la política: el desafio del socialismo en nuevos escenarios'. Em: Observatorio Social de América Latina, N. 33. Buenos Aires: CLACSO, 2013, ps. 15–37.

Obuchi, Richard K. (coord). Gestion en rojo. Evaluación de desempeño de 16 empresas estatales y resultados generales del modelo productivo socialista. Caracas: IESA, 2011.

Parra Luzardo, Gastón. De la nacionalización a la apertura petrolera. Derrumbe de una esperanza. Caracas: Banco Central de Venezuela, 2012.

Pérez Alfonso, Juan Pablo. Hundiéndonos en el excremento del diablo. Caracas: Banco Central de Venezuela, 2011.

Plan de la Patria. Segundo Plan de Desarrollo Económico y social de la Nación (2013–2019). Caracas: Ediciones Correo del Orinoco, 2013.

Posado, Thomas. 'L'État regional du Bolívar au Venezuela. Reflet du désalignement entre le gouvernement chaviste et le mouvement ouvrier'. Mouvements des idées et des luttes. N. 76. Paris, La Découverte, 2013.
Ramonet, Ignacio. Hugo Chávez. Mi primera vida. Conversaciones con Hugo Chávez. Caracas: Vadell Hermanos Editores, 2013.
Ramos, Felippe. Entrevista a América Economia Brasil, 16/04/2014. Disponível em: http://americaeconomiabrasil.com.br/content/oposicao-radicalizada-na-venezuela-perde-forca-porque-protestos-mais-violentos-pioram-econom. Acesso em 9/9/2014.
Rangel, Jose Vicente. De Yare a Miraflores, el mismo subversivo. Entrevistas de José Vicente Rangel al comandante Hugo Chávez Frías (1992–2012). 3ª ed. Caracas: Correo del Orinoco, 2014.
Sanahuja, José Antonio. 'Regionalismo post-liberal y multilateralismo en Sudamérica: El caso de UNASUR'. In: Serbin, Andrés; Martínez, Laneydi; Ramanzini Júnior, Haroldo; El regionalismo 'post–liberal' en América Latina y el Caribe: Nuevos actores, nuevos temas, nuevos desafíos. Anuario de la Integración Regional de América Latina y el Gran Caribe 2012. Buenos Aires: Coordinadora Regional de Investigaciones Económicas y Sociales, 2012.
Tinker Salas, Miguel. Una herencia que perdura. Petróleo, cultura y sociedad en Venezuela. Caracas: Editorial Galac, 2014.
Webber, Jeffery; Carr, Barry. The new Latin American left. Cracks in the Empire. Lanham: Rowman & Littlefield Publishers, Inc., 2013.
Weisbrot, Mark; Johnston, Jake. 'Venezuela's economic recovery: is it sustainable?' Center for Economic and Policy Research, 2012. Disponível em: <http://www.cepr.net/index.php/publications/reports/venezuelas-economic-recovery-is-it-sustainable>. Acesso em 20/6/2014.

Interviews and conversations

Caracas, July 2014:.
Barros, Pedro Silva. Head of IPEA mission in Venezuela.
Cerezal, Manuel. Advisor at Banco Central de Venezuela.
Derli. MST activist in cooperation mission in Venezuela.
Micilene. MST activist in cooperation mission in Venezuela.
Ramos, Felippe. Researcher at IPEA mission in Venezuela.
Toledo, Alexis. Vice Minister of Comunas y Movimientos Sociales.
Caracas, November 2015:.
Cerezal, Manuel. Advisor at Banco Central de Venezuela.
Constant Rosales, Hector. Diplomat and professor at Universidad Central de Venezuela.

Figueroa, Amílcar. Left leader, PSUV cadre.
Lira, Bárbara. Researcher.
Ramírez, Kenneth. Director of Consejo Venezolano de Relaciones Internacionales – COVRI.
Ramos, Felippe. Researcher at IPEA mission in Venezuela.
Medellín, November 2015:.
Lander, Edgardo. Soci.
Montevidéu, December 2015:.
Urbina, Elvis. 2015. Venezuela National Coordinator at COSIPLAN. Montevideo, December 2015.
La Paz, July 2016:
Villegas, Pablo. Centro de Documentación e Información Bolivia (CEDIB)

Concluding Remarks

Abelardo Ramos, Jorge. História da Nação Latino-Americana. 2a ed. Revisada. Florianópolis: Insular: 2012 (1968).
Assadourian, C.S.; Cardoso, C.F.S.; Ciafardini, H. et al. Modos de producción en América Latina. Bogotá: Cuadernos del Pasado y Presente, n. 40, 1973.
Blackburn, Robin (org.). Depois da queda. O fracasso do comunismo e o futuro do socialismo. 3. ed. São Paulo: Paz e Terra, 2005.
Fernandes, Florestan. Capitalismo Dependente e classes sociais na América Latina. 2. ed. Rio de Janeiro: Zahar, 1975.
Furtado, Celso. A economia latino-americana. São Paulo: Companhia Editora Nacional: 1986.
Furtado, Celso. O mito do desenvolvimento econômico. Rio de Janeiro: Paz e Terra: 1974.
Galeano, Eduardo. El fútbol al sol y sombra. Buenos Aires: Siglo XXI, 1995.
Lenin, V.I. O Estado e a Revolução. São Paulo: Hucitec, 1986.
Luxemburgo, Rosa. Isabel Loureiro (org.). Textos escolhidos. 3 volumes. São Paulo: Unesp; Fundação Rosa Luxemburgo, 2017.
Mariátegui, José Carlos, 1990. Temas de Nuestra América. 11ª edição (Lima: Amauta).
Martí, José. Obras Escogidas. 3 tomos. La Habana: Editorial de Ciencias Sociales, 2000.
Mészaros, Istvan. Beyond Capital. Nova Iorque: Monthly Review Press, 1996.
Rostow, W.W. Etapas do desenvolvimento econômico. 5a ed. Rio de Janeiro: Zahar, 1974 (1960).
Sánchez Vázquez, Adolfo. Filosofia da práxis. São Paulo: CLACSO e Expressão Popular, 2007.
Svampa, Maristella. Del cambio de época al fin de ciclo. Gobiernos progresistas, extractivismo y movimientos sociales en América Latina. Buenos Aires: Edhasa, 2017.

Index

Abelardo Ramos, Jorge 281
Acción Democratica 13
Acción Ecológica 130–31
AcerBrag steelworks 161
Achacachi 101
Acosta, Alberto 123–26, 128–29, 132–33, 135, 167, 279
Aerolíneas Argentinas 76, 85
AFP 191–92, 196
African National Congress 3
agrarian reform 53–54, 94, 97, 138, 140, 145, 148, 151, 172–73, 176, 197, 200–201, 213, 226, 228
agribusiness 45–46, 51, 53, 55, 86, 96, 102, 108, 114, 119, 132, 137, 144, 145, 147, 155, 239
Aguayo, Luis 149, 151
Alanism 198, 203, 210, 218
ALBA 5, 21, 33–34, 118–19, 135, 163–64, 168, 244, 277
Alckmin, Geraldo 65
Alcoa group 162
Alderete, Alberto 146, 150, 151
Alfonsín, Raul 75, 76, 89
Alianza País 124, 127, 128, 130–32, 133–37
Allende, Salvador 96, 171–74, 181
Almaraz, Alejandro 99, 110–12, 114–16
Almeyda, Clodomiro 177
Alstom 161
Altamirano, Carlos 177
Alumar 44
Alunorte 44
Álvarez, Victor 26
Alzugaray Treto 256
Amazon 53, 105, 122–23, 128, 158, 215
Ambev 44
American Hispanic War 11
Ames, Rolando 209
Amoedo, João 65
Amorim, Celso 146
Andean-Amazonian Capitalism 105
Andean Development Corporation 164
Andeism 208
Anderson, Benedict 205
Andréz Pérez, Carlos 17–18
Ángel Beltrán, Miguel 224

Angola 267
anti-capitalist forces 283
anti-capitalist imagination 285
anti-capitalist projects 35
anti-PT 59, 65–68, 166
APRA 198–201, 203–5, 208, 211, 218
Aracruz Celulose 42
Arantes, Pedro 52–53
Arbenz, Jacobo 7
architecture, new regional financial 164, 166
Argaña, Luis María 147
Argentina 1–2, 21–22, 70–73, 75, 77, 79, 83–85, 87–89, 139, 144–45, 161, 164–65, 272–74, 276, 278–79
Argentinazo 79–80
armed forces 30, 34, 87, 92, 176, 180, 200, 207, 210, 213, 218
armed struggle 4, 19, 173, 177, 222, 234, 240, 242, 273
army 16, 20, 26, 30, 33, 205, 207, 211, 217, 222–23, 231, 236, 239
Aronson, Bernard W. 212
Asange, Julian 137
Assis Brasil-Iñapari 161
AUC 234–35, 237
autocoup 211
autonomy 22, 33, 35, 47, 58, 102–3, 106–7, 227, 232, 241, 248, 274, 284, 287
Avella, Aida 223
Avellaneda 78
Ayacucho 206–9, 212
ayllu 99
Aylwin administration 182
Aymara 93, 111, 119
Aymara bourgeoisie 113, 119
Ayoreo 147
Azellini, Dario 28

Bachelet, Michelle 180, 183, 187, 193–94
Bagua massacre 217
Banzer, Hugo 96–97, 100–101
barbarism 1–4, 275–76, 280–81, 286
Barrantes, Alfonso 202–3, 205
Bartolina Sisa 106, 112
Belaúnde Terry 199, 202

Belo Monte Dam   45, 162
Benjamin, Walter   4, 286
Bertin meat company   162
Betancourt Doctrine   14
Betancourt, Rómulo   95
binomial system   178, 184, 195
Blair, Tony   10, 19
Blanco, Hugo   201
Blas Riquelme   152
blockades   7, 101, 151, 247, 261
   economic   251
BNDES   42, 44, 145, 159–66, 277
BNDESPAR   160–62
Bobbio, Noberto   72
Boff, Leonardo   104
Bogotazo   227
boliburguesía   21
Bolívar, Simón   11, 19, 180
Bolivarianism   1, 23, 28, 35–6, 88, 168–69, 279
Bolivarian process   7, 13, 23, 25–26, 31–34, 36, 273, 275–77
Bolivarian Revolution   11, 18, 20, 22, 35
Bolivarian socialism   21, 26
Bolivia   1–3, 6–7, 9, 92–95, 98, 100–101, 103–7, 111–12, 117–19, 121, 133–34, 144–46, 161–62, 200–201, 271–76
Bolsa Família Program   46, 53, 54, 59, 160, 275
Bolsonaro, Jair   64–68
Boulos, Guilherme   63
Bourdieu, Pierre   105
Bourgeois Autocratic State   278
bourgeois-democratic revolution   70, 72
bourgeoisie   6, 25, 48, 80, 131–32, 278
   commercial   111, 113
   country's   236
   dependent   6, 263
   financial   122
   national   16, 70–72, 82, 90
Brasiguayo Question   8, 138–39, 141, 143, 145, 147, 149, 151, 153, 155
brasiguayos   138, 141–42, 144–46, 150, 152
brasiguayo space   141
Brasil Foods   43, 160
Brazil   1, 4–8, 33–34, 37, 39–45, 51–57, 63, 67, 69–70, 138–41, 143–45, 151–52, 154, 156, 162–65, 167–69, 225, 272–73, 275–76, 278–79
Brenco group   162
Brezhnev, Leonid   174

British Guiana   11
Bucaram, Abdalá   125
Buen Vivir   104
Bunge   143

cabildos   100–01
CAE   184, 187–88
CAF   164, 166
Cajamarca   219
Caldera, Rafael   18
Camargo Corrêa   161–62
cambas   103
Campero, Ariana   116
Campora, Hector   73
Canada   154, 158, 162, 215
Candia Amarilla, Rubén   154
Canese, Ricardo   154
capitalism   26, 45, 121, 123, 125, 127, 129, 131, 133, 135, 137, 263, 267–68, 282, 284, 28–89
   dependent   6–7, 88
   peripheral   45, 245
   shock   175, 232
capitalist restoration   5, 257, 289–90
Capriles, Henrique   31
Caracazo   10, 17, 31
carapintadas   76
carbon market policies   136
Cardenas, Victor Hugo   99
Cardoso, Fernando Henrique   40, 59–60, 157, 280
Cardoso administration   46, 53, 158
Cargill   143, 153
Carmona, Pedro   131
carperos   151
Cartes, Horacio   9, 138, 153–54
cash transfer programs   46, 55, 86, 129, 133, 275
Castañeda, Jorge   205
Castaño brothers   235, 238
Castro, Cipriano   11
Castro, Fidel   12, 26, 156, 244, 246, 248, 251–52, 256, 259, 271
   Raul   252, 257, 258–62
castrochavismo   221, 242
Cavallo, Domingo   76, 126–27
CDRs   27, 245
Cely, Nathalie   131
Cementos Avellaneda   161

INDEX

Central America   75, 230, 241
Central American   12, 205, 226
Central Obrera Boliviana   112
Centro Democratico   238
Cepeda, Iván   224
CGT   72, 87
Chaco aqueduct   161
Chaco War   94, 96
Chapare   98, 111, 119
Chaparina   109
Chávez, Adolfo   109–11
　second   168
Chávez, Hugo   5, 8, 10, 17–19, 20–28, 30–35, 105, 109–11, 118, 156, 164, 168, 214, 273
Chavism   20, 22, 27, 31, 33–34, 276
Chevron   84, 123
Chile   1, 3–5, 7, 9, 102, 171–73, 175–97, 210, 213, 231–32, 272–74, 277, 279
　contemporary   183, 186, 196
Chilean Christian Democracy   172
Chilean Constitution   179, 187
China   21, 81, 104, 132, 144, 160, 185, 212, 217, 256–57
cholets   113, 119
Chonchol, Jacques   172–73, 175
Christ from the robbery   43
Chulavitas   228
Chuquisaca   115
Chuschi   206
CIA   95, 212, 246
CIDOB   106, 109–10, 112, 119
Cimitarra River Valley   233
Cisneros Visquerra, Luis   207
Citizen Constitution   38, 61
citizen credit   182, 184, 196
citizenization of politics   127
Citizen Revolution   2, 121–22, 127–28, 130–31, 133–35, 273
　self-described   128
Clarín   86, 90
classes, conciliation of   39, 90
class struggle   7, 15, 24, 67, 72, 120, 178, 221, 227
clientelism   23, 34, 116, 142, 274
Clinton, Bill   251
Cobos, Julio   85
coca   100, 111, 233
cocaine   111–12, 216, 229, 233
coca leaf   100, 104, 111–12, 118, 229

cocaleros   100, 106, 108, 111–12
Cochabamba   96, 100, 105, 110, 112
Codelco   176
Cold War   7, 72, 110, 141, 178, 195, 244, 251, 271, 273, 283
Collor, Fernando   39, 66
Colombia   1, 3–5, 7–9, 30, 64, 67, 135, 137, 221–25, 227–41, 243, 271, 273–74, 277, 279
Colombian guerrillas   222, 228–29
Coloradism   153
Colorados   138, 147–48, 151, 153–55
commodities   45, 50, 111, 143–44, 155, 179, 185, 196–97, 271, 275–76, 278
commodity boom   81, 89, 160, 165
commodity consensus   278
Communal Councils Law   22
communal state   21, 26–28, 33, 35
Commune, Paris   291
communism   3, 38, 212, 227–28, 262–65, 268, 282, 284, 289–91
community   105, 113, 136, 215, 217, 223, 228
community justice   109, 119
CONAIE   125, 127, 130–31
CONAMAQ   99, 106, 109
Concertación   1, 177–78, 180–85, 190–91, 193–95, 273
Concertación governments   180, 184–85, 187
Condor, Operation   96, 140, 175
CIDOB   106
Conga mining project   215–6, 220
Conisur   109
constituent assembly   19, 35, 100–101, 106, 128, 132, 136, 196, 201, 232, 241
constituent process   118, 206, 231
constitution   3, 5, 113, 115, 128, 130, 136, 158–60, 177–79, 184, 213, 215, 231–32, 250, 275
　new   92, 105–6, 118, 262
construction   28–29, 105, 110, 114, 116, 119, 133, 140, 145, 161–63, 165
　civil   43, 51, 111, 160–61, 277
　financing   161
　housing   21
consumption   15–16, 23–24, 27, 33–34, 41, 44, 54–55, 57, 119–20, 133–34, 137, 183–84, 263–65, 267, 286–87
consumption patterns   15, 23–24, 27, 33–34, 57, 119, 184, 252, 263, 284–87

continuities 14–15, 61, 89, 127, 157, 171, 185, 220, 239
  colonial 92
  macroeconomic 156
  structural 79, 157
Contreras, Manuel 175
Convivir 234
cooperation 263, 281
  economic 181, 288
  south-south 167
cooperatives 21, 113, 254–55
cooperativism 220, 254, 258
cooptation 110, 127, 130, 274
Copei 14, 18
Córdoba, Piedad 224
Cordobazo 73
Corfo 173
Coroníl, Fernando 15–16, 24
corralito 77–78
Correa, Rafael 1, 18, 121, 124–32, 134–35, 137, 273
Correismo 134–35
corruption 15–16, 18, 23, 27, 58–60, 112, 137, 142, 166, 204, 210, 213, 215, 219–20
corruption scandals 30, 39, 43, 58, 87, 124, 161, 181, 194, 196
Cosiplan 159, 164, 166–67
Council for Mutual Economic Assistance 247
counterinsurgency 75, 229–30, 235
counterrevolution 6, 136, 271, 289, 291
counterrevolution, permanent 6–9, 222, 270
coup 6, 9–12, 14, 18, 20, 59–61, 63–64, 66–67, 71, 131–32, 152–55, 171, 175
  alleged 131
  failed 33, 76
crisis 17, 23, 30–31, 39–40, 45–46, 70–71, 83, 86–87, 102–3, 124–26, 133–35, 165–66, 184–85, 191, 193–94, 251–52, 279
  capitalist 276
  diplomatic 162
  economic 39, 42, 59, 131, 166, 195, 202, 249
  global 55, 132, 160
  humanitarian 30
CSUTCB 97, 101
CTA 83, 87
CTEP 80, 83
CTV 14, 22

Cuba 3–5, 7–8, 22, 31, 164–65, 174, 244–57, 259–68, 272, 277, 285
cultural emancipation 286
cultural revolution 119, 270
cultural self-reference 285
Cunha, Eduardo 59
CUP 250, 253
Curuguaty 152, 155
Cutipa, Luis 112

Dacal, Ariel 260, 262, 268
Dardot, Pierre 41
Dávalos, Pablo 127
Dayuma 128, 136
DEA 106, 111, 118
debt crisis 10, 16, 92, 124–25, 177, 203, 229, 271–72
debts 19, 53, 76–77, 81, 87, 161, 188–90, 192, 203, 248
  external 25, 70, 76–77, 98, 154, 213
  public 12, 57, 185
decolonization 111, 286–87
Degregori, Ivan 205–8
de-industrialization 45–6, 70, 76, 176, 182
democracy 13–14, 97, 131, 135, 142, 171, 177, 183, 185, 194, 199, 248, 251
Democratic Center 238
democratization 33, 37, 56, 88, 143, 155, 171, 241, 258–59, 283, 287, 290–91
denationalization 46, 60, 70, 76, 80, 82, 229
Deng Xiaoping 256
depeasantisation 13, 143
dependence 4, 6, 8, 16, 23–24, 27, 34–35, 85, 90, 263, 270–71, 275, 278, 280–81
depoliticization 61, 194, 214, 260
Deposition of Lugo in Paraguay 138–39, 141, 143, 145, 147, 149, 151, 153, 155
development 1, 5, 42, 45, 82, 84, 108, 112, 120–21, 164, 167, 280, 282–85
  dependent 2
  entrepreneurial 259
  national 72, 256
developmentalism 3, 42, 45, 157, 165, 167, 169, 171, 175, 272
developmental regionalism 159, 167
development myth 34, 124
Díaz-Canel, Miguel 262
dictatorship 37–39, 49–50, 64–65, 67, 73–76, 80–83, 88–89, 96–98, 125, 139–42,

INDEX   335

147–48, 150, 171, 175–78, 180–87, 193, 195, 227–28, 245, 272
Diez Canseco   201–2
Digcoin   112
discipline   31, 65, 87, 116, 211, 213, 232, 250, 261
disciplining   27, 40, 155, 250, 253
discourse   42, 48, 87, 92, 127, 149, 181, 209, 235, 239, 252
  alternative   220
  anti-party   210
distribution   16, 21, 24, 41, 76, 111, 255
dogmatism   38, 218, 247–48, 258, 261, 264
dollarization   30, 89, 121, 124, 126–27, 129, 134
Dominican Republic   14, 33, 161, 165
Dória, João   65
drugs   68, 233
  illicit   241
drug trafficking   97, 111–12, 119, 214, 216, 219, 223, 229–30, 233–34, 236, 238
Duhalde, Eduardo   78–79
Duque, Iván   243
Durand, Francisco   216
Dutch disease   12, 16, 24
Duvalier   14

Eastern Europe   248–49
East European countries   247
ECLA   157, 172–73, 200, 245, 272
ecology   120–21, 123, 125, 127, 129, 131, 133–35, 137, 266, 283
economic aid   95, 101
Economic Development Programs   43
economic diversification   34, 116, 283
economic growth   2, 42, 45, 50–51, 55, 78, 81, 133, 135, 137, 141, 215, 220
  myth of   2, 169, 287
Ecuador   1–3, 6, 8–9, 18, 121–25, 127, 131–33, 135, 161–62, 164, 167, 273–76, 278
Ecuadorian State Oil Corporation   123
education   51, 57, 62, 179, 186, 188, 192, 196–97, 248, 250, 257, 260, 266
El Alto   102, 113
El Caguan   235
electoral frauds   214, 228
Eletrosul   162
ELN   228, 234
El Niño   126
El Salvador   229
El Universo   130

emergency   210–11, 213, 228
Emergency Economic Law   76
emigration   126, 143, 155
employment   10, 19, 50, 58, 90, 248, 253, 257
  formal   17, 23, 133
  public   87, 134
enclave   145, 226, 236, 271
equality   179, 249, 250, 255, 261, 263, 265, 279, 282, 284, 286–90
  values of   253, 268
Erdogan   64
Escobar, Pablo   230, 235, 238
Escoto, Miguel d'   104
establishment   9, 19, 94, 140, 149, 176, 179, 199
ethnic discourses   99
ethnicity   92, 118, 120
Eurocommunism   38, 181
Europe   38, 184, 282
European experiments   280
European Social Democracy   177
European Union   135, 251
Evoism   93
evolution   46, 50, 95, 105, 145
  economic   183, 281
  gradual   82
exploitation   6, 8, 82, 84, 89, 122–23, 169, 185, 220, 262
  class   291
  historical foreign   102
exploration   84, 162, 186
export corridors   158, 277
expropriation   20, 103, 107, 143, 146, 150–52, 173, 227
Extra   21, 116
extractivism   93, 119, 130, 134, 136, 217–20, 278, 283
extradition   230, 236

Falabella stores   196
Falkland Islands   75
FARC   214, 221, 228, 231, 233, 235, 240, 242–43
Farouk, Yanine Díaz   230
fascism   64, 68
fascist inclinations   227
Favero, Tranquilo   138, 151
Felcn   112
Fernandes, Florestan   6, 24, 37, 245, 263, 270, 278, 290
Fernández Estrada, Julio Antonio   260–62

FEU   252, 268
Fibria   43, 160
Fides   110
FIFA   57
financial capital   40–1, 45, 47–48, 55, 74, 124, 170, 272
financialization   2, 42, 135, 181, 184, 196, 287
financial markets   81, 191, 211
financial speculation   25, 238
financial system   75, 81, 186
fiscal adjustment   17, 58, 232, 253
fiscal austerity   42
fiscal deficits   85–6, 89, 252
fiscal pedals   59
fiscal responsibility law   40–41, 59, 184
Fogel, Ramón   150
Fondo Indígena   112
Fonplata   164, 166
forajidos   127
Foreign Affairs   42, 145–46, 159, 176
foreign capital   12, 23, 31, 77, 82, 250, 256, 261
foreign companies   13, 107, 144, 255–56
foreign debt   11, 80, 128, 132
foreign exchange   7, 11, 16, 29, 31, 35, 125, 176, 249–50
   abundance of   10–11, 15, 24, 271
foreign investment   40, 103, 107, 134, 182, 185, 215–16, 250–51, 253, 256
Fox, Vicente   158
France   65, 172
Francis, Pope   104
Franco, Frederico   152
freedom   22, 136, 172–73, 179, 187, 237, 248, 263, 265, 285–86
   creative   197, 264
free trade agreements   158, 183–84, 214, 232, 236, 277, 283
Free Trade Area   21, 102, 158–9
Freire, Paulo   260
Frente Amplio   1, 194, 196, 219
Frente Nacional   228
Frente Patriotico Manuel Rodríguez   177
Frondizi, Arturo   72
Frondizi, Silvio   72
Fujimontesinismo   203, 213
Fujimori, Alberto   203, 209–15, 217–19, 232
Fujimori, Keiko   219–20
Fujimorism   198–99, 211

fujishock   7, 210
Fundación Lazos   222
Fundación Sol   190
Fundación Tierra   109–10
funds   47, 108, 112, 118, 140, 151, 160, 166, 191–92
   vulture   81, 87, 90
Furtado, Celso   11, 14, 23–24, 27, 34, 284–85, 287

Gaitán, Jorge Eliécer   226–27
Gaitanism   227
Galán, Luis Carlos   230–31
Gallegos, Romulo   14
Galo Plaza   122
Garcés, Joan   175
García, Alan   198, 203–5, 208–9, 214, 218–19, 226–27, 253, 262
Garcia, Marco Aurelio   168
García Linera   96, 105–6, 110, 113, 116, 118
García Marquez, Gabriel   225–6
García Meza   97
gasolinazos   108, 119
Gas War   100
Gaviria, César   232
genocide   212, 233
geopolitical   139, 141, 247
Ghaddafi, Muammar   19
globalization   1–2, 132, 272
Global South   3
Gómez, Laureano   226–28
Gonçalves, José Botafogo   170
Goni   99, 101
Gonzalo, President   208
Gorbachev, Mikhail   248
Gott, Richard   19, 96, 248–51
Gramsci, Antonio   28, 286
Gran Mision AgroVenezuela   21
Gran Misión Vivienda   21
Grez, Sergio   178
GRFA   200–201, 220
Gringo   83
Growth Acceleration Program   43
growth peaks   215
Guanche, Julio Cesar   248, 252, 260
Guarani aquifer   143
Guatemala   7, 229
Guatemalan Civil Self-Defense Patrols   234

INDEX 337

guerrillas   200, 203, 206, 212, 221, 223–24, 229–31, 233–37, 240–42
Guevara, Ernesto Che   96, 104, 246–47, 265
Gutiérrez, Lucio   127
Guzmán, Abimael   206, 212
Guzmán, Jaime   177

Haddad, Fernando   56, 63–65, 67
Haiti   14, 67, 101, 165, 225
Halperin Donghi, Tulio   225
Harvey, David   238
Haya   198, 202
Heleno, General Augusto   67
Helms-Burton Act   251
herbicide Roundup   143
Hernández, Rafael   257–58
Hobsbawm, Eric   221, 225
Honduras   168
horizon   26, 35, 46, 54, 120, 181
    continent's civilizing   286
    national   45, 94
    neo-developmental   167, 170
    utopian   220
Huancavelica   215
Huilca, Pedro   213
Humalla, Ollanta   165, 198, 214, 217
human capital   258–59, 268
human rights   19, 75, 130, 149, 231
hydrocarbons   83–84, 89, 108, 110, 113, 119
    nationalization of   103, 107, 118
hyperinflation   76, 89, 92, 98, 204

Ibarra, Velasco   123
Ibis   110
IDB   42, 140, 158–59, 164, 166
ideology   39, 45–6, 48, 52, 62, 82, 88, 91, 157, 169, 195, 255, 257, 261, 283, 285
    capitalist   263
    communist   289
IIRSA   5, 53, 108, 158–59, 161, 164, 166–67, 169–70, 277–78, 283
Ilia, Arturo   72
illusion   3, 34, 45, 47, 56, 188, 194, 263–64, 267, 274, 284
IMF   29, 40, 55, 76–78, 95, 102, 124, 128, 167, 203, 211, 213, 272
impeachment   9, 37, 39, 48, 55, 58–59, 62–63, 139, 154–55

impeachment process   59, 154–55, 215
imperialism   7, 156, 245, 251, 258, 261, 267, 271, 274, 278–79, 290
imperialist onslaught   10, 18
import substitution industrialization   226, 271
Inacap   188
Inambari   163, 216
Inco   162
INDEC   85–86
independence   72, 93, 122, 134, 190, 226, 247, 283, 286
    second   279
INDERT   143, 146, 149–52
India   3, 64, 160
Indian Revolution   97
Indians   92, 106, 111, 169, 200–201
indigenous   19, 101, 103–5, 109, 111, 121, 130, 136, 200–1, 206, 220
indigenous march   119, 163
indigenous movements   99, 106, 108, 126–27, 130–31, 143, 162
indigenous municipalities   107
indigenous organizations   111–2, 125, 127, 135
industrialization   13, 21, 23, 38, 42, 44, 79, 95, 102, 112, 116, 172, 247–48, 272, 280, 282
inequality   3–4, 6, 27, 34, 39, 80, 169, 190, 250, 257, 265, 270, 275, 280
infantile environmentalism, indigenism   121, 135
inflation   17, 23, 28–30, 42, 47, 50, 73, 76, 86–87, 114, 117, 204, 211, 213, 271–72
inflationary pressures   29, 58, 85, 98
infrastructure   53, 123, 129, 166, 159, 253, 283
infrastructure works   16, 137, 275
INREDH   130–31
insurgency   61, 205, 208–10, 212, 229–31, 233–37, 239–40, 242, 276
integration   2, 5, 8, 156, 158, 163, 167, 170, 200, 203, 277, 279–81, 285, 287
    continental   279, 285, 287
    counter-hegemonic   164
Integrationist projects   280–81
Inter-American Commission on Human Rights   231
Inter-American Development Bank   42, 158
internationalization   160, 165, 167, 170, 271, 277, 287

International Nickel Company of
    Canada 162
Iran 21, 120
Israel 231, 236
Israeli advisers 230
Itaipu 141, 143, 154
Izquierda Unida 218

Jamaica 33
January agenda 103
Japan 214
Jara, Victor 173
Jaramillo, Bernardo 231
JBS-Friboi conglomerate 42, 160–62
Jirau plant 162
Juana Azurduy program 117
Juancito Pinto program 117
June Days 55–56
Juriti 162

Katarism 97, 105, 120
Kennedy, John F. 95
Kerensky 173
Kichwa 131
Kirchner, Cristina 70–1, 85, 70–1, 79, 82–5, 87, 90, 273
Kirchner, Néstor 1, 2, 70, 79, 81–2, 86, 89, 273
Kirchnerism 71, 79–80, 82–83, 85, 87–88, 90, 279
Kirchners 70, 79, 82, 87, 89
Kissinger, Henry 174
Klein, Naomi 175, 181, 210, 231
kollas 103
Korean War 228
Kuczynski, Pedro Pablo 215, 219

Lagos, Ricardo 1, 180, 183
    Lagos government 184, 187
Lagunita Country Club 25
land distribution 142, 150–51
Lander, Edgardo 23, 31, 36
Landless Rural Workers Movement
    (Brazil) 32, 53
land occupations 147, 153, 172, 200
landscapes 52, 122, 196, 200, 219, 229, 239–40, 263, 274–75, 279, 288
    alternative civilizing 285
Lara Bonilla, Rodrigo 230

Larrea, Gustavo 130
Latam airlines 119
Latin America 5–8, 94–95, 98, 101, 157, 159, 220–21, 248–49, 263–64, 272, 279–80, 282, 285–86, 288, 290
Latin American Organization of
    Solidarity 247
Latin American Revolution 9, 279–80, 282
Laureate International 187
Lava Jato operation 48, 59
Laval, Christophe 41
Leal, Eusebio 269
Lebanon 231
Lechín, Juan 95–6
Lenin 19, 289
Leninism 209
Leninist bet 292
liberalism 12, 42, 128, 205, 227
liberalization 15, 41, 76, 195, 258
    economic 25, 72, 135, 177
    financial 175, 229–30
Limia Díaz, Ernesto 247
Lineamientos 253, 255–56
Living well 104, 119, 121, 220
Loma Negra 161
López Maya, Margarita 22, 28
López Obrador, Andrés Manuel 3, 274
López Pumarejo, Alfonso 226
Lugo, Fernando 1, 7, 138–39, 141, 143, 145, 147, 149, 151–55, 273
Luksic 191
Lula, Luis Inácio 1, 18, 21, 37–39, 41, 45, 47, 59, 62–68, 146, 156–57, 160, 163–64, 168, 273, 276
Lula administrations 161, 165
Lula government 46, 50, 146, 157, 159
Lulaism / Lulism 37, 39, 41, 43, 45, 47, 49, 51, 53, 55, 57, 59–61, 63–69, 278
Lulista mode of regulating social
    conflict 46, 49
Luxemburg, Rosa 279, 290, 292

M-19 223, 231–32
Macri, Mauricio 70, 85, 87–88, 90
Macron, Emmanuel 65
Maduro, Nicolás 7, 26, 31–33, 35–6, 168
Maduro government 27, 276
Magdalena Medio 222, 230–31, 234

INDEX 339

magic state 16, 27
Mahuad, Jamil 126
Malpica, Carlos 199
Malvinas 75
Mao 205
Maoism 209
Mapuche 184–85
maquiladoras 154–5
Mariana 45
Mariátegui, José Carlos 207, 209, 217, 280
mariateguista 199
Mariel 256–57
marijuana 229, 233
Marinho, Luis 63
Markas 99
Martí, José 265, 281, 285
Martínez Heredia, Fernando 246–48, 252, 258, 267–68, 289
Marx, Karl 60
Marxism 19, 173, 209, 266
Marxist guerrilla 218
massacres 96, 153, 222, 226, 230, 234, 266, 291
mass movement 100, 206, 240
 radicalized 226
Matos Mar, Jose 203
Matte 191
Media Luna 102, 118
Medina, Nilson 145–46
Meirelles, Henrique 65
Mendoza, Verónika 219
Menem, Carlos 77–78, 84, 87–88
Menemato 70, 76–77, 82
mensalão 48
Mercal 21
MERCOSUR 21, 25, 158, 170, 183
Mesa Gisbert, Carlos 97
Mesoamerican Plan 158
Mészáros, István 288
Mexican Revolution 289
Mexico 3, 38, 158, 213, 224–25, 234, 273–74, 277
Miami 158, 244, 251, 268, 286
middle class 13, 50–51, 56, 58, 72, 77–78, 80–81, 87, 126–27
middle class populism 87
militarization 33, 230, 232, 237–38
Military-Peasant Pact 96

Millennium Foundation 110
Minha Casa Minha Vida program 43, 53–4
MIR 98–99, 174
Misión Barrio Adentro 21
Misiones Ribas 21
missions 20, 22, 26, 33, 67, 73, 165
misti 206–7
MNR 94, 97–98, 120
modernities 55, 195, 265
 alternative 136
modernization 6, 49, 55–57, 133–36, 284, 287
Modi, Narendra 64
Mommer, Bernard 14–5, 17
Monedero, Juan Carlos 20, 25
Monsanto 143, 154
Montecristi 128, 136
Montesinos, Vladimir 210, 213–4
Montoneros Peronistas 73
Morales, Evo 1, 18, 92, 98, 100, 103–09, 115–6, 118–19, 121, 128–29, 146, 270
 brother 111
Morales Bermúdez 201
Moreno, Lenin 137
Morlote, Luis 261
Moro, Sergio 65
Moulian, Tomás 182, 183, 196
Movement for Socialism-Political Instrument 99
movements 1–2, 5, 7, 48–49, 52–56, 77–78, 82, 98, 100–101, 112, 193, 207–08, 237–38, 270–71, 287
 guerrilla 202, 205, 229
Movimiento Emancipador Peronista 80
Moxos-Villa Tunari 161
Moyano, Hugo 87
Moyano, Maria Elena 212
MRB-200 19
MRTA 209, 212
MST 32, 53–54
MTL 77, 83, 89
MTL governista 81
myth 46, 66, 172, 274, 280, 282

Ñacunday 146, 151–52, 155
Napoleon 27
narcoguerrilla 230
narcolavado 129
narco-terrorism 238

narcotrafficking   230, 235
Nationalist Democratic Alliance   98
National League of Carperos   151
National Liberation Army   228
neo-developmentalism   157, 167, 169, 170
neodevelopmentalist project   41, 44, 46
neodevelopmentism   2, 39, 42
neoliberal adjustments   41, 210
neoliberal fundamentalism   70, 171, 175, 220
neoliberalism   1–7, 41–42, 45–47, 49, 64,
　　92–93, 97–98, 100, 157, 181, 196–97, 210,
　　229, 232–33, 271–72
　inclusive   2, 59, 64, 68
　multicultural   99
neoliberalism with a human face   181
neo-Pentecostalism   55, 206, 266
new Peruvian left   199, 201
New Republic   38, 61, 64–66, 226
Newsweek   43
NGOism   110
Nickson, Andrew   140
non-alignment   173
North-Rurrenabaque-El-Chorro Project   161
Norwegian Norsk Hydro   44
Nuestra America   244
Nueva Mayoría   178

OAS   161, 163
Obama, Barack   43, 156, 168, 244, 268
October agenda   102
Odebrecht   43–4, 161–62, 165
OEA   173, 226, 246
oil   10, 12–13, 15, 24, 76, 84, 107–8, 125, 129, 132, 160
　dependence on   23, 27, 34–35
　sowing   13, 16, 24, 31
Onganía, Juan Carlos   73
OPEC   14–15
Ordoñéz, Alejandro   224
Oviedo, Lino   148

PAC   43, 53
Pachacutik   125, 127, 136
Pachamama   118, 128
Pacific Alliance   277
Pacific War   102
Palacio, Alfredo   127
Palau, Tomas   143, 149–50

Paley, Julia   183
Panama   11, 19, 111, 224, 226
Pandora's Box   63
paradox   3, 107, 113, 155, 159, 214, 216, 220,
　　258–59, 261, 276, 278
paradoxical   139, 159, 282–83
Paraguay   1–2, 4, 7–8, 138–39, 141–51, 153–55,
　　161, 164, 168, 273, 275–76, 278–79
paramilitaries   223, 228, 230–31, 234–38
paramilitarism   230–31, 234, 236, 238
Paranaguá   140
Paraná River   154, 161
parapolitics   221, 223, 232, 235, 241–42
parasite feeding   13
parasite of nature   24
Pardo Leal, Jaime   231
participatory budgeting   39, 52
partidocracy   125, 127
Partido Sociedad Patriotica   128
parties   37–39, 47–48, 56, 58–61, 63, 65, 67,
　　97, 99, 102, 115–16, 127, 177–78, 198–99,
　　201–2
　alternative   243
　center-left   98
　conventional   18, 124, 200–201, 229
Patiño, Simón   95
Patria, Plan de la   23, 26, 31
Patria Roja (PR)   201
Patriotic Agenda   115
Paz Estenssoro, Victor   95, 98, 272
Paz Zamora, Jaime   98
PCP   199–200, 206
PCP Patria Roja   201
PDVSA   15, 20, 34
peace process   9, 221, 231, 235, 239–42
peasant movements   26, 96, 151–52, 199, 240, 273
Pease, Henry   205
penguin revolt   193
People's Liberation Army   232
Peredo, Osvaldo   109, 115
Perez Compac   161
Perez Jimenez   14
period, special   31, 249, 251–53, 255,
　　265, 268
periphery   1, 3–4, 45, 90, 201, 209, 263, 265,
　　269, 282
　urban   233, 238

INDEX   341

Perón, Juan Domingo   70–73, 88
Peronism   70–76, 79–80, 88–90
Peru   4–5, 43–44, 161, 164–65, 167, 199,
    202, 206, 210–11, 215–17, 220, 272, 274,
    277, 279
  neighbors   93
Peru Brand   217, 220
Petro, Gustavo   243
Petrobras   54, 58–9, 161, 166
Petrocaribe   21, 33, 163
picketers   77–78, 83
Pilgrim's Pride Corp   161
Pineiro Harnecker, Camila   254, 258–9, 261
Piñera, José   177
Piñera, Sebastián   177, 184, 191, 193
Pinochet, Augusto   1, 175, 177–78, 180, 182,
    184, 210, 232
Plan Colombia   7, 149, 221, 226, 235–36,
    277
Plan Patriota, so-called   236
plurinationalism   119–20
  repressing   113
plurinationality   107, 118, 128, 136
PMDB   48, 58, 65
Podemos   106
polarization   173, 240
  fake   169
  ideological   226
  political   57, 227
Popular Action   199, 211
Popular American Revolutionary
    Alliance   199
Popular Front   171–72, 194
Popular Unity   98, 173, 195, 231, 265
popular uprisings   6, 10, 94
populism   86–7
  fiscal   42
populist demagoguery   38
Porto Alegre   127
positives, false   222
post-neoliberal   157, 167
post-neoliberalism   158
post-neoliberal regionalism   157, 169–70
Prada, Raul   110
Pradel, Gumercindo   109
privatizations   40–41, 52, 57, 76–7, 80, 84, 177,
    179, 182, 211, 213
  generalized   213

progress   2, 4, 34, 41, 95, 172, 228, 235, 267,
    282–85
  alliance for   95, 172
  capitalist   282
  ideology of   2, 282–83
  paradigm of   34, 284–85
progressive expectations   37, 39
progressive governments   2, 4, 6, 8, 157, 159,
    170, 244, 274–76, 290
  so-called   274
progressive intelligentsia   79
progressive wave   1–7, 9, 21, 70, 88, 92, 121,
    244, 263, 270–71, 273, 275–79
progressivism   1–6, 8, 37, 121, 169, 276, 278
  limits of   36, 277
PSUV   22, 28
PT   37–40, 47–48, 51–52, 56–57, 59–68, 104,
    156, 159, 163, 165–66, 273, 276
PT administrations   39, 44, 49, 52–53, 61–62,
    165–66
Puebla-Panama Plan   158
Puerto Rico   11
Puerto Stroessner   140
Pueyrredón Bridge   78
Punto Fijo Pact   10, 14, 16–19, 34, 169, 228

Quechua   111, 200, 207, 212
Queiroz Galvão   161
que se vayan todos   78, 127
Quijano, Aníbal   200, 203, 213
quinoa   114, 217
Quispe, Felipe   101
Quito   122
Qullasuyu   99

racism   103, 206, 266, 287
Radical Civic Union   72, 76
radicalism   88, 197
radicalize   101, 263, 265, 274
Radical Party   172
Ralito Pact   235
Ramonet, Ignacio   27
raspacupos   30
real neoliberalism   171, 173, 175, 177, 179, 181,
    183, 186–87, 191–97
  dimensions of   194, 197
Real Plan   40, 50, 169
Red Derecho   223

reform   6–7, 9, 38, 41, 173, 178, 191–93, 222, 252, 258, 271
　constitutional   183, 239, 256, 262
　economic   204, 258
　financial   74
　social   38, 95, 271
　social security   117, 157, 177
　structural   83, 213
　tax   80, 85, 107, 204, 213
　urban   49, 52–54, 245
regional integration   4–5, 8, 33, 157, 164–65, 167, 170, 270–71, 276–79, 281, 283–84
　project of   8, 157, 159, 166, 168
regionalism, open   157–59, 167, 170
regression   49–50, 55, 60
　conservative   271
Renta Dignidad program   117
rentier state   14, 31
rentism   15, 42, 245
repression   73–75, 79, 97, 102, 119, 130, 136, 140, 163, 175, 177, 181, 184, 194–95, 197, 199, 227, 234, 236
Repsol   84
revolution   5, 92–93, 95, 172–74, 208, 222, 244–49, 251–53, 257–58, 260–61, 263–65, 267–71, 274–75, 282–83, 288–91
　permanent   264
Revolutionary Vanguard   199
Revolutionary Workers Party   95
Reyes, Raúl   224
rhetoric   22, 45, 79, 85, 90, 119, 132, 136, 150, 170, 172, 212, 218, 224, 236, 238–39
　anti-imperialist   21
　counter-terrorist   221
　populist   204
　revolutionary   33, 200, 273
Rice, Condoleeza   168
Rivera Cusicanqui, Silvia   105, 109, 113
Rockefeller Standard Oil   84
Rodrigazo   73
Rodrigues, Roberto   146
Rodríguez, General Andrés   147, 150
Rodríguez, José Luis   253, 257, 265
Rodríguez, Simón   18–9, 26
Rojas Pinilla, General   223, 227–8
Rojas Villagra, Luis   144, 149
Romero, Carlos   119
Romero, José Luis Martin   259
rondas campesinas   209

Rostow, W. W.   280
Rousseff, Dilma   7, 39, 43, 49, 57–59, 61–63, 165, 169
Rulli, Javier   143
Russian Revolution   279, 282, 291

sabotage   10, 18, 131, 151, 235
Sachs, Jeffrey   98
Said, Edward   208
Sainz, Hugo   110
Salary Bonus Program   43
Salcedo, Guadalupe   228
Samaniego, Lilian   154
Sampaio Jr, Plinio   42, 45–46, 63
Samper, Ernesto   233
Sánchez de Lozada, Gonzalo   98–9, 107, 224
Sandinista Revolution   229
Sandinistas   290
Santa Cruz   79, 102–3, 106, 110, 114–15
Santa Elisa   44
Santos, Gregorio   219
Santos, Juan Manuel   9, 221, 239–42
Saravia, Ramiro   105
Sarayacu   136
scandals   48, 112, 165–6, 213
Schavelzon, Salvador   107
Scioli, Daniel   88
segregation   93, 187
self-management   22, 39, 52, 254, 259–60, 264, 288
self-organization   105
Senderistas setbacks   212
Sendero Luminoso   199, 201–2, 205–13, 218
Senderoism   198, 203
Shell   12
Sherman, Wendy   168
Shining Path   7, 199, 205
shock   148, 210–11, 218, 257
Shuar leaders   131
Sicad   29
Sidor   31–32
Siles Zuazo   98
Silva, Golbery Couto e   141
social change   18, 33, 38, 46, 58, 148, 226, 229, 236, 276, 279
social conflicts   55, 94, 131, 133, 216–17, 228
social contradictions   25, 102, 118, 195, 208, 226
Social Democratic Party   136

socialism   18, 21, 26, 35, 38, 169, 171, 173, 175, 195, 257, 259, 280–81, 284, 286, 288–89
   dependent   266
   real   244
   rentier   24
socialist   25, 28, 32, 173, 199, 208, 245–46, 252, 256–57, 267
Socialist International   202
socialist market economy   256
Socialist Party   173, 177, 194–95
socialist realism   264
socialists   1, 10, 19, 171–73, 175, 180–81, 183–84, 195, 257, 259, 272–73
socialist transformism   275
socialist values   258
social movements   37, 47–49, 97–98, 104–5, 109, 119, 127, 130, 132, 149, 226, 228, 230, 241, 272–76
   government of   105, 111
social protest   100–101, 125, 224, 226, 230, 238–39, 273
social revolution   36, 119, 221
social rights   179, 196, 232, 252
   commodification of   177, 184, 197
sociedad abigarrada   7, 92–93
   variegated   7, 92–93, 120, 169, 271
SocioBosque   135
SocioPáramo   135
Souchaud, Sylvaine   141
soup kitchens   77, 81, 89
South Africa   3, 160, 182
South American Integration   5, 156–57, 159, 161, 163, 165, 167, 169–70, 283
sovereignty   2, 5, 107, 122, 134–35, 168, 172, 246, 249, 265, 267–68, 278–79, 284–85, 287, 289
soviets   174, 246–47, 263–65, 284, 286, 289
Soviet Union   31, 211, 229, 244, 246–48, 262–63, 272, 282–83, 288, 291
soy   83, 86, 111, 142–45, 160
soybeans   83–84, 119, 143–44
   expansion of   138, 143, 145, 147, 217
Spanish Civil War   289
Special Development Zone   256
stability   40, 64, 131, 171, 180–83, 189, 194–95, 215, 220, 233, 247
stabilization   95, 211, 213
Stalin, Josef   181
Stalinism   289

Standard Oil   12
Starn, Orin   208
state   13–17, 32–33, 71–72, 76–78, 81–82, 93–94, 101–05, 107, 112–15, 134–36, 171–73, 186–88, 196–203, 207–10, 230–35, 249–50, 252–55, 261–62, 266–69, 288–91
   bourgeois   136, 173, 266
   plurinational   118
state repression   98, 100, 102, 147, 220
state terrorism   80, 89, 175, 181, 195, 200, 212, 273
Stroessner, Alfredo   139, 141–42, 147, 150–51
Stronismo   153
structural adjustment   2, 6, 40, 46, 61, 63, 76, 89, 124, 157, 164
student revolt   194
students   49, 51, 55, 105, 186–88, 193, 197, 206, 213, 224, 228, 246, 252
subsidies   16, 27, 33, 51, 85, 90, 108, 144, 154, 187, 190, 214, 255
Sumak Kawsay   121, 128, 169
   constitutional precept of   129
Svampa, Maristella   86–87
Swift & Co   161
Syngenta   145

Tablada   250
Tacna   215
Tacutu River   161
Taiwan   144
Tambogrande   216
Tambs, Ambassador Lewis   230
Tapia, Luis   93
Tarija-Bermejo Highway   161
TCOs   99, 114
Techint   161
Teixeira, Ulisses Rodrigues   151, 155
Tejada, Sergio   219
Telesur   22, 163, 168
Televen   25
Tella, Chancelor Guido di   76
Temer, Michel   48, 61–62, 66–7, 161, 276
   out with   63
territories   93, 99, 109, 111, 122, 141, 145, 213, 215, 223, 228
   autonomous   111
   national   151, 223
terror   74, 181, 212, 235
   war on   224

terrorism 10, 18, 131, 149, 176, 209, 235–36, 238
terrorists 208, 237, 242
Thatcher, Margaret 75
Third World 3, 195, 248, 256, 265
Thorstensen, Vera 170
Thousand Days War 226–27
tierras excedentes 142
tierras fiscales 114
tierras mal habidas 142
timber 176, 185
Tinker Salas, Miguel 13–14
Tipnis 108–9, 110, 112, 119, 162
Toledo, Alejandro 214, 219
Toledo, Alexis 26
Toribio Merino 180
Torres, Javier 210
Torricelli Act 251
Torrijos, Omar 19
Toucans 56, 63–66
trade liberalization 40, 76, 233, 284
  multilateral 277
trade union movement 62, 72, 98, 189
trade union organization 60, 71
trade unions 14, 26, 47, 83, 88, 237, 272
traffickers 155
  drug 231, 233, 238–39
transgenic 36, 53, 84, 118, 137, 142–3, 267
transition 26, 38, 148, 178, 195, 201, 268, 271–72, 289–90
  negotiated 201
Trinidad, Simon 230
Triple Alliance 139, 144
Trotskyists 95, 199, 201
truce 149
Trujillo 14
Trump, Donald 64
Tupac Amaru 200
Túpac Amaru Revolutionary Movement 209
Tupac Katari 101, 119, 200
Tuto Quiroga 106

UDP 98–99
UNASUR 5, 25, 55, 135, 156, 159, 163–64, 168–69, 273, 277–79
underdevelopment 6–7, 10–11, 14–15, 23–24, 34–35, 119, 123, 195, 245, 247–48, 263, 271, 288
UNESCO 260

Únete 219
Unidad Popular 7, 96
Unión Patriótica 231
Union Sindical Obrera 222
United Fruits Company 226
United Left 199, 202–3, 205
United Nations 55, 104, 165
United Nations Development Program 129, 185, 238
United Self-Defense Forces of Colombia 234
United Socialist Party of Venezuela 22
United States 5, 7, 64, 75–76, 94–96, 119–20, 168, 226, 229–30, 244–47, 250–51, 268, 273–74, 277–78, 286–87
Unitel 116
Unity Pact 109, 112
Universal Church 62
Uraba 234
Uribe, Álvaro 5, 8, 221, 231, 234–35, 236–42
Uribe accords 231
Uribe bloc 242
Uribe politics 9
Uribism 64, 221, 241
Uruguay 1, 4, 6, 8, 18, 22, 90, 161, 164, 273, 276
Uslar Pietri, Arturo 13
utopia 2, 28, 31, 45, 90, 135, 171, 195–96, 268, 286

Vadillo, Alcides 98, 111
vagabonds 130
Valdés Paz, Juan 255–57, 262
Vale 44, 160–612
Vargas, Getulio 38
Vargas Lleras, Germán 242
Vargas Llosa, Mario 204, 210, 218
Vatican 154
Vázquez, Tabaré 1, 18
Velasco Alvarado 19, 96, 199–202, 217
Velasquism 201, 206, 218
Venevision 25
Venezuela 1–3, 5, 7–10, 12–19, 21–28, 31–36, 123–24, 128, 161, 164–65, 167–69, 271–73, 275–77
Vicente Gómez, Juan 12
Vietnam 257
Villa El Salvador 201
Villarán, Susana 219

violence   7, 64–66, 120, 199, 207, 210, 215–16, 221–23, 227, 233–35, 238–42
Violencia   222, 227
Vladivídeos   213
Votorantim   42, 161

water   68, 85, 100, 113, 130–31, 179, 190, 198, 208, 215, 217, 220, 241
Water War   100
wave   2, 58–59, 78, 103, 116, 162, 193
  reactionary   63
  repressive   231
workers   16–17, 32, 41, 47, 50–51, 53, 58, 60–61, 71–73, 82–83, 94–97, 162, 179, 189–92, 197, 226–28, 252–55, 259, 286, 291–92
  rural   96, 141, 149, 151, 233, 260, 288
World Bank   42, 46, 52–53, 55, 100, 117, 128, 135, 140, 148, 204, 211
World Cup   55, 57, 165, 222
World Social Forum in Porto Alegre   127
World Trade Organization   55, 170

Xingu River   162

Yasunidos   130
Yasuní-ITT initiative   129, 132, 135–36
Yeltsin, Boris   248
Yom Kippur   123
YPF   76, 84–85
YPFB   95, 99, 107, 118
Yungas   111

Zamora, Ezequiel   19
Zamora government   99
Zapata   205
Zapatismo   273, 290
Zapatista principle   104
Zavaleta Mercado, René   92–94, 103, 120, 169
Zero Hunger program   39
Zucolillo, Aldo   153–54
Zuluaga, Iván   240
Zuma, Jacob   3

www.ingramcontent.com/pod-product-compliance
Lightning Source LLC
Chambersburg PA
CBHW071331080526
44587CB00017B/2803